THE TRINITY GUIDE
TO THE BIBLE

THE
TRINITY GUIDE
TO BIBLE
THE

Richard H. Hiers

TRINITY PRESS INTERNATIONAL

Trinity Press International
P.O. Box 1321
Harrisburg, PA 17105

Trinity Press International is a division of the Morehouse Group.

Cover art: *Arcosolio di Balaam.* Roma Catacomba delle pitture in via Latina. Pontifical Commission for Archaeology of Sacred Sites at the Vatican.

Design: Corey Kent

Library of Congress Cataloging-in-Publication Data
Hiers, Richard H.
  The Trinity guide to the Bible / Richard H. Hiers.
    p. cm.
  Includes bibliographical references and indexes.
  ISBN 1-56338-340-3 (alk. paper)
    1. Bible—Introductions. I. Title.

BS475.3 .H54 2001
220.6'1—dc21   2001027466

Printed in the United States of America

01 02 03 04 05 06   10 9 8 7 6 5 4 3 2 1

CONTENTS

ABBREVIATIONS

Old Testament

Gen	Genesis
Exod	Exodus
Lev	Leviticus
Num	Numbers
Deut	Deuteronomy
Josh	Joshua
Judg	Judges
Ruth	Ruth
1 Sam	1 Samuel
2 Sam	2 Samuel
1 Kgs	1 Kings
2 Kgs	2 Kings
1 Chr	1 Chronicles
2 Chr	2 Chronicles
Ezra	Ezra
Neh	Nehemiah
Esth	Esther
Job	Job
Ps/Pss	Psalms
Prov	Proverbs
Eccl	Ecclesiastes
Song	Song of Solomon (or Canticles)
Isa	Isaiah
Jer	Jeremiah
Lam	Lamentations
Ezek	Ezekiel
Dan	Daniel
Hos	Hosea
Joel	Joel
Amos	Amos
Obad	Obadiah
Jonah	Jonah
Mic	Micah
Nah	Nahum
Hab	Habakkuk
Zeph	Zephaniah
Hag	Haggai
Zech	Zechariah
Mal	Malachi

Old Testament Apocrypha

1 Esdr	1 Esdras
2 Esdr	2 Esdras
Tob	Tobit
Jdt	Judith
Add Esth	Additions to Esther
Wis	Wisdom of Solomon
Sir	Ecclesiasticus (or Sirach)
Bar	Baruch
Let Jer	Letter of Jeremiah
Pr Azar	Prayer of Azariah and the Song of the Three Young Men
Sus	Susanna
Bel	Bel and the Dragon
Pr Man	Prayer of Manasseh
1 Macc	1 Maccabees
2 Macc	2 Maccabees
3 Macc	3 Maccabees

4 Macc	4 Maccabees
Ps 151	Psalm 151

New Testament

Matt	Gospel according to Matthew	2 John	2 John
Mark	Gospel according to Mark	3 John	3 John
		Jude	Jude
Luke	Gospel according to Luke	Rev	Revelation
John	Gospel according to John		
Acts	Acts		
Rom	Romans		
1 Cor	1 Corinthians		
2 Cor	2 Corinthians		
Gal	Galatians		
Eph	Ephesians		
Phil	Philippians		
Col	Colossians		
1 Thess	1 Thessalonians		
2 Thess	2 Thessalonians		
1 Tim	1 Timothy		
2 Tim	2 Timothy		
Titus	Titus		
Phlm	Philemon		
Heb	Hebrews		
Jas	James		
1 Pet	1 Peter		
2 Pet	2 Peter		
1 John	1 John		

TABLE OF DATES

6 B.C.	Birth of Jesus
A.D. 64	Christians persecuted in Rome by authority of Nero
66–70	Jewish war for liberation from Rome
70	Jerusalem captured, temple destroyed by Romans
79	Eruption of Mount Vesuvius, which buries Pompeii
96	Christians in Asia Minor persecuted by Romans

INTRODUCTION

This introductory volume is intended to provide those who wish to read some or all of the books of the Bible, including the Old Testament Apocrypha, with a survey of their historical contexts, their major literary forms, and their authors' or editors' principal concerns. Readers from any or no particular religious tradition or denominational background may find this book instructive. As a convenience, the symbols B.C. and A.D. will be used rather than B.C.E. (Before the Common Era) and C.E. (Common Era). Many of the interpretations proposed here are necessarily tentative, and readers are encouraged to draw their own conclusions from the biblical texts and from their own reading of secondary sources.[1] At the same time, this book attempts to present, if often in general terms, the substance of current scholarly consensus in matters of interpretation.

Readers should plan to give their attention primarily to the biblical text itself. The chapters of this book, therefore, are quite limited in length and indicate only basic features of each biblical book. Significant biblical passages that illustrate various points are frequently cited, usually in parentheses or endnotes. Similar or contrasting statements or ideas found in other biblical writings are often noted, usually by means of the abbreviation *cf.* ("compare"). Each subchapter describing features of individual biblical writings or books is meant to be understandable by itself. Consequently, some matters are repeated from time to time.

As for the organization of the book, the table of contents sets out the general framework. This table includes a list of the books of the Bible in the order in which they are examined here. Readers may wish to mark the first page of this list for easy reference, since the order in which the books of the Bible appear varies considerably from one modern version of the Bible to another. The situation is further complicated by the fact that Jewish Bibles include neither the Old Testament Apocrypha nor the New Testament, while Christian Bibles all include the New Testament but differ as to which, if any, of the apocryphal writings are to be regarded as Scripture.

A table of dates immediately precedes this introduction. Since most of the biblical writings refer to or reflect the impact of particular events, readers will find it helpful to refer to this table in order to correlate biblical peoples' concerns or developing institutions or practices with the contemporary circumstances. Readers may also find it helpful to develop their own more extended outlines of major biblical events, by placing significant figures in their historical settings or contexts.

Three background essays follow immediately after this introduction and constitute part I of this book. These three essays may help readers understand the biblical books in broader contexts. Since, to a great extent, biblical faith came to expression in connection with events—past, present, and anticipated—the first essay, which traces the basic features of the historical context, is especially important. Most of the biblical writings can be considered within certain broad categories of biblical literature. The second essay summarizes some of the principal literary and editorial features of biblical writing, and the third focuses on a number of central themes in biblical religion and faith.

There are several ways to use these essays. Since they all refer to a wide range of events, writings, and beliefs, they may be more helpful after the reader has worked carefully through several of the books of the Bible. On the other hand, reading these essays before undertaking more detailed study of particular books could provide a useful overview. Another option would be to read and review them from time to time during the course of one's study of the Bible.

Part II begins with an overview of the Old Testament, followed by subchapters introducing each of the Old Testament books. From the standpoint of Judaism, what Protestant Christians call the Old Testament constitutes the entire body of Jewish Scripture. These books are considered in the order or sequence traditional in Christian Bibles.

After a brief overview, part III introduces the Old Testament Apocrypha, which includes the Deuterocanonical writings, as they are characterized in Roman Catholic tradition.[2] Until the sixteenth century, the apocryphal writings were included within the Old Testament section of all Christian Bibles. Even modern versions differ as to their placement: Some locate the Apocrypha between the Old Testament and the New Testament, while others set the Apocrypha apart, following the New Testament. Since the apocryphal or Deuterocanonical writings by and large were composed and reflect historical developments between the time the latest Old Testament books were written and the beginning of the New Testament period, these writings are considered in this book immediately following the Old Testament. In addition, the Apocrypha is construed broadly so as to include not only the Deuterocanonical writings, but also 1 and 2 Esdras and the Prayer of Manasseh, which Catholicism views as not fully canonical; 3 Maccabees and Psalm 151, which are contained in Eastern Orthodox Bibles; and even 4 Maccabees, to which the Greek Orthodox Church accords a secondary status.

Part IV introduces the New Testament and the various books it comprises. These were all relatively early Christian writings but not necessarily the earliest. For example, some noncanonical writings such as *1 Clement* and the *Epistle of Barnabas* may have been composed before 1 and 2 Timothy and 2 Peter. Part IV is therefore captioned "The New Testament, or Canonical Early Christian Writings."

The book concludes with an index of topics and names of persons in biblical times. Boldface citations there refer to pages where technical terms that may be unfamiliar to many readers are defined or explained. Topics or issues that relate to more than one biblical book are also noted here. Thus, these boldface index citations serve a glossary function.

A list of suggested reference works and readings relating to the Bible as a whole and to individual books of the Bible appears at the back of this volume. A number of excellent study Bibles reflecting modern textual scholarship are available in English translation.[3]

Although other translations have been published more recently, the Revised Standard Version (RSV) provides a more literal and precise translation,[4] and at the same time preserves some flavor of the old King James Version, which in turn often reflects underlying Hebrew, Aramaic, and Greek expressions or idioms.[5] The biblical texts quoted in this book generally follow the RSV translation, but readers are invited and encouraged to consult other modern translations as well.[6]

This book is intended to help readers identify and understand the basic beliefs and concerns indicated in each of the biblical writings. It does not attempt to intimate what meanings the texts should have for modern readers. The present significance of biblical texts may be very important. However, each reader's own understanding will be better served by beginning with the effort to grasp what meanings the biblical speakers, writers, and editors may have found and expressed in and for their times. In this way, the book may serve indirectly to suggest the continuing and contemporary relevance of many biblical texts, for those who appreciate the intentions and meanings of the biblical writers in their own time will be better able to recognize how those intentions and meanings may relate to matters of faith and life today.[7]

Readers are urged to remain open to words and meanings of the biblical text and the biblical writers' intentions. The Bible may not always say what readers would like it to say. Lack of interest in or respect for what the biblical writers intended can all too easily result in substituting the modern reader's notions and prejudices for the biblical authors' beliefs and concerns. The present book should prove useful as a guide to persons studying either independently or in church seminars or college classes.

NOTES

1. A number of secondary studies are noted from time to time in this book as suggested reading for those who want to engage in more specialized studies. Hundreds of books and articles on biblical topics are published every year. Titles mentioned in this book necessarily are only a small sampling.

2. These include most of the writings otherwise classified as the Old Testament Apocrypha. In Catholic tradition, they are considered part of Scripture and included in appropriate places in the Old Testament section of Catholic Bibles. See the introduction to part III.

3. Among these are the following: *The New Oxford Annotated Bible with the Apocrypha*, Revised Standard Version (New York: Oxford University Press, 1977); *The New Oxford Annotated Bible with the Apocrypha*, New Revised Standard Version (New York: Oxford University Press, 1991); *The New English Bible with the Apocrypha, Oxford Study Edition* (New York: Oxford University Press, 1976); *The Oxford Study Bible, Revised English Bible with the Apocrypha* (Oxford: Oxford University Press, 1992); *The Catholic Study Bible, New American Bible* (New York: Oxford University Press, 1990); *The New Revised Standard Version, Catholic Edition and Student Edition* (Oxford: Oxford University Press, 2000); and *The HarperCollins Study Bible*, New Revised Standard Version, 3d ed. (San Francisco: HarperSanFrancisco, 2001).

4. The translation of the biblical text in the NRSV is basically the same as in the RSV. The principal difference is that the translators of the NRSV undertook to employ gender-inclusive or gender-neutral language where they found it appropriate. In some instances, the basis for such language is not clearly evident in the underlying texts. Readers are encouraged to consult and compare at least two different modern translations in the course of studying texts of particular interest to them.

5. The King James Version (KJV) was originally published in 1611. Since then, the English language has changed significantly, as anyone knows who attempts to read unannotated versions of Shakespeare's plays. Additionally, more ancient biblical manuscripts are now known to scholars than was the

case when the KJV was published: for example, the New Testament Chester Beatty Papyri, discovered in 1931 but dating back into the second century A.D., and the Dead Sea Scrolls, discovered in 1948 but dating perhaps as early as the first century B.C.

6. Neither the New English Bible (NEB) nor the Revised English Bible (REB) translations includes 3 or 4 Maccabees or Psalm 151.

7. Suggested reading: Paul J. Achtemeier, *Inspiration and Authority: The Nature and Function of Christian Scripture*, rev. ed. (Peabody, Mass.: Hendrickson, 1999); Darrell Jodock, *The Church's Bible: Its Contemporary Authority* (Philadelphia: Fortress, 1989); and Henning G. Reventlow, *The Authority of the Bible and the Rise of the Modern World* (Philadelphia: Fortress, 1985).

PART I
Background Essays

A. THE HISTORICAL CONTEXT:
Main Events and Developments,
1500 B.C. to A.D. 100

Most of the biblical drama took place on a stage just slightly larger than the state of Vermont, known first as the land of Canaan,[1] then Israel, and later as Palestine.[2] Portions of the land also went by other names during the biblical period, such as Judah, Judea, Samaria, and Galilee. North to south, "from Dan to Beersheba," was 150 miles, while the greatest width, from Gaza to the Dead Sea, was barely sixty miles. Located on the southeastern end of the Mediterranean Sea, the land served as a corridor between the great empires of the Tigris-Euphrates Valley and Egypt. A number of smaller nations or peoples were situated nearby: the Philistines, Edomites, Moabites, Ammonites, Syrians, and Phoenicians, for example. To a considerable extent, the history of Israel, Judah, and the Jewish people is the story of the interactions with these occasionally friendly but generally intrusive and sometimes overwhelming neighbors. The reported biblical traditions, however, are more interested in the internal history: the events and meaning of events from the perspective of the faith-understanding of Abraham's descendants.

Abram and Sarai, the first of the fathers and mothers of Israel, migrated from Babylon (Chaldea) and sojourned in Syria (Aram) before going on into Canaan. The stories of Abraham and Sarah,[3] Isaac and Rebekah, and Jacob, Leah, and Rachel—the principal "patriarchs" and "matriarchs" of Israel—may recall real persons and events from the fifteenth century B.C. or even earlier. As the story is told, Jacob was renamed Israel and became the father or grandfather of those persons for whom the twelve tribes of Israel were named. A number of names and practices mentioned in biblical narratives are corroborated by archaeological evidence, though the stories themselves may be somewhat legendary.

The Joseph saga at the end of Genesis explains how the people of Israel, still a large family or clan, came to find themselves in the land of Egypt. Time passed, probably more than one generation, and the Hebrews multiplied. The Egyptians, fearing their growing numbers,

1

subjected them to slavery, probably during the reign of the famous pharaoh, Ramses II. Under Moses' leadership, however, the Israelites escaped from Egypt into the Sinai wilderness, perhaps about 1230 B.C. Here they wandered for "forty years," receiving, through Moses, God's law or covenant. The Canaanites and various other peoples had already occupied most of the fertile lowlands of Canaan. The invading Israelites, led by Joshua, succeeded in conquering or settling the central hill country of Canaan, along with some of the plateau east of the Jordan River. Unhappily for the Israelites, the Philistines arrived about the same time (ca. 1200 B.C.) and quickly proceeded to occupy the fertile southern coastal plain and, within two centuries, nearly the entire land of Canaan.

The time between 1200 and 1000 B.C. is known as the period of the judges. During that period, the tribes of Israel (which included Gilead and Bashan besides the traditional twelve) were, at best, loosely united in a confederation led, occasionally, by able charismatic judges and prophets, the last and perhaps greatest of whom was Samuel. The judges mainly seem to have been local heroes who came forward in times of crisis and singlehandedly, or with volunteers from, at most, a few tribes, tried to cope with neighboring marauders or oppressors. An editor of the book of Judges periodically comments before or just after describing particularly chaotic and gruesome scenes, "In those days there was no king in Israel; every man did what was right in his own eyes." In retrospect, it is clear that the political structure of the confederation proved inadequate to cope either with internal dissension and, at times, fratricidal conflict between or among the tribes of Israel, or with recurrent external threats to the nation's existence—in particular, the Philistine menace. Around 1000 B.C., after the Philistines had decisively overwhelmed Israel at Shiloh and captured the ark of the Lord, Samuel was induced to anoint Saul, a Benjaminite, as king of Israel. Saul began his career after the fashion of the judges, leading volunteer guerrilla forces to rescue the village of Jabesh-gilead from besieging Ammonite troops. After this success, the people of Israel made him their king. For a while, Saul succeeded in establishing a precarious independent Israelite nation. But his kingship was weakened by internal problems, and the Philistines eventually proved too much for Israel, defeating Saul and his army at Mount Gilboa.

David, a Judahite, had earlier been anointed by Samuel to replace Saul, but became king only after Saul's death. He was then made king of Judah by its leaders. Only after surmounting certain major obstacles was he also made king of Israel. Under David, the people of Israel and Judah were united into one nation. Under David's dynamic leadership, the united kingdoms of Israel and Judah succeeded in both throwing off Philistine domination and compelling other nearby nations to keep their distance. Years later, David's reign was seen as the golden age, and later hopes for the future often took the form of longing for another king or messiah (i.e., anointed one) from the house (i.e., lineage) of David. Yet David was strangely incapable of dealing with problems occasioned by the lust and ambition of his own sons, whose misdeeds closely resembled his own offenses against Bathsheba and Uriah, if not also against the house of Saul. One son raped a half-sister and afterward was murdered by her brother, who later led the Israelites in revolt against David. David became old and senile without having arranged for someone to succeed him. When he failed to install his surviving oldest son as king in his place, Solomon became king through a palace revolution engineered by his mother and the prophet Nathan.

Solomon became famous both for his wisdom and for the material splendor of his reign. But Solomon's luxury was paid for, in part, by the forced labor of his northern subjects, the Israelites, who resented this oppression by a southern (Judahite) ruler. A later commentator also condemned Solomon for his apostasy and worship of foreign deities. When Solomon died, his son Rehoboam arrogantly rejected the appeal by Jeroboam and the elders of Israel for relief from the heavy yoke of Solomon. Thereupon, the Israelites renounced Rehoboam and the house of David, revolted and established their own separate kingdom, Israel, with Jeroboam as king (ca. 926 B.C.). This revolt marked the end of the united kingdom and the beginning of the period of the divided monarchy.

The Northern Kingdom, Israel (also known as Ephraim or Samaria), continued under its own kings—who came from nine different, mostly short-lived, family dynasties—down to 722 B.C., when Assyria took it over. The Southern Kingdom, Judah, was ruled by David's descendants (with one exception, Queen Athaliah) and continued as a separate and more or less independent nation until 586 B.C., when it was annexed by the Babylonian empire, then the dominant power in the Near East. The period of the divided monarchy was complicated and sometimes chaotic, as the period of the judges had been earlier. At its beginning (ca. 926 B.C.), Israel and Judah were at war with each other, and soon the latter was raided by Egypt (ca. 922). At times, Israel and its northern neighbor Syria warred against each other; once, at least, Israel and Judah were allied against Syria. Toward the end of the period (ca. 734), Syria and Israel combined against Judah, intending to compel the latter to join in a triple alliance against Assyria in order to try to check that empire's advance, as the three small kingdoms had done before in 853.

Some prophets had appeared before the time of the divided monarchy: Moses, Miriam, Balaam, Deborah, Samuel, and Nathan, for example. Now many others came forward. Micaiah, Elijah, Elisha, and others played prominent roles in the early years of the Northern Kingdom, advocating worship of Yahweh (God) and condemning Baal and other "foreign" (non-Israelite) gods and the kings, priests, prophets, and people who served them. The first two classical prophets, Amos and Hosea, also appeared in the North, in about 740. These two denounced the people and particularly the leaders of Israel for their apostasy (i.e., turning from Yahweh), their worship of other gods, and their violations of the covenant requirements of kindness and justice within the community. Each declared that Yahweh would bring Israel to an end. That end came, at the hands of Assyria, in 722.

Judah survived, paying tribute to Assyria as the price of independence. The reign of Manasseh (ca. 687–642), the longest of any of the kings of Israel or Judah, was marked by religious syncretism, cruel oppression, and compliance with Assyrian domination. But hope dawned with the accession of Josiah to the throne of Judah in 640. Josiah sponsored a major religious institutional reform (ca. 622) inspired by the requirement set forth in the newly discovered "book of the law" that God should be worshiped in only one place. This requirement, along with several institutional accommodations necessary to implement it, appears in Deuteronomy 12–19. The requirement to offer sacrifices in only one place apparently was unknown in earlier biblical traditions (which report, without misgiving, sacrificial worship at several different places). Many interpreters suggest that the laws calling for and implementing worship at the one place (Jerusalem) were added to the text of Deuteronomy sometime during the seventh century B.C. in order to counter the persistent tendency of Judahites to worship other gods at the old Canaanite cult shrines outside of Jerusalem. Josiah ordered the renovation of the Jerusalem temple and the destruction of all other places of worship, and also asserted Judah's independence from Assyria. But now the Babylonians were on the move. By 598, Judah had become a Babylonian vassal state. After Judah tried to rebel in 586, a Babylonian army stormed into Jerusalem, burned the city, destroyed the temple and much of the city's system of walls, and carried away most of the remaining leaders as captives.

The Babylonian conquest of Judah in 586 marked the beginning of the period of the exile. The terms "Jew" and "Jewish" came into use at this point in the biblical tradition, for there was no longer a kingdom of Judah. Now it was their religion and their culture that gave the people identity. Though the prophets Jeremiah and Ezekiel encouraged the exiles to believe that God was still with them, the life of some exiles was bitter and anguished (see Ps 137), as was that of those Jews who had remained in their homeland (see Lamentations). Persia, in the meantime, had become the preeminent power in the Middle East. By defeating the Babylonians in 540, Cyrus, the Persian emperor, became the liberator of the Jewish people. Judah and Jerusalem were still part of the Persian empire, but in 538 Cyrus decreed that exiled peoples might return to their homelands, and many exiled Jews did so. Thus, the exile is said to have ended in 538, though, in fact, many Jews remained in Babylon for several centuries afterward.

The Jewish exiles who returned to what had been their country at first busied themselves with rebuilding their homes and trying to reestablish their livelihoods. But crops failed, and many suffered from continuing poverty. Eventually the temple was rebuilt (ca. 515), but despite assurances by the prophets Haggai and Zechariah, conditions did not improve greatly. The walls and gates of Jerusalem were rebuilt under the direction of Nehemiah (ca. 444), a redoubtable Jewish leader commissioned by the Persians as governor of that portion of their empire. Malachi, the last of the biblical prophets, appeared about this time, insisting that Yahweh required full tithes and unblemished sacrificial animal offerings. By around 400, the entire biblical law (Exodus through Deuteronomy) was codified and promulgated, evidently under the auspices of temple priests and Ezra the scribe. This written law, or Torah, was to be the basic standard for all subsequent Jewish faith and life.

Shortly thereafter, the Greeks, led by Alexander the Great, rapidly expanded into a world empire, overwhelming the Persians in 333. By 331, the Jews were living under these new masters. For several centuries afterward, Greek (or Hellenistic) culture was a major influence upon Judaism and also, in due course, upon Christianity. Following Alexander's death in 323, his leading generals contended for supremacy and ended up dividing the empire among themselves. One of them, Seleucus, established himself in Syria and began a dynasty there to the north of Israel. Another, Ptolemy, did the same in Egypt. From 301 to 198, the Jewish people were ruled by the Ptolemies,[4] then after 198, by the Seleucids. The Seleucid emperor Antiochus IV ("Epiphanes," or "God manifest," as he named himself), moved, it seems, by enthusiasm for Greek culture, decided to stamp out Judaism and require Jews to worship Greek gods. Many Jews were persecuted for their religion, and in 168, a group of Jews took up arms against their Syrian oppressors. Judas Maccabeus was the most famous of the leaders in that era of resistance and eventual independence (of sorts), which came to be known as the Maccabean or Hasmonean period. Religious freedom was restored and the title "king" reinstituted, though none of the Maccabean kings was descended from David. The period was marked by constant plotting and intrigue, as evidenced in the books of 1 and 2 Maccabees.

The independent Jewish kingdom ended in 64 B.C., however, when the Roman general Pompey annexed Judea as part of the Roman empire. Jews continued to have religious freedom under Roman rule, though largely through the influence of a series of shrewd Edomite (Idumean) powerbrokers: Antipater, his son Herod ("the Great"), and the latter's son Antipas and grandson Agrippa. Herod the Great rebuilt the temple (which had fallen into disrepair since 515), making it into a magnificent edifice (sometimes called "the temple of Herod"), and presided over a period of material prosperity.[5] Many Jews, however, resented Herod's harsh ways and the fact that he was an Edomite and an agent for foreign overlords.

At his death in 4 B.C., Herod's jurisdiction was partitioned among his sons. Antipas was made tetrarch of Galilee, and Archelaus tetrarch over Samaria, Judea, and Idumea. Archelaus proved incompetent and was replaced by a series of Roman officials known as procurators, who were generally neither competent nor popular. The fifth of these, Pontius Pilate, was removed from office in A.D. 36. The Romans later put Agrippa over these provinces. He was popular with the Jewish people, but when he died in A.D. 44, a second series of procurators took over. Some of these deliberately provoked Jewish religious sensibilities, for instance, by allowing Roman legions to march through Jerusalem bearing images of the emperor as god.

In A.D. 66, under the leadership of the Zealots, the Jewish people revolted against Rome. Under the emperor Titus, the Romans laid siege to Jerusalem and, in A.D. 70, overan it and destroyed the temple.[6] The Jewish sectarian community at Qumran, where the Dead Sea Scrolls had been copied and preserved, was also overrun at this time. With no temple, there was no longer a place for sacrificial worship, and the Sadducees, who had been associated with the temple priest-hood, lost their leadership role. Instead of offering sacrifices, knowing and observing other aspects of the law now became the central fea-tures of Judaism. The Pharisees, with their teachers (rabbis) and their developing oral law or tradition, became the main authorities for Judaism then and subsequently. Synagogues, places of instruction in the law, already to some extent had replaced the temple as institu-tional centers for Judaism.

From its beginnings in Galilee and Judea, Christianity spread over the Mediterranean world in large part, it seems, through the efforts of Paul and his fellow missionaries. All of the first Christians had been Jews, and many continued to observe Jewish law and tradition. Paul insisted that the gospel, or "good news," was for gentiles (non-Jews) as well as for Jews, and he personally established a number of gentile Christian congregations. James (Jesus' brother) and Peter, also known as Cephas, were the main leaders of the early churches in Jerusalem and Antioch, respectively, where certain Jewish practices evidently were retained for some time. Paul and Peter may have been executed in Rome at the time of the emperor Nero's persecution of Christians there in A.D. 64. Christians in Jerusalem abandoned that city shortly before or during the war of A.D. 66–70, after which Christianity became increasingly a gentile religion.

Several other kinds of problems arose among second- and third-generation Christians. One of increasingly urgent importance was that of identifying and defining correct teachings and proper moral standards. At that time, there was no overall structure of church gov-ernance, nor were there as yet any generally accepted creeds or doc-trines, nor was there even a complete consensus as to which Christian writings should be considered authoritative. False teachers, heresies, and immoral conduct were central concerns in the New Testament writings dating from around 110 to 140. Another recurrent problem throughout the New Testament period was the fact that the expected parousia, or return of Jesus, had not yet occurred. Christians in Asia Minor, particularly in the Roman province of Asia, faced another seri-ous crisis in the mid-90s. Roman authorities there evidently were enforcing a requirement that everyone, including Christians, worship an image of the Roman emperor (perhaps the current emperor, Domitian). Those who failed to make the offering were subjected to severe persecution. Christians in post-New Testament times also were subjected periodically to similar persecution. That situation, and much else, of course, changed radically when, toward the end of the first quarter of the fourth century A.D., the emperor Constantine converted to Christianity and established this faith and its emerging institutions as the official religion of the Roman Empire.

B. THE BIBLICAL LITERATURE

The Bible comprises the preserved traditions and writings of a series of religious and sometimes political communities, reflecting the full range of their experiences and concerns during more than twelve hundred years. We find here what we might call biographies and histories; "last words," dirges, and eulogies; sermons and parables; folk songs, hymns, and love songs; architectural plans and military strategies; diaries, detective stories, melodramas, and romances; ritual and criminal laws; blessings and curses; moral admonitions and advice; prophecies and political commentaries; scientific and psychological observations; genealogies; aphorisms; theologies of history; fragments of myths; letters and tracts; apocalyptic visions; and various prayers. The variety and richness of this literature may confuse readers who expect to find only "religious" material in the Bible. Nevertheless, the Bible tells one story: the story of God, creation, and humanity, focusing particularly on God's special peoples. A number of categories or genres of writing can be identified.

Arrangement or Order of Appearance

Approximately the first half of the Old Testament consists of historical narratives (along with other kinds of traditions) that set out the main events and periods from earliest times to around 400 B.C. in story form, mainly in prose composition. Interpreters commonly identify three main collections or sets of writings: the Tetrateuch (Genesis through Numbers, "four books" edited under priestly auspices, ca. 400 B.C.), the Deuteronomic History (Deuteronomy through 2 Kings, edited ca. 550 B.C.), and the Chronicler's History (1 Chronicles through Nehemiah, edited ca. 350 B.C.). The Pentateuch (the first "five books" of the Bible) includes both narratives (from the creation stories to the death of Moses) and, in Exodus through Deuteronomy, the basic law codes. It concludes with the Israelites still in the wilderness but moving toward the land of Canaan. The books from Joshua through 2 Kings continue the story of Israel and Judah, starting with their occupation of Canaan and continuing into the beginning of the exile. First and 2 Chronicles recapitulate and revise the narrative from Adam to the end of the exile, while Ezra and Nehemiah carry it forward to about 350 B.C. The Old Testament writings from Esther through Malachi all were written or are set in the context of the historical period described in the last two of these three sets of works, namely, the Deuteronomic and the Chronicler's Histories.

The story of Esther is placed in the Persian period but probably was written somewhat later. The Psalms, some of which date from pre-exilic times, served as hymns or liturgical prayers in the second temple.[7] The wisdom writings—Job, Proverbs, Ecclesiastes, Wisdom of Solomon, and Ecclesiasticus (also known as Sirach)—reflect Persian and Hellenistic influence and probably were composed between the fifth and second centuries B.C.

The Song of Solomon is grouped with Ecclesiastes and Proverbs because these writings were popularly believed to have been written by Solomon. Three collections of relatively early prophets' oracles and reported activities are then set out at some length: Isaiah, Jeremiah, and Ezekiel. Lamentations was inserted after Jeremiah, probably because it was commonly thought that Jeremiah wrote it. Lamentations, like the apocryphal writings Baruch and the Letter of Jeremiah, gropes with the problem of the exile and related events for traditional faith and understanding. Daniel, also set in the time of the exile (though probably written much later), follows Ezekiel.

The Old Testament closes with the book of the Twelve, namely, twelve relatively brief writings consisting largely of prophetic oracles, attributed to or concerned with the twelve prophets, Hosea through Malachi. These were probably all inscribed on a single scroll originally, which came to be called "the book" of the Twelve. The Hebrew canon, on the other hand, closes with its third section, the Writings, commonly placed in the following order: Psalms, Job, Proverbs, Ruth, Song of Songs (or of Solomon), Ecclesiastes, Lamentations, Esther, Daniel, Ezra-Nehemiah, and 1 and 2 Chronicles. The Law, or Torah (Genesis through Deuteronomy), and the Prophets (including not only the prophetic books but also Joshua, Judges, and 1 Samuel through 2 Kings) constitute the first and second parts of the Hebrew scriptures.

The Old Testament Apocrypha includes a number of writings that in early times were regarded as authoritative, if not as Scripture, in Jewish and Christian circles. First Esdras reviews the history of the Jewish people from Josiah to Ezra, while 2 Esdras is a philosophical treatise in the form of an apocalypse. Several stories written between the fifth and second centuries B.C. give indications of Jewish life and interests during these years: Tobit, Judith, Additions to Esther, Susanna, and Bel and the Dragon. These works are principally concerned with encouraging Jews to remain faithful to their traditions and practices, and to keep themselves from becoming too much like their pagan friends and neighbors. In particular, these writings caution readers to refrain from worshiping the gods and from adopting the moral standards and customs of non-Jews. The books of 1, 2, 3, and 4 Maccabees pick up Jewish history and lore from the time of Alexander the Great, reporting in some detail, if not always accurately, on events and intrigues during the years from about 170 to 125 B.C.

The New Testament, as it is called in Christian traditions, begins with four accounts of Jesus' ministry, words, death, and resurrection: the four Gospels. The first three, called the Synoptic Gospels, are quite similar: Matthew and Luke apparently followed Mark's narrative framework and drew many of Jesus' sayings from another common source, the hypothetical Q (from the German *Quelle*, meaning "source").[8] Luke continues with a second volume, Acts, which describes the early church's, and especially Peter and Paul's, activities.

Epistles, or letters, purportedly written by Paul are arranged approximately in order of length, from Romans to Philemon. Paul's letters date from the early 50s A.D. and contain his thoughts and advice, usually for churches he himself had founded. Many interpreters attribute Ephesians and Colossians to a Deutero-Pauline author, 2 Thessalonians to another unknown writer, and the Pastorals (1 and 2 Timothy; Titus) to a still later author, possibly a follower of Paul, around A.D. 110. Epistles thought to have been written by other early Christian authorities follow next, again in approximate order of length, from Hebrews to Jude. Those not addressed to particular churches or persons are called "catholic" (general or universal) epistles. Last, appropriately, comes the Revelation to John, known more simply as Revelation or the Apocalypse. It begins with a series of admonitions in the form of seven short letters to seven churches in Asia Minor and includes numerous reported visions and psalms or hymns, all concerning the imminent deliverance awaiting Christians who remain faithful despite persecution.

Major Categories or Literary Genres

Poetry

A few biblical books consist almost entirely of poems, some of which were originally also songs or hymns—for example, Lamentations,

Psalms, and the Song of Solomon. Poems, songs or hymns, and prayers are found embedded in many other books, such as Genesis 49, Exodus 15, Numbers 24, Deuteronomy 32, Judges 5, Jonah 2, Tobit 13, Judith 16, Luke 1, and Revelation 19. Ordinarily, prophetic oracles, wisdom sayings, and prayers are in poetry. Biblical poetry takes the form of a short statement followed by reiteration or repetition in different terms of all or part of the idea first stated (in effect, A/A, B/B, etc.). There is no rhyme, but literary critics at times believe they can distinguish meter or cadence.

Law

Many biblical laws are similar to those of other ancient Near Eastern peoples, such as the Babylonians, the Hittites, and the Assyrians. But most are distinctively Israelite in their understanding that it was God who gave the law to his people through Moses for their own good, in order to maintain the right relationship between God and people and to preserve the welfare of the community (cf. Deut 10:12–13). The laws as such are in the form of authoritative pronouncements stating what is to be done and what is not to be done. Those that specify what is or is not to be done under certain circumstances are sometimes called "casuistic" laws. From time to time, the laws were collected and to some extent organized by topics. These collections are known as codifications or codes.

Exodus 34:10–26 may be a fragment of an early Israelite law code, which scholars sometimes call the Ritual Decalogue. The first complete law code is the Covenant Code or Book of the Covenant (Exodus 20–23). A number of laws found in the Covenant Code are reproduced in the Deuteronomic Code, or D (Deuteronomy 5, and most of chaps. 12–26), which, however, consists largely of new laws.[9] Leviticus 17–26 record a somewhat similar code, commonly called the Holiness Code or H, which again consists largely of new laws. The Priestly Code (sometimes labeled PC) includes most of the other ritual and sacrificial laws found in Exodus, Leviticus, and Numbers. These collections probably were codified at different times in various circles within the Israelite-Judahite-Jewish communities between 1200 and 400 B.C.

Prophets

The prophets were spokesmen and spokeswomen for God to the people of their time. Some of the earliest prophets were women, such as Miriam and Deborah. Typically, a prophetic oracle begins with the declaration, "Thus says the Lord." The oracles or prophetic declarations themselves are usually in poetic form. Several of the prophetic books also contain descriptive or narrative prose. Early prophets included cultic, court, or group prophets, as well as individuals. Balaam, an early non-Israelite (Numbers 22–24), in some respects was a prototype of later Israelite prophetism. Several prophets have prominent roles in 1–2 Samuel and 1–2 Kings, such as Samuel himself, Nathan, Elijah, Elisha, Micaiah, Isaiah, and Huldah.

Several of the prophets to whom whole books are dedicated are called "classical prophets" because of their emphasis on Yahweh's requirements both of fidelity to him and of justice and mercy in dealing with other persons in the community. Hosea, Amos, First Isaiah, Micah, Jeremiah, and sometimes Ezekiel and Second Isaiah are regarded as the classical prophets. "Postclassical" prophets (Joel, Obadiah, Nahum, Habakkuk, Haggai, Zephaniah, Zechariah, and Malachi) tend to emphasize Judah's special status vis-à-vis foreign nations and/or the importance of properly offering sacrifices in the temple.

Wisdom

Wisdom was an international type of literature, as demonstrated by comparing biblical texts with extant Egyptian, Babylonian, and Edomite wisdom writings. Several biblical wisdom books are traditionally associated with Solomon, an internationalist par excellence. The typical literary form is the aphorism, a short admonition or comparison. Interests include such matters as court etiquette, prudential and moral advice, and observations about natural phenomena, particularly human motives and behavior. The main writings are Proverbs, Ecclesiastes, Job, Wisdom of Solomon, and Ecclesiasticus (or Sirach).[10] Certain psalms, such as Psalms 34 and 37, and various sayings in chapters 4 and 12 in Tobit and in the Synoptic Gospels also exemplify typical wisdom interests and format. Such sayings are sometimes called "proverbial" or "gnomic."

Apocalyptic

The apocalyptic writers generally state that they are revealing secrets communicated earlier in the form of dreams or visions either to the author (e.g., Revelation) or to some person in antiquity (e.g., Daniel, 2 Esdras). These secrets gave meaning to persons living in the period in and for which they were revealed, which often was a time of tribulation or persecution. Typically, apocalyptic writers vividly describe what is to take place in the last days of the present age and picture the glorious conditions of life in the new, coming, or messianic, age. The characteristic apocalyptic message is that those who are persecuted (Daniel, Revelation) or troubled (2 Esdras) should endure their trials and tribulations in hope and confidence, for God or a supernatural power of some sort will soon intervene and deliver those who remain faithful to God and live rightly in the meantime. The main biblical examples are Daniel, Revelation, and Matthew 24 = Mark 13 = Luke 21 (the "little apocalypse" or "Synoptic apocalypse"). Other biblical writings, such as Isaiah 24–27, Joel, Amos 9, Zechariah 14, 2 Esdras, Additions to Esther 11, 2 Thessalonians, and 2 Peter, also contain apocalyptic passages. Several other apocalypses are found in the Pseudepigrapha: for example, *1-2 Enoch*, the *Sibylline Oracles*, and *2-3 Baruch*.

Narratives, Gospels, Parables, and Letters

Several other literary types or genres are amply represented in biblical tradition. The former category is illustrated throughout the biblical writings, for example, the J and E narratives from Genesis to 1 Kings, numerous short stories (or novels) such as Ruth, Esther, Tobit, Judith, and the four books of Maccabees. Narratives figure prominently in the New Testament, as well, particularly in the first three Gospels and the book of Acts.

Gospels constitute a unique literary genre, one found only in the New Testament and other early Christian literature, such as the Gospel of Thomas. Gospels are narratives, and typically report Jesus' activities. They are distinctive in that they also present collections of Jesus' sayings and purport to describe all, or substantially all, of his public career, including his execution under Roman authority. Three of the New Testament Gospels also include accounts of his resurrection appearances. Gospels were written both to preserve recollections of first and second generation Christians and to provide resources for the faith and life of the emerging Christian communities. They may derive in part from early Christian preaching.

One of the typical forms of Jesus' teaching or preaching, as reported in the Gospels, is the parable. Parables are also narratives or stories, usually quite short ones, about persons (or sometimes other beings) who have acted prudently or imprudently, righteously or otherwise. Typically, a parable calls forth the hearer/reader's response, prompting examination of his or her own life and values in light of the story. For instance, the Parable of the Good Samaritan (Luke 10:29–36) challenges the hearer/reader to ask, "Am I like the Samaritan, who gave assistance, or like the Priest and Levite who passed by on the other side of the road?" Parables also are found in the Old Testament; for example, Jotham's parable (Judg 9:7–15), Nathan's story about the rich man and the poor man (2 Sam 12:1–6), or the parable of the forest and the sea (2 Esdr 4:13–18). The entire book of Jonah may have been written as a parable.

The epistle appears commonly in the New Testament in virtually every writing from Romans to Revelation. Some of these were actual letters, written to known persons and communities. Others, though in the form of letters, were more likely essays or tracts, written for contemporary Christian readers generally. Epistles, or writings in formal letter style, are also found in other biblical literature (e.g., Ezra 5, Jeremiah 29, 1 Esdras 2, the Letter of Jeremiah, and Additions to Esther 16).

Sources and Editorial Units

Many of the traditions were remembered and passed on by word of mouth perhaps for generations or even centuries before being written down. Later writers or editors occasionally added to earlier writings in order to correct, clarify, or supplement the texts before them. Some of the earliest biblical writers may have been more collectors and editors of tradition than authors. These editors may have either been single individuals or groups representing individual schools of interpretation. For example, there may have been several Deuteronomic editors and probably many priestly editors.

The earliest such editor was the Yahwist, designated J, who gathered and set down a wide range of material, some of it probably dating from much earlier times, around 950 B.C. This writer regularly used the divine name YHWH or Yahweh,[11] which is translated as "the LORD" in most English translations, and as "Jehovah" in some earlier translations. J apparently lived in Judah, and the material he collected probably represents southern, or Judahite, tradition. Some interpreters suggest that he may have been a court archivist in the time of David or Solomon. The J material appears in Genesis, Exodus, Numbers, Deuteronomy, Joshua, Judges, 1 and 2 Samuel, and early chapters in 1 Kings. Later southern tradition, sometimes designated A, then follows in the rest of 1 and 2 Kings. The J theology of history may be seen particularly in Genesis 2–4 and 6–13, in 2 Samuel 11–20, and in 1 Kings 1–2. J's critical appraisal of human pretension and cruelty, and his interpretation of events in terms of Yahweh's sovereign justice and mercy prompt some modern interpreters to view J as a precursor to the kind of prophetic understanding of human affairs that is found later in the classical prophets such as Hosea, Amos, Isaiah, and Jeremiah.

The northern traditions were collected about the same time (ca. 950–850) by E, so called because the divine name Elohim, usually translated as "God," is used regularly in texts attributed to this source. A later northern editor, sometimes called B, may have completed the collection around 722. The E or B material is found intermittently from Genesis 20 through Exodus, in Numbers, Deuteronomy, Joshua, and in 1 Samuel through 2 Kings 17. In E traditions, God often is said to communicate with people through dreams. Northern traditions characteristically take a negative stance toward kingship in Israel, holding that God alone is Israel's king.

Sometime after the fall of the Northern Kingdom in 722, perhaps around 650, its traditions were combined with those of Judah by a redactor or editor, referred to generally as RJE, into a composite collection commonly designated JE. By that time, it may have become clear to people in Judah that the Northern Kingdom, Israel, was extinct. Southern writers had already begun to use the name Israel when referring to the surviving kingdom of Judah. In effect, Judah had inherited the name of Israel and probably also many of the traditions of the North. JE represents the combination resulting from incorporation of these northern traditions into existing southern traditions. Modern critics generally hesitate to differentiate between the J and E components of JE in many parts of the text. The fact that the combination took place under southern auspices may account for the relatively fragmentary character of E compared to J in the biblical narrative as we have it.

The presence of duplicate or conflicting versions and details in the writings from Genesis through 2 Kings may be understood, at least in part, by recalling that the editors, J, E, and RJE, were collectors of traditions and sometimes of earlier collections, some of which had come down in variant and possibly multiple forms. These editors evidently were more concerned to preserve what they had collected than to trim possible discrepancies or differences found in the traditions they honored. Biblical editors may have occasionally added their own interpretations and comments as well.

Not all modern interpreters regard J and E as early writings or documents. Many scholars, particularly Scandinavian, see the so-called J and E material primarily as oral traditions that were remembered, modified, and passed along by word of mouth until finally set down, perhaps as recently as 400 B.C. It should also be recalled that the "documentary hypothesis," which posits the existence of early documents J, E, D, and finally P, is just that: a hypothesis.[12] It may be the best current explanation of the process by which the present biblical traditions in Genesis through 2 Kings came together, though it is not unchallenged. None of the "documents" it posits, however, has been found; and it may be that in time a new scholarly consensus or paradigm will develop to better account for the data.

The Priestly tradition (P) includes both narrative and legal materials. The legal portion, known as the Priestly Code (PC), is concerned primarily with procedures to be followed by priests in offering sacrifices in the temple or its portable predecessor, the tent or tabernacle. P material appears in all of the first four books, the Tetrateuch, which may have been put into their present form by the P editor or editors (RP) around 400 B.C.[13] P, unlike traditions dating before 450 B.C., consistently distinguishes between priests and Levites. In P, priests are characterized as the sons of Aaron, while Levites are relegated to the role of assistants to the priests. P traditions assume that Israelites always worshiped in one place at a time—first the portable tent or tabernacle, and later the Jerusalem temple. P laws include more numerous sacrificial offerings and more elaborate ritual procedures than are to be found in the earlier law codes.

Following the Tetrateuch, the next major editorial unit is the Deuteronomic History, which includes Deuteronomy, Joshua, Judges, 1 and 2 Samuel, and 1 and 2 Kings. At its core is the Deuteronomic Code, or D (Deuteronomy 5, 12–26), much of which may date from the time of the judges. The commandment in Deuteronomy 12 that Israel must worship in only the one place (implicitly, the temple in Jerusalem) was probably added in the seventh century B.C. in order to curb the worship of Canaanite gods. Such worship continued to be associated with the numerous shrines throughout the land. Earlier traditions contain no strictures against worship at these places. Chapters 12–19 of Deuteronomy provided for a number of adjustments in cultic practice that were necessary in order to implement the new requirement of worship in only the one place. For example, Israelites, or more precisely, Judahites, might now slaughter farm animals for food in their local towns without offering them in sacrifice. Rural Levites, who previously had earned their livelihood by officiating as priests at the local shrines, were now added to the welfare rolls or lists of persons to be cared for—along with orphans, widows, and sojourners—because they had no independent means of support. In theory, such rural Levites were to be accorded the same status and perquisites as the Levites who were priests in the Jerusalem temple. Since for many it was a long way to Jerusalem, Judahites might now sell the tithes of their harvests locally, carry the proceeds with them, and buy food and offerings in Jerusalem rather than be obliged to haul the heavy loads of tithes there. The dating of D before P is the keystone of the documentary hypothesis set forth late in the nineteenth century by Julius Wellhausen. Since the D tradition requires Israel's worship in one place but the P tradition assumes it, and for various other reasons, such as the many new types of offering found in P laws, it seems likely that P represents a later perspective or understanding than D. Biblical scholars generally agree that P was also later than J or E traditions.

The Deuteronomic Editor or Historian (designated DH or RD), writing around 550 B.C., interpreted the past in accordance with the prophetic theory of history but with particular attention to the requirements of the Deuteronomic law: that only Yahweh should be worshiped and that such worship was to take place, once the temple was built, only in Jerusalem. DH thus structures the period of the judges in terms of a repeated cycle of Israel's apostasy, God's punishment ("he gave them over to plunderers") and deliverance through the prowess of a judge, who judges all Israel for so many years, then dies, and the cycle of apostasy begins again. DH evaluates the kings of Israel and Judah according to their exclusive devotion to Yahweh and their diligence in destroying the "high places" (shrines of Canaanite and other foreign gods). No northern and only a few southern kings receive good marks from DH.

The third main editorial collection is the Chronicler's History: 1 and 2 Chronicles, Ezra, and Nehemiah. In these works, history and religion are reviewed with special attention to David, Jerusalem, the temple, priests and Levites, and the "books of the law" (here perhaps the PC or the whole Tetrateuch, but more likely the whole legal corpus from Exodus through Deuteronomy). Critics suggest that the Chronicler may have been a Levite, a singer, or perhaps Ezra himself. The Chronicler's viewpoint is similar to that of P in that the offering of sacrifices is the central interest and that only priests may officiate at such ceremonies while Levites are relegated to lower status. The Chronicler's collection probably was assembled and edited around 400 to 350 B.C.

Additions to and combinations of other material within single books, as in the case of Isaiah, Zechariah, and 2 Corinthians, along with other types of editorial activity, such as borrowing and interpolation, are noted in the introductory chapters on the separate books of the Bible.

Canon, Manuscripts, and Translations

Canon

The term "canon" derives from the Greek, *kanon*, meaning a "measuring rod." As applied to biblical writings, it came to mean "normative" or "authoritative," with the further sense of having been officially approved. Canonical writings are those that, whether by deliberate choice at a particular time, or through usage over a longer period, have come to be considered Scripture. The following section first overviews the process by which Jewish scriptures, or Old Testament, was recognized as authoritative, and then considers briefly the formation of the New Testament as additional Christian Scripture.

At what point did the biblical writings come to be regarded as canonical, that is, officially scriptural? The Covenant Code (Exodus 20–23) possibly was the law of the land as early as 1200–1000 B.C. The Deuteronomic law was authoritative for the Judahites by the seventh century B.C. if not earlier,[14] and the Priestly Code was so regarded for Judaism by about 400 (Nehemiah 8). A Greek translation of the Pentateuch known as the Septuagint (designated LXX) was made beginning perhaps as early as 250 B.C. and supplemented in following centuries by other writings.[15] According to Jewish tradition, learned rabbis at Jamnia around A.D. 90 decided to retain as Scripture only those writings then known in Hebrew or Aramaic, perhaps on the assumption that these were more ancient and consequently more authoritative than those in Greek or other "modern" languages.[16] The latter were excluded from the Jewish canon. In time, many of these writings originally in the LXX but subsequently excluded from Jewish scriptures, along with a few later writings, came to be known as the Old Testament Apocrypha.

Discovery of the Dead Sea Scrolls in 1947 shed further light on the nature of Jewish religion and the question of canon in the final two centuries B.C. and the first century A.D.[17] The first scrolls were found by accident in a cave near the Dead Sea, and more scrolls subsequently were located in nearby caves. The greater number of these scrolls have become available to scholars only in recent years. At first, many popular writers and a few imaginative scholars jumped to the conclusion that the scrolls somehow demonstrated that Jesus was a renegade member of the Qumran community that had produced them, and that he and thus also Christianity should now be considered discredited. Subsequent and more careful reading of the scrolls, however, has found no connection with Jesus or early Christianity, but it has led to the recognition that Judaism at that time was more complicated than had been supposed. The scrolls provide a wealth of information about this branch of sectarian Judaism and its scriptures. They include many writings not previously known, such as the *War Scroll*, the *Manual of Discipline*, and the *Thanksgiving Psalms*. But the scrolls also include at least fragments of most of the writings eventually included in the canon of Jewish scriptures. The most complete such text is the Isaiah scroll. Since the scrolls are dated prior to Jamnia, they indicate that at least in this sectarian community, writings that later were included in the traditional Jewish canon were honored as at least authoritative. It is not known to what extent the Jamnia rabbis may have known of or considered the other writings esteemed by the Qumran community.

Early Christian communities, increasingly composed of gentiles more than Jews, apparently preferred to use the Greek Bible and preserved the apocryphal books as part of their scriptures. Catholic and Eastern Orthodox Bibles still include most of the apocryphal writings, but beginning with Martin Luther in the sixteenth century, Protestants reverted to the Hebrew canon of Jamnia for their Old Testament.[18] The early churches did not yet have a New Testament, but some of their writings evidently were intended to be authoritative at least for their particular readers.[19] A collection of Paul's letters may have been circulating among gentile Christian churches as early as A.D. 90. Such a collection could have served as the model for the collection of seven letters at the beginning of the book of Revelation (composed ca. A.D. 96). Second Peter, written around A.D. 120–140, refers to Paul's letters as authoritative "writings" or "scriptures."[20] The earliest known New Testament canon was Marcion's (ca. A.D. 140). This was selected and edited in accordance with Marcion's own heretical views. By the end of the second century A.D., more orthodox Christian leaders began listing the writings they thought scriptural or otherwise, and they achieved some consensus on this. The present New Testament canon was generally agreed to by around A.D. 400.

Some thirteen Coptic codices (bound papyrus volumes) were discovered at Nag Hammadi in 1945. These included an extensive "library" of early Christian literature, all of which was excluded from the eventual New Testament canon. These writings provide a much more complete and detailed picture of the developing beliefs of gnostic

Christianity, a major movement especially in North African Christianity that began perhaps as early as the first century A.D. The core belief in gnosticism is that salvation, often thought of as liberation from the physical to a spiritual realm, is through *gnosis*, or knowledge. Such knowledge was shared by sectarian or relatively isolated communities.[21] Some commentators believe that the substance of the Nag Hammadi materials confirms the wisdom of the church fathers who excluded them from the New Testament canon that was in process of formation from the second century through the first half of the fifth century. Others have suggested that the New Testament canon should be reopened to include at least some of this newly found early Christian literature.[22] Scholarly discussions continue about whether there was a pre-Christian gnosticism or whether the kind of gnosticism represented in the Nag Hammadi codices emerged out of Christian beliefs. Scholars think it likely that some of these writings, including perhaps the Gospel of Thomas, originally were nongnostic but then edited or revised in order to accord with gnostic concerns.

Manuscripts and translations

No original biblical manuscripts survive. What we have are copies of copies. Aside from the Dead Sea Scrolls (ca. 150 B.C.–A.D. 70), extant Old Testament manuscripts date no earlier than the ninth century A.D. Copyists, including the Masoretes (scribes who added Hebrew vowel points during the period from A.D. 600 to 950), generally exercised great care, with the result that relatively late Old Testament manuscripts may be fairly reliable renditions of much earlier copies. There are, however, numerous textual errors and multiple versions. Translators have to choose among Hebrew, Aramaic, Syriac, Latin, and other ancient textual versions, and sometimes must finally resort to conjecture.[23] Some New Testament manuscripts found in 1931 date as early as the late second and third centuries A.D.,[24] but most New Testament manuscripts are more recent. Early manuscripts are in Greek, Latin, Syriac, Ethiopic, and other languages. Some four hundred thousand textual variants appear among the New Testament manuscripts, but the probable meaning of most passages is fairly clear.

Around A.D. 390, a scholarly monk, Jerome, produced a Latin translation of the Bible that was to become the standard Bible of most Western Christians for more than a thousand years. It was called "the Vulgate" because it was written in the "vulgar," that is, common language of the time: Latin. It was based on Jerome's judgment regarding the reliability of the manuscript versions available to him. The Vulgate was later translated into English (the Old Testament at Douay in 1607; the New Testament at Rheims in 1582) in order to counter the influence of Protestant English Bibles, which often followed Luther's German translation. The past 170 years of textual and linguistic discoveries and research have yielded substantial information not previously available. Modern versions reconstruct and translate the text using the results of this scholarship. Readers often find it instructive to consult more than one translation of biblical texts, since different translations often bring out fresh nuances and sometimes render a given text in new ways that are nevertheless faithful to the underlying ancient languages.

The editors of the Revised Standard Version (RSV) tried to preserve as much of the familiar language of the King James Version (KJV) as is both intelligible to modern readers and accurate in the light of modern knowledge. The KJV itself was a revision of earlier versions going back, for example, through the Bishop's Bible (1568) and the Coverdale translation (1535) to Tyndale's translation (1526–1534). Many of Tyndale's phrases still may be found in the RSV. The translators of the New English Bible (NEB), on the other hand, decided to recast the meaning of the text in different language, adopting many modern British idioms. The RSV (1946–1952) and NEB (1970) were translated by Protestant scholars but have since been endorsed by American and British Catholic authorities. The Jerusalem Bible (1966) is an English version of a 1956 translation by French Catholic scholars in Jerusalem. The New American Bible (1970) is a fresh translation by American Catholic scholars. A new inclusive-language version of the New Testament portion appeared in 1987 (the Revised New Testament of the New American Bible), replacing the 1970 version. The New Revised Version (NRSV), based on the RSV, was published in 1989. Its principal feature is the use of gender-inclusive language. The Revised English Bible (REB), also published in 1989, generally follows the New English Bible translation but often renders the text into more conventional modern English.

C. BASIC THEMES AND ISSUES IN BIBLICAL FAITH AND UNDERSTANDING

Mainline biblical faith affirms one God as creator and source of all that is, as the one whose merciful bounty provides for the needs of all his creatures, as the Sovereign over the history of nations and the little histories of individual persons, and as the one who in his own good time will restore and transform the world that has been disfigured and degraded by human depravity into a renewed or new realm where all creatures shall flourish before him, doing his will and enjoying his blessings forever.

Yet it would be a mistake to assume that the biblical peoples were always or inevitably devoted to the one God. Again and again, Hebrews, Israelites, Judahites, and Jews pursued their love affair with other gods: the golden calf, the gods of the Canaanites (whose favor was closely linked with successful agriculture and animal husbandry), the gods and goddesses of other nations, and the little man-made godlings or idols of hearth and home. From Moses to Elijah, to Hosea and Second Isaiah, to the Letter of Jeremiah and the stories of Bel and the Dragon in the Apocrypha, religious leaders and writers called on their people to choose which god they would serve. Thus, one of the core issues in biblical faith is this continuing struggle between proponents of faith in the one God, and the popular and persistent worship of other deities. Such worship was not only an affair of the masses. At times it was abetted by leaders, for example, by Aaron, Moses' brother, and by kings of Israel and Judah (such as Solomon, Ahab, and Manasseh). Sometimes it was ordained by foreign overlords (as in Daniel 3, 1 Maccabees 1–2, and Revelation 13, 14, and 20).

The biblical writings are nearly all theocentric: If human figures are on the stage, it is always God who is the director. God is not thought of abstractly, as a being in or by himself, but always in relationship to the world, which God created and rules, and to human beings and other creatures. The biblical writings testify to a particular relationship with Israel and, in the New Testament, to Jesus, the church, and the world. These relationships—in the past, the present, and the future—are at the center of biblical faith and understanding.

The Creation

In many Eastern and gnostic religions, the material world is regarded as evil, an illusion, or a mistake to be endured or overcome. Not so here: God created the heavens and the earth, and found all that he had made very good (Genesis 1). In the story of the flood, God spares not only a core of human survivors but also the progenitors of all other species of life, and not just those useful to people. *All living creatures* were to "breed abundantly . . . and be fruitful and multiply upon the earth" (Genesis 6–9). The whole created order of beings is tended by God's wondrous power and good will;[25] its existence occasions awe and celebration.[26] Life in the world, including sexuality and material prosperity, is affirmed as good. Hopes for the future center first on coming into the promised land, a "land flowing with milk and honey," and later, on life in a fruitful and peaceable kingdom on a renewed or transformed earth, commonly visualized with Jerusalem or Zion in its midst.[27] Only in the New Testament is it sometimes suggested that the fulfillment of life is to be in heaven.[28]

The Human Condition

Humanity is part of the good world of beings created by God. The creation story attributed to the Priestly source (P) in Genesis 1 declares that God made male and female in his own image and gave them dominion over other creatures of the earth.[29] The Yahwist (J) tradition is less optimistic: In the J creation story, the first human, *ha adam*, like other creatures, is made from the dust of the earth (*adamah*) and, as a result of disobedience, is destined to return to the dust (Genesis 2–3). The P and J versions together encompass the biblical appreciation of the ambivalence of human nature and destiny. Humanity is "little less than God" (Ps 8:5) but is not God. When human beings try to put themselves in God's place or ignore God's commands, catastrophe results, usually for others as well as themselves (Genesis 3–4; 6–9; 11).

The number of persons characterized as righteous in the later biblical traditions is quite small: Abraham (perhaps), Kings Hezekiah and Josiah,[30] Job, Tobit, Judith, Esther (of the Additions), Susanna, and a few people commemorated in the books of Maccabees. However, even the writings that are most pessimistic about human nature and destiny (Ecclesiastes and 2 Esdras) understand that people have the capacity to respond faithfully to God and considerately and justly to other persons—and must bear responsibility for failing to do so.

Death, Resurrection, Eternal Life

Since Adam's disobedience, all of humanity has had to face death. The hope for the resurrection of the dead appears only in a few late Old Testament texts: Daniel 12:2, perhaps Isaiah 26:19 and Ezekiel 37, and in 2 Maccabees 7:9–14. In the New Testament, it is generally expected that those who have died will be raised at the parousia, when Christ returns. They will then face divine judgment, along with those who are still alive at the time, after which the righteous will enter the kingdom of God. Paul sometimes states that those still alive will be "changed" or transformed before entering their heavenly common-wealth. Throughout most of the biblical period, hope for the future was expressed mainly in terms of the continuation of one's name and family and of the people of Israel or Judah in coming generations. Hope for eternal life after death or the immortality of the soul is found a few times in the Bible.[31] Most New Testament texts that give expression to the hope for life in the coming kingdom of God suggest that those who enter it will experience eternal life there.[32]

Good and Evil

All creation, including humanity, was made good by God. If God is good and all-powerful, why does he allow or cause bad things to happen to good or innocent people? This issue is sometimes called the "theodicy" problem. Abraham poses it when bargaining with Yahweh over the fate of Sodom and Gomorrah (Gen 18:22–33), and it is addressed thematically in the book of Job. Why then is there disobedience, fratricide, homicide, injustice, suffering, and death?

In some biblical traditions, what may seem evil is attributed to God's acting for his own purposes, for instance, hardening Pharaoh's heart (Exodus 10) or tormenting Job. In the OT, however, evil is usually understood to arise out of the anxious and arrogant will of people to gain power and glory over others or to put themselves in the place of God. "The imagination of man's heart is evil from his youth" (Gen 8:21), nevertheless, people also can obey God and love their neighbors.[33] This dual capacity is the basic dynamic of the biblical story of humankind's, and particularly of Israel's, life under God's sovereignty. Many Old Testament prophets looked for that future time when God would transform the human heart so that obedience, love, and the knowledge of the Lord would prevail on earth.[34] In the meantime, the story of humankind and of Israel is one not only of faithfulness and obedience but also—and more typically—of mistrust and disobedience, and of God's varied responses of judgment and steadfast love. Fairly late in the Old Testament period, another explanation for bad things happening was noted: the idea of chance or fate, which is indifferent to human deserving (Eccl 9:11–12).[35] The "devil" is mentioned, somewhat incidentally, as a source of evil in the Wisdom of Solomon 2:24, and a demon plays a prominent role in the book of Tobit. In the New Testament, Satan and his demons emerge as instigators of illness and suffering, as well as of faithlessness and wrongdoing.[36] Satan is also known here as "the Evil One,"[37] and sometimes, though not always, as "the devil." In a few New Testament writings, the present world is said to be under his power (1 John 5, Revelation). Nevertheless, the New Testament writings all maintain that human beings are accountable for their decision whether to serve God or other masters and are responsible before God for how they act in relation to other persons.

Israel and Other Nations

Chapters 1–11 of Genesis tell the stories of the first human beings: their creation and that of the rest of the world and its other inhabitants including creatures of all kinds, the first human pair's eating of the forbidden fruit, the first fratricide, a subsequent homicide, the flood, and the building of the city and the tower. Thereafter, according to the stories, people were scattered abroad over the earth, separated by nations and languages,[38] alienated from one another and from God. In this problematic and inauspicious setting, Abraham is called both to *be blessed* and to become a great nation and also, somehow, to *be a blessing* to all the families of the earth (Gen 12:1–3).[39] The rest of the biblical story represents a series of fulfillments or partial fulfillments of these promises and tasks. In some traditions, the emphasis is on the role of Abraham's descendants as a blessing to other nations or peoples; in others, the blessings seem reserved more, or even exclusively, for Israel, Judah, or the Jewish people.

The promise that Israel would be a blessing to other nations is exemplified in many prophetic and narrative traditions. Thus, the "floating oracle" of Isaiah 2:2–4 and Micah 4:1–3 looks forward to a wonderful era of international peace and other blessings. Isaiah 19 visualizes Israel in the latter days as "a blessing in the midst of the earth," along with Egypt, characterized as God's people, and Assyria, said to be the work of his hands. Zechariah looks for a time when the survivors of all nations will go up to worship Yahweh in Jerusalem each year (Zechariah 14). Through the evil scheme of Joseph's brothers, God brings it about that people from many nations are kept alive in time of famine (Genesis 50). Jonah's grudging message enables the Ninevites (Assyrians) to be spared otherwise certain destruction. Ruth, a Moabite, is a model for fidelity and devotion, and is also King David's great-grandmother. Two of the most righteous people in the Old Testament were non-Israelites: Noah and Job. In the New Testament, Jesus refers to a Samaritan as an exemplar of responsive neighbor-love (Luke 10) and promises that people will come from all the earth to sit at table in the kingdom of God (Luke 13). A Roman centurion testifies to Jesus' divine status (Mark 15:39), an Ethiopian is among the early converts to Christianity (Acts 8), and, at least after Paul, Christianity becomes open to believers from all nations and races.

On the other hand, a narrower, more exclusive point of view is to be found in many biblical texts. When Israel enters Canaan, the indigenous peoples are to be slaughtered (Deuteronomy 7) or at least enslaved (Judges 1). Ammonites and Moabites are forever to be barred from the congregation of Israel (Deuteronomy 23). Ezra and Nehemiah ruthlessly "cleansed" Israel of foreign wives and children for the sake of the "holy race" or of ancient grievances (Ezra 9–10; Nehemiah 13). Xenophobia, fear of foreigners or strangers, surfaces particularly in writings reflecting the experience of persecution or defeat (e.g., Esther; Psalm 137; Nahum; 3 Maccabees). Some of the prophets looked for a messianic age in which other nations (i.e., gentiles) either have been destroyed or are made to serve the Jewish people (e.g., Joel, Obadiah, Haggai). Is Israel chosen by God for special, even unique, privilege, or is it chosen to be a blessing, a "light to the nations" (Isa 49:6)? Both kinds of understandings are found in the Old Testament. A similar issue arises in the New Testament: Are Christians to love and do good to their enemies or to only fellow believers? Is salvation reserved only for the few, or is it open, potentially, for all?

The God of Past, Present, and Future

The God of biblical faith was not known through philosophical speculation or mystical contemplation. Rather, he was known and remembered through his actions and interactions in history. God had called the fathers and mothers, used the evil intentions of Joseph's brothers for the good of many peoples, and led Israel, through Moses, out of Egypt, thereby showing not only his good intentions toward Israel but also his power to make good his will and word in the world. Through Moses, God had given Israel his law, and under Joshua, brought them into the land of Canaan, true to his promises to the fathers (Josh 21:43–45). The Deuteronomic editor of Judges reports that because of Israel's apostasy, God periodically subjected them to oppressors, but afterward would send deliverance through the various judges (Judg 2:11–23). Hosea looked to the past to understand the present relationship between God and Israel: "Out of Egypt have I called my son."

But because the Israelites had forgotten God, he also proclaimed, "they shall return to the land of Egypt" (Hos 11:1, 5). The prophet known as Second Isaiah saw in the exodus from Egypt a clue to a new deliverance in store for the exiles in Babylon (Isa 43:14–21). Not only was the God of Israel the same as the one who had acted in the past, but the people identified themselves with those who had gone before: "A wandering Aramean was my father. . . . And the Egyptians . . . laid upon us harsh bondage. . . . And the LORD brought us out of Egypt . . . and gave us this land" (Deut 26:5–9).[40] The New Testament writers not only tell stories about Jesus and the early church but also claim to be part of the continuing story of Israel that began with Abraham.

The present was understood with reference to both past and future. God who acted before is the same who now rules and overrules Israel and the nations. God's law, given in ancient times to Moses, is also the law for "this day," a recurrent phrase in Deuteronomy 5–11, for God's will and purposes for his people are unchanged. Emphasis in the Law and the Prophets alike is always upon the here and now. Now is always the time for faithfulness to God and for keeping God's commandments! Similarly, in the New Testament, Paul and John stress the present decision of faith in relation to what God has already done in Christ and the possibility and demand for a life now lived according to the Spirit in the way of love.

The promises to Abraham and Sarah (Genesis 12 and 17) pointed toward a future fulfillment. The Old Testament prophets expected God to act in judgment against foreign nations because of their pride and cruelty, but particularly against his own people, Israel and Judah, who had forsaken the covenant. They also looked for God's action in restoring the fortunes of his people and sometimes those of other peoples as well. This expectation was decisive for the present: If the people returned to the Lord, they might avert his wrath; if they looked to the Lord for deliverance, they need not despair. Some visions of hope for the future include the promise of a new king or messiah from the house of David (Isaiah 9 and 11; Ezekiel 34); others do not (Isaiah 2 and 19; Jeremiah 31; Daniel 7; Hosea 2; Zechariah 14). Jesus also called on his hearers to repent, claiming that the kingdom of God and the time of judgment were near. Most of the New Testament writers also summoned their readers to right action then, while there was still time, before the coming of Christ. At that time, God would make all things new. Those found fit for the kingdom would then enter into the blessings of life together and with God in a transformed heaven and earth.

NOTES

The Historical Context

1. The Canaanites had been there since about 3000 B.C. Canaanite cultural and religious influences on early Israel have been examined in recent decades following the discovery and translation of the Ras Shamra (or Ugaritic) texts. For information on Canaanite religion, see Mark S. Smith, *The Origins of Biblical Monotheism: Israel's Polytheistic Background and the Ugaritic Texts* (New York: Oxford University Press, 2000); David P. Wright, *Ritual in Narrative: The Dynamics of Feasting, Mourning and Retaliation Rites in the Ugaritic Tale of Aqhat* (Winona Lake, Ind.: Eisenbrauns, n.d.).

2. After annexing the former homeland of the Jewish people in the first century B.C., the Romans renamed it Palestine in honor of the Philistines, who had dominated it a thousand years before.

3. Initially named Abram and Sarai. See Gen 17:1–16.

4. Strangely, little is known about the experience of the Jewish people during this period of Egyptian rule. Some of the biblical writings may have been composed then, but none of them provides any particular information about the times. Third Maccabees, which has the Egyptian period as its setting, is highly legendary in character.

5. Portions of Herod's temple remain to the present time, notably the "Western Wall" and the now-subterranean "Warren-Wilson arch."

6. See the depiction on the Arch of Titus in Rome.

The Biblical Literature

7. The Prayer of Manasseh and the Prayer of Azariah and the Song of the Three Young Men, also psalm-like in form and content, probably were written after the book of Psalms was completed. Psalms are found in many other books of the Bible.

8. See the overview to part IV.

9. Many of the new laws found in Deuteronomy 12–19 concern what appears to be a major institutional revolution in the late eighth or sometime in the seventh century B.C. These laws stipulate that sacrificial worship may take place only at the central shrine (in due course, identified as the Jerusalem temple), and make a number of adjustments or accomodations in light of this new requirement.

10. In the present book, the name Sirach will be used to designate this writing.

11. *Jahwe* in German, hence the symbol J. German scholars were the first to identify and label this hypothetical source.

12. The documentary hypothesis came to classic expression in Julius Wellhausen, *Prolegomena to the History of Ancient Israel* (New York: Meridian, 1957), originally published in 1878.

13. Some interpreters believe that traces of P editing can also be found in Deuteronomy.

14. See 2 Kings 22–23.

15. The term "Septuagint" may refer to a variety of ancient, mainly Greek, writings, used as Scripture by Jews in the last two centuries B.C.E., and by both Jews and Christians in the first century or two of the Common Era. As to the problematic nature of the Septuagint, see Melvin K. H. Peters, "Septuagint," in *The Anchor Bible Dictionary* (New York: Doubleday, 1992), V: 1093–1104.

16. There is very little reliable evidence that rabbis actually met at Jamnia, much less what criteria they may have used in determining which writings were to be regarded as canonical. "Jamnia" may best be understood as a symbol for the process—whatever it may have been—whereby the Jewish canon eventually took shape.

17. Oxford University Press is currently publishing critical scholarly texts in its *Discoveries in the Judean Desert Series*. For a relatively brief overview of the scrolls and their significance, see one or more of the Bible dictionaries listed under suggested reading following the introduction to this book. See also *Eerdmans Commentaries on the Dead Sea Scrolls* (Grand Rapids: Eerdmans, 2001).

18. See the overview to part III.

19. See, e.g., Mark 13:14; John 20:30–31; 1 Cor 14:37–38; Rev 22:18–19.

20. The Greek term used in 2 Peter is *grammata*, which can be translated either way.

21. Interpreters think it likely that the Corinthian Christians who valued "knowledge" and "spiritual gifts" were influenced by or else giving expression to gnostic beliefs.

22. Some members of the Jesus Seminar favor so doing. See, e.g., Robert W. Funk, *The Five Gospels: What Did Jesus Really Say?* (San Francisco: HarperSanFrancisco, 1997), which includes the *Gospel of Thomas*, one of the Nag Hammadi gospels, along with Matthew, Mark, Luke, and John.

23. The alphabetized footnotes in many English translations refer, often in general terms, to such different sources.

24. The Chester Beatty papyri.

Basic Themes and Issues in Biblical Faith and Understanding

25. See Sir 18:13: "The compassion of man is for his neighbor, but the compassion of the Lord is for all living beings."

26. See Job 38–39; Psalm 104, 148; Isaiah 40; and the Song of the Three Young Men.

27. See, e.g., Isaiah 2, 11, 19; Jeremiah 33; Ezekiel 47; Hosea 2; Amos 9; Revelation 21–22.

28. See, e.g., John 14; Philippians 3. It is unclear whether "the eternal age," "safe and healthful habitations," or "world to come" anticipated in 2 Esdras were visualized as in heaven or in a transformed earth.

29. Such dominion may have been meant to extend only to the time of the flood. The "dominion" authorization is not repeated after the flood to its human survivors. Moreover, in much of biblical tradition, it is clear that dominion belongs to Yahweh or God.

30. See 2 Kgs 18:5; 22:2.

31. See Isaiah 25; 2 Esdras 4–9; Wisdom of Solomon 3–6; 8; 4 Maccabees 7–8; 10; 14–18; John 6; cf. Luke 16:19–31.

32. See, e.g., Matthew 25; Mark 10; 1 Corinthians 6; 15.

33. See Sir 10:19, which highlights the ambivalence of human potentiality.

34. See, e.g., Isa 11:1–9; Jer 31:33–34; Ezek 36:26–27; Hos 2:19–20.

35. See also Tob 2:1–10, where Tobit's blindness results from chance circumstances.

36. The appearance of Satan as an independent, supernatural, evil being resolves, in a way, the earlier theodicy problem: why God, who is good, and presumed to be all-powerful, causes or allows bad things to happen. But now, with Satan causing evil in the world, the question arises whether God is all-powerful after all. Apocalyptic writings, such as the book of Revelation, express the hope and expectation that in time Satan will be defeated and the exclusive rule of God again established on earth and over all that is.

37. According to Matt 6:13, Jesus taught his followers to pray that they might be delivered from "the Evil One."

38. This is the human condition as described both after the flood (Genesis 10, in the P tradition) and as punishment or to prevent further human pretentions following the building of the city and the tower (Genesis 11, in the J tradition).

39. Cf. Gen 17:15–21, which adds that the promises are to be fulfilled through Isaac, who would be born to Sarah, Abraham's wife.

40. See also Deut 6:20–25. These recitations, sometimes called "cultic credos," may have been part of an ancient ceremony during the time of the judges, when the tribes or their leaders gathered to renew the covenant. Note that they look to the history of God's dealings with his people in order to understand both who he is and who they are.

PART II
The Old Testament, or Hebrew Scriptures

OVERVIEW

The term "Old Testament" was coined by Christians to distinguish the scriptures Christianity had inherited from and shared with Judaism from those written by and for the emerging Christian communities in the first and second centuries A.D. To the present time, many Jews prefer to use terms such as "the Hebrew Scriptures" or, simply, "the Bible." According to ancient tradition or legend, leading Jewish rabbis who met in Jamnia around A.D. 90 determined which of the many writings that had been considered inspired or authoritative at one time or another in Jewish circles should be included in or excluded from the Jewish canon. Those writings that were included at Jamnia constitute the present Jewish Bible. In the sixteenth century, Martin Luther decided that the Christian Old Testament should be limited to the writings accepted by the Jamnia rabbis.[1]

Jewish tradition divided its sacred writings into three categories: the Law, the Prophets, and the Writings (or Holy Writings). The Law includes the first five books, Genesis through Deuteronomy, which in traditionalist Judaism and traditionalist Christianity came to be called "the five books of Moses" and among scholars are known as the Pentateuch ("five books"). In Judaism these writings are also known as the Torah ("law") and are regarded as the basis for Jewish life. The Talmud ("teaching") and later rabbinical commentaries concentrate on interpreting the meaning of the Torah for Jews who wish it to guide their lives. The Prophets includes the historical books of Joshua, Judges, 1 and 2 Kings, and 1 and 2 Samuel, as well as the lengthy books of Isaiah, Jeremiah, and Ezekiel, and the shorter writings contained in the book of the Twelve, that is, Hosea through Malachi. The Writings include all other books, such as Psalms, Proverbs, Ruth, Job, and Esther.

The Bibles of first- and second-century Christianity consisted of the Septuagint and some other Greek versions. These Bibles included several writings omitted by the Jamnia rabbis. There was as yet no generally accepted collection of writings known as the New Testament. One early prominent Christian reader, Marcion, may have made the first collection of Christian scriptures, in about A.D. 140. Marcion observed that the world as he knew it was marked by misery, violence, death, and decay, and he doubted that the God who had made it could be good. He also observed that, according to what would later be known as the Old Testament, Yahweh delighted in bloody sacrifices. Marcion concluded that the God of these scriptures was a malevolent deity, quite different from the One whom Christianity had come to worship. Marcion proposed to dispense with both Jewish scriptures and the God known through them.[2] The rest of Christianity decided not to go along with Marcion, branded him a heretic, and affirmed that the God known in the Bible was the God of Christianity and that what later came to be known as the Old Testament was to be part of the Christian Bible.

Exactly which books or writings should constitute the Old Testament was a matter of some disagreement among later Christians. The Septuagint included a number of writings that, for one reason or another—including the fact that, at the time, they were not known to exist in Hebrew or Aramaic—the rabbis at Jamnia excluded from their canon. These writings, now referred to as the Apocrypha, included such important works as Ecclesiasticus (or Sirach), the Wisdom of Solomon, Tobit, and Judith. These writings continued to be regarded as Scripture by nearly all Christians until the time of the Protestant Reformation, when they were relegated to the apocryphal category by Protestants. Most of the writings of the Apocrypha remain in Catholic and Eastern Orthodox Bibles to the present time. These writings are examined in part III of this book.

At least some of another group of writings also, for a while, served as Scripture for many early Christians; these are known collectively as the Pseudepigrapha. Jude (a New Testament book), for instance, quotes one of these writings, *1 Enoch*, as Scripture. *Second Enoch, 2 Baruch, the Book of Jubilees*, and the *Testaments of the Twelve Patriarchs* are other particularly important pseudepigraphic writings.[3] Several of the writings in the Pseudepigrapha include Christian commentary, and some of them may have been written by Christians.

The first half of the Old Testament consists mainly of stories and historical reports arranged roughly in chronological order, beginning with the creation and following the course of events in the life of the Hebrew, Israelite, Judahite, and Jewish people down to approximately 400 B.C., the era of Nehemiah and Ezra. Here we have what probably were three separate collections of stories and historical traditions:

1. *The Tetrateuch* ("four books," Genesis, Exodus, Leviticus, and Numbers). These books were put in their present form by Priestly editors (commonly designated P or RP; ca. 400 B.C.). These writings may include much earlier narrative and legal traditions, as well as more recent compositions by Priestly authors.

2. *The Deuteronomic History* (comprising Deuteronomy, Joshua, Judges, 1 and 2 Samuel, and 1 and 2 Kings) was assembled and edited by a writer (or writers) influenced by the Deuteronomic reform who lived during and perhaps near the end of the exile. This collector-author-editor is commonly designated the Deuteronomic theologian or the Deuteronomic historian (DH). DH probably wrote around 550 B.C.[4]

3. *The Chronicler's History* (consisting of 1 and 2 Chronicles, Ezra, and Nehemiah) may have been assembled and edited by an unknown writer, commonly designated the Chronicler, around 350 B.C.[5] This third unit provides a brief summary and revision of history from the earliest times through the period of the exile, and adds new accounts of the return of the exiles and the reconstitution of Jerusalem and the temple through the time of Nehemiah and Ezra.

The second half of the Old Testament includes a variety of writings, some, such as Amos and Hosea, dating from as early as the eighth century B.C. The most notable writings include the book of Psalms, the wisdom writings (Proverbs, Ecclesiastes, and Job), the three longer prophets (Isaiah, Jeremiah, and Ezekiel), and the prophets of the book of the Twelve (Hosea through Malachi). The second half also includes Esther, which follows Nehemiah, perhaps because both purport to have been written in the Persian period; the Song of Solomon, which follows Ecclesiastes and like it from early times was thought to have been written by Solomon; Lamentations, which follows Jeremiah both because it was once commonly believed that Jeremiah had written it and because it describes the course of events in Jerusalem after the beginning of the exile; and Daniel, which probably dates from the second century B.C. but purports to have been written in the time of the Babylonians and thus appropriately follows Jeremiah and Ezekiel. Though not part of the book of the Twelve, Daniel is similar in content to some of the more apocalyptic prophets contained there and so is plausibly placed next to it.

All of the present Old Testament writings are placed in settings that suggest they were composed by around 400 B.C. Later Judaism evidently considered sacred only those writings that were written prior to that time. Most of the apocryphal and pseudepigraphic writings similarly are ascribed to relatively ancient authors or seers, though they were probably composed well after 400 B.C.[6]

Studying the Bible would be simpler if the traditions about a given period all dated from that period. Such, however, is not the case. For example, the first story we find in the Bible, the first creation narrative (P), probably was not written down until around 400 B.C., while the second creation account (J) may have been written as early as 950 B.C. The point to bear in mind is that a given tradition should be seen not only as a recollection of what took place at the time the events supposedly happened but also, often primarily, as a source of insight into the religious and cultural beliefs and concerns of those who set the tradition down. Thus, although P stories in Exodus and Numbers may tell us very little about the experience of Israel during its wandering in the wilderness after coming out of Egypt, they do provide a great deal of information about the beliefs and concerns of Jewish leadership in Jerusalem around 400 B.C. From this perspective, all biblical traditions are of historical and religious value, even if they tell us more about the times in which they were written than about the times or events they describe. Therefore, even 1 and 2 Chronicles are important sources, at least for Jewish beliefs and practices around 350 B.C.

Frequently, of course, the records are contemporary with, or at least close in time to, the events described. Examples include the court history in 2 Samuel 11–20 and 1 Kings 1–2, much of the tradition in prophets such as Amos, Hosea, Isaiah, Jeremiah, Nahum, and Obadiah, and the memoirs of Nehemiah. Nevertheless, it is helpful to keep track not only of the main outline of historical periods and events but also of the approximate dates, as they can best be determined, and perspectives of the biblical sources or writers to whom we are indebted for this great wealth of tradition.

For assistance in navigating through the long and complex periods in which the Old Testament events occurred and were remembered, see the table of significant dates in ancient world and biblical history on pages x–xii, and the summary of major events and periods in biblical history in the first essay of part I. Readers are urged to consult these resources frequently, particularly since much of the Old Testament faith developed in the context of events in time and space: those remembered from the past, those experienced in the present, and those anticipated for the future.

Genesis

The title "Genesis" comes from the Greek Bible and means "beginning" or "origin." It was the first word translated from the Hebrew text, which begins, "In [or "at"] the beginning." Genesis 1–11 form the prologue and setting for all that follows in the Bible. Here we see stories about early humanity before the days of the first fathers and mothers of Israel. There are the two creation stories, followed by the story of the man and the woman in the garden, the stories of the two brothers and the descendants of Cain and Seth on down to Lamech, the story of the flood, and the story of the city and the tower.

The two creation stories complement each other. In the first story, 1:1–2:4a (P),[1] the transcendent God calls creation into existence by his word, summoning the waters and the earth to bring forth all other kinds of living creatures, and last of all makes "man," both male and female, in his own image. What was meant by the "image of God" (Latin, *imago dei*) has been interpreted in many different ways by ancient and modern commentators. It is noteworthy that both male and female are said to share that image. Possibly the "image" refers to humanity's creative gifts or to its moral capacity. Here we see humankind in the most positive light, as somehow like God. The primordial couple are then instructed to "be fruitful and multiply," to "fill" and "subdue" the earth, and to have "dominion" over the creatures of the sea, air, and earth (1:28).[2] In these early days, humans and all other creatures were vegetarians (1:29–30). Afterward, God affirms that everything he has made is very good, and he rests on the seventh (Sabbath) day.

In the second, but more ancient, creation story in 2:4b–25 (J), Yahweh God[3] forms "man" (*adam*) from the watered dust of the ground (*adamah*) and puts him in the Garden of Eden to tend it. Yahweh God then forms the beasts and birds from the ground, in the same way he had made the man, with the purpose of giving the man a companion and helper (2:18–24). The man then names the beasts and the birds, but they do not fill the empty place in his life. Therefore, Yahweh God makes woman (*ishshah*) from the rib of the male (*ish*). "This at last" was the companion the man was looking for. The Hebrew word for man, *ha adam* (translatable also as "earth creature"), becomes in English the proper name Adam.[4] The narrator then explains the affinity between men and women: Originally they were "one flesh." Explanations like this of existing phenomena on the basis of what happened to people in primordial times are referred to as "etiological" explanations or stories. Many such stories or comments appear in the pages of Genesis.

In Genesis 3 (J continued), we come to the garden scene. The woman, renamed Eve, persuaded by the serpent, and then the man, who needs no further persuasion, break the one commandment given them by eating the forbidden fruit, that of the "tree of the knowledge of good and evil."[5] Immediately they recognize their nakedness, attempt to hide from each other, and then try to hide from Yahweh God when they hear him walking in the garden "in the cool of the day." The man blames the woman (and Yahweh, who gave her to him), and the woman blames the serpent. Contrary to popular understanding, the serpent is not identified as Satan either here or anywhere else in the Old Testament; instead, the serpent is merely the most subtle of all the wild creatures Yahweh God has made (Gen 3:1).[6] All three are subjected to various penalties. The serpent must now go about on its belly, and in the future its descendants and humans will be enemies. The man and the woman are expelled from the garden, but Yahweh God provides them with suitable clothes. Now they are mortal, for their way to the tree of life, of which they have not yet eaten, is barred (3:22–24). But the human experiment is not put to an end, for the man and the woman will come together and have offspring (4:1–2).[7]

In Genesis 4 (J continued), these two offspring present their offerings to Yahweh. For unstated reasons not relevant to the story, Yahweh accepts Abel's offering but not Cain's. Cain's reaction is to become angry and jealous of his brother. Though cautioned to accept what has happened, Cain now tries to overrule Yahweh's choice and make himself number one by killing his brother, thereby committing the first fratricide. Yahweh banishes Cain from his homeland but tries to protect him from vengeance at the hands of Abel's kinsmen by somehow marking him. Some generations later, Cain's descendant Lamech, who in the J tradition appears to be the father of Noah, kills a man and then brags about it to his wives (4:23–24). Human depravity continues to spread. The P tradition introduces Seth as the original couple's third son, and a more auspicious forebear of Lamech and thus of Noah and later humankind, in 4:25–5:27. The P tradition generally has a more optimistic view of human nature and destiny than the J material.

In Genesis 6–9, where J and P are intertwined, Yahweh finds the human imagination "only evil continually" (J) and determines to destroy all flesh. However, he decides to spare Noah, a righteous man (according to P), along with his family and an ark full of two (P) or seven (J) pairs of each kind of animal, bird, and "everything that creeps on the ground." Some of those additional pairs are required in the more primitive J narrative because in that version Noah was going to sacrifice one or more of all the clean (ritually suitable) animals and birds immediately after leaving the ark (Gen 8:20).[8] The additional pairs enable all species of life to survive, so that they may be fruitful and multiply upon the earth (8:15–19). Noah's preservation of all kinds of living creatures has been called the first "endangered species act."[9] Significantly, the P covenant in Genesis 9 includes not only humans, but "every living creature . . . for all future generations" (9:8–16)."[10]

In a final episode appended to the flood story, Noah plants a vineyard, makes wine, becomes drunk, and lies naked in his tent (9:20). Inadvertently, Ham, one of Noah's sons, sees his father in this condition. Emerging from his stupor, Noah curses Canaan, Ham's son, saying that Canaan (or his descendants) would be slaves to his brothers (or their descendants).[11] The story may have been intended to justify Israelites' later enslavement of some Canaanites.[12]

In the last of these stories from Genesis 1–11, the episode of the Tower of Babel (J), people, heedless of Yahweh, try to secure a great name and destiny for themselves by building a city and a tower "with its top in the heavens" (11:4). These people, representing, it seems, all humankind, do not disobey any expressed divine command. They merely pretend to be self-sufficient, to be masters of their own destiny. Yahweh "comes down," confuses their language, and scatters them "over the face of all the earth." This story accounts etiologically for the division of humankind into different ethnic and language groups, and also, perhaps, for the ruins of a great city. Once, it was felt, humankind was all one people. But since known history, humankind has been divided. Again we see an etiological story, to explain why human groups are mutually alienated from each other.

The J stories present a discernible theology of history: Humanity violates the conditions of life before Yahweh and experiences disruption of community and alienation from Yahweh, yet is permitted to continue to exist, though under increasingly circumscribed conditions. Once living in peace and harmony with each other and with Yahweh in the garden, humans are now divided, "scattered abroad," unable to understand one another's language. It is in this setting that Abram, later called Abraham, appears. He is born, marries, and goes with his family from Chaldea to Canaan in the closing verses of chapter 11. By structuring the traditions in this way, the narrator implies that Abraham is somehow to be understood as Yahweh's answer to the fractured and alienated condition of humanity. This interpretation is made more explicit in the first few verses of chapter 12.

Before turning to these verses, however, some additional features of chapters 1–11 are to be noted. Readers often wonder, for instance, where the wives of Cain and Seth might have come from. As the stories are told in their present sequence, these women, as well as would-be avengers of Abel, appear from nowhere. In fact, minor details suggest that the stories in these chapters once circulated separately. Noah is said to be the "first tiller of the soil" (9:20), but Adam and Cain both tilled it before him. Humankind is twice separated by languages and locations (chapters 10 and 11). Lamech's sons are described as the fathers of all nomads, musicians, and metalworkers (4:19–22), but as the story is told, they would all have perished in the flood. Neither the first collector and arranger of the J stories nor RP, who later edited Genesis, seems to have been bothered by these apparent inconsistencies. Their concern, evidently, was not so much with literal history as with the preservation of these old traditions so that through them, they could try to understand and explain the meaning of the human situation in their own times. To the extent that these traditions were regarded as ancient, they were considered authoritative and not to be discarded, even though they might fail to present a completely coherent narrative or ideological perspective.

The mythical fragment about the "sons of God," who resemble the lustier type of Greek deities, and the "daughters of men" (6:1–4) is only partly assimilated to the more developed biblical faith. The new race of demigods resulting from the infusion of immortality into humankind might have lived forever were it not for the limit of 120 years, a limit exceeded by only a few subsequent biblical figures.[13] Presumably the "Nephilim," who were apparently these mixed divine-human progeny under a different name, would have perished in the great flood, which follows immediately, but they appear later on in Numbers 13:33. Etiological interests recur frequently in Genesis 1–11, typically in the form of answers to implicit questions about why things are as they are: Why do men and women desire to be "one flesh"? Why do snakes have no legs? Why do women have pain in childbearing? Why must men toil for their bread? Why must all men and women die? Why are the nations divided?

Genesis 1–11 records these ancient stories about the origins and early days, years, and millennia of humankind, and of other life forms or creatures as well. These chapters form the prelude to the biblical traditions that follow. Beginning in Genesis 12, attention shifts to the story of Israel, starting with its forebears: the fathers and mothers of that special people who through Yahweh's blessings and for his own purposes are called into being.

In Genesis 12:1–3, Yahweh calls Abram, later renamed Abraham, to leave his hometown in Haran and go to the land of Canaan, and promises to make him a great nation and to make his name great. (Compare 11:4, where the builders of Babel aspire to make a name *for themselves*.) Yahweh also promises Abram that he will be a blessing to, or the envy of, other nations.[14] Yahweh blesses Sarai, later called Sarah, Abram's wife, and promises, notwithstanding her advanced age, not only that she will bear a son but also that she will become the mother of kings and nations and that Yahweh will establish his covenant with her son Isaac (Gen. 17:15–21). The remainder of the biblical story, both in Genesis and in the Bible as a whole, records the fulfillment or partial fulfillment of these commands and promises. Abraham is the central figure in chapters 12–26. Isaac appears mainly to connect Abraham with Jacob, whose dealings with Esau and Laban are described in chapters 27–35. There are few independent traditions about Isaac, and he appears mainly as a passive and shadowy figure. Sarah, Rebekah, and Rachel, on the other hand, emerge as definite and significant persons in their own right.

The account of God's covenant of circumcision with Abraham (17:1–4) probably comes from P, which characteristically is interested in ritual or "priestly" matters. Most of the remaining Genesis traditions come from J, but some E material appears, often blended with J as JE. Chapters 20 and 22 appear to derive mainly from E. Both P and E traditions in Genesis generally use the divine name Elohim, translated as "God." In Genesis, the J tradition is distinguishable by its use of the divine name Yahweh, commonly translated in English Bibles as "the LORD." It is sometimes said that the J tradition is earlier than E material, and that the two collections of tradition are to be dated around 950 and 850 B.C., respectively. The more significant point is that J represents southern, or Judahite, tradition, while E consists of northern, or Israelite, materials. The symbols J and E, like P, are used sometimes to designate the collectors and editors of these respective materials, and sometimes to refer to the biblical texts attributed to these collectors and editors.

Abraham is remembered for his faithfulness and obedience to God but also for his mistrust and his conniving or deceit. These modes of response almost alternate in the Abraham stories. Abraham goes, as

Yahweh commands (12:4), but, fearing for his life, lets Pharaoh take Sarai as his wife (12:10–20). Later, after separating from Lot, Abraham is promised all the land he sees, along with innumerable descendants. Commendably, he goes and builds an altar to Yahweh (13:8–18), but then doubting that Yahweh God will give him the promised offspring (15:2–3) has a son, Ishmael, by another woman, Hagar (16:1–4). On the positive side, Abraham agrees to be circumcised (chap. 17), and Yahweh promises that, notwithstanding her advanced age, Sarah will bear him a son (18:10–15). Though Sarah laughs at the idea, Abraham apparently preserves a straight face. Yahweh honors Abraham by consulting him about the fate of Sodom, and Abraham, to his credit, goes so far as to remind Yahweh that as "Judge [*shophet*] of all the earth," he should "do right" (*mishpat*)[15] and not destroy the righteous with the wicked (18:16–33).[16] Abraham then bargains with Yahweh, who finally agrees to spare Sodom if only ten righteous persons can be found there. Here we see Abraham as a model of superlative faith and moral conduct. But then, again fearing for his life, Abraham gives Sarah over, this time only briefly, to the Philistine king Abimelech (chap. 20).[17] Isaac at last is born (chap. 21), and in due course Abraham meets the supreme test of faith by preparing to sacrifice this special and only son through whom alone, it seems, the promise of Genesis 12:2a can be fulfilled. The story may function etiologically to explain why Israelites no longer sacrifice their firstborn sons.

Time passes and Isaac grows up. Abraham is now getting old. He sends his servant to find a wife for Isaac from among his kinsmen. The servant travels to Nahor, near Haran, in Aram or Syria. There the servant prays for guidance and comes upon Rebekah, Abraham's grand-niece and Laban's sister (24:1–15). The narrator emphasizes that the decision whether to marry Isaac is left to Rebekah (24:5, 8, 58). She agrees to go with the servant, and she and Isaac marry and have twins, Jacob and Esau. The boys grow up, and Jacob becomes the central narrative figure. Jacob coolly extorts Esau's birthright (25:29–34),[18] deceives his blind, old, dying father, Isaac, in order to swindle Esau out of his blessing (27:1–40),[19] and then prudently goes to visit Uncle Laban in Haran to escape Esau's revenge (chap. 27). There Jacob falls in love at first sight with his cousin Rachel while also noticing the size of her father's herds, a sure indicator of his wealth (29:9–11). Laban, an Aramean, who also has an eye for acquirable wealth (24:29–31), tricks Jacob into marrying Leah, another daughter first and thus into fourteen years of indentured service (29:15–30).

Years go by. Jacob has eleven sons and a daughter and gains title to most of Laban's movable property (with God's help, of course). He correctly senses that Laban and his sons are displeased and that the time has come to leave (31:1–3). One day while Laban is away, Jacob steals off with everything he claims as his own (31:17–21). Laban's posse overtakes Jacob, but warned by God in a dream (31:22, E) and unwilling to bring harm to his own daughters and grandchildren, Laban in exasperation calls on God to keep an eye on Jacob, in the words of the Mizpah benediction (31:49–50).

Jacob returns to Canaan, anxiously sending large bribes ahead to placate Esau (32:1–21). An ancient myth (largely unassimilated) about a night demon tells of Jacob's wrestling at Peniel (meaning "the face or presence of a god") with a man or god who must flee before daybreak. This being blesses Jacob and renames him Israel (32:22–32, JE). Here, as elsewhere in Genesis, etiological interests are apparent. In P, Jacob is renamed Israel under less primitive circumstances, near Bethel (35:9–15).

The story of Shechem's rape of Jacob's daughter Dinah, his subsequent love for her, and her brothers' vicious revenge is told in chapter 34. Jacob objects to his sons' conduct on prudential, not moral, grounds (34:30). A separate story is set out in chapter 38, that of Judah, who has married a Canaanite woman, and his daughter-in-law Tamar. Tamar cleverly compels Judah to observe the traditional requirement of levirate marriage after her husband dies and his other sons fail to do their duty.[20] Here, however, the obligation of the brother-in-law (*levir*, in Latin) is assumed by the widow's father-in-law.

The saga of Joseph and his brothers in Genesis 37 and 39–50 is one of the early masterpieces of world literature.[21] J and E traditions are carefully blended. In J (the southern source), Judah protects Joseph, who is sold to Ishmaelites; in E, Reuben pleads for Joseph, who is sold to Midianites. Here, as elsewhere in the E tradition, God typically communicates with people through the medium of dreams. In this story, Jacob's doting affection for Joseph, one of the two sons of his beloved Rachel, which he expresses by dressing him up like little Lord Fauntleroy (37:3–4),[22] together with Joseph's tactless recitation of his seemingly pretentious dreams, prompts his brothers to try to get rid of him. Joseph survives, is taken to Egypt, where he is recognized for his ability to interpret dreams, and is made czar of agriculture. Worldwide famine brings all the earth, including his brothers (who apparently are not bright enough to think of the idea themselves; 42:1–2), to Egypt to buy grain. This gives Joseph an opportunity to get back at them and, curiously, to add to the misery of his father, to whom he has neglected to send word that he has been alive and well in Egypt all these years (chaps. 42–44). Theologically, Joseph's achievements there represent

God's providential care for Israel and for all the families of the earth (41:57; 45:5–7; 50:20). Thus, we see here an early, partial fulfillment of the promise in the J tradition that the descendants of Abraham, Isaac, and Jacob would be a blessing (12:2–3; 26:4; 28:14). Historically, the Joseph story serves to bring Jacob and his family from Canaan into Egypt, where the story of Israel begins in the book of Exodus.

Exodus

Two important eras and two decisive events are remembered in Exodus. The eras are Israel's experience of bondage in Egypt and of the subsequent wandering in the wilderness. The two critical events were God's delivering Israel out of Egypt and his giving Israel the law through Moses. The traditions, including some very early ones, are preserved by J, E, and P. The E tradition introduces the divine name Yahweh ("the LORD") in 3:13–15. J used this name from the start (Gen 2:4b); in P it is first revealed in Exodus 6:2–3. Previously, both E and P have used the name Elohim (originally a plural form meaning "gods," but in biblical times a proper name for God).

At the close of the book of Genesis, Jacob, or Israel, and his family have settled in the land of Egypt as sojourners (resident aliens) or economic refugees. According to Exodus 1, the people of Israel multiply greatly and are made slaves and put to work on various Egyptian building projects under the reign of a new pharaoh (possibly Ramses II, ca. 1290–1223 B.C.) who fears their growing numbers. The Egyptians try to limit Israelite population growth by ordering the two Hebrew midwives to kill any newborn Hebrew boys (1:8–22). The Israelites groan in bondage, crying to God for help (2:23)—though later, in the wilderness, their recollection of their former life in Egypt will be much more positive (14:10–12; chap. 16).

In the meantime, Moses, spared by his mother's ingenuity from Pharaoh's plan to kill all newborn Hebrew sons, is adopted and raised by Pharaoh's daughter (2:1–11). Grown to young manhood, Moses kills an Egyptian who was beating a fellow Hebrew. The next day, Moses attempts to mediate between two brawling Hebrews; they object to his efforts on their behalf, as his fellow Israelites will again and again in the wilderness, and ask sardonically if he means to kill them as he killed the Egyptian. Fearing lest that incident come to the authorities' attention, Moses seeks refuge by fleeing to Midian, all the way across and to the east of the Sinai Peninsula. There he marries Zipporah, the daughter of a Midianite priest (named Jethro in E, Reuel in J). But at the "burning bush" (3:1–2), God calls on Moses to lead the Israelites out of Egypt. Moses is reluctant to accept this assignment, but Yahweh answers all his objections and appoints Moses' brother Aaron to assist him (3:11–4:17). An early and largely unassimilated myth tells of Moses' vicarious circumcision along the way, whereby Zipporah shrewdly thwarts Yahweh's arbitrary attempt to kill him (4:24–25).[23]

Moses and Aaron proceed to perform wonders and evoke plagues in order to persuade Pharaoh as to God's power.[24] Pharaoh, however, remains unimpressed until God sends the "destroyer," who kills the firstborn of the Egyptians but passes over the houses of Israel (12:21–24, J).[25] At last, Pharaoh is convinced, and not only allows but orders Moses, Aaron, and all the people of Israel to leave the country immediately (12:21–33).[26]

All now looks hopeful for the Israelites. But then Yahweh hardens Pharaoh's heart, the better to "get glory" over him (14:4),[27] and Pharaoh sends a great army after the terrified Israelites. Nevertheless, Yahweh rescues them by the Sea of Reeds (Red Sea).[28] One version visualizes a "wall of water" on either side of the escaping Israelites that later engulfs the pursuing Egyptians. The early song attributed to the prophet Miriam (15:20–21) and in expanded form to Moses himself (15:1–18) pictures the action somewhat differently. Here Yahweh throws the Egyptian horses and riders into the sea! Whatever may have actually happened, the exodus (*ex hodos*, meaning "way out" or "departure" in Greek) is commemorated in many later writings as a major milestone, indeed, as the event in which God called Israel into existence as a people.[29] Thus, it can be said that the history of Israel as a people, if not yet a nation, begins with the exodus from Egypt.[30] Scholars generally date the Israelites' escape from Egypt at around 1230 B.C.[31]

The wilderness epoch (ca. 1230–1200 B.C.) is marked by "murmuring" or complaining (chap. 16) and by apostasy and idolatry (chap. 32) on the part of the Israelites. Through all this time, Moses attempts to mediate between Yahweh and his often, if not chronically, ungrateful and unruly people.[32] During this period, as the story is told, Yahweh gives Israel "the law." The books of Leviticus, Numbers, and Deuteronomy also describe Israel's experience in the wilderness and set forth several versions of the laws God gives to Moses there for the purpose of structuring and guiding the affairs of his newly freed people.

The Covenant Code, delivered orally to Moses on the mountain (Mount Sinai in J), is reported in Exodus 20–23 (E). This first extensive codification of Israelite law may date from as early as 1100 B.C.[33]

In the memory and faith of Israel, it was not just any god but the God who brought them out of Egypt who gave this law (20:2). The first two of the Ten Commandments, or Decalogue, require exclusive fidelity to this God; the last eight serve to promote and preserve the well-being of the community. The Third Commandment (20:7) probably warns against committing perjury (cf. Jer 5:2). The Fourth Commandment proclaims the Sabbath as a day of rest not only for Israelite families but also for their servants and cattle and for sojourners. The Fifth and Tenth Commandments refer to internal attitudes, namely, honoring father and mother and not coveting others' possessions, wives, or servants. Numerous other commandments follow in chapters 21–23; these too require faithfulness to God and a few refer to sacrifices and festivals, but primarily they require the maintenance of right relationships within the community.

Thus, one can speak of the vertical and horizontal dimensions of Israelite law: what is owed to God and what is owed to neighbor or the community. The horizontal laws specify what is to be done if wrongdoing occurs; for example, injuries to animals or to slaves or to other persons resulting from negligence must be remedied by full restitution or some other form of just compensation (21:33–22:15). If a man intentionally steals or destroys his neighbor's property, he must pay multiple or punitive damages (22:1, 4, 7, 9). Criminal and civil laws are not differentiated. The "law of retaliation" applies only when a pregnant woman is injured by brawling males (21:22–25). Slaves, widows, orphans, sojourners, the poor, and both domestic and wild animals are to be protected or provided for.[34] All these commandments, not just the Ten, are remembered as the words and laws of Yahweh.[35] After receiving these commandments, Moses records them and reads this "book of the covenant" to the Israelites. They pledge their obedience, and he consecrates them with the "blood of the covenant" (24:3–8).

Chapters 25–31 and 35–40 (P) mainly contain laws regarding descriptions of the design of the tabernacle and its furnishings, the duties and prerogatives of Aaron and his sons (the only persons who may be priests, according to P), and procedures for the ordination of priests. Chapters 32–34 consist principally of J and E traditions, including the famous episode of the golden calf. Upon the mountain, Yahweh says to Moses, "*Your* people, whom *you* brought up out of the land of Egypt, have corrupted themselves." Moses, undaunted, replies, "O Yahweh, why does thy wrath burn hot against *thy* people whom *thou* hast brought forth out of the land of Egypt?" (32:7–11).

Here Moses barely dissuades Yahweh from destroying Israel (32:7–14), and Aaron lamely "explains" the presence of the calf: "I threw [the gold] into the fire, and there came out this calf" (32:24). Yahweh speaks with Moses "face to face" (33:11), or, as another tradition has it, Moses sees Yahweh's back but not his face (33:20–23). In chapter 34, Moses again goes up Mount Sinai to receive another and somewhat different set of commandments, sometimes called the Ritual Decalogue (34:11–28, J). It is possible that this chapter gives another ancient version of the tradition of making covenant that is found in chapters 19–24 (E).

Leviticus

The title of this biblical book is misleading: Levites are mentioned only in 25:32–33. The book primarily contains laws concerning priests, sacrifices, festivals, and ritual purity. Biblical tradition prior to about 450 B.C. does not distinguish between priests and Levites; in these early traditions, in order for a man to be a priest, he must be a Levite, that is, from the tribe of Levi. The distinction first appears in the P tradition, around 450–400 B.C. Leviticus includes two major literary components: the Holiness Code (H) in chapters 17 through 26, and P laws (part of the Priestly Code, or PC) in the other chapters. All purportedly were spoken by Yahweh to Moses in the wilderness (1:1). Like most of Exodus, Numbers, and Deuteronomy, Leviticus is set in the wilderness period (ca. 1230–1200 B.C.). By the time the Pentateuch was put in its final literary form (ca. 400 B.C.), Jews generally believed that all legal traditions, including those that modern scholars date well after the time of Moses, were revealed to Moses and transmitted by him to Israel during the wilderness years.

H, the Holiness Code, which appears to have been the third codification of Israelite-Judahite law,[36] may have been composed by rural priests or Levites around 650 B.C., about the same time that J and E, the southern and northern narrative traditions respectively, were being combined to form JE. The Northern Kingdom, or Israel, was then defunct, and the Southern Kingdom, or Judah, had fallen heir to northern traditions that it preserved by weaving them together with its own. The laws in H stress Yahweh's holiness and the requirement that Israel be holy (*qadosh*), that is, separate or different from the ways of other nations (18:3; 19:2; 20:23–26). Commonly the laws in H are sanctioned by the refrain "I am Yahweh your God." They pertain to sexual practices, priestly purification, sacrifices, and festivals, but also to love of neighbors (19:18) and strangers (19:34) and to justice, including obligations to the poor and to sojourners (e.g., gleaning privileges for poor people and aliens [23:22]) and a uniform law for both strangers and native Israelites (24:22). Here the *lex talionis,* or law of retaliation (24:19–20),[37] applies only to disfigurement (mayhem in modern American statutes), but an implicit principle of limited retribution or compensation also appears in several other laws (e.g., 24:17–18, 21). In chapter 25, the land is to keep Sabbath: Whatever grows by itself the seventh year is to provide food for citizens, slaves, sojourners, domestic animals, and wildlife (25:2–7; cf. Exod 23:10–11). The law of the jubilee year (Lev 25:8–55) requires the return of unredeemed rural property to original owners and the freeing of indentured servants in the fiftieth year. The underlying rationale for the land ethic of Leviticus 25 is that ultimately the land belongs to Yahweh, not the people: "The land is mine; for you are strangers and sojourners with me" (25:23).[38] Chapter 26 consists of admonitions about the life-and-death importance of keeping the commandments, ordinances, and statutes set out in H.

Elsewhere in Leviticus, as in Exodus and Numbers, we see large segments of the fourth and most extensive collection or codification of law, sometimes designated the Priestly Code, or PC. The PC describes mainly burnt, cereal, peace, sin, guilt, thank, and wave offerings, several of which are not mentioned in the earlier codes. The PC, like the P tradition generally, distinguishes between priests and Levites, relegating the latter to the role of assistants to the former. Several laws focus on what Aaron and his sons (the priests, now distinguished from Levites) are to do with the blood, fat, kidneys, livers, entrails, and so forth of the sacrificial animals. Choicer portions belong to the priests as their due (7:28–36). Clean and unclean animals are to be differentiated (chap. 11). Priests and others are to attend to human diseases and discharges with various therapeutic procedures and offerings (chaps. 13–15).

Procedures for the Day of Atonement (Yom Kippur) are described in chapter 16: Various animals are to be sacrificed at the tabernacle or tent of meeting (which functions in P and PC as an early prototype of the temple at Jerusalem), and a goat is to be sent to Azazel, a wilderness spirit of some sort, to make atonement (thus, the later expression, "scapegoat"). No one may eat the blood of either domestic or wild animals, "for the life of every creature is its blood" (17:10–14). Because life comes from God, it must be returned to him by pouring the blood out on the ground.[39] The book of Leviticus concludes with the summary statement, "These are the commandments which Yahweh commanded Moses for the people of Israel on Mount Sinai" (27:34). Yet both Numbers and Deuteronomy, which follow immediately after Leviticus, consist largely of additional laws. These writings, like Leviticus and Exodus 15–40, also have as their setting the period of Israel's wandering or sojourning in the wilderness between Egypt and the promised land, the land of Canaan.

Numbers

Israel is still in the wilderness, between bondage in Egypt and the promised land of Canaan. Several narrative sections deriving mainly from J and E are included in chapters 11–14, 16, 20–25, and 32. The greater part of the book continues the P laws (Priestly Code or PC), which appear at length from Exodus 25 through Leviticus and Numbers. The PC was the fourth major collection or codification of laws, set down sometime between 450 and 400 B.C., probably by priests who presided over the offering of sacrifices at the temple in Jerusalem. These laws are typically presented as instructions spoken by God to Moses, supplementing those initially given on Mount Sinai. The entire Tetrateuch (Genesis, Exodus, Leviticus, and Numbers) was probably edited by RP, the Priestly redactor or editor, around 400 B.C.

This book's title derives from P's characteristic interest in the numbers, names, and locations of the Israelite tribes, their leaders, and their families. The P laws relate mainly to sacrificial offerings and ritual purity. P tradition distinguishes priests (Aaron and his sons) from Levites. The latter were to attend to the tabernacle and its furnishings and merely assist the priests.[40] The distinction between priests and Levites does not appear in writings dated before ca. 450 B.C. P narratives refer frequently to the tabernacle, or tent of meeting (which is rarely mentioned, if at all, in the earlier J, E, or DH traditions). This was visualized as a portable prototype of the Jerusalem temple, which, when the P authors were writing, had been the only proper place of worship for some two hundred years. P seems to assume that Judah and the Jewish people had always been obliged to worship in just one place: first the tabernacle, and then, when it was built, the temple.

Primary responsibilities and choicest perquisites are reserved for priests (see, e.g., chaps. 4 and 18). Special P laws in Numbers include the cereal offering of jealousy, a kind of trial by ordeal for a wife whose husband suspects her of infidelity (chap. 5); the law of the Nazirite, a man or woman who practices a temporary ascetic withdrawal (chap. 6); Passover, which must be kept also by sojourners (chap. 9); and laws of inheritance, including provisions for daughters if a family has no sons.[41] Other P laws in Numbers include provisions for keeping vows or making contracts—women's contracts being subject to fathers' or husbands' approval (chap. 30)—and establishing cities of refuge and other cities for Levites (35:1–8).[42]

One P narrative concerns what modern judges call "a case of first impression" under the law prohibiting work on the Sabbath. Did a man who gathered sticks on that day violate the law? The answer came when Yahweh gave Moses further directions, and the violator was stoned to death (15:32–36). Another P story tells what happened when some men who were not descended from Aaron, and thus were not, under Priestly law, legitimate priests, claimed equality with Moses and Aaron, on the theory that "all the congregation are holy" (16:3). To settle the matter, Yahweh caused the earth to open up beneath these dissidents and "swallow them up, with their households," while fire consumed all their followers (16:30–35). The moral to the story is "a reminder to the people of Israel, so that no one who is not a priest, who is not of the descendants of Aaron, should draw near . . . before Yahweh" (16:40).

J and E narratives report Israel's repeated complaining about life in the wilderness and their hankering for the good old days in Egypt. Fed up with all the complaining, Moses on one occasion proposes to disown Israel (chap. 11); another time Yahweh determines to disinherit them, and Moses only just barely persuades him to relent (chap. 14). Miriam and Aaron protest Moses' marriage to a black (Cushite) woman, and envy his unique status as prophet and leader. In punishment, Miriam is turned snow white with leprosy until Aaron petitions Moses and prays to God for forgiveness (chap. 12). Israelite scouts report that Canaan is fruitful but filled with huge inhabitants (chaps. 13–14). Only Caleb and Joshua are confident that they can occupy it. Again (chap. 20) the people of Israel pine for the comforts of Egypt. Following Yahweh's instructions, Moses strikes a rock that brings forth water (20:2–11, 13; cf. Exod 17:1–7)—an act of faithlessness, according to later tradition, which serves to explain why Moses was not allowed to enter the promised land (Num 20:12; Deut 32:48–52).

Chapters 22–24 (J and E) picture Balak's persistent efforts to induce the non-Israelite prophet Balaam to curse Israel. Balak is king of the land of Moab, which the Israelites are passing close to, if not cutting across, while journeying on their way to Canaan. Their presence makes Balak nervous, so he sends for Balaam, a professional execrator, to come and put a curse on Israel. As the story is told—possibly combining two different versions—it is unclear whether God wishes Balaam to go or not. According to 22:20, God tells Balaam to go ahead. Yet two verses later, God is angry because Balaam has gone, and Yahweh's angel blocks the path. Balaam's ass, seeing the angel, refuses to proceed. Balaam, who does not see the angel, beats the ass, whereupon she reproaches Balaam for so treating her. Balaam shows no surprise at hearing her speak, and concedes that she is in the right, especially after the angel becomes visible to him, too, and points out that the ass has saved his life. Balaam then proceeds to the capital of Moab but insists that he can only speak what Yahweh commands. To Balak's intense chagrin, Balaam repeatedly pronounces blessings on Israel rather than curses, even adding one final, gratuitous blessing after Balak has dismissed him (24:10–19). The episode's point comes to expression in the comforting assurance that there is no enchantment or divination against Israel (23:23). Strangely, P tradition later condemns Balaam (31:8, 16), possibly confusing Balaam, son of Beor, with the story of Israel's apostasy at Baal-Peor (25:3).

The book of Numbers concludes the collection of traditions about early times that was edited in priestly circles around 400 B.C. What follows is an earlier collection of traditions, commonly designated the Deuteronomic History, which begins with the book of Deuteronomy.

Deuteronomy

The title means "second law." Chapters 5 and 12–26, together designated the Deuteronomic Code (D), constitute the second earliest major codification of Israelite law, the first being the Covenant Code (Exodus 20–23). Much of the legal material in Deuteronomy 12–19 and 26 was evidently added well after the original codification of the laws in chapters 20–25. The original codification, which incorporated, with some variations, several laws found in the Covenant Code,[43] may have been set down as early as the period of the judges. Most of the book purports to have been spoken by Moses to Israel in the wilderness.

Chapters 1–4 are an introduction by the Deuteronomic editor (also known as the Deuteronomic historian or, simply, DH) both to the book of Deuteronomy and to the entire Deuteronomic History, which, omitting Ruth, extends through 2 Kings. Some modern scholars posit two different Deuteronomic editors, one working around 600 B.C., the other around 550 B.C. For simplicity, we refer only to one such editor designated here as DH, who wrote around 550. The

generally accepted theory is that DH drew on earlier Judahite traditions (commonly designated as J down to ca. 950 B.C. and as A thereafter) and Israelite accounts (E down to perhaps ca. 850 B.C. and B
thereafter) along with some other sources, and arranged them in their
present order, commenting occasionally, particularly in Deuteronomy,
Judges, and 1 and 2 Kings. DH was looking back into history, trying
to make sense of what had occurred over the course of the previous
several centuries of Israel's history. Drawing on the prophets, who had
explained the meaning of current events and those pending in their
own times in accordance with Yahweh's righteousness, DH retrospec-
tively viewed the frequent disasters that had come upon Israel and
Judah as Yahweh's punishments for their forsaking him and the
requirements of the Covenant, in particular, for their turning from
Yahweh (apostasy) and worshiping other gods (idolatry). Writing in
the middle of the sixth century B.C. after the defeat of Judah and the
destruction of its capital, Jerusalem, DH regarded the Deuteronomic
requirement that Israel worship only in one place (implicitly,
Jerusalem) as a key criterion in appraising the kings of Israel and
Judah. DH was probably unaware that this requirement (along with a
series of laws making various accommodations to it) may well have
been added to the text of Deuteronomy less than a century earlier.

In these first chapters, Moses reviews previous events in the wilderness
(where the Israelites are still wandering), emphasizing the need to keep
Yahweh's ordinances and statutes, including the Ten Commandments
(4:13–14), which are set out in chapter 5. According to this editor, the
covenant was made at Mount Horeb, not Mount Sinai (5:2; 29:1).
Perhaps these are different names for the same mountain.

Chapters 6–11 include a series of sermons or speeches by Moses
calling for fidelity to Yahweh and his "commandments, statutes, and
ordinances." Some material may derive from an ancient ceremony of
covenant renewal, practiced perhaps as early as the time of the judges
(ca. 1200–1000 B.C.).[44] The great commandment to love God is
included in 6:4–5. These sermons insist that Yahweh is bringing Israel
into the land of Canaan for his own reasons, particularly, his love for
them, not because of their importance or merit (7:6–9; 9:4–8). They
warn that once Israel is in the promised land, the people shall surely
perish if they neglect the commandments, forsake Yahweh, and worship other gods. So-called cultic credos recalling the people's history
(6:20–23; 26:5–9) may have been recited at the ancient ceremony of
covenant renewal. The sermons express the understanding that Yahweh
gave the law to the people of Israel for their own good because of his

love for them. The law serves beneficially to structure the community; moreover, by keeping the law, Israel can avoid incurring Yahweh's wrath. In addition, Yahweh is particularly concerned for the welfare of "the fatherless," "the widow," and "the sojourner"; therefore the Israelites should do likewise (10:18–19).

Chapters 5 and 12–26 consist largely of new laws, while retaining several of those found in the earlier Covenant Code. The added laws pertain to sacrifices and festivals but also to justice and compassion within the community.

The principal innovation introduced by the Deuteronomic reform is the idea that when the Israelites enter the promised land, they are to destroy all the shrines where the indigenous peoples serve their gods and thereafter to worship at only one place: Jerusalem (12:2–14). Jerusalem is not named, probably because the authors of this new requirement were aware that the Israelites did not even occupy that city until the time of David (2 Sam 5:6–9), and that the temple was not built there until the reign of Solomon (1 Kings 6), more than two centuries after Moses. According to earlier legal and historical traditions, at first the Israelites had been free to worship at many places and had done so for many generations without apparent qualms.[45] The new law requiring centralized worship evidently was introduced prior to or in connection with the Deuteronomic reform carried out under King Josiah of Judah, around 622 B.C.[46] The requirement that Yahweh be worshiped only at the one place evidently was intended to counter the Judahites' continuing tendency to worship deities other than Yahweh at these local shrines.

With this requirement in effect, however, a number of adjustments were necessary. Because many people lived far from Jerusalem, provision was made for local slaughter of animals for food (12:15–16, 20–22). The major festivals, however, were to be observed in Jerusalem by all males every year (16:5–17; cf. Tob 1:6). Tithes of crops that proved too bulky to be carried to Jerusalem could be sold and the proceeds used to buy food to "eat before Yahweh" there (14:22–27). The closing of the local shrines meant that the Levites who had been priests at these shrines were now out of work. Provisions were made to meet their needs. They could sell their patrimony and move to Jerusalem, where they were supposed to have the same duties and rights as the Levites who were priests there (18:6–8). The Levites who remained in their towns or local rural areas, now having no livelihood, were to be provided for along with widows, the fatherless, and sojourners (12:18–19; 14:27–29). Secular judges were to be appointed to replace the local Levites, who, as priests, formerly were available to settle claims (16:18–20; cf. 17:8–13). And secular cities of refuge were to be set aside to replace the cultic shrines that previously served as sanctuaries for persons who committed manslaughter (19:1–10).

Several due process provisions are included in Deuteronomy 19. The cities of refuge were designated as places where persons could flee for protection pending trial (19:1–10). In addition, at least two witnesses must give evidence to sustain any criminal charge (19:15), and malicious witnesses who give false testimony are to receive the same punishment that those they accused would have suffered had the accused been found guilty (19:16–20). In this context, the *lex talionis* is applied to punishment of such false witnesses (19:21).

The *herem*, or the sacred destruction or slaughter of the indigenous peoples of Canaan, also is stipulated in order to prevent apostasy that might result from contact with them. The *herem* is a recurrent theme in Deuteronomy and the Deuteronomic History. To what extent it accurately represents ancient Israelite practice is uncertain. Judges 1:27–35 and some other texts suggest that it was not carried out systematically. Certain related neighboring peoples were to be tolerated but excluded from the Israelite community (23:3–8).

Various laws provide protection for the poor (15:7–11), laborers (22:8; 24:14–15), slaves and escaped slaves (15:12–18; 23:15–16), newly married males (24:5), day laborers (24:14–15), debtors (24:10–13), sojourners, orphans and widows (24:19–22), and offenders (25:3). These laws, some of which derive from Exodus 20–23, emphasize Yahweh's compassion for his people. Some are also concerned with conservation and respect for animal life (20:19; 22:1–4, 6–7; 25:4).

Chapter 27 ordains a ceremony in which Israel gathers at Shechem to ratify the covenant, invoking curses on those who violate the laws (cf. 11:26–29); chapters 28–30 (probably composed by DH) reiterate the life-and-death importance of faithfulness to Yahweh and his commandments.[47]

Chapters 32 and 33 include, respectively, a psalm attributed to Moses, and Moses' blessing of the tribes of Israel.[48] In Deuteronomy 32:48–52, Yahweh tells Moses that he will see the promised land, but not go there. Chapters 31 and 34 (J and E) report Moses' appointment of Joshua to be his successor and Moses' death at the age of one hundred and twenty (cf. Gen 6:3).

Deuteronomy concludes the Pentateuch, or the five books of the Law or Torah, popularly ascribed to Moses. Several hundred verses of these books are attributed to Moses in the text, for example, his two psalms or songs (Exod 15:1–18; Deut 31:30–32:43) and numerous speeches to Israel and conversations with Yahweh and others. But nothing in these texts suggests that anyone in biblical times thought that Moses authored the first five books as such.

The book of Deuteronomy is also the first part of the Deuteronomic History, which also includes Joshua, Judges, 1 and 2 Samuel, and 1 and 2 Kings. The book of Joshua continues the narrative from Deuteronomy 34, which is set in the closing years or months of Israel's long sojourn during the wilderness era.

Joshua

The book has two main sections. In the first (chaps. 1–12), Joshua brings the Israelites out of the wilderness and into the promised land, which, with Yahweh's help, they completely conquer. In the second (chaps. 13–21), the land is apportioned among the various Israelite tribes. Principal sources include J (the Judahite tradition, set down perhaps ca. 950 B.C.) and E (the Israelite tradition, possibly recorded ca. 850 B.C.). Here the Deuteronomic editors (DH) continue their retrospective account of Israel's history that began with the book of Deuteronomy and runs through 2 Kings. These writings, sometimes called the Deuteronomic History, include the present books of Deuteronomy, Joshua, Judges, 1 and 2 Samuel, and 1 and 2 Kings. Writing around 550 B.C., DH contributed several interpretive and summary passages by way of understanding or interpreting Yahweh's purposes for and dealings with his people Israel over the course of time.[49]

Joshua 1 continues the story left off in Deuteronomy 34. Joshua has now succeeded Moses as Israel's divinely appointed leader. DH's narrative commentary conveys the impression that, under Joshua's leadership and with Yahweh's support, Israel completely overran the land of Canaan, killing off all the indigenous peoples.[50] Theologically, DH characterizes these events as the fulfillment of all the promises to the fathers: Yahweh thus gave the people this land as their *possession* or *inheritance*, and gave them *rest*.[51] Several passages, however, indicate that the conquest was less than complete.[52] Modern historians dispute whether Israel's occupation of the land was primarily through conquest or by more peaceful and gradual settlement of largely unoccupied areas.[53] The reported tribal allotments are probably somewhat idealized; very likely, the several tribes managed to settle where they could, with periods of conflict as well as times of peaceful relations with their neighbors.[54]

Various DH passages emphasize the *herem*, which required killing indigenous peoples, possibly lest any survivors tempt the Israelites to worship their gods.[55] Nevertheless, in later years, Israelites, Judahites, and Jews evidently would be tempted again and again to worship other gods: We find such practices condemned (and sometimes ridiculed) from Hosea and Isaiah, through the times of Ezekiel and Second Isaiah, on down to relatively late writings such as the Wisdom of Solomon, the Letter of Jeremiah, and Bel and the Dragon. Various passages probably attributable to DH affirm that if Israel would keep the laws of "this book" (probably referring to Deuteronomy), the nation would prosper (1:7–8), but if it served the gods of foreign peoples or intermarried with foreigners, it would "perish quickly from off the good land" (23:1–16).[56]

Two important institutional practices are authorized in Joshua: inheritance by daughters and cities of refuge for persons who have committed manslaughter, that is, unintentional homicide. Both are represented as carrying out earlier provisions ordained by Yahweh through Moses. Joshua 17:3–4 describes the time when the five daughters of Zelophehad claimed their father's inheritance.[57] Joshua 20 describes the establishment of five cities of refuge where the unintentional "manslayer" may obtain sanctuary pending further inquiry or trial.[58]

Early traditions in Joshua (mainly J and E) recall a number of memorable scenes: the harlot Rahab's clever protection of the Israelite spies at Jericho—hiding them on the roof, then letting them down by a rope from her window in the city wall, and finally marking her window by a scarlet cord (chap. 2); Israel's crossing the Jordan River on dry ground while the ark of the covenant—symbolizing the power and presence of Yahweh—causes its waters to stop, piling up in a heap (chaps. 3–4);[59] the mass circumcision of the entire new generation of male Israelites (5:2–7); and the dramatic capture of Jericho, as its walls fall flat (though without harming Rahab or her household) after the trumpets blow and the people shout (chap. 6).[60]

The story of the capture of Ai by ambush and the slaughter of all its inhabitants—all while Joshua holds out his javelin—is told in chapter 8. Joshua then builds an altar at Shechem and holds a ceremony of covenant ratification or renewal there, featuring the reading of "the book of the law" (8:30–35).[61] The Gibeonites (Hivites), a nearby tribe, wishing to be spared the notorious *herem*, send a peace delegation who, equipped with moldy bread and worn-out clothes, pretend to have come from a far country, and thereby beguile the Israelites into making a covenant to let them live (chap. 9). The five

Amorite kings who attacked Gibeon for making peace with Israel are then defeated by Yahweh and Israel on the day the sun and moon stood still (10:1–15). Joshua's headquarters for a time was at Shiloh (18:1–10), but Shechem was the main place for tribal meetings to renew the covenant (chap. 24).[62] Here we find another cultic credo whereby the people of Israel were to recite the historic deeds of Yahweh on behalf of his people (24:2–13).[63] Here as elsewhere in the Old Testament, the focus is on what Yahweh has done and will do, and on his people's obligations, rather than on doctrinal propositions about him. An oath of fidelity to Yahweh and his law is also part of this ceremony (24:14–27).

The book concludes with a report of Joshua's death and burial and a tribute to him somewhat like DH's characteristic epitaph to many of the judges: "And Israel served Yahweh all the days of Joshua" (24:31). As the biblical story was told, the period of the conquest or settlement of Canaan by Israel was now at an end. The approximate date was 1200 B.C. Next would follow the chaotic period of the judges.

Judges

The Israelites are now in Canaan, having conquered or settled the land. But the Canaanites and other peoples have "persisted in dwelling" there, and, together with several neighboring nations, cause Israel much grief. Israel's political structure, such as it was, in this era (ca. 1200–1000 B.C.) was a confederation of tribes loosely united but occasionally divided against one another. The main institutional expression of their unity was the periodic ceremony of covenant renewal usually held at Shechem, which is evidenced in Deuteronomy 11 and 27, and Joshua 8 and 24, though not mentioned in the book of Judges. An editor, possibly DH,[64] comments thematically in the concluding chapters of this book, "In those days there was no king in Israel; every man did what was right in his own eyes" (21:25). From this editorial perspective we may infer that the politics of rugged individualism failed to cope with the serious problems that were gradually overwhelming the nation. What Israel needed, it seemed, was a strong central government, namely, a king. The editor clearly recognized that the Israelite confederation was unable to cope either with external enemies or with internal dissensions.

As to external enemies, at first Israel manages to hold its own. Under the leadership of Deborah, a prophetess and judge (4:4–5), certain Israelite tribes get together and defeat a coalition of Canaanite kings. This victory is credited in large part to another woman, Jael, who dramatically kills the Canaanite general Sisera while he sleeps (4:21) or drinks out of a "lordly bowl" and so is unable to see the blow coming (5:25–27). The Song of Deborah, one of the earliest fragments of biblical tradition, reports sardonically that some Israelite tribes failed to come when they were called (5:13–18), clearly a bad sign for the future of the confederation. Nevertheless, according to DH, there follows a forty-year period of rest (5:31).

But then come hostile Midianites and others, stealing and destroying Israelite crops. This time, Gideon is summoned by Yahweh to deliver Israel. Through a surprise attack featuring some startling special effects in the middle of the night, Gideon, leading troops from the tribes of Manasseh, Naphtali, and Asher, defeats the Midianite invaders (chaps. 6–7). The Israelites then propose to make Gideon their king and to found a royal dynasty, but he refuses on the grounds that only Yahweh should rule over Israel: "I will not rule over you, and my son will not rule over you; Yahweh will rule over you"(8:22–23). Here we see an example of the Northern or early Israelite view that Yahweh alone is king and that human kings would encroach on Yahweh's status as such.[65] Again there is peace, of sorts, for a while. But then Philistines and Ammonites oppress Israel. Jephthah, "a mighty warrior," now assumes leadership in connection with the Ammonite crisis. Jephthah and the people of Gilead (here represented as one of the tribes of Israel) manage to subdue the Ammonites, though Jephthah's tragic vow costs the life of his daughter, his only child (chap. 11).[66] The Israelite tribe of Ephraim, though summoned to help, fails to come until after the battle (12:2). The Philistines, however, soon prove too much for Israel. Stories about the exploits of the physically powerful but mentally and morally negligible hero, Samson, serve to distract and comfort the original listeners or readers, but they do not alter the fact that the Philistines have become rulers over Israel (15:11) and remain so for some time.[67]

The Israelite confederation also proves unable to deal with problems of internal disorder. The Ephraimites, aspiring to the grandeur of being the number one tribe in Israel (cf. Gen 48:8–20), and perhaps desiring a share in the spoils of battle, berate Gideon for not calling them to help fight the Midianites. His diplomatic answer averts conflict (8:1–3), but when the Ephraimites repeat their performance with Jephthah, who has just defeated the Ammonites, bloody civil war breaks out in Israel, even while the Philistine menace grows on the horizon (12:1–6). In the particularly gruesome series of stories that conclude the book (chaps. 17–21),[68] the tribe of Benjamin is nearly destroyed in a genocidal frenzy by the rest of Israel. It is rescued from extinction only by the Israelites' belated anxiety lest a tribe should be lacking in Israel (21:3). Thereupon, they proceed to massacre another Israelite community (Jabesh-gilead), sparing only one hundred virgins to be wives for the surviving Benjaminite males. When that number proves insufficient, other Benjaminite males forcibly abduct young women from the old Israelite town of Shiloh (chap. 21). Clearly the storyteller means to justify the establishment of the monarchy in Israel as a way out of the moral and political chaos characteristic of the time of the judges.

DH structures the period in terms of a cyclical theology of history, as set forth in 2:11–23: Israel commits apostasy by worshiping other gods; Yahweh then punishes Israel through plundering or domination by enemy nations; the Israelites cry or groan under oppression; after some time, Yahweh has pity on them and delivers them through a judge who, either single-handedly or as leader of one or more tribes, overcomes the enemy of the moment, and then rules for a time, "judging" all Israel. The judge dies, Israel again commits apostasy, and the cycle repeats itself again and again. In this framework, DH presents such diverse figures as Ehud, Shamgar, Deborah, Gideon, Tola, Jair, and Samson. Some of these may have been local or tribal leaders at one time or another, but it is unlikely that any of them actually judged or ruled over all Israel. For a while, Gideon's son, Abimelech, sets himself up as king over part of Israel, rules by brutal violence, and then perishes, unregretted by all, when an unnamed woman drops a millstone on his head (chap. 9).

Notwithstanding DH's formulaic characterization of the judges as persons who delivered and then ruled over all Israel, the biblical traditions themselves indicate that the judges were temporary, local figures who appeared in times of crisis and, through their own powers and leadership, often with Yahweh's help, managed to rescue some tribe or group of tribes from immediate danger. Either DH or possibly an earlier commentator had no doubt that Israel needed a king to deal with its recurrent and catastrophic external and internal crises. Comments to that effect conclude or introduce several episodes illustrative of this theme: 17:6; 18:1; 19:1; and 21:25, the book's concluding sentence. In Christian Bibles, the book of Ruth follows Judges and introduces David (Ruth's great-grandson), who was to become king par excellence. In Jewish scriptures (and following Ruth in Christian versions), the books of Samuel then describe the establishment of the monarchy in Israel: Saul's troubled kingship over Israel and David's later accession to the thrones first of Judah and then also of Israel.

Ruth

This short story, set in the chaotic and slaughterous "days when the judges ruled," is all the more remarkable in that its gentle heroine is not an Israelite but a Moabite. Moreover, she turns out to be King David's great-grandmother.

The author's references to Israelite custom in "former times" (4:7) might suggest that he or she was writing relatively late in the history of Judah. The present story presupposes David's rise to fame (4:17–22), and interpreters who view it as a polemic against the kind of ethnocentrism, if not xenophobia, represented in Ezra and Nehemiah usually date it in postexilic times. Probably the law (or practice) of levirate marriage has evolved since its earlier formulation in Deuteronomy 25:5–10.[69] But the same considerations could suggest that at least the core of the story may be relatively ancient. No eyebrows are raised when Judah marries a Canaanite woman or when Moses marries a Midianite (Genesis 38; Exodus 2, 18).[70] The story of Ruth may antedate the rise of the kind of intense ethnocentrism found in postexilic times. Conceivably, the law of levirate marriage set out in Deuteronomy 25:5–6 was meant to limit the obligation to the brother(s) of the deceased, as against the kind of custom represented in Genesis 38 and the book of Ruth, where the obligation extends to a widow's father-in-law or the next nearest male kinsman, whoever that might be. In any case, it is not possible to date the story of Ruth with certainty.

The practice of levirate marriage evidently is presupposed.[71] According to Deuteronomy 25:5–6, if brothers dwell together and one of them dies without having a son, his brother is obliged to marry the widow, and their first son is to bear the dead brother's name. If the surviving brother refuses to do his duty as *levir*, the widow is authorized to bring the matter before the city elders and otherwise apply social pressure. Levirate marriage functioned, and very likely was intended, to provide support for the widow and any daughters she might have had. It was probably understood that a son born of such a union would inherit from his father. From the story of Judah and Tamar (Genesis 38), we learn that the obligation might devolve on a second brother-in-law or even the father-in-law. At the time of the story of Ruth, we see that the obligation (or privilege) extends to whoever might be the deceased's nearest male kinsman.

In the story of Ruth, a man from Judah, his wife Naomi, and their two sons sojourn in Moab.[72] There the man dies, as do the sons, after marrying young Moabite women. Naomi's daughters-in-law, Orpah and Ruth, both propose to go with Naomi, who now plans to return to Judah. She urges them to remain with their own people in Moab, telling them they ought not wait to remarry until any sons she might yet have could grow up.[73] Nevertheless, in her famous statement of steadfast devotion, "Entreat me not to leave you . . . ," Ruth insists on abiding with Naomi (1:16–17). Together they return to Judah. There Ruth gleans, picking up after the reapers as she is entitled to do under the law (Deut 24:19–22), in the fields of Boaz, an older man who takes kindly to her. Apparently Ruth does not yet know that Boaz is a kinsman of her deceased husband (2:19–20).[74]

Winter is coming, and Naomi is concerned to find "a home" for Ruth in order "that it may be well" with her. She advises Ruth how to let their kinsman, Boaz, know that she would like him to become her husband (3:1–4). Ruth approaches Boaz at night on the threshing floor, and he is delighted by her proposal (3:6–11). But there is a complication, namely, a still nearer kinsman who, in effect, holds the first option. The next morning, Boaz goes with this kinsman to the city gate and gathers a quorum of ten elders, who form a kind of court of record. Boaz begins by discussing a parcel of land Naomi evidently had inherited from her husband, which, according to Boaz, she is now selling.[75] The kinsman is willing to purchase or redeem the parcel, but Boaz then tells him that if he buys the field from Naomi, he is also buying the widow (the Hebrew text does not say which widow) "in order to restore the name of the dead to his inheritance" (4:4–5). There is no known basis in law for linking land redemption with levirate marriage. Perhaps Boaz was bluffing. At any rate, hinting that no sensible man would want to marry Ruth, "the Moabitess,"[76] and thus be obliged to provide an inheritance for her offspring, Boaz elicits the kinsman's refusal.[77] The kinsman now takes off his own sandal, an interesting vestige, perhaps, of the harsher requirement set out in Deuteronomy 25:8–10.[78] Now that the nearer kinsman has waived his option, Boaz can exercise the "right of redemption" himself and marry the widow Ruth.

Ruth and Boaz receive a special blessing from the elders and all those at the gate (4:11–12) and are married. Interestingly, their son is characterized as *Naomi's* next of kin (or restorer or redeemer) and son, as if Ruth had carried him as a surrogate parent. This son is to be the grandfather of the great King David (4:18–21). This circumstance and the favorable representation of Ruth here contrast notably with the negative view toward Moabites expressed in Deuteronomy 23:3–4 and toward marriage with foreigners generally in several other biblical writings.[79] That David later leaves his parents for safekeeping as guests of the king of Moab may corroborate this account of his Moabite lineage (1 Sam 22:3–4).

1 Samuel

Eli and Samuel are introduced both as priests who preside over the "yearly sacrifice" at Shiloh, and as judges (5:18; 7:15). Samuel is also described as a prophet (3:20) or seer (9:19). The book depicts an era in which Israel is at war against the Philistines. In desperation, the Israelites bring their secret weapon, the ark (representing Yahweh's presence and power), out against this enemy who has been oppressing them since the days of the judges,[80] but to no avail. The Philistines defeat Israel and capture Shiloh and even the ark (chap. 4). Old Eli falls over dead, and his daughter-in-law, dying in childbirth, hopelessly names the newborn baby Ichabod ("Gone is the glory," 4:21–22). Following these catastrophic events, some tales are told about the Philistine god Dagon's obeisance to the ark and the Philistines' returning it to the Israelites (chaps. 5–6). These stories probably were intended to console latter-day Israelites by showing that Yahweh was still powerful, even though Israel had been ignominiously defeated. Although Israel experiences some relief in Samuel's time (chap. 7), the Philistines continue to rule the land (13:19–22). Samuel's sons, like Eli's, are corrupt,[81] so in order to provide needed leadership for the nation, Samuel anoints Saul and later David as kings. Duplicate and sometimes triplicate versions of several episodes are reported, deriving from J, E, and other sources. Though they are part of the larger Deuteronomic History, 1 and 2 Samuel contain little obvious commentary by DH.

The northern tradition (E) views the people's desire for a king as rejection of Yahweh. According to this tradition, Samuel opposes the idea of kingship, yields only reluctantly (8:1–9; 10:17–24), and warns what it will be like to have a king (8:10–18). Samuel's reported views reflect both Israel's commitment to the theocratic ideal (cf. Judg 8:23) and also, probably, its unhappy experience under Solomon's tyrannical rule (see 1 Kgs 5:13–14; 12:3–4). In southern tradition (J), however, Samuel anoints Saul without hesitation, as Yahweh commands, after Saul comes to him looking for his father's lost asses (chap. 9).[82]

Judah's experience of kingship under David and Solomon was more positive when J was writing (ca. 950 B.C.).

Saul's career begins about 1000 B.C., after the manner of the judges, with his bold rescue of Jabesh-gilead from the Ammonites (chap. 11). Under Saul, Israel gains initial successes against the Philistines. These successes are all the more remarkable considering the extent of Philistine power and control at the time (13:19–23). Saul nevertheless fails to satisfy Samuel (13:8–15; chap. 15), who denounces him and anoints David to be king in his place. It is some time, however, before David actually becomes king. Arguably, Samuel acted unfairly in denouncing and rejecting Saul. As noted in 1 Samuel 13:8, Saul had "waited seven days, the time appointed by Samuel," and Saul had reason to believe that he had to act as he did under the circumstances, given Samuel's failure to come. In chapter 15, Samuel calls on Saul—who already had enough to do given the Philistine menace (14:15)—to "punish" the Amalekites for an ancient grievance (15:2; cf. Exod 17:8–16). Samuel ordered Saul to destroy not only the Amalekites but all their livestock (15:3). Saul, very likely wishing to be able to feed and pay his army, spared the best of the captured livestock, as Joshua had done earlier (Josh 8:2, 27).

Notwithstanding Samuel's opposition, Saul manages to free part of Israel from Philistine domination. David, a Judahite, appears on the scene as one of Saul's warriors. By then, readers already know that Samuel has anointed David to become king and successor to Saul (16:1–13). One version of David's rise to prominence is the perhaps legendary story of his victory over the Philistine giant, Goliath (chap. 17).[83] In time, Saul becomes jealous of David's popularity (18:7–8) and suspects, perhaps correctly, that David hopes to supplant him as king. David learns of Saul's resolve to kill him, and escapes with the assistance of his wife, Michal, Saul's daughter (chap. 19). Seeking refuge in Gath, a Philistine city, David is recognized as the famous Philistine-slayer. To escape retribution, he pretends to be crazy. (In the ancient Near East, madmen were thought to be touched by divine power and were treated with caution.) Achish, king of Gath, exclaims that he already has enough madmen in his entourage (21:10–15), so David is allowed to move on. David then gathers a band of debtors and malcontents, the beginning of his own standing army (22:1–3). Saul now obsessively tracks David through the wilderness, while the Philistine storm clouds gather against Israel.

Chapter 25 indicates David's modus operandi at this time. He sends ten of his band to ask the wealthy Nabal for a "donation" on the basis that they have "protected"—that is, not yet stolen—his sheep or attacked his shepherds.[84] After Nabal indignantly (and imprudently) declines to be shaken down and sends David's men away empty-handed, his intelligent (and beautiful) wife Abigail quickly makes amends. When he learns what has happened, Nabal dies of what once was called a fit of apoplexy. David then takes Abigail as one of his wives. Soon David becomes a vassal or mercenary of the Philistine king Achish. Now David spends his time raiding non-Israelite villages, all the while telling Achish that he has been plundering Judahites and related peoples. Samuel is now dead, so unlike Saul (chap. 15), David is not obliged to destroy the spoils as required by the *herem* doctrine; instead, he uses them to maintain his army and give presents "to his friends, the elders of Judah" (chap. 27; 30:26–31), who later show their appreciation by making him king. David kills the men and women of the villages he has raided, not because of the *herem* but to prevent their telling on him to Achish (27:8–12). Dead men and women tell no tales.

The Philistines are now ready to fight Saul and the army of Israel, and Achish is ready to have David join them in the campaign. Some of the Philistine lords question David's loyalty, however, so he and his men are sent back, just in time as it turns out, to retrieve their wives, children, and possessions, which have been carried off by some Amalekites (chaps. 29–30). While David is thus honorably occupied, the Philistines defeat Israel on Mount Gilboa. Saul and most of his sons perish, but their bodies are respectfully buried by the grateful men of Jabesh-gilead. Once again, there is no king in Israel. The situation seems hopeless.

2 Samuel

This writing might well be entitled the book of David. It reports David's rise to power following Saul's death, his great achievements as well as his great offenses against his subjects and against Yahweh, and, subsequently, a series of catastrophes that are interpreted as Yahweh's judgments against David for these offenses. Second Samuel is part of the Deuteronomic History, which starts with the book of Deuteronomy and (excepting Ruth) extends through 2 Kings. The main source in 2 Samuel is J, though some E tradition may also be found here. What is sometimes called "the court history" (chaps. 11–20 and 2 Kings chaps.1–2) may be an earlier piece preserved by J or perhaps composed by J himself.

It is no simple matter for David, a Judahite, to become king of Israel. Though he is quickly made king of Judah, he becomes king over Israel only after several complications are resolved (chaps. 2–5). His reign over both kingdoms (ca. 990–965 B.C.) marks the beginning of the United Monarchy. But it is a precarious union. During David's reign, the North (Israel) makes two serious efforts at secession (chaps. 15–18; 20). As a Judahite, David needs to convince the Israelites that he is a legitimate successor to Saul. His famous lament over Saul and Jonathan (chap. 1) may have been published with this purpose in mind. Saul's career as king of Israel began with his rescue of Jabesh-gilead, one of the Israelite tribes (Judg 21:8). Now David sends a message to the men of Jabesh-gilead (2:5–7), clearly inviting them to regard him as their king.

No sooner is David made king of Judah than war games between Israel and Judah degenerate into full-scale war (chaps. 2–3), no doubt to the delight of the Philistines. Saul's general and cousin, Abner, disgruntled because Ishbosheth, Saul's oldest surviving son and Israel's nominal king, has reproached him for going to bed with Saul's concubine, proposes to bring Israel over to David's side. Significantly, David stipulates that first Michal, Saul's daughter (for whom David otherwise has shown little regard), must be restored as his wife (3:13). Evidently David wishes to be in a position to gain Israel's loyalty by qualifying as Saul's son-in-law and thus as a member of the royal family of Israel. Abner delivers Michal to David, persuades the elders of Israel to accept David as their king, and promises to gather all Israel to David to make a covenant with him as such. But then David's commander, Joab, prompted by jealousy and desire for revenge, murders Abner, thereby creating a major public relations problem. David orders public mourning, composes a lament, and makes it clear to the Israelites that he is innocent of Abner's death (3:31–39)—but without lifting a finger to punish Joab, whose services he still needs. Next, two assassins, sensing David's ambition and hoping that he will reward them, bring him Ishbosheth's head. David has no need of these two and has them publicly executed. He also has Ishbosheth's head properly buried. Persuaded at last, Israel makes him their king too (5:1–5). Now, for the first time, Israel and Judah are united under a single king.

David and his men take Jerusalem from the Jebusites, making it the capital of the united kingdom. He has the ark of Yahweh brought into Jerusalem, offers sacrifices before it, and proposes to build a "house" or temple—the precursor of the Jerusalem temple (6:1–7:7). In short order, David proceeds to defeat, or otherwise come to terms with, the

Philistines and most of Israel's other erstwhile enemy nations—a remarkable accomplishment considering the Philistines' initial, virtually complete supremacy. The prophet Nathan, according to a relatively late source, declares that David's house and kingdom will "be made sure for ever" (chap. 7). Evidently in order to secure this end, David hands Saul's two surviving sons and five grandsons over to the Gibeonites for execution, on the pretext that they have an old grievance to settle against Saul (21:1–14; cf. 9:1). Shimei, a kinsman of Saul's, accuses David of murdering Saul's family and reigning in its place (16:5–8). David does spare Mephibosheth, Jonathan's lame son, but keeps him under house arrest (chap. 9).

Second Samuel 11–20 and 1 Kings 1–2 constitute the great literary, historical, and theological masterpiece of the period. The writer of this court history may well have been a contemporary of David's and Solomon's, and some scholars suggest that this author was none other than J, who collected and edited southern traditions around 950 B.C.

This court history begins with a less than flattering portrayal of King David's latter years. The writer describes the course of events vividly but with exceptional economy of words: "It happened, late one afternoon . . ." David, no longer leading his troops in battle, one afternoon looks down from the palace and sees Bathsheba bathing. He has her brought to him and sexually assaults her. Since she is a married woman, David thereby also commits adultery. On learning that she is pregnant, he tries to cover his tracks by sending for Uriah, her husband, so that the latter will go home and "father" the child. But, in striking contrast to David, Uriah is too devoted to his comrades in the field to indulge in such pleasures. So David cynically sends him back with a message instructing his friend Joab, his army commander, to arrange to have Uriah killed in battle. Afterward, David takes Bathsheba as another of his wives. The prophet Nathan then tells David the parable of the little ewe lamb, thereby catching the conscience of the king and causing him to pronounce judgment upon himself. Nathan now declares that the sword shall not depart from David's house (chap. 12). The ensuing events fulfill that declaration, sometimes reenacting David's offenses through a series of offenses committed by his own sons against members of his own family.

In what follows, we see not only a series of events that implicitly represent Yahweh's judgment against David in the form of evil arising against him out of his own house (12:11); we also see David's sons struggling for power. In theory, the oldest son succeeds the king once he dies. But David, though increasingly decrepit, is in no hurry to die.

His oldest son, Amnon, rapes his half-sister, David's daughter, Tamar. Two years later—and thus with premeditation, or "in cold blood"—Absalom, the next oldest son, has Amnon murdered. Now Absalom is in line to succeed David. But David lives on. After some political maneuvering (15:1–9), Absalom declares himself king, precipitating renewed war between Israel and Judah. Joab, going against David's order to spare Absalom, has him killed while he is caught by his head in the lower branches of an oak tree (chap. 18). For a while, Israel and Judah again are ruled by David (chap. 19). But the kingdom again comes apart as the Israelites once again secede, this time under the leadership of Sheba, a man of Saul's tribe (chap. 20). The stories in 1 Kings 1–2 will complete the pattern of evil arising against David out of his own household. Adonijah, now David's oldest surviving son, expects to be king soon, since the old man finally is about to die. But Solomon's mother and the prophet Nathan conspire to bring about a palace revolution that leapfrogs Solomon onto the throne over several older brothers. Solomon then conducts a bloody purge of possible rivals and dissenters, including his own brother Adonijah.

Chapters 21–24 of 2 Samuel assemble miscellaneous leftover traditions about David: stories about Philistine giants (including Goliath, here reportedly killed by a certain Elhanan), a psalm virtually identical to Psalm 18 (22:2–51), another psalm purporting to be the last words of David (23:1–7), a catalogue of David's mighty men, and the story of his numbering Israel and Judah, inspired by God but nevertheless sinful, and therefore punished by plague (chap. 24).[85]

1 Kings

The period covered here extends from the last days of David (ca. 965 B.C.) through the reign of Ahab (ca. 875–850 B.C.) and includes the era of Solomon, the breakup of the united kingdom, and reports of intermittent warfare among Israel, Judah, and Syria. Early prophets figure prominently, anointing, advising, and condemning kings, according to the word of Yahweh. First Kings is part of the Deuteronomic History (edited by DH) that begins with Deuteronomy and ends with 2 Kings. Sources include Judahite (J and A) and Israelite (E and B) traditions, among others. DH's commentary on the kings and their faithfulness (or lack thereof) to Yahweh appears fairly regularly in summary formulas.[86]

As the book opens, King David is now quite old and evidently somewhat senile but still has not appointed a successor. His oldest surviving son, Adonijah, assuming that his father will soon be dead, celebrates in anticipation of his own installation as king (1:5–10). David has never been able to cope with Adonijah (1:5–6) or any of his other sons (2 Samuel 13–19). For reasons of his own, Nathan conspires with Bathsheba to beguile the befuddled David into thinking that he has promised that Solomon, a much younger son, will become king (1:11–27). The ruse succeeds, Solomon is quickly enthroned, and David soon dies. Solomon promptly conducts a political purge, sending his henchman Beniah to kill possible rivals and dissenters, including his brother Adonijah and old Joab (even as he clings to the altar, a supposed sanctuary), on various slight pretexts (chap. 2).

Solomon is remembered positively in several ways, beginning with his piety, as expressed in his famous prayer in 3:5–9. He is especially remembered for his wisdom, a trait illustrated by his resolution of the competing claims of the two harlots for the one living infant (chap. 3). In later years, he was credited with authorship of many wisdom writings, including much of Proverbs, Wisdom of Solomon, and, by implication, Ecclesiastes. He is also famous for the luxury and extravagance of his court (chaps. 4 and 10) and as the builder of the temple and several (rather larger) royal palaces (chaps. 5–7). A euphoric commentator epitomizes the era: The people "were as many as the sand by the sea; they ate and drank and were happy" (4:20).

But as the story unfolds, Solomon provokes increasing resentment on the part of the Israelites because of the heavy yoke of forced labor he imposes upon them (12:4). DH notes another negative trait, Solomon's unprecedented apostasy, but generously suggests that Solomon's foreign wives were to blame for turning his heart to other gods, and that this apostasy occurred only in his old age (11:4–8). Nevertheless, DH blames Solomon for the ultimate breakup of the kingdom, interpreting it as Yahweh's judgment against Solomon's apostasy (11:9–11).

Solomon's son and successor, Rehoboam, enjoys playing the role of Oriental potentate even more than his father did. Rehoboam goes to Shechem so that Israel may ratify and inaugurate his kingship, little thinking he needs the consent of the governed. Refusing to heed the Israelites' plea for relief from the harsh treatment they suffered under Solomon, Rehoboam arrogantly tells them that now it will be much worse for them. As a result, "Israel departed to their tents," leaving Rehoboam and his successors to rule only over Judah (chap. 12). Thus, Israel and Judah, united most of the time under David and his son Solomon, break apart ca. 926 B.C., never again to be reunited. Never again did a descendant of David rule over Israel.

Jeroboam, anointed by the prophet Ahijah (11:29–39), is made king of Israel. Southern tradition regards him, along with all Israelite kings, unfavorably. DH accuses all northern kings of apostasy: Necessarily, none of them worshiped at the Jerusalem temple as required by Deuteronomy 12. DH, writing about 550 B.C., assumes that this requirement—then probably less than a hundred years old—was part of the original Mosaic law. Much of the time, during the period of the divided kingdoms that follows, Judah and Israel are at war with one another (14:30).

The very idea of kingship is always portrayed as suspect in early Israelite tradition.[87] None of the northern kings enjoyed the sense of divine authorization experienced by or claimed on behalf of the house of David in the South (see 2 Sam 7:11–17). In the North, kings and their entire families often are assassinated by would-be successors. One such pretender, Baasha, kills off Jeroboam's family and makes himself king, in accordance with "the word of Yahweh" (15:27–30). The prophet Jehu then denounces Baasha, who dies after a reign of two years. His son Elah and all his male kinsmen are then killed off by Zimri, another pretender, who lasts just seven days (chap. 16). After more civil war, Omri becomes king of Israel, an important one, according to extrabiblical sources. It is he who establishes Samaria as the capital of Israel. Afterward, the Northern Kingdom is frequently referred to as Samaria, as well as Ephraim and, of course, Israel.

The prophet Elijah is introduced in chapter 17. His special status is shown in a story that tells how ravens bring him food while he is in hiding. His miraculous powers are indicated by his multiplying the contents of a widow's jar of meal and cruse of oil. He also brings her son back to life through prayer and a kind of CPR procedure (17:20–22; cf. 2 Kgs 4:32–35).

Omri's son Ahab and his Phoenician wife Jezebel then rule Israel. On Elijah's orders, King Ahab gathers all Israel and four hundred and fifty prophets of Baal to take part in a contest at Mount Carmel (chap. 18). Baal's prophets call on him to light their sacrificial fire, but there is no answer. Call louder, Elijah mockingly urges them. Perhaps Baal is musing, or visiting the outhouse, or is asleep. They call louder and even lacerate themselves, but there is still no answer. Then Elijah calls on Yahweh, whose sacrifice is immediately consumed by fire from heaven. Elijah orders the prophets of Baal killed, and then the rains come, ending the three-year drought Elijah had previously called for in order to show that Yahweh, not Baal, sends the rain (chaps. 17–18).[88] Jezebel does not share Ahab's reluctance to violate the rights of subjects who do not care to comply with royal desires. When Naboth declines to sell his ancestral vineyard, which Ahab covets, she has him falsely charged with treason and summarily executed, and then she "gives" the vineyard to Ahab.[89] Thereupon, Elijah pronounces Yahweh's word against both Ahab and Jezebel (21:17–24). Both subsequently are killed in separate, dramatic circumstances, thereby fulfilling Elijah's prophecy.

Syria, the small kingdom just north of Israel, at one time is allied with Israel against Judah; at another, with Judah against Israel (16:16–20). On one occasion, after three years without war (22:1), Israel plans to seize some territory back from Syria. Ahab calls on Jehoshaphat, king of Judah, who is at this point allied with him as a vassal or junior partner, to join in the campaign against Syria. Unimpressed by the four hundred sycophantic prophets in the court of Ahab, Jehoshaphat asks if there is not yet another prophet of Yahweh of whom they may inquire. The prophet Micaiah (the last syllable of whose name, like Elijah's, signifies that he is an adherent of Yahweh) is consulted. Having been warned by one of Ahab's officials not to rock the boat, Micaiah sardonically tells Ahab, "Go up and triumph." But Ahab knows that Micaiah never prophesies good about him, and charges him to tell the truth. Micaiah then declares that Ahab will die in battle. Ahab thinks it is a big joke (22:18), goes to war, and is fatally wounded by a Syrian archer.

2 Kings

Second Kings continues the history of the separated kingdoms of Israel and Judah and concludes the Deuteronomic History. As in 1 Kings, Israelite kings uniformly are condemned for apostasy, while Judahite kings (who at least occasionally worship at the Jerusalem temple) generally receive qualified praise (e.g., 2 Kgs 15:1–5; 16:17–20). All the kings of Judah were descendants of David.

As in 1 Kings, the chronology of 2 Kings is complicated by the system of relative dating (e.g., 2 Kgs 8:16, 25), and the fact that many kings have similar or identical names. Israel and Judah each have kings named Jehoram, Ahaziah, and Jehoash (not to be confused with Israel's king Jehoahaz), and Judah later has a king named Ahaz (not to be confused with Israel's king Ahab or the kings Ahaziah). Two different kings named Jeroboam rule over Israel. Israel's king Pekahiah is followed by Pekah, while Judah's Jehoiakim is followed by Jehoiachin. The prophet Jehu is to be distinguished from the king by that name.

To make matters worse, some kings have more than one name: The kings Jehoram are also known as Joram, and the kings Jehoash as Joash, while Jehoiachin is also known as Jeconiah (1 Chr 3:16; Esth 2:6) and simply Coniah (Jer 22:24, 28). Readers are advised to have on hand one of the standard lists of the kings of Israel and Judah.[90] Occasionally reports conflict, for instance, as to the year Ahab's son Jehoram began to reign over Israel (1:17; cf. 3:1).

Prophets continue to anoint, advise, and condemn the kings. Jehu's rebellion (ca. 842 B.C.) is instigated by Elisha (chap. 9), and his slaughter of the house of Ahab is said to have Yahweh's prior approval (10:30), though Hosea later declares otherwise (Hos 1:4–5). Jehu succeeds in becoming king of Israel and comes close to taking over Judah as well (2 Kings 10). Most of the classical prophets appear during the later years of Israel and Judah, the period set out in 2 Kings; they are Amos, Hosea, Isaiah, Micah, Jeremiah, and Ezekiel.

Alliances continue to shift uncertainly, as Syria, Israel, and Judah combine with or against one another and other nations, notably, Edom, Moab, Assyria, and Egypt. Between 926 and 722 B.C., Israel has nineteen kings from nine different dynasties or families, who are commonly overthrown by revolution or assassination. In Judah, on the other hand, the only break in the line of nineteen Davidic kings, beginning with Rehoboam, from 926 to 586 B.C., is Athaliah, the first and only queen in either Israel or Judah (9:29; 11:1–16).

Second Kings begins with a series of tales about Elijah and his younger associate and future successor, Elisha. Elijah calls down fire on three platoons of Israelite soldiers sent by King Ahaziah, evidently to arrest him (chap. 1). In the next chapter, accompanied by a group of fifty prophets ("the sons of the prophets"), Elijah and Elisha approach the Jordan River. Elijah parts the water with his mantle, and the two prophets cross over. Elijah is then taken up into heaven by a whirlwind, accompanied by a chariot and horses of fire.[91] Elsewhere, too, Elijah is associated with fire (1 Kings 18). Later traditions look for Elijah, prophet of repentance par excellence, to return to earth before the time of judgment.[92]

Elisha now proceeds to use his "double share" of Elijah's spirit to perform a series of wonders. He takes Elijah's mantle and parts the Jordan, purifies the water at Jericho with salt, calls two bears out of the woods to attack some small boys who have insulted him by calling him "baldy" (chap. 2), prophesies the defeat of Moab by Israel, Judah, and Edom (chap. 3), multiplies the contents of a widow's jar of oil so she can pay her debts, cures a wealthy Shunammite woman's infertility and restores her son to life, renders edible a pot of poisoned pottage, feeds a hundred men with twenty loaves of bread and some ears of grain (chap. 4), cures the Syrian Naaman's leprosy, but inflicts his servant Gehazi with it for taking graft (chap. 5), retrieves a lost axe head by making it float to the surface of the Jordan River, uses ESP to eavesdrop on the Syrian king, blinds the army of pursuing Syrians and then orders the king of Israel to give the Syrian army a great feast, after which the Syrians peaceably return home (chap. 6), foretells relief from a great famine (chap. 7), instructs the Shunammite woman on how to survive a seven-year famine, and predicts Hazael's succession to the Syrian throne and his subsequent infliction of evil upon the people of Israel (chap. 8).[93]

Major events occur during these years (ca. 850–586 B.C.). In 853, at the battle of Qarqar, the three small kingdoms of Syria, Israel, and Judah, temporarily allied, succeed in blocking Assyrian expansion into their territory. Nevertheless, the Assyrians reappear over a century later, in 738, and this time Israel must pay tribute to purchase a few more years of independence. Hoping to compel Judah to join them against the advancing Assyrians, Syria and Israel together besiege Jerusalem (ca. 734; see Isaiah 7–8). But Ahaz, king of Judah, turns to Assyria for help, and even pays a large bribe. Assyria obligingly attacks and overruns much of Syria and Israel (15:29; 16:1–9). In 722 B.C., Assyria moves decisively against Israel, now bringing that kingdom to an end. Never again is there a kingdom of Israel. As Amos anticipated, it has "fallen, no more to rise" (Amos 5:2). DH interprets this final disaster as Yahweh's judgment for Israel's chronic apostasy (17:7–23). Now only the southern kingdom of Judah remains from what was once, under David and Solomon, the united kingdoms of Israel and Judah.

Judah manages to preserve at least nominal independence for nearly another 140 years. In 701, Sennacherib's Assyrian army surrounds, but does not enter, Jerusalem (see 2 Kgs 18:13–19:37; Isa 36:1–37:38). King Hezekiah rules Judah during much of the troubled period, beginning, perhaps, as early as 728 (2 Kgs 18:1, 9–10) until around 687. DH credits Hezekiah with having been uniquely faithful to Yahweh, who in turn caused him to prosper (18:3–6; cf. 23:25). But Isaiah reproaches Hezekiah, perhaps for having imprudently shown all the royal treasures to a visiting delegation from Babylon (20:12–19). Hezekiah is succeeded by his son, Manasseh, famous chiefly for his apostasy, idolatry, and syncretism (i.e., combining the worship of Yahweh with worship of other gods), and for slaughtering innocent people in Jerusalem (21:2–16). Shortly after the end of the long reign of Manasseh—the worst southern king ever, according to DH (21:1–16)—Josiah is enthroned in Judah. He is the best king in DH's "book" (22:2; 23:25). He restores the temple (ca. 622), removing foreign and idolatrous cults in compliance with the newly rediscovered "book of the law," probably Deuteronomy, which now contains the requirement of worship in only the one place (see Deuteronomy 12–19; 2 Kings 22–23). According to the "pious fraud" theory, the ink was barely dry on the new chapters in Deuteronomy when the book was "found."[94] It may well be, however, that the centralized worship requirement and attendant adjustments in law and cultus were added as part of a reform movement that developed earlier, perhaps during the years of the apostate Manasseh, or even earlier, under the reign of Hezekiah.

In the late seventh century B.C., Babylon emerges as the most powerful empire in the ancient Near East. In 598, its emperor, Nebuchadnezzar, carries off Jerusalem's treasures, leading families, craftsmen, and King Jehoiachin (24:10–16). Then in 587, Judah's King Zedekiah rebels against the Babylonians, who, after a terrible year-long siege, destroy Jerusalem, including the temple, and take most of the remaining citizenry to Babylon (cf. Psalm 137). This catastrophe marks the end of the kingdom of Judah and the beginning of the exile. Never again did a descendant of David sit on the throne of Judah. In fact, never again was there a kingdom of Judah at all—though in the second and first centuries B.C. there would emerge a Jewish kingdom that endured some hundred years.[95]

Sources used by the writer-editor of 2 Kings may have included northern (B) stories about miraculous deeds by Elijah and Elisha, as well as considerable southern (A) material. Additionally, as in 1 Kings, references are made to chronicles of the kings of Israel and Judah that are no longer extant. (These are not the same as the books of 1 and 2 Chronicles found in the Old Testament.) Two sections duplicate, largely verbatim, portions of Isaiah and Jeremiah: 2 Kings 18:13–20:19 (cf. Isa 36:1–39:8); and 2 Kings 24:18–25:21 (cf. Jer 52:1–27).

Writing several decades into the exile, DH, the editor of the Deuteronomic History, tries to make sense of the grand, tragic, and chaotic events and times dating back to the days when Moses and Israel were in the wilderness. This much is clear: Yahweh had made good his promise to bring Israel into the land of Canaan and give it to them as an inheritance and a possession. Had Israel (and Judah) remained faithful to Yahweh and his covenant, they would have continued to enjoy his favor there. But Israel and Judah had worshiped other gods and otherwise failed to obey Yahweh's ordinances, commands, and statutes. Consequently they experienced divine judgment in the form of disaster and defeat at the hands of their enemies. Thus not only the Northern Kingdom (2 Kgs 17:7–18) but also the Southern (2 Kgs 17:19–20; 24:1–4) perished because their people and leaders had broken covenant with Yahweh. DH concludes his work with the pathetic note that the exiled King Jehoiachin is allowed to live out his life as an honored prisoner of the Babylonians (25:27–30). Yet DH achieved his goal. The kings and their kingdoms were gone, possibly forever, but Yahweh is still God. All that happened made sense within the framework of the theology of history presented by DH to his fellow exiles. And now, though the people of Judah were still in exile, hope remained that, just as Yahweh had brought his people from bondage in Egypt into the promised land, so he might again be with and for his people in some great act of future redemption.

1 Chronicles

The final editor of 1 and 2 Chronicles, Ezra, and Nehemiah is usually referred to as "the Chronicler." Some interpreters suggest that Ezra, himself remembered as "the scribe," might have been the Chronicler. Whoever brought them together, these four books constitute the third of the three edited segments of biblical historical tradition that constitute the first half of the Old Testament. Certain clues, including the distinction between priests and Levites (e.g., 9:10–16) and reference to Persian coins (1 Chr 29:7), suggest that Chronicles was written no earlier than 450–400 B.C., and possibly as late as 350 B.C. The present 1 and 2 Chronicles originally formed a single book.

First Chronicles 1–9 provide a genealogical recapitulation of world and Israelite history from Adam to the time of David. Curiously, the Babylonian exile (ca. 586–539) is reported at 9:1, and 9:2–34 seem to describe the population of Jerusalem after the exile. But then the scene shifts backward to the time of Saul (ca. 1000).[96] Chapter 10 reports Saul's death, and chapters 11–29 concentrate on David's reign. Like the priestly authors and editors of much of Genesis through Leviticus, the Chronicler was interested in genealogies, including those of early humanity, but particularly of the sons of Abraham and Israel. Relatively few women are named; for example, there is no mention of Eve, Sarah, Rebekah, Leah, Rachel, or Ruth. Little is said about what anyone did, apart from having sons, until the time of David.

Religious functionaries (priests, the sons of Aaron, and Levites, the sons of Levi) are accorded special prominence (see chaps. 6; 9; 23–26). Levites are particularly important as assistants to priests in the tabernacle (which, as in the P tradition, appears as a portable prototype of the Jerusalem temple), with gatekeepers and musicians also filling important roles. In all probability these latter classifications had not existed in the time of David or Solomon but did figure prominently in temple rituals at the time the Chronicler wrote.

Earlier biblical materials are used when suitable to the Chronicler's purposes. Traditions that might cast doubt on David's virtue are omitted, such as his working as a mercenary for the Philistines (1 Samuel 27; 29–30), his dancing naked before the ark (2 Sam 6:12–22), the Bathsheba-Uriah episodes and David's subsequent condemnation by Nathan and the ensuing chaos within David's household (2 Samuel 11–20), and his arranging for the extermination of Saul's family (2 Sam 21:1–6; cf. 1 Chr 10:6). There is no mention of warfare between Judah and Israel (cf. 2 Samuel 2–3); instead, even before Saul's death, various Israelite groups seek David as their leader and afterward unanimously make him their king (chaps. 11–12). David's prominence is emphasized in that he is described as having all but built the temple: He receives the plans from God, works out the details, assembles building materials and workers, as well as priests and Levites to staff the temple, and he prays for Solomon to have wisdom to see it to completion (chaps. 22; 28–29).

Satan appears in the Bible for the first time at 21:1. He, rather than Yahweh (cf. 2 Sam. 24:1) incites David to take a census.[97] The Chronicler's theological commentary on history somewhat resembles that of DH, in that Israel and Judah experience catastrophe at the hand of God because of their unfaithfulness (e.g., 5:25–26; 9:1). Like the wisdom writers, however, the Chronicler also suggests that individuals are brought to account in this life for their misdeeds (e.g., 10:13–14).

Chronicles may contain accurate information about priestly and Levitical families in the postexilic period. Moreover, one should not be surprised to find revisionist, idealized, or sanitized historical writing in any era. Yet much of what appears here seems to derive from pious imagination; for example, the reports that Zeruiah was David's sister (2:16), that Joab was the first man into Jerusalem (11:6), that Reuben lost his birthright because he had committed incest (5:1), that Elhanan killed not Goliath but Goliath's brother (20:5; cf. 2 Sam 21:19), that over three hundred thousand troops from all twelve tribes of Israel came in full battle dress to make David king (chap. 12), that David commanded over a million Israelite soldiers and nearly half a million from Judah (21:5), and that David purchased the future site of the temple for six hundred gold shekels (21:15–22:1).[98]

Solomon, the Chronicler assures us, was chosen by David, God, and the people of Israel (23:1; 29:1, 22), and all the mighty men and all the other sons of David pledged him their allegiance. No mention is made of either the palace revolution that put Solomon on the throne or his purge of dissenters and possible rivals (including Joab and Solomon's own brother Adonijah, as in 1 Kings 1–2). The ideal-ized view of history presented by the Chronicler has led some inter-preters to suggest that he may have meant to picture here a future messianic era, modeled on the golden age of David's kingship.

2 Chronicles

The retelling of history begun in 1 Chronicles continues here, down to the time of the exile (ca. 586 B.C.). The book's last verses anticipate the first few of the book of Ezra, which carries the account into the post-exilic period. The Chronicler again repeats much of earlier biblical writ-ings (here, drawing from 1 and 2 Kings), omitting and supplementing in accordance with his concerns. The Chronicler emphasizes the impor-tance and virtues of Levites.[99] Again, temple worship is the central interest, with special roles assigned to priests and Levites, respectively. These functionaries had not been differentiated in 1 and 2 Kings or in any other sources written before 450 B.C. It is likely that 2 Chronicles was written about 350, as a single book along with 1 Chronicles.

Julius Wellhausen's comment that one might as well try to hear the grass growing as hope to learn anything about the history of ancient Israel from Chronicles may have been overly severe, though undoubt-edly we do have here a revisionist history written from a particular religious and political perspective.[100] In any event, we may learn a great deal from Chronicles about the interests of an important segment of Judaism in the fourth century B.C.

The first nine chapters portray Solomon as an ideal king, who is remembered especially for his construction and dedication of the original temple. Nothing is said here about Solomon's subjecting the people of Israel to forced labor (cf. 1 Kgs 5:13–14), a policy that fueled their secessionist resentment (cf. 1 Kgs 12:3–4), or about his apostasy, which in 1 Kings 11 is the stated reason for the breakup of the kingdom of Israel-Judah shortly after his death.

Generally, the Chronicler holds the view that Judah (the Southern Kingdom) is the true "Israel." He has little to say, and less that is favorable, about the Northern Kingdom. Most of the southern kings are said to have been good, but the Chronicler's attention is directed mainly to religious leaders. Military and political events are less significant than faithful worship of Yahweh expressed through offering sacrifices and other temple rituals, which are carried out under the auspices of the priests and various orders of Levites. When the Chronicler wrote, the Jewish people were no longer an independent nation but only a province of the Persian empire, or possibly of a later foreign empire, and thus were bound together primarily by religious and cultural ties.

Kings Hezekiah and Josiah are remembered chiefly for keeping the Passover in Jerusalem (chaps. 30 and 35). Catastrophes that befall certain kings are explained as God's judgment for sins that were unreported in earlier tradition, such as Jehoram's wretched end (chap. 21), Uzziah's leprosy (26:16–20), and Josiah's untimely death at the hands of Pharaoh Neco, which is explained here on the somewhat implausible basis of Josiah's failure to heed the "words of Neco from the mouth of God" (35:20–24). On the other hand, Manasseh, the worst king of all according to 2 Kings 21, nevertheless repents, the Chronicler tells us (33:12–17), evidently to account for the extraordinary length of his reign.[101] These features of Chronicles may have been prompted by familiarity with the emerging orthodox wisdom theology (represented in Proverbs), according to which the righteous are rewarded with long life while the wicked soon suffer or perish. Several times, however, 2 Chronicles holds out the hope that God will forgive those who repent and pray to him.

Second Chronicles concludes the Bible in modern Hebrew editions, where it is classified with the Holy Writings. Unlike 2 Kings, which leaves off in the time of the exile, 2 Chronicles reports the Persian monarch Cyrus's edict of liberation, which, as in Ezra, includes the promise that he will undertake to build a new temple in Jerusalem (36:22–23).[102] By the time the Chronicler was writing, the rebuilt temple had been standing for a century and a half.

Ezra

The author, probably the Chronicler, who may have been Ezra himself, continues his story from 2 Chronicles, starting with Cyrus's proclamation ending the exile (ca. 538 B.C.), through the rebuilding of the temple (ca. 515 B.C.), and down to the time of Ezra. In the books of Ezra and Nehemiah, Ezra is generally referred to as either "the priest" or "the scribe" or both.[103] Biblical scholars generally agree that 1 and 2 Chronicles, Ezra, and Nehemiah together constitute a single literary or editorial unit, the third of the historical collections that make up approximately the first half of the Old Testament.[104] Literary or editorial connections between the books of Ezra and Nehemiah are apparent. For instance, Ezra 2:1–3:1 duplicates Neh 7:6–73 nearly verbatim. The description of Ezra's activities and prayer in Neh 8:1–9:37 may have derived from an earlier version of the book of Ezra.

It is possible that Ezra was appointed governor of Jerusalem and its environs, which then constituted a Persian province. At any rate, as the story is told, King Artaxerxes has authorized him to spend huge sums of money to pay for sacrificial offerings in Jerusalem, to teach the returned exiles the laws of God and of Persia, and to see that these laws are enforced by appointing magistrates and judges (7:25–26). It is not clear whether the author was thinking of Artaxerxes I (ca. 465–425 B.C.) or Artaxerxes II (ca. 400–350 B.C.). Most interpreters place Ezra in the latter period. One section is written in the first person, as if indeed by Ezra himself (7:27–9:15).

The writer is mainly interested in the second temple, its reconstruction, furnishings, and staff: all central features of Jewish life in his time. As in Chronicles, the people usually are referred to as Israelites (e.g., 2:2; 6:16), though the term Jews also appears here regularly for the first time in the Old Testament (e.g., 4:23; 5:1; 6:7–8).[105] Since Israel and Judah no longer exist as nations, the people's identity now is experienced primarily in terms of their common religion and culture. Thus, the temple and ritual observances are of basic importance in Ezra. The author states that the Persian kings Cyrus and Darius not only commanded that the temple be rebuilt but even proposed to pay all the costs (6:1–12). Even the king of Assyria helps (6:22). Later, the Persian king Artaxerxes sends Ezra to Jerusalem laden with gifts of silver and gold, and with permission to take whatever more he can find "in the whole province of Babylonia" for sacrificial offerings and anything else needed for the temple (chap. 7). Such concern and generous support for the temple on the part of foreign rulers is not recorded elsewhere other than in 2 Chronicles 36:22–23 and the apocryphal 1 Esdras (chaps. 4–6).

Also in chapter 7, Ezra is associated with the law, particularly with laws relating to temple sacrifices and ritual propriety. Here, he is referred to as "the scribe of the law," and is instructed by King Artaxerxes to teach "the laws of your God" (7:25). Ezra is also represented as the great teacher of Jewish law in Nehemiah 8.

As in Chronicles, the writer likes to count and name "the heads of the fathers' houses" (chaps. 2, 8). Here, too, priests are distinguished from Levites (e.g., 6:16, 18). Priests, Levites, and related temple functionaries are accorded special privileges (7:24). The attention given to Levites has suggested to some interpreters that the author himself may have been a member of that order.

Like Nehemiah before him, Ezra is appalled to find that fellow Jews, especially priests and Levites, have married foreign women, thereby contaminating what Ezra calls the "holy race" (9:2) and "holy place" (9:8). He tears his clothes and pulls out his own hair, prays to God (chap. 9), and undertakes to propitiate God by requiring the culprits to make confession, sacrifice rams as guilt offerings, and separate themselves from these foreign women (chap. 10). The book concludes with a list of Levites who, to the author's apparent satisfaction, were required to put away these wives along with their children (10:44).

Nehemiah

This book concludes the Chronicler's narration, which began in 1 Chronicles with Adam and lists his (mainly male) descendants down to the time of the exile. As in 1 and 2 Chronicles, Ezra, and the book of Numbers, considerable attention is given to the names and numbers of families, particularly Levites and related temple personnel (chaps. 10–12). Here, as in 1 and 2 Chronicles, Ezra, and the Priestly tradition, priests are distinguished from Levites. Most other material seems to come from what may have been Nehemiah's memoirs or diary.

Nehemiah, a cupbearer[106] to the Persian king Artaxerxes, hears that things still are not well in Jerusalem, even though it has been nearly a hundred years since the end of the exile. A devout and dynamic personality, Nehemiah asks God for help and Artaxerxes for permission to go there and take charge of rebuilding the city. Arriving in Jerusalem, he tours it inconspicuously, observes its ruined condition, decides what needs to be done, assembles the local Jews and their leaders, and calls on them to get to work (chap. 2). Under his direction, the city gates are repaired, and in only fifty-two days, the walls are restored—to the dismay of the troika of jealous neighboring provincial officials, "Sanballat the Horonite, Tobiah the servant, and Geshem the Arab." Informed of their plotting, Nehemiah posts guards and even arms those who work on the walls (4:6–23). Learning that, contrary to biblical law, some Jewish officials and nobles have been exacting interest and foreclosing against fellow Jews, causing some even to sell their sons and daughters as slaves or indentured servants, Nehemiah gathers them together and tells them in no uncertain terms to stop charging interest and to return the properties they have taken. For the record, he notes in his diary that, unlike former governors of Judah, he has refrained from collecting the customary perquisites of office, both because he fears God and because such servitude would have been a burden on the Jewish people there (chap. 5). His enemies continue to plot against him and now hire various prophets to try to scare him into hiding in the temple. Scornfully, Nehemiah refuses to panic: "Should such a man as I flee?" (6:10–14).

Later, Nehemiah returns to Jerusalem, evidently for a second term as governor. With characteristic vigor he corrects various other abuses, including treading wine presses, hauling grain, and selling fish and sundry wares on the Sabbath, and threatens to "lay hands on" any future Sabbath violators (13:1–22). Finally, discovering that certain Jews have married women of Ashdod, Ammon, and Moab, he "cursed them and beat some of them and pulled out their hair," making them forswear such marriages in the future (13:1–3, 23–27). Nehemiah comes across as a forcible and fearless leader, a man of direct and decisive personal action, who is not ashamed to pray to God or ask him to remember him for his good deeds.

Nehemiah probably lived in the time of Artaxerxes I. The restoration of the Jerusalem wall, a major event in postexilic Judaism, is dated about 444 B.C. Ezra suddenly appears in chapters 8–9 as if he were one of Nehemiah's contemporaries, but Ezra's promulgation of the law (perhaps the Pentateuch) by the Water Gate (chap. 8) more likely is to be dated in the time of Artaxerxes II (ca. 400–350 B.C.). This scene suggests the central importance of law (Torah) in Judaism of the fourth century B.C. We may also see here the beginning of the midrash tradition of paraphrasing translations and interpretations of the law for the edification of the general populace (8:7–8). The scene is somewhat reminiscent of the ancient Israelite ceremonies of covenant renewal, when the law was read and affirmed by those present.[107] But now there was no longer an independent nation of Israel. Instead, the Jewish people were part of the much more extensive Persian empire.

Together, the books of 1 and 2 Chronicles, Ezra, and Nehemiah are the last of the historical writings in the Hebrew Bible. In Christian Bibles, the writings from Genesis through Nehemiah report events in

more or less chronological order. In various ways, they recall historical events and periods in the life of the Hebrew-Israelite-Judahite-
Jewish people from earliest times to approximately 400–350 B.C. The
books that follow, from Esther to Malachi, are arranged more according to categories of literature—such as short stories or novellas, wisdom writings, "Solomonic" writings, psalms, longer prophets, and
shorter prophets—than in historical sequence.

Esther

Esther, along with Ruth, Judith, and Susanna, are memorialized in
separate books or writings bearing their respective names. Each of
these books or writings could be characterized as a short story or
novella. Esther appropriately follows Ezra and Nehemiah, which also
are set in the time of the Persian monarch Ahasuerus, or Artaxerxes I
or II, and thus sometime between 465 and 350 B.C. The story is more
plausibly read as imaginative literature, however, than as objective history. As told, it may reflect Jewish experience or fears of persecution
in later times. Apart from a quite indirect or implicit allusion to
divine providence (4:14), the secular substance and tone of the book
are remarkable: No one prays; there is no mention of God, the law,
the temple, or even the Sabbath; no one keeps kosher; and no eyebrows are raised over Esther's marriage to a gentile (cf. Ezra,
Nehemiah, and Additions to Esther). Religious interest is limited to
the festival of Purim (9:26–32), which is "explained" in connection
with unintelligible references to casting "Pur" (3:7; 9:24). The point
of the festival, like that of the book, is clear, however: to celebrate the
defeat of would-be persecutors of the Jews, epitomized in the despi-
cable Haman.

The story contains several notable, even melodramatic scenes:
Queen Vashti's refusal to display her beauty for the entertainment of
guests at the king's seven-day banquet and the consequent consternation in the royal court at the prospect of a revolutionary women's
movement breaking out all over the empire (1:10–18); Ahasuerus's
Miss Universe Pageant, won, of course, by Esther, who is made queen
(or number one harem girl) in place of the now demoted Vashti
(2:1–17); Esther's cousin and guardian Mordecai's happening to learn
of a plot to assault King Ahasuerus and his duly reporting the matter;
the same Mordecai's resolute refusal to bow before Haman, the king's
newly appointed head honcho, and that self-important worthy's exasperation at such effrontery (3:2; 5:9, 13); and Esther's brave appearance

before the king, who, to her enormous relief, does extend his golden scepter, thereby sparing her life, and even offers her half his kingdom (4:10–5:3). In the central, climactic sequence, the king's insomnia prompts him to have "the book of memorable deeds" read, after which he decides to honor Mordecai (6:1–3)—just in time to assign this task to Haman, who has arrived at the king's palace bright and early, intending to arrange for Mordecai's execution.

Haman pretentiously imagines that he, himself, is the man the king means to honor, and sketches out a pompous, public, royal parade featuring himself clad in the king's robes and seated on the king's horse—while the horse wears a royal crown. But then Haman learns that he must heap these honors, omitting no detail, on none other than Mordecai, his enemy! The most melodramatic moment in the book, if not the Bible, is Esther's denunciation of Haman and the king's unfortunate misconstruction of that wretched man's posture as he falls upon her couch to plead for mercy (7:6–8).

In the story, Haman, offended by Mordecai's refusal to bow and scrape before him (3:2–5), persuades King Ahasuerus "to destroy, to slay, and to annihilate all Jews" (3:13). Through Esther's courageous intervention, the king changes his mind and has Haman hanged on the same gallows he had prepared for Mordecai. Because, so it was believed, under Persian law the king's decree, once given, could not be revoked, the king can only grant Esther and Mordecai authority to send word throughout the empire that the Jews are to defend themselves by killing all who may attack them (8:8–14). Construing the edict a bit broadly, Jews then preemptively massacre "those who hated them": eight hundred in Susa and seventy-five thousand in the provinces, along with Haman's ten sons (9:6–16). A certain morbid redundancy may be noted in the two reports of the hanging of Haman's sons (9:13–14, 25) after they have already been killed (9:6–10, 12).

The story ends with Esther installed in Haman's house and Mordecai wearing the king's signet and royal garb (8:12, 15), elevated to the post of second-in-command over all the empire, and eulogized in terms reminiscent of statements reserved in Kings and Chronicles for the kings of Israel and Judah (10:2–3). Probably the story was meant not only to entertain with its humor and melodrama and to explain the origins of the festival of Purim (which is not grounded in the law or Torah), but also to encourage readers facing persecution in the author's time and perhaps in later times with the hope that they too might triumph over their enemies. The apocryphal Additions to Esther contribute still more moments of drama as well as a number of clues with respect to Jewish religion and culture in the closing century or two before Christ.

Job

In broad terms, Job represents the wisdom genre of literature.[108] Several segments are indistinguishable in form and substance from material found in Proverbs and Sirach. Yet, as we shall see, there are important differences. The book of Job could also be classed with the more philosophical biblical writings, especially Ecclesiastes and 2 Esdras, which likewise raise, sometimes rather bluntly, basic questions about the meaning (or meaninglessness) of life.

Interpreters disagree about when the book was written, which parts may have been added later, and even its main purpose. Surprisingly, Job is not an Israelite, Judahite, or Jew but rather a citizen of Uz (probably in Edom); yet he worships Yahweh and leads a life of exemplary righteousness.[109] The book begins with a prose prologue (chaps. 1–2) and ends with a prose epilogue (42:7–17), both of choice literary and dramatic quality. The chapters between are mainly poetic in form and include three cycles of discourses in which Job complains and is reproached in turn by each of his three "friends," Eliphaz, Bildad, and Zophar (chaps. 3–27); a somewhat extraneous psalm in praise of wisdom (chap. 28); Job's concluding summation in his own defense (chaps. 29–31); the youthful Elihu's rather verbose remarks (32:6–37:24); God's two answers "out of the whirlwind" (38:1–40:2; 40:6–41:34); and Job's two replies (40:3–5; 42:1–6).

Textual problems are suspected in the third cycle, in which lines typical of his friends' viewpoint are attributed to Job.[110] The wisdom poem (chap. 28) adds a flavor of orthodoxy to the book, affirming, as do many passages in Proverbs, that the fear of the Lord is (the beginning of) wisdom. Elihu's commentary probably was inserted by a later interpreter to show what the latter considered Job's real fault (surely he must have had one!): his pride (33:17; 37:24).[111] The second of Yahweh's answers, which portrays Behemoth and Leviathan, the latter as a prototype of a medieval or Chinese dragon, may have been a later addition intended to illustrate the limits of human knowledge and power. The prologue and epilogue may derive from an earlier story that was then expanded by the three cycles of speeches and Yahweh's reply. In the prologue, Job is remarkable for his patience (1:20–22; 2:10), but he is not so characterized in the poetic section (e.g., 21:4). Yet both the prose and poetic sections refer to Job's children (1:13–19;

8:4), his vanishing kinfolk and close friends (19:13–19; 42:11), and both contain masterful touches of irony.

The book is concerned with the problem of evil or theodicy (God's righteousness). Job is uniquely righteous and prospers (1:1–3), as indeed he should, according to orthodox wisdom theology (e.g., Prov 14:11; 15:6). He is described as the richest man in all the east. But then, for no apparent reason, he experiences one catastrophe after another: His herds are stolen, his servants are massacred by marauders, his children all die in a windstorm, and he himself is covered with loathsome sores (chaps. 1–2).[112] Such is his misery that his wife advises him to get it all over with: "Curse God and die" (2:9). Job does not curse God, but he does curse the day he was born (chap. 3); he desires to die (6:8–9) and objects that the wicked flourish and the poor perish while God takes no notice (21:7–33; 24:1–12). In particular, Job maintains that he is innocent and that God is punishing him unjustly (10:2–7; 23:10–12). Repeatedly, in language borrowed from the courtroom, Job protests that God is not giving him a fair trial.[113]

Job's "comforters" are adherents of orthodox wisdom theology, according to which God rewards the righteous with long, happy, and prosperous lives but cuts off the wicked in the midst of their sinning or at least makes their lives miserable (e.g., 4:7–9; 15:20–35). On these premises, they conclude that since Job suffers, he must have sinned. They question whether any man can really be righteous before God (4:17; 25:4–6), assert that Job's children perished because they sinned (8:4); advise him to seek God, that is, to repent,[114] tell Job that he deserves worse punishment than he has so far received (11:1–6) and that by complaining he is sinning even more (15:2–6), and falsely charge him with numerous fictitious iniquities (22:4–11). Job is not deceived by these "miserable comforters" (16:2). He perceives that they blame the victim because they themselves fear calamity (6:21) and wish to "magnify themselves" against him (19:5). He sardonically denounces their pretensions to absolute wisdom: Too bad, he says to them, that when you die, "wisdom will perish with you" (12:2).

In his answers to Job, Yahweh reviews the wonders of creation, implying that human beings cannot know the ways of God, a point reiterated by Elihu: "Behold, God is great, and we know him not" (36:26). Yahweh's speeches "out of the whirlwind" declare that he has created the world for purposes that go beyond human desires for knowledge and fulfillment (chaps. 38–39; 40:15–41:34). And Yahweh cares for all creation and all creatures, not only for humankind.[115] For example, Yahweh has given the wild ass the steppe and saltland for his dwelling place (39:5–8), the eagle the rocky crag (39:27–30), and the mountains for all wild beasts to play upon (40:20). Job acknowledges that Yahweh's ways transcend his understanding, now that he "sees" God. Since no theophany (appearance of God) is reported, "see" here means that Job understands and accepts Yahweh's transcendence.

Yahweh now restores Job's fortunes (exactly doubling the numbers of livestock he had before; 42:10). Only then do his relatives and other erstwhile friends (who conveniently disappeared entirely during the time of Job's poverty and affliction; 19:13–19) turn up to feast (at Job's expense), show him sympathy (which he no longer needs), and bring him gifts (now that he is doubly the richest man in all the east)—again the ironic touches. Job then has another seven sons and three daughters[116] (presumably the ideal numbers of each), and afterward lives 140 more years (notwithstanding the limit of 120 years prescribed in Gen 6:3). Was all this told with a straight face, or did the author perhaps mean to parody the orthodox wisdom theology that Job attacks directly in his speeches?

In the epilogue, Yahweh says that Job has spoken rightly about him but that his three "comforters" have spoken falsely. The comforters had claimed that God always rewards the righteous and punishes the wicked and that Job was wrong to complain about the way God was treating him. Yet when Job acknowledges that God's ways are unsearchable, his fortunes are restored, as if the orthodox wisdom theology is somehow true after all! Perhaps the author meant that a person is rewarded for faith in God but that such faith paradoxically includes recognizing that in this life the righteous may have to endure inexplicable catastrophes and tragedies.

Possibly the author meant Job to represent the Jewish people, who collectively experienced suffering beyond what they believed was deserved during several centuries following the exile.[117] Some interpreters see in Job's affirmation "I know that my redeemer lives" (19:25–27) the hope for vindication after death, if not resurrection.[118]

As the story is told, it is Satan—Yahweh's attorney general[119]—who first challenges the orthodox wisdom theology: "Does Job fear God for nought?" he asks (1:9). Satan insinuates that God makes it worth Job's while to be righteous, implying that such righteousness is tainted by self-interest. It is not Satan, however, but Yahweh who initiates the testing of Job by directing Satan's attention to him (1:8). Satan proceeds to wager that once he brings calamity upon Job, Job will turn from Yahweh, and Yahweh accepts the wager. But even then, Satan acts only with Yahweh's permission (1:12; 2:6). Job does not turn from God, but rightly complains that God is not treating him fairly. Thus, whatever else the author may have intended, the story of Job affirms that, appearances notwithstanding, God ultimately is in control of human destiny and may be trusted even by those who experience devastation.

Psalms

The present book of Psalms probably was the hymnal and prayer book of the postexilic, or second, temple. Psalms generally are prayers or songs written in poetic form, which were either recited by individuals or sung as hymns on various ceremonial occasions. Many are found outside the book of Psalms, such as the songs of Moses (Exod 15:1–18), Miriam (Exod 15:21), Deborah (Judges 5), and Judith (Jdt 16:2–17), and prayers, such as those found in Jeremiah 12:1–13, Jonah 2:2–9, Luke 1:46–55, and in whole books, such as Lamentations and Obadiah.

The book of Psalms presents the biblical faith in microcosm: creation (Pss 104; 148), history (Pss 105; 106), the law (Ps 119), the word of Yahweh (81:8–16), and wisdom (Pss 1; 37). In and above all, God's help is sought for and praised for his many blessings. The book of Psalms constitutes one-tenth of the Old Testament's pages. As now arranged, its psalms are grouped into five "books," each ending with a distinctive formula of blessing (after Pss 41; 72; 89; 106). Psalm 150 is the finale to the book as a whole: "Let everything that breathes praise the Lord!"[120] Numerous psalms traditionally are attributed to David, but many are assigned to others, such as Asaph, the sons of Korah, and even to Ethan the Ezrahite (Ps 86), Moses (Ps 90), and Solomon (Pss 72, 127).[121]

A later editor would supply what he or she thought appropriate settings for several of the psalms assigned to David (e.g., Pss 3; 18; 56; 59). Instructions at the beginning frequently appear, advising "the choirmaster" or "leader" as to hymn tunes (e.g., Pss 8; 12; 45; 80) or instrumental accompaniment (e.g., Pss 4; 5; 54).[122] The term *selah* often appears, indicating places where the choir, instrumentalists, or readers should pause a moment before going on. Liturgical directions sometimes are indicated (e.g., 118:24; 129:1–2). It is not likely that copies of the psalms were available to the entire congregation. Often the congregation was to repeat a particular response: In Psalm 136, the repeated response is written out in full.[123] Some psalms borrow from others.[124] Occasionally the editor who numbered the psalms arbitrarily divided single hymns or poems in two (e.g., Pss 9–10; 42–43).

Form critics have identified certain types of psalms: for instance, enthronement, royal, lament, and thanksgiving. The first type celebrates God's enthronement in the heavens and his sovereignty over creation and all nations (e.g., Pss 46; 93; 97). Some of these may derive from an ancient ceremony in which Yahweh was symbolically re-enthroned each year. Royal psalms apparently were sung at the coronation of the kings of Judah (Pss 2; 21; 72; 110).

Lament psalms are the most common, the greater number in the form of prayers for help by individuals in distress.[125] Typically these call on God, ask his protection from or vengeance upon personal enemies, pray for deliverance from death (Sheol, or "the pit"), invoke God's steadfast love, and affirm that he will indeed help or has already done so, and that the petitioner will pay his vows, offer sacrifice, or praise God in the assembly.[126] Some are less concerned with personal enemies than with forgiveness of sins (e.g., Pss 38; 51), God's help in maintaining a righteous life (Pss 119; 141), and anxiety in the face of sickness or the brevity of life (Pss 39; 88). Like Job, some psalms charge God with neglecting to do justice and call on him to arise and make things right (Pss 10; 58). Communal laments concern the sufferings of Israel (or Judah, or the Jewish people) as a whole and often ask God to crush the nation's enemies (Pss 60; 80; 83). Some evidently refer to the exile experience.[127]

Psalms of thanksgiving or praise, both individual and communal, also are numerous. Usually these offer thanks to God for deliverance from enemies or Sheol, for forgiveness, or for victory against national enemies.[128] Some of the hymns praise God for his greatness as manifested in creation,[129] for his mighty deeds in history (Pss 66; 78; 105), or for both (Ps 136). Like the Yahweh speeches in Job, the creation psalms affirm that Yahweh's concerns extend beyond human needs and desires: He causes "the grass to grow for cattle" (104:14); "rocks are a refuge for badgers" (104:18); young lions seek their food from God (104:21); he gives food to the beasts (generally) and young ravens (147:9); the sea teems with innumerable "living things both great and small," and Yahweh made Leviathan, the great sea creature, "to sport in it" (104:25–26).[130]

Many psalms, however, do not fit into these categories. Some are of mixed character, that is, both lament and thanksgiving (Pss 40; 89; 139), royal and lament (Ps 61), or thanksgiving and enthronement (Ps 103). Moreover, various other types can be identified: wisdom,[131] moral admonition and exhortation,[132] and encouragement or hope.[133] Psalm 23 voices confidence in God's continuing providential care.

Several eulogize Zion, Jerusalem, or the temple, the national and religious capital.[134] Zion, the mountain in Jerusalem on which the temple was built, sometimes stands for the temple, and sometimes for the whole city of Jerusalem. Some of these psalms may have been sung by people coming to Zion to offer sacrifices or participate in the three main festivals that, under seventh-century Deuteronomic law, were to be observed there.[135] In Psalm 82, God addresses the unrighteous gods (probably those of other nations) in the heavenly council. Another unusual psalm advises a king's new bride about her prospective role (45:10–17).

Like the prophets, the psalmists place differing values on sacrificial worship and hold divergent views on the relation between Israel and other nations. Portions of several psalms oppose or transcend sacrificial offerings,[136] while other passages commend sacrifices.[137] Psalms 68, 72, and 149 express hope for Israel's triumph over foreign nations, while others call upon all nations, and even all creation, to praise the Lord.[138]

Proverbs

Proverbs is the principal example of wisdom literature in the Old Testament.[139] Wisdom writings appear in many other countries and cultures, ancient and modern.[140] Wisdom writers' reflections generally are presented in poetic form, in which each statement typically is followed by a repetition of the underlying idea, but in different terms or imagery. Frequently the wisdom writers use aphorisms or short, often pungent, sayings—in brief, proverbs. These commonly offer pointed descriptions and comparisons and generally constitute advice or admonitions about attitudes and conduct. There are also longer collections or ruminations on such topics as the perils of association with "loose women" (7:5–27; 9:13–18), the merits of wisdom (8:1–36), undesirable aspects of experiencing inebriation (23:29–35), the futility of dealing with fools (26:1–12), and the surpassing value of a good wife (31:10–31).

Commonly the writer assumes the role of a father addressing his son; one exception is Proverbs 6:20, which commends adherence to one's mother's teaching. Chapter 31 is attributed to the mother of an otherwise unknown King Lemuel of Massa (31:1). Wisdom (*Hochmah*), a feminine being herself, also speaks occasionally (1:20–33; 8:1–9:6).[141] Much of the book is ascribed to Solomon (1:1; 10:1; 25:1), but other persons also are credited with many of the sayings (24:23; 30:1; 31:1). A number of different concerns or foci appear in Proverbs.

Several proverbs, particularly in the final chapters, show a kind of prescientific interest in observing and classifying phenomena on the basis of some principle of similarity.[142] Most such proverbs refer to human characteristics.[143]

Quite a few sayings advise youths and aspiring nobles how to make a favorable impression upon the mighty (18:16; 22:11) or how avoid doing otherwise.[144] Some advise rulers or kings themselves how best to proceed in order to achieve desirable results or stay out of trouble.[145]

The majority of the sayings appear to be addressed to general readers and concern what we might call etiquette and morality. Prudence is particularly commended. Thus, readers are urged to avoid contention (3:30; 26:17), evil companions (1:10–19), angry men (22:24–25), fools (14:7), and gossips (20:19). They are admonished frequently to shun harlots and adulteresses.[146] A person should stay clear of danger (22:3; 27:12), act with caution and discretion (14:15–17), be slow to anger (14:29; 19:11; 29:11), answer softly (15:1), ignore insults (12:16), maintain discreet silence (17:27–28), not waste words on scoffers and fools (9:7–8; 23:9), abjure excessive indulgence in pleasures (12:11; 21:17), avoid imbibing too much wine (20:1; 23:20–21), and refrain from oppressing the poor and afflicted (22:16, 22–23) or from moving ancient landmarks (22:28; 23:10). Diligence and work are recommended repeatedly, in contrast to the way of the "sluggard" or lazy bones (24:30–34; 26:14–15).[147] Yet one ought not strive to gain wealth either (28:19). There are also positive admonitions to be responsive to the needs of the poor,[148] and to be kind to one's animals (12:10).

Some sayings primarily offer practical advice, such as how to get along with one's neighbors (3:28–29; 25:17; 27:14), and ideas about agriculture (12:11; 14:4; 27:23–27), diet (eating honey, but not too much; 24:13; 25:16), and building construction (24:27). The writer recurrently bemoans the fate of those who dwell with a contentious woman or wife, thereby, perhaps, revealing his own unhappy marital experience.[149] One saying suggests the writer's exasperation at having to try to teach wisdom to inattentive or slow learners: "Why should a fool have a price in his hand to buy wisdom, when he has no mind?" (17:16). Throughout Proverbs, the reader is urged to listen to instruction ("my commandments"), love wisdom, and bring up children accordingly, not sparing the rod.[150]

Numerous sayings affirm that in this life the righteous are rewarded and the wicked punished. Thus, the righteous may expect to live long and prosperous lives, while the wicked are likely to experience poverty, misery or other trouble and early death.[151] This understanding is commonly designated the "orthodox wisdom theology." It surfaces elsewhere, for example, in Sirach and Psalm 37 but is questioned in Job and Ecclesiastes. The orthodox wisdom theology is similar to the prophetic and Deuteronomic theologies of history, which held that if or when Israel (or Judah) broke covenant with Yahweh, he would or did punish the nation with disaster. An important difference, however, is that the orthodox wisdom theology focuses on the situation of individuals, not that of nations as a whole. Like many of the prophets, the writer of Proverbs urges that justice and righteousness are more acceptable to Yahweh than sacrifices (21:3).

Although wisdom as such is frequently personified and praised, the insistence that wisdom comes from God and that the beginning of wisdom is fear of (i.e., reverence for) him pervades Proverbs. Several sayings affirm God's providence or sovereignty over human affairs (16:9; 19:21; 20:24). Basic themes in the legal tradition are reiterated: The law and commandments are to be kept;[152] the rights of the poor and the orphan are to be protected;[153] just weights are to be used (11:1; 20:10, 23); father and mother are to be honored;[154] true witness or testimony is to be given (12:17; 19:5, 9); and impartial justice is to be rendered (24:23–25). Generally, righteousness is equated with wisdom and wickedness with foolishness.

Ecclesiastes

The anonymous author of this book calls himself Qoheleth, meaning one who holds forth, probably as teacher, in a *qahal*, or assembly. Like other wisdom writings, Ecclesiastes consists largely of short, detached sayings, though there are a few longer passages (e.g., 2:1–11 on the quest for pleasure, and 12:1–7 with its striking images of aging and death). Several sayings reflect interests common to the wisdom tradition, such as those in Proverbs: scientific observations and comparisons (4:9–12; 11:3), advice to those aspiring to royal favor (8:2–5; 10:4, 20), and other prudential or practical advice (7:9; 10:10; 11:4, 6). Sloth is deplored (10:18), work is commended (9:10), wisdom praised (7:11–12, 19), and the way of fools condemned (7:6; 10:3, 12–15).

Yet Qoheleth (or "Preacher," RSV; "Speaker," NEB, REB; "Teacher," NRSV) repeatedly questions traditional wisdom motifs or doctrines. He disputes the value of work (1:3; 2:18–23) and even doubts the worth of wisdom: "In much wisdom is much vexation, and he who increases knowledge increases sorrow" (1:17–18).[155] Qoheleth particularly challenges the claim of orthodox wisdom theology that the righteous are rewarded and the wicked punished in this life (7:15; 8:14). Job likewise questioned that claim.

Moreover, contrary to common biblical affirmations and assumptions, the Preacher's key theme is the proposition that all is vanity ("emptiness," NEB; "futility," REB), that is, futile, senseless, without meaning (1:2, 14).[156] Like the ancient Greeks, he holds that time and chance happen to everyone (9:11) and that history, like nature, is doomed to repeat meaningless cycles (1:4–10; 3:15). His appraisal of humanity is pessimistic: Though God made humans upright (7:29), no one is so righteous as to do good and never sin (7:20).[157] Indeed, human hearts are full of evil and madness (9:3). Even human creativity is inspired by the envy of people toward their neighbors (4:4). Humankind's desire for money is insatiable (5:10).[158] In Qoheleth's view, the human scene is characterized by oppression and injustice (4:1; 8:9).

The writer frequently takes an agnostic stance on ultimate questions: "Who knows" what is good for people during their lifetime, or what will happen after their death (3:21; 6:12)? God has "put eternity into man's mind," but humans cannot know the ways of God—not even "the wise" who claim to know the answers (3:11; 8:16–17). Evidently Qoheleth agrees with the author of Job that the answers to life's ultimate questions are unknowable.[159] Thus, he concludes, corroborating the experience of all students everywhere and in every era, "Of making many books there is no end, and much study is a weariness of the flesh" (12:12).

The shadow of death falls across all human activity. Wise and foolish, righteous and wicked alike come to the same end (2:15–16; 9:1–3). The fate of humans is the same as the fate of beasts: All are from the dust, and all will turn to dust again (3:19–20; cf. Gen 3:19). The dead are more fortunate than the living, and those unborn even more so, since they have not seen the injustices committed under the sun (4:2–3). The Preacher does not look for any life beyond death; moreover, he holds that after people die, they and their deeds, whether wise or foolish, good or evil, will be forgotten by those who come after; their love, hate, and envy will have perished with them and they will have no more share in all that is done under the sun (2:16; 9:56). The phrase "under the sun" recurs thematically throughout the book, generally in texts that point to the fewness of a person's days or to the folly and injustice that characterize human existence.

Taking the role of Solomon in chapters 1 and 2, the author reports that he has tried to find meaning in pleasure (2:1–10) but discovered that this is merely "vanity and a striving after wind" (2:11). Work too proves pointless and futile (2:18–23). Nevertheless, though all are doomed to die, Qoheleth recommends that a man seek enjoyment in eating, drinking, toil (2:24–25; 3:12–13; 8:15), and companionship with his wife whom he loves (9:9). Such at least will distract him from considering the brevity of his life (5:18–20). Offering sacrifices may be foolish and futile (5:1; 9:2), but Qoheleth, or a later editor, commends keeping God's other commandments (12:13).

Certain passages seem to run counter to the book's usual agnosticism and gloom. The excellence of wisdom is affirmed, after all (2:13–14a; 9:13–18a); the righteous and wicked *do* receive fitting recompense (2:26; 8:12–13); people *will* be judged for their deeds (3:17; 11:9b; 12:14). These may be later editorial "corrections" or part of the author's own, perhaps paradoxical, perspective. Throughout, readers are admonished to fear (i.e., have reverence for) God, even if his ways are unknowable.[160] Such also seems to have been the message of the story of Job.

Song of Solomon (or Canticles)

Traditional Judaism and traditional Christianity often have read this book as an allegorical statement of God's love for Israel[161] and of Christ's love for the church ("the bride of Christ"), respectively. It has been known traditionally also as "the Song of Songs." As it stands, the book contains one or more poems concerning the love of a man and a woman for each other. Alternately, female and male speakers address their respective lovers, with occasional comments by companions or a chorus (NEB and REB supply captions indicating who is speaking). Some or all of the poems may originally derive from secular wedding songs[162] or love ballads. Solomon is mentioned from time to time (1:1; 3:7, 9–11; 8:12; and perhaps 6:13, where *Shulammite* may mean "bride of Solomon"). In 6:8–9, the male tells his beloved that she is the fairest of sixty queens and eighty concubines. These numbers of consorts likewise suggests Solomon, the famous lover (or owner) of even more wives and concubines than that (1 Kgs 11:3). Though scholars generally doubt that Solomon wrote it, most think that the book was included in Scripture because the Jewish authorities who eventually decided which writings were to be accorded that status believed that Solomon was its author.

Periodically, the female cautions or adjures the daughters of Jerusalem not to waken love (or her lover) until it (or he) is ready.[163] Thematically, the man tells the woman, "you are beautiful, my love," and proceeds to picture her attributes through various charming images and comparisons (1:15; 4:1–8; 6:4–7). In the many descriptions of the lovers and their visits to gardens, orchards, and fields, we find numerous comparisons and allusions to delightful trees, flowers, fruit, scents, birds, and animals, as well as to gold, ivory, and jewels. These descriptions express the characteristic biblical affirmation of the goodness of all that God has made.[164] The male occasionally calls his beloved "my sister" (4:9–10; 5:1–2), an idiomatic term of endearment found also in Tobit (e.g., Tob 7:16; 8:4, 7). Twice he goes off and must be sought by his would-be lover (3:1–4; 5:2–8). His later disappearance provides the woman occasion to describe her lover to the "daughters of Jerusalem" (5:9–16). Again, thematically, love and the lovers' kisses are compared favorably to wine (1:2; 4:10; 7:9). Lovers generally—or perhaps guests at a wedding party—are encouraged to "eat . . . and drink: drink deeply" (5:1). A notable poem in praise of love is included at 8:6–7.

As with other biblical traditions, physical love between man and woman is valued highly among the blessings of life in the created world.[165] Only the corruption of this relation through adultery, exploitation, or promiscuity is deplored in the law and by the prophets and wisdom writers.

Isaiah

This book contains traditions from several different periods. Isaiah is named only rarely, and not at all after chapter 39. Nevertheless, most of the sixty-six chapters are attributed either to the Isaiah who prophesied in Jerusalem (ca. 742–690 B.C.) or to his disciples (see 8:16) or "school." Chapters in the book from later times reiterate basic Isaianic themes, such as God's holiness and sovereignty over nations, and the assurance that those who look to God as their Maker and King need not fear. Certain other prophets, such as Micah and Habakkuk, also echo some of these themes and may well have been influenced by Isaiah. The present book of Isaiah may include writings from as many as four different prophets that span a period of some five hundred years.

Most of chapters 1–23, 28–33, and 36–39 seem to derive from or relate to the original Isaiah, often designated "Isaiah of Jerusalem." However, many of the "oracles against foreign nations" (e.g., chaps. 13;

21; 23) evidently presuppose later circumstances and probably were composed by later writers. Chapters 36–39 essentially duplicate 2 Kings 18–20, from which they may derive. A psalm (of lament) attributed to King Hezekiah is included at 38:10–20.

Several major events occur during Isaiah's career. In 738 B.C., Assyria invades Israel, which, for a time, purchases its survival by paying tribute to the Assyrian king, Tiglath-pileser, known as "Pul" in 2 Kings 15:19–20. A few years later, kings Rezin of Syria and Pekah of Israel try to induce Ahaz, king of Judah, to join them in an alliance against Assyria. When Ahaz declines, Syria and Israel besiege Jerusalem, the capital of Judah, hoping to force that country to join such an alliance. Ahaz, however, asks for help from Tiglath-pileser— of all people (2 Kgs 16:5–9). These events (ca. 735–734 B.C.) prompt Isaiah's famous Immanuel and Mahershalalhashbaz prophecies (Isa 7:1–8:8), in which he warns Ahaz that Yahweh will be with Judah in the form of devastation wrought by Assyrian armies before the newborn child grows beyond infancy (7:15–20; 8:3–4). In 721, Assyria overruns Israel, bringing that kingdom to its end (1 Kgs 17:1–8). Judah survives, though sometimes having to pay massive tribute. Twenty years later, Assyria lays siege to Jerusalem, but then, for one reason or another, withdraws (Isaiah 36–37).

Isaiah is the first known prophet to carry on his work in Judah. While his contemporaries Amos and Hosea prophesy against Israel in the North, Isaiah proclaims the word of Yahweh against Judah, the Southern Kingdom, for its faithlessness, injustice, and oppression. Isaiah especially emphasizes the rule of God over history. Because of her injustice, luxury, pride, and indifference to Yahweh,[166] Judah will experience his rule as judgment in the form of invasion by Assyria.[167]

Yet at times Isaiah promises that Yahweh will protect Jerusalem (33:20–22; 37:33–35). In due course, Yahweh also will punish Assyria for its pride (10:12–19). Moreover, he will bring back a remnant of his people and establish his rule over all the earth. That will be the "peaceable kingdom," the time when the wolf and the lamb, the leopard and the kid, the calf and the lion, the cow and the bear, the serpent and the little child shall all dwell together: "They shall not hurt or destroy . . . for the earth shall be full of the knowledge of Yahweh as the waters cover the sea" (11:6–9). Some passages tell of a new king from the family of David (9:2–7; 11:1–5); others look for the transformation of history and creation without mention of a messiah or king (e.g., 2:2–4; 29:17–21). All nations will then worship Yahweh and be his people.[168] Isaiah 19:19–25 anticipates that in the coming restored era, Egypt and Assyria—remembered mainly for oppressing Israel—would not only be present. Yahweh himself would bless them—Egypt as his "people" and Assyria as "the work of [his] hands." Then Israel would be "a blessing in the midst of the earth."[169]

In the meantime, Yahweh does not desire animal sacrifices or pious ceremonies; instead, he asks that his people "cease to do evil, learn to do good, seek justice, correct oppression, defend the fatherless, [and] plead for the widow" (1:10–17). Because Yahweh is holy and lifted up, he is against all that is proud and lofty, especially the pride of people (2:11–17). Those who trust him may look for deliverance (7:4; 10:24–27), but those who seek foreign alliances lack faith and will perish along with such helpers (31:1–3). Isaiah offers several "signs" to reinforce his message,[170] and gives at least two of his sons symbolic names: Shearjashub (7:3) and Mahershalalhashbaz (8:1–4).[171]

An anonymous prophet commonly designated "Second Isaiah" is credited with most of the sayings found in chapters 34–35 and 40–55. These evidently were set down in the latter years of the exile, perhaps as late as 540 B.C., slightly after the time of the Deuteronomic historian. Animus directed against Edom in chapter 34 probably reflects the prophet's recollection of that nation's role in assisting Babylon to destroy Jerusalem in 586 (see Obadiah). Only wildlife will possess the land of Edom in years to come and they shall possess it forever because Yahweh has cast his lot for them (34:11–17).[172] Second Isaiah is mainly concerned to assure the exiles, who are still in Babylon, that the time for punishment is past (40:2), that Yahweh is preparing a smooth and safe highway in the wilderness (35:1–10; 40:3–4) for their return to Zion (Jerusalem), and that the time for them to go forth is at hand.[173] Then the desert or wilderness will blossom, and the "redeemed" of Yahweh all will "come to Zion with singing; everlasting joy shall be upon their heads" (35:10).

Like Isaiah of Jerusalem, Second Isaiah affirms the holiness, majesty, and sovereignty of God. But now Yahweh is going to do a "new thing" (43:19), that is, deliver his people, rather than punish them (cf. Jer 28:8–9). Thus, speaking for Yahweh, Second Isaiah repeatedly assures the exiles, "Fear not, I am with you" (41:10, 13; 43:5). Like Isaiah of Jerusalem (6:5; 17:7), Second Isaiah hails Yahweh as Israel's Maker and King, but now also as Israel's Redeemer (43:15; 44:6; 54:5). Yahweh appoints the Persian emperor Cyrus as his messiah (anointed) to overthrow Babylon and release the exiles (45:1–6).

Creation and exodus imagery merge with and give promise of a new beginning and deliverance.[174] Like Hosea, Second Isaiah declares that Yahweh is prompted to act because he loves his people.[175] He proclaims that Yahweh has created all that is and alone is God (40:12–28; 43:10–11; 44:6–8); thus, some modern interpreters view Second Isaiah as the first biblical proponent of theoretical monotheism. Since only Yahweh is God, all other "deities" are bogus, and worship of man-made gods or idols is necessarily pathetic and futile (40:18–20; 44:9–20), a theme developed in later times.[176] The several "servant of Yahweh" passages present a problem for interpretation. Is Cyrus, the liberator of the exiles, who is named Yahweh's shepherd and anointed, the one so designated (44:28; 45:1)? Or does the prophet mean that the servant is Jacob (Israel) or perhaps the exiles (42:18–43:7; 43:8–13; 49:1–6)? Or is the servant some other person (52:13–53:12), possibly the prophet himself (50:4–11) or a future messiah?[177]

Chapters 56–66 may come from a later Isaianic prophet who lived in Jerusalem after the exile but before the temple was rebuilt, perhaps around 520 B.C.—the time also of Haggai and Zechariah (chaps. 1–8)—and also afterward, for a decade or two. This sometimes so–called Third Isaiah likewise emphasizes Yahweh's transcendence and holiness (57:15) and names him Israel's Redeemer (60:16b). He prophesies that Jerusalem will be restored, that Yahweh's glory will come upon the Jewish people, and that all will enjoy permanent prosperity and possession of the land (chaps. 60–61). There is no mention here of a Davidic king, but a radically transformed era is expected— indeed, a new heaven and a new earth that will incorporate the "peaceable kingdom" in which all kinds of creatures will dwell together in harmony (65:17–25; cf. 11:1–9). Like Haggai and Zechariah, Third Isaiah anticipates that the wealth of other nations will then flow into Zion (60:5; 61:6).[178] Later, Christian Christmas tradition would draw on passages such as 60:1–7 for inspiration in reconstructing some of the circumstances of Jesus' birth.[179] The "grapes of wrath" imagery in 63:1–6 refers to Yahweh's future trampling down of Judah's oppressors. Yet when Yahweh transforms heaven and earth, "all flesh" will worship him in Jerusalem.[180]

In the meantime, Sabbath observance is important, but Third Isaiah repudiates sacrificial offerings in favor of doing justice and caring for the needy (58:6–9; cf. 56:7). Yahweh has made all things; they are already his, so he has no need for animal sacrifices (66:1–4).[181] Like earlier prophets, Third Isaiah proclaims Yahweh's judgment against the Jewish people for their apostasy and covenant violations (57:1–13; 59:1–15). Here we encounter the first biblical text to look for the eternal torment of the wicked (66:24).[182]

Chapters 24–27 generally are attributed to a later prophet, sometimes designated "Fourth Isaiah," who may have lived in the third or second centuries B.C. This prophet looks for God's deliverance not only from foreign nations, but from cosmic or supernatural powers (24:21–23; 27:1). Yahweh will punish the whole earth (chap. 24) but then will establish a new age "for all peoples"; there will be feasting and wine, the dead will be raised, death itself will be swallowed up forever, and, at the sound of a great trumpet, the people of Israel will gather to worship Yahweh in Jerusalem (25:6–8; 26:19; 27:12–13).[183] The sayings in Fourth Isaiah are eschatological, that is, they refer to events expected at the end of history and to the conditions of life in the expected new age. As in Third Isaiah, however, there is no mention of a coming messiah or king from the line of David.

Jeremiah

Like Isaiah, but a hundred years later, Jeremiah prophesies in Judah, especially Jerusalem, for several decades. Some narratives and oracles can be placed in identifiable settings, but they are not all in chronological order. Jeremiah's career begins during the reign of Josiah, around 626 B.C. (1:2), shortly before the Deuteronomic reform, and extends through the initial conquest of Judah by Babylon in 598, its final defeat in 586—when the Babylonians destroy the temple, the palaces, larger houses, and the walls of Jerusalem (chap. 52)[184]—and into the first years of the exile. He is last seen in Egypt, condemning those Jews (Judahites) who have fled there and have not only failed to repent for their past wickedness but continue to ignore Yahweh's law and statutes while idolatrously worshiping the "queen of heaven," perhaps the goddess Ishtar (chaps. 43–44).

In the years before 598, and down to 586, Jeremiah generally prophesies that Yahweh will bring doom and destruction upon Judah because of its many offenses (e.g., chap. 6). But, especially after 586, he begins to proclaim that Yahweh will restore the fortunes of his people (e.g., 30:18–22). Throughout the book, Jeremiah declares that Yahweh intends both "to pluck up and break down" and "to build and to plant" (1:10; 31:28; 45:4), images respectively of divine judgment and redemption.

Yahweh will punish the people of Judah, Jeremiah repeatedly warns, because of their apostasy, disobedience (7:21–26; 32:26–35), complacency (5:11–17), corruption (5:25–29), injustice (8:10), pride (13:9), and other forms of wickedness and iniquity. All classes of persons have acted wrongly: kings, prophets, priests, and common people (2:4–8; 5:1–5, 30–31). Like the other classical prophets, Jeremiah, speaking for Yahweh, condemns those who have practiced oppression and failed to judge justly the causes and rights of the vulnerable members of the community (5:25–29). Because they do not wish to hear about their wickedness or Yahweh's pending judgment, the authorities ridicule, beat, and imprison Jeremiah from time to time, and more than once threaten his life. He is nearly lynched when he announces that Yahweh will destroy the temple, in which people have put so much trust (chaps. 7; 26). His advice to submit to Nebuchadnezzar as the agent of Yahweh's judgment is viewed by many as treason (38:1–28).[185] In turn, Jeremiah frequently berates both the false prophets and priests who tell people what they want to hear by proclaiming peace when there is no peace.[186]

Like Moses (Exod 3:11–4:17) but unlike Isaiah (Isa 6:6–8), Jeremiah is a reluctant prophet (Jer 1:4–10). More than other prophets, Jeremiah identifies and sympathizes with his fellow Judahites. Thus, he suffers great anguish in his role as spokesman for Yahweh's judgment against his people. Despite being commanded otherwise by Yahweh (7:16; 11:14), he persists in praying for the nation (14:7–9, 19–22); moreover, in his "confessions" or complaints, Jeremiah unfolds his intimate feelings of grief and anger at his lot and that of his people, while also giving vent to his desire for vengeance against his persecutors.[187] Yet Yahweh repeatedly assures Jeremiah that he will make him "a fortified city" and admonishes him to stop feeling sorry for himself and get on with his task as prophet (1:4–19; 12:1–6; 15:10–21).

Notwithstanding his complaining, Jeremiah stands his ground in crisis after crisis, effectively declaring Yahweh's word despite official opposition. Thus, after being beaten and put in stocks by Pashur, the priest in charge of the temple, Jeremiah declares that Yahweh will especially punish Pashur and his friends (20:1–6). After the prophet Hananiah breaks the yoke bars that Jeremiah has worn to symbolize Judah's pending subjugation to Babylon, Jeremiah comes back with the word that Yahweh has not authorized Hananiah and will cause the latter to die within the year (28:1–17). After being banished from the temple, Jeremiah dictates the words of Yahweh and sends his secretary Baruch to read them there. When King Jehoiakim destroys that scroll (after it was confiscated by the temple authorities), Jeremiah dictates another, this time pronouncing further doom, specifically on Jehoiakim, his friends, and his associates (36:1–36).

Once the Babylonian ax falls in 586, Jeremiah declares that Yahweh will restore his people, both Israel and Judah. He will bring them back (16:14–15), make a new covenant with them, one written in their hearts (31:31–33), an everlasting covenant (32:36–41; 50:4–5). A few passages refer to a new king or "branch" (cf. Isa 11:1) that will spring up from the house of David. This new king's reign will be marked by peace and justice (Jer 23:5–6; 33:14–16). Most of Jeremiah's oracles of hope for the future, however, include no mention of a coming messiah or king. Chapter 29 reports the substance of a letter that Jeremiah wrote to the people of Judah who had been deported to Babylon in 598. In it, he urges them to recognize what has happened as Yahweh's doing and to settle down there and seek the welfare of that city, assuring them that in due time Yahweh will give them "a future and a hope" (29:4–14). Jeremiah particularly emphasizes Yahweh's love for his people (31:3). Like Hosea, Jeremiah compares Yahweh's intended relationship with the people of Israel and Judah both to that of a husband and wife (2:2; 3:20; 31:32) and father and son (3:19; 31:9, 20), relationships that, though violated by his people, Yahweh means to restore in order to fulfill his own purposes.

Some later chapters (e.g., 36–45) may have been composed by Baruch. Also, some material may have come from later times. Certain passages suggest that Jeremiah was a proponent of the Deuteronomic reform, which established the Jerusalem temple as the sole place for sacrificial worship.[188] He may well have been, though sometimes he seems to say that Yahweh is opposed to all sacrificial offerings.[189] Like Third Isaiah but unlike earlier prophets, Jeremiah may have commended Sabbath observance, though it could be that the principal text so indicating, 17:19–27, was added by a later advocate of such observance.[190] The oracles against Babylon (chaps. 50–51) appear contrary to both Jeremiah's view that the Babylonians were God's instrument of judgment against Judah and his advice that the exiles in Babylon seek that city's welfare (chap. 29). Many scholars think it likely that these oracles were composed and added to the Jeremiah scroll by a later writer or editor.

It may be that Jeremiah was in the "school" of Isaiah.[191] Jeremiah clearly shares Isaiah's emphasis on Yahweh's sovereignty over nations and his assurance that Yahweh would both bring catastrophic judgement upon his people for breaking the covenant and then in his own time, restore them to favored status.[192] And, like Isaiah, Jeremiah occasionally refers to Yahweh by the circumlocution "the Holy One of Israel."[193] But Jeremiah did not simply repeat what Isaiah had said.

Clearly he was a major figure in his own right, as was his contemporary, the prophet Ezekiel.

Lamentations

Traditionally, the book is ascribed to Jeremiah. Several passages recall, and some may incorporate, that prophet's words.[194] Scholars commonly assign the writing to other hands, however, partly because after 586 B.C., Jeremiah's message clearly and consistently was one of certain hope for the future that Yahweh would surely bring. Such certainty is lacking in Lamentations.

Lamentations consists of a series of poems or psalms that express and commemorate the anguish of the Jewish people who remained in Jerusalem (Zion) after the Babylonians overran it in 586.[195] The Jewish exiles who were deported to Babylon long bitterly for Zion (Ps 137). But things are hardly better for the captive Jews who continue to dwell amid Jerusalem's ruins. The siege was terrible: People starved or killed their own children for food (2:20; 4:9–10), the city was burned (4:11), and the temple was destroyed (see 2 Kgs 25:1–12). Famine is still severe, and the humiliated survivors are subjected to physical abuse and hard labor (Lam 5:1–13). The vividness of these recollections suggests that the poems were written not long after the events of 586, perhaps within a decade or two.

Remarkably, the catastrophes experienced by these survivors are perceived as Yahweh's judgment against the Jewish people because of their transgressions (1:5; 2:17).[196] This understanding of the meaning of history contrasts markedly with that of Obadiah, who devotes his entire book to the condemnation of Edom, which had aided Babylon as it pillaged and devastated Jerusalem. It contrasts even more sharply with the perception of these events expressed in Psalm 137, where Jewish exiles in Babylon vent their white-hot fury by calling on Yahweh to take vengeance upon Edom and pronounce their blessings on anyone who would massacre Babylonian children. Neither Obadiah nor the author of Psalm 137 acknowledges the hand of Yahweh in the disasters of 586. The understanding found in Lamentations, on the other hand, reflects the warnings of the prophets to the effect that Yahweh would punish—indeed, destroy—this people if they continued to forsake him and his covenant.[197] Lamentations 2:17 acknowledges that they had been so warned and that what Yahweh had purposed and ordained had now come to pass. The Deuteronomic historian, writing a few decades later, likewise recognizes the exile as Yahweh's judgment against Judah and its people for breaking covenant.[198]

Nevertheless, the writer cries out for Yahweh to avenge and help the Jewish people.[199] Like Second Isaiah, the author of Lamentations declares that the time of punishment is over and that the exile must soon end (4:22a; cf. Isa. 40:2). Trusting in Yahweh's steadfast love, the poet dares to hope that Yahweh will not forever cast them off (3:22–33). But that hope is by no means a certainty, and the book closes with the haunting question to Yahweh: "Or hast thou utterly rejected us?" (5:22). The old covenant between Yahweh and his people had been broken. Whether Yahweh would again be with and for them remained to be seen.

Ezekiel

Ezekiel's career as prophet begins in the final years of Judah's existence as an independent nation and continues a decade or more, into the period of the exile. The earliest date indicated is around 593 B.C., five years after the first deportation (1:2); the latest, perhaps, is 573 (40:1). Much of Ezekiel's time is spent among fellow exiles in Babylon by the river Chebar, though occasionally he visits Jerusalem, at least in visions (8:3–11:25). A few chapters (e.g., 3–7; 12; 16) possibly report somewhat earlier activity in Jerusalem. The account of Ezekiel's call to be a prophet is characteristically vivid: The voice of Yahweh tells him to eat a scroll and then speak the words written on it to "the house of Israel."[200] In Ezekiel, as in much other biblical tradition written after the fall of the Northern Kingdom, "Israel" generally refers to the surviving Southern Kingdom, Judah. Throughout the book, Yahweh typically addresses the prophet as "son of man," a term equivalent to "man" (as in Ps 8:4), connoting his lowly condition before God. Here it may also connote Ezekiel's special status as Yahweh's prophet.

Like Jeremiah, his contemporary, Ezekiel proclaims not only doom and destruction but also hope for the future. Before the end in 586, Ezekiel declares that Yahweh will punish Judah and Jerusalem for their various offenses. Like the other classical prophets, Ezekiel focuses on two dimensions of transgressions: those against Yahweh and those that take the form of injustice, oppression, and unresponsiveness to the needs of others in the community. Like Hosea and Jeremiah, Ezekiel characterizes the people's persistent worship of other gods as harlotry (chaps. 16; 23). Israel and Judah always have been nations of rebels, a stubborn people (2:3–4), but Judah is even worse than her late sister

(16:51; 23:11): She continually fails to keep Yahweh's ordinances and statutes and worships other gods at pagan shrines (5:6; 6:13; 11:12; 20:28). Such passages resemble Deuteronomic language and suggest that Ezekiel may have shared the ideals of the Deuteronomic reform of 622 B.C., which had instituted the requirement that sacrifices be offered only in one place, Jerusalem.[201] Ezekiel also condemns his contemporaries for violating the horizontal dimension of the covenant: They have shed innocent blood; dishonored their parents; wronged the poor, sojourners, orphans, and widows; committed adultery and incest; taken interest, and practiced extortion (22:6–12). Everyone— princes, priests, prophets, and ordinary people alike—has done wrong in these ways (22:23–29). Not a single righteous man—for whose sake the nation might be spared—is to be found (22:30).[202] Because of these offenses, Ezekiel declares that Yahweh will send pestilence, famine, and the sword against Jerusalem and the whole nation of Judah or "Israel" (chaps. 5–7). When disaster befalls them, his people will know that he is Yahweh (7:27).

Yet, once the Babylonians capture and demolish Jerusalem and take most of its remaining citizens into exile, Ezekiel declares that Yahweh will gather his people and bring them back to their own land (28:25; 36:24), give them a new heart and a new spirit so that they will "walk in his statutes," that is, willingly and gladly obey his laws (11:19–20; 36:26–27), and make an everlasting covenant of peace with them (37:26). Wild beasts will be banished from the "prosperous plantations" that Yahweh will give to his people, who will then be the sheep of his pasture (34:25–31).

The most famous of Ezekiel's images of hope for the future is his vision of the valley of dry bones (37:1–14). Just as the bones come together again and are brought to life, so "the whole house of Israel" will be restored to nationhood. When their fortunes are restored, they shall once more know that Yahweh is their God (39:25–28).[203] Like Isaiah and Jeremiah, Ezekiel looks for a king from the house of David who will then rule in righteousness (34:23–24; 37:24–25). Ezekiel may even have meant that David himself would return (cf. Mal 4:5). Moreover, through his demonstration with the two sticks, Ezekiel gives assurance that this king will rule over a reconstituted Israel that will be united with Judah into one nation, as in the golden days of yore (37:15–23).

More frequently than other prophets, Ezekiel describes complex visions and allegories (e.g., chaps. 16; 17; 24) and acts out symbolically the disasters Yahweh is going to inflict as judgment upon the people of Jerusalem and Judah, thereby engaging the attention of passers-by, after the fashion of modern guerrilla theater performers (e.g., chaps. 4–5; 12; 24). Lest any of his hearers or readers suppose that his prophecies are for "times far off," Ezekiel insists that Yahweh means them for those alive at the time and that the prophesied events will occur without delay (12:21–28).[204] Another of his memorable visions describes a representation of Yahweh's transcendent but all-seeing presence among the exiles in Babylon, the mobile "chariot" with wheels within wheels (chaps. 1; 10). Jeremiah too assured the exiles that Yahweh was with them (Jeremiah 29).[205] In later theological terms, this vision symbolized Yahweh's omnipresence. The prophet's sense of Yahweh's transcendence is expressed in his remarkable circumlocution: "Such was the appearance of the likeness of the glory of Yahweh" (1:28).

Earlier prophets sometimes emphasized individual responsibility for keeping the covenant, but Ezekiel does so systematically: The old proverb, "The fathers have eaten sour grapes, and the children's teeth are set on edge," will no longer apply; instead, individuals are to be accountable for their own offenses (18:1–24).[206] Even prophets are liable if they fail to warn the wicked (3:16–21; 31:1–9). The righteous shall live, while the sinner shall surely die, but the righteous can lapse, and sinners can change their ways; therefore, the prophet calls the wicked to repent, for Yahweh takes no pleasure in the death of anyone (18:30–32). We find a similar emphasis on individual rewards and punishments in this life in the wisdom writings (e.g., Prov 10:2–3, 27–30).

Like many other prophetic books, Ezekiel contains several "oracles against foreign nations" (chaps. 25–32; 35), some of which may have been added after Ezekiel's time. Like such oracles in other prophetic writings, these point to Yahweh's sovereignty over all nations, promising or warning that he will judge them, and not only Israel or Judah, for their pretension and wickedness (e.g., Isa 10:12–19; Amos 1:3–2:3). Some such texts also may be tinged by a spirit of xenophobia or desire for national revenge.[207]

The book of Ezekiel closes in chapters 40–48 with a detailed description of an ideal future temple and various laws concerning sacrifices, priests, and Levites. Since these interests appear to reflect the influence of emerging Priestly (P) tradition recorded, perhaps, between 450 and 400 B.C., some interpreters suggest that these chapters are the work of a later prophet, apocalyptic seer, or priest. Here the sons of Zadok are distinguished from the other sons of Levi, and only the former may minister at Yahweh's altar.[208] Earlier traditions make no distinction between priests and Levites, but the P tradition and Chronicles insist that only the "sons of Aaron" may be priests, while Levites may serve only in lesser sacerdotal capacities. Chapters 40–48 make no mention of David or a king or messiah descended from him, even though these chapters, broadly speaking, depict conditions of life in the messianic age to come. Instead, the priestly sons of Zadok are to be the central leadership figures (44:15–31). Their task is to preside over the offering of sacrifices in the temple of the new age. Later prophets, notably Haggai, Zechariah, and Malachi, would continue to accentuate the importance of the temple and ritual observances there, especially the offering of proper sacrifices.

In chapter 47, the prophet, or a later apocalyptic editor, looks for the preternatural abundance of fish and fruit in the new era, when all kinds of trees will bear fresh fruit every month.[209] Other postexilic and intertestamental texts likewise look for superabundant harvests or food in the coming age.[210] Various New Testament texts also anticipate that the righteous will eat and drink together in the coming age.[211]

Some prophets looked only for the glorification of Israel, Judah, or the Jewish people in the coming age. Ezekiel, on the other hand, seems to be among those others who declared that gentiles would have a share in the blessings of life in that new era (37:28; 47:22–23). Several other prophets likewise looked for the inclusion of other nations in that future era.[212]

Daniel

The ostensible setting of this book is the period from the beginning of the exile—dated, oddly, in the third year of Jehoiakim, or 606 B.C. (Dan 1:1)—and extending into the reign of the Persian king Cyrus (ca. 558–530 B.C.). Cyrus is a major figure in biblical history: It was he who conquered the Babylonians and issued his famous decree in 538 allowing Jewish exiles to return to their former homeland. As the story is told, Daniel and some of his friends are chosen by the Babylonian king Nebuchadnezzar to serve in his court. The king gives Daniel the name Belteshazzar, not to be confused with Belshazzar, and soon Daniel is interpreting the king's dreams (chaps. 2–4). Daniel also interprets King Belshazzar's famous vision of the handwriting on the wall (chap. 5), and later, during the reign of the Medes and the Persians, his own dreams and visions (chaps. 7–12). Like Joseph, whom Pharaoh honored for interpreting his dreams, Daniel serves these kings in various high official capacities when he is not being persecuted for refusing to abandon traditional Jewish practices.

Several dreams and visions refer to developments in later centuries, particularly the rise and breakup of the Greek empire (chap. 11) and the oppressive reign of a later king who seems to fit the description of the Syrian tyrant Antiochus IV ("Epiphanes"), known to us from 1 Maccabees.[213] The resemblance is so considerable that many interpreters have concluded that Daniel was written during the reign of Antiochus IV or in the early Maccabean years (ca. 170–160 B.C.). The book is concerned with religious persecution of the sort first experienced, so far as we know, at that time. Much of it is explicitly apocalyptic in form: The words and visions purport to have been revealed to persons living in earlier times, but to have been "shut up and sealed" (8:17, 26; 12:4, 9) until the proper time, evidently that of the persecution under Antiochus IV. Intervening history is represented by a variety of symbolic figures, beasts, and horns. Second-century Jews, looking back to the time of Daniel and taking his interpretations as prophecies of things to come, could see that history had unfolded in accordance with this now unsealed or revealed plan. Thus, they would be encouraged to believe that the time of deliverance promised in the book would soon come to pass as well, since God had long known, if not also ordained, everything that was to happen.

The stories about Daniel and his friends all have the same point: Even though all may seem hopeless, God will deliver those who continue to trust him, refuse to worship other gods, and keep Jewish tradition despite persecution. Thus, Shadrach, Meshach, and Abednego, Daniel's three friends who, like him, keep kosher (chap. 1)[214] and refuse to worship the golden image, are rescued miraculously from the fiery furnace by God's angel (chap. 3).[215] Likewise, Daniel, who persists in praying to his God despite Darius's decree, is saved from the lions, again by the angel (chap. 6). Moreover, the several dreams, visions, and the supernatural handwriting on the wall all reveal that Daniel's God (identified as Yahweh only in chap. 9) rules over human kingdoms, notwithstanding the arrogant presumptions of certain kings,[216] and that these kingdoms will endure only for a time, after which God will establish his rule on earth through his saints (faithful Jews) forevermore.[217]

The mysterious power of God is expressed in a particularly dramatic way in two instances. A stone "cut out by no human hand" smashes the great image representing the four kingdoms (2:34; see also 8:25). Another time, only the fingers of a man's hand appear and write on the wall—the eerie effect of which is not lost upon King Belshazzar (5:5–6). The latter scene, one of the most vivid in the

Bible, gives Daniel occasion to interpret the ominous words, "MENE, MENE, TEKEL and PARSIN," thereby demonstrating again that God is in control of history, and that God puts down those who exalt themselves, lord it over the Jewish people, and fail to honor him (6:13–30).

The "son of man" dream or vision of Daniel's in chapter 7 has several distinctive features. Biblical tradition generally is reluctant to describe God, perhaps to avoid transgressing the prohibition against making likenesses of him (Exod 20:4; Deut 5:8). Ezekiel, for instance, cautiously characterizes Yahweh's enthroned presence: "Such was the appearance of the likeness of the glory of Yahweh" (Ezek 1:28b). Daniel 7:9 not only describes the throne (which, as in Ezekiel 1, has fire as well as wheels) but also "one that was ancient of days," namely, God, along with his raiment. "Ancient of Days" (7:13) is a circumlocution, that is, a way of referring to God without using his name. Beginning in the third or second century B.C., Jewish tradition increasingly tended to avoid naming God, perhaps to avoid inadvertent contravention of the Third Commandment (Exod 20:7; Deut 5:11).

The term "son of man" as such does not appear here; instead, 7:13 refers to "one like a son of man," who is pictured ascending to the Ancient of Days on or with the clouds of heaven. As the vision goes on, this "person" is to be given "dominion and glory and kingdom" forever (7:14). Later, the report tells that "the saints of the Most High," that is, Jews who remain faithful despite persecution, will receive the kingdom and dominion forever (7:18, 22, 27). Many scholars conclude from these texts that Daniel (or the apocalyptic seer who wrote in his name) used the expression "one like a son of man" to stand for those righteous Jews who would receive dominion over the kingdoms of the earth once their persecutors were overcome. There is no mention of a messiah or Davidic king in the book of Daniel.

The basic message of the book of Daniel, as of most apocalyptic writings, is this: Readers are urged to keep the faith and endure to the end, for God will deliver those who do so. A time of unprecedented tribulation or persecution is expected just before the final deliverance (12:1). This expectation is shared by other Jewish and early Christian writers, who sometimes look for accompanying cosmic manifestations as well.[218] One of the few Old Testament passages that mentions resurrection, Daniel 12:2–3 offers hope for those who have perished, perhaps in the course of persecution.[219]

The earliest known versions of other Old Testament books were written in Hebrew; however, Daniel 2:4b–7:28 is first known in Aramaic. Another distinguishing feature of Daniel is that the writer uses the term "Chaldeans" in a special sense—as "wise men," in company with magicians, enchanters, sorcerers, and astrologers (2:2; 5:7). Elsewhere in the Old Testament, Chaldeans is synonymous with Babylonians. Further traditions about Daniel and his friends are included in the Greek Bible, or Septuagint, and in later Catholic Bibles. In Protestant editions, these other traditions are placed in the Apocrypha under the heading of Additions to Daniel and include the Prayer of Azariah and the Song of the Three Young Men, Susanna, and the stories of Bel and the Dragon.

Hosea

Hosea is the first of twelve relatively short writings that, together, are often designated "the book of the Twelve." Most of these consist largely of prophetic sayings or writings.[220] The book of the Twelve concludes with Malachi.

Hosea prophesied in Israel (Ephraim, Samaria, or the Northern Kingdom) between 750 and 725 B.C., about the same time as Amos. Despite numerous textual problems (see footnotes in RSV, NRSV, NEB, and REB), his message is clear: Because the people of Israel have forgotten Yahweh and his law or covenant, Yahweh will reject, indeed, destroy them. And yet, in various ways, Hosea declares that Yahweh nevertheless loves his faithless and degraded people, Israel, and intends to restore them after all.

For Hosea, Israel's fundamental offense is infidelity or apostasy. Forgetting Yahweh who brought them from Egypt (2:13; 8:14; 13:46), the people of Israel commit harlotry (5:3–4; 9:1) by persistently worshiping other gods, such as the fertility gods (Baalim or Baals) of Canaan or various man-made idols (8:4–5; 11:2; 13:2). This pattern is expressed memorably in Hosea's comparison of Israel with his faithless wife, Gomer (chaps. 1–3). Moreover, worship of the fertility gods entails recourse to cult prostitutes (4:13–14), making the characterization of Israel's apostasy as harlotry especially apt. In addition, Israel has turned to foreign alliances instead of to Yahweh (5:13; 8:9–10), and, forgetting Yahweh, has pretended self-sufficiency (10:13–14; 12:8; 13:5–6). Israel's history, Hosea declares, shows this pattern to be chronic: "as in the days of Gibeah" (9:9; 10:9; cf. Judges 19–20) or Baal-peor (9:10; cf. Numbers 25). Hosea also objects that Israel's having a human king is contrary to Yahweh's purposes (8:4; 13:10–11). Evidently Hosea, himself a northerner, shares the northern belief that kings or would-be kings of Israel usurp Yahweh's role as

King of Israel.²²¹ In these several ways, Hosea says, Israel has turned from Yahweh to other gods, thereby violating the vertical dimension of the covenantal requirement: "no other gods besides me" (Exod 20:3 or Deut 5:7). In a sweeping indictment, Hosea declares that there is no knowledge of Yahweh in the land and also no faithfulness or kindness (4:1; 5:4).

The horizontal dimension of the covenant—the basic commandments governing conduct within the human community—also have been violated. Israel is condemned for its bloody deeds (1:4; 6:8–9), evil works (7:2), false balances, and oppression (12:7). Israel has violated most of the Decalogue's basic horizontal prohibitions: "There is swearing, lying, killing, stealing, and committing adultery" (4:2). The people of Israel love to offer sacrifices, but what Yahweh desires is steadfast love (6:6; 8:11–13).

Because of her many offenses, Israel will experience Yahweh's judgment in the form of Assyrian oppression. Literally or symbolically, Israel will go back to Egypt, the land of bondage (8:13b; 9:3, 6; 11:5). Yahweh's repudiation of Israel is symbolized in the names the prophet gives the children of Gomer, his harlotrous wife: *Lo Ruchamah* ("Not pitied," 1:6) and *Lo Ammi* ("Not my people," 1:8). The name of another son, *Jezreel*, represents Yahweh's condemnation of Jehu's murderous revolution instigated by the prophet Elisha a century earlier (2:4; 2 Kgs 9:1–10:36). Although Hosea often says that Yahweh will (merely) punish Israel,²²² he also sometimes goes further and declares that Yahweh intends to destroy the nation and its people, to bring them to an end.²²³

Yet, elsewhere Hosea speaks as if Israel might yet repent and return to Yahweh (5:15–6:3; 14:1–3), seek him, and practice righteousness and steadfast love (10:12), and—as if to summarize the burden of the Law and the Prophets—at last hold fast to "love and justice" (12:6). To be sure, Yahweh will hedge faithless Israel about and punish her (2:6–13), but afterward will restore her and again treat her as his bride (2:14–16), making a new covenant with her, and also with "the beasts of the field, the birds of the air, and the creeping things of the ground"—establishing or reestablishing his kingdom where all creatures and all creation will dwell together in peace (2:28).²²⁴ Life in this new era will be marked by six central biblical norms: righteousness, justice, steadfast love, mercy, faithfulness, and, perhaps all-inclusively, knowledge of Yahweh (2:19–20). Hosea also pictures Yahweh's love for Israel as that of a father for a wayward son: "It was I who taught Ephraim to walk. . . . How can I give you up, O Ephraim! . . . My compassion grows warm and tender. . . . I will not again destroy Ephraim" (11:3–9).

As the text stands, the core issue remains unresolved: Will Yahweh destroy his people, or will he sustain them with his love despite all that they have done? In one passage, it is a matter of Yahweh's justice and condemnation (11:5–7); in the next, of his compassion (11:8–9). Both moods recur throughout the book, which concludes with further oracles of doom (13:3–16), followed by assurances of Yahweh's love and support (14:4–7). In fact, not long after Hosea's time, Israel was destroyed by Assyria (722 B.C.). But that was not the end of the biblical story of Yahweh's dealings with his people.

Joel

This book consists entirely of prophetic sayings or oracles and offers no particular evidence concerning the prophet or his time. Its numerous references to Zion (i.e., Jerusalem) and Judah suggest that he lived in or near Jerusalem. The oracle against Edom (3:19) points to a date after 586 B.C., when the Edomites helped Babylon destroy Jerusalem and capture its people.[225] Evidently the temple ("house of God") has been rebuilt (1:14; 2:17), which would indicate a date after 515. However, because of locusts, drought, and fire, crops have failed to such an extent that sacrificial offerings are suspended (1:4–20).[226] From Haggai (ca. 520) and Malachi (ca. 450 B.C.) we learn that crop failure became a serious problem after the exile. Possible echoes of Malachi hint that Joel was set down after 450 (2:11b, 31b; cf. Mal 3:2; 4:5b). Mention of Greeks (3:6) may suggest a date no earlier than the fourth century, while the book's eschatological sections (2:28–32; 3:14–15, 18) accord with beliefs found in Jewish sources dating from the third and second centuries B.C.

Joel's message contains four motifs. The first is that Yahweh's judgment will come upon the Jewish people in the form of various catastrophes (1:1–2:11). Already fields, orchards, and pastures are in ruins, meaning, evidently, that Yahweh has begun to punish the Jewish people. There is little or no food for persons, domestic cattle, and sheep, or water for wildlife (1:16–20).[227] Earlier traditions also saw that other creatures suffered as a result of human depravity (Gen 6:5–7; Hos 4:1–3). And more catastrophes will soon follow: The day of Yahweh is near. It will be a day of darkness, gloom, and destruction from the Almighty.[228] The menacing army pictured in 1:4–7 and 2:2–10, whether locusts, foreign troops, or both, is sent by Yahweh to execute his word (2:11).[229]

"Yet even now," Joel declares, Yahweh calls his people to return: "Rend your hearts and not your garments" (2:12–13). This is Joel's second motif: Because Yahweh "is gracious and merciful, slow to anger, and abounding in steadfast love, and repents of evil" (2:13), he may yet bless them if they repent.[230] Thus, the prophet's declarations about catastrophes already experienced and those that are near seem to be meant as warnings to prompt his Jewish contemporaries to repent (Heb. *shub*, literally, "to return" or "turn around") while there is still time to do so. Neither Joel nor any of the other biblical prophets seem to have been interested simply in predicting the future.

The third motif is the prophet's message of hope. As if in response to their petition, Yahweh then assures his people that he will indeed restore their fortunes and never again put them to shame (2:18–27). Wildlife ("beasts of the field"), wilderness pastures, fruit trees, and vines also will take part in this great restoration (2:22; cf. 3:18). In addition, Yahweh will bestow his spirit, the gift of prophecy, upon "all flesh" and warn them through apocalyptic portents so that they may repent "before the great and terrible day of the Lord comes" (2:28–32). Judah will then enjoy abundant wine, milk, and water, and be inhabited forever (2:19, 21–26; 3:18).

The final motif concerns foreigners or gentiles. In the coming era of restoration, foreigners will have no place in Jerusalem (3:17b).[231] Moreover, Joel promises that "in those days" Yahweh will gather all nations for judgment and wreak vengeance on them for the acts of violence they have committed against the people of Judah (3:1–21).[232]

Amos

Several prophetic books are placed before his, but Amos may have been the earliest of the classical prophets, although Hosea and Isaiah may have been near contemporaries. Though a southerner from Judah, he delivered his oracles in Israel.[233] Much or all of Amos's message may have been spoken at Bethel, one of the major northern cities (7:10). Amos's prophetic activity is generally dated in the middle of the eighth century (1:1), possibly as early as 745 B.C.

Amaziah, the priest in charge of the northern sanctuary at Bethel, is not pleased to see Amos there, and tries to disparage and dismiss him as a two-bit "seer" or fortune-teller and a carpetbagger (7:12; cf. 1 Sam 9:6–9). Amos insists that he is not a professional prophet; rather, he is a shepherd from Judah who has experienced Yahweh's call to go and prophesy to Israel (7:14–15). Moreover, he adds some further words from Yahweh about the miserable fate in store for Amaziah and his family (7:16–17).

Amos begins by announcing Yahweh's intention to punish a series of foreign nations for their respective crimes (1:3–2:3). Very likely a gathering crowd of Israelites cheers him on as he proclaims Yahweh's judgment against Syria, certain Philistine cities, Tyre, Edom, Ammon, and Moab for their various acts of cruelty not only against Israel but against each other.[234] But then, using the same formula, he abruptly declares that Yahweh will punish Israel for its own offenses (2:6–16). Here, no doubt, the cheering suddenly stopped. The special relation Yahweh has had with Israel as "chosen people" in the past now becomes the basis for special condemnation: "You only have I known of all the families of the earth; therefore I will punish you for all your iniquities" (3:1–2). In popular religion, the "day of Yahweh" was thought to be that time in the future when Yahweh would defeat Israel's enemies and pour down unqualified blessings on his people. Amos turns that around: "Woe to you who desire the day of Yahweh! . . . It is darkness and not light" (5:18–20). No wonder Amaziah views Amos as a troublemaker and orders him to leave "the king's sanctuary" (7:10–12).

In particular, Amos declares that the people of Israel have violated the horizontal dimension of the covenant. They have failed to provide justice in the local courts ("the gate"); instead, the wealthy and powerful have been exploiting the righteous, poor, and needy, the very people whose interests the covenant requires them to protect (2:6; 5:11a; 8:4–6). They have also committed other offenses against persons in the covenant community (2:7–8, 12). Moreover, both the men and women of Israel have been living in ease and luxury without regard to the plight of the poor and needy or to the future of the nation. Therefore, Yahweh, who is just, will surely bring judgment against them (3:15–4:1; 6:1–6). The people of Israel think they can multiply their transgressions but then make everything all right by offering sacrifices. They love to offer sacrifices, but Yahweh will not be bought off by religious services and offerings (4:4–5; 5:21–23); what he does require is justice and righteousness (5:15, 24).[235] Amos, like Jeremiah after him, implies that Yahweh never asked for sacrifices in the wilderness, the time when the law was given to Moses, and hints, perhaps, that Yahweh never did ordain sacrificial offerings (Amos 5:25; Jer 7:21–23; cf. Isa 1:12–17). The term "classical prophets" generally is used to designate those prophets who, beginning with Amos, emphasize this horizontal dimension, that is, Yahweh's requirements of justice, righteousness, mercy, and, especially, concern for the poor, the needy, the widow, and the orphan. Yahweh repeatedly has tried to warn Israel, Amos says, by bringing famine, drought, blight, mildew, locusts, pestilence, and conquering enemies upon them. "'Yet you did not return to me,' says Yahweh" (4:6, 8, 9, 10, 11). Now time has run out; doom is nigh: "Prepare to meet your God, O Israel" (4:12).

Like Jeremiah after him, Amos pleads with Yahweh for the nation (7:1–6) but ultimately to no avail. Amos depicts not only devastation and decimation (3:12; 5:3) but the total destruction of Israel and the Israelites.[236] A few passages hint that it still may not be too late: that Israel may yet seek Yahweh and live (5:4, 6, 14–15). But otherwise, Amos's message is one of certain and impending doom. Because Israel has violated the covenant, particularly the covenant obligation of the rich and powerful to look out for the well-being of the poor and needy, Yahweh will bring disaster upon the whole nation.

Interpreters generally regard most of the present ending of the book (9:9c–15) as a supplement appended after the disastrous events of 586 B.C. in order to give hope to the exiles of Judah or their later Jewish descendants. The transition from 9:8b to 9:8c seems abrupt and even contradictory: "I will destroy it from the surface of the ground; except that I will not utterly destroy" it. The declaration that sinners will die (9:10) is more like Ezekiel's and the orthodox wisdom theology's emphasis on individual retribution than Amos's characteristic focus on Yahweh's pending judgment on the nation of Israel as a whole. David's "booth" (9:11), that is, the line of Judahite kings, had not yet fallen in the time of Amos—nor was Amos generally concerned with Judah. That Yahweh was going to restore the Davidic line would, of course, have been good news to Jews living under the dominion of foreign empires following 586 B.C.[237] As in other late prophetic and apocalyptic writings, we see in 9:13 the prospect of a restored or transformed fertility of the ground, once the new or messianic age has dawned (cf. Joel 3:18). However, Yahweh's promise to restore the fortunes of his people Israel and make them forever secure in their land (9:14–15) is congruent with assurances found in the other classical prophets: Hosea, Isaiah, Jeremiah, Micah, and Ezekiel. It may be that Amos, like these other prophets, believed that after Yahweh had punished his special people, he would make a new beginning with them. If Amos had not so believed, a later prophet or editor did, and added these oracles to complete our present book of Amos.

Obadiah

This is the briefest writing in the book of the Twelve, the collection of relatively short prophetic books, Hosea through Malachi, that follows the longer prophets, Isaiah, Jeremiah, and Ezekiel. Obadiah either lived through or otherwise knew of the destruction of Jerusalem by Babylon in 586 B.C. His book consists largely of a declamation against Edom, which not only had gloated and rejoiced over Judah's "day of calamity" or "distress" but actively joined in plundering Jerusalem and rounding up Jewish fugitives (vv. 10–14). For this, Obadiah proclaims, Yahweh will destroy Edom and its people; not a survivor of them will remain (vv. 9–10, 18). Other writings from this period and afterward express similar hatred for Edom.[238] Obadiah also condemns Edom for its pride (vv. 3–4).

Edom was the small nation south of Judah and the Dead Sea. There had been little interaction between Edom and Judah in previous centuries, probably because the Negeb Desert made travel difficult between the two. However, Edomite wisdom was recognized in biblical tradition (Jer 47:7), and Job was evidently an Edomite (Job 1:1). That Edom should have turned against Judah was especially bitter, since according to ancient tradition (Gen 25:36), the Edomites were descendants of Esau, Jacob's twin brother (see Obad 10–12). Edomite hostility toward Judah and Jerusalem may have been fueled by recollection of their ancestors' treatment at the hands of David (2 Sam 8:13–14).

Like Amos, Obadiah affirms Yahweh's universal justice: All nations soon will be punished according to their deeds (vv. 15–16).[239] The "day of Yahweh" (v. 15) is a term used by many prophets to refer to the time when Yahweh will punish Israel, Judah, or other nations for their wickedness. It also often designates the time when Yahweh will act to restore Israel, Judah, and, sometimes, other nations. Here, like other prophets, Obadiah expresses the belief that this day is near: It will not be long before Yahweh acts to requite the nations for their evil deeds.

Unlike Jeremiah, Ezekiel, the author(s) of Lamentations, and the Deuteronomic historian, Obadiah does not characterize the catastrophic events of 586 as Yahweh's judgment against the people of Judah for breaking the covenant. But like Jeremiah, Ezekiel, and Second Isaiah, he holds out hope that the Jewish exiles will be restored. In fact, he seems to say that only "the house of Jacob" (the exiled people of Judah, if not also of Israel) will survive the time of judgment; other nations will "be as though they had not been" (vv. 16–17). The exiles will repossess not only their own land (v. 17b) but also the land that formerly belonged to other nearby nations (vv. 19–20). The newly constituted kingdom will be Yahweh's (v. 21). The idea here is similar to that expressed in Daniel 7: In the coming era, the Jewish people will have dominion, if not over all the earth (cf. Zech 14:9), at least over their own and several neighboring lands.

As in Daniel, Joel, and many other apocalyptic and prophetic texts, there is no reference to a future Davidic king or messiah; however, Obadiah 17 is one of the very few biblical passages that designate Jerusalem or Judah a *holy* place.[240] Obadiah's nationalistic vision of the future era is somewhat similar to Joel's (Joel 3:1–17, 19) and Nahum's, but contrasts sharply with the declarations of several other prophets, such as Isaiah (11:10; 19:19–25),[241] Jeremiah (e.g., 48:47; 49:39), Ezekiel (47:22–23), Micah (4:1–4), and Zechariah (2:11; 14:16–17), to the effect that some or all other nations will also have a share in the blessings of life in the coming age.

Jonah

This is a parable about a man whose God is too great and too merciful to suit him. Summoned by Yahweh to go to Nineveh (the capital of hated Assyria)[242] and "cry against it," Jonah boards a ship bound for Tarshish, in the opposite direction, hoping desperately to escape Yahweh's presence, as the narrator states three times in the opening verses (1:3a, 3b, 10b) lest readers miss this important point. But why did Jonah wish to escape from Yahweh's presence? To understand that is to understand the point of the story. The narrator proceeds to explain subtly but clearly through numerous significant details.

Here is Jonah on board the ship, headed for Tarshish, contrary to Yahweh's instructions. But Yahweh is lord of wind and sea and stirs up a great storm. The pagan sailors pray to their gods while Jonah sleeps in the ship's hold. Finding him there, the pagan captain orders Jonah to get up and pray to his own god (Yahweh). There is no indication that Jonah does so. The sailors then cast lots to see who is responsible for their trouble. When it turns out to be Jonah, he admits that he fears Yahweh "who made the sea and the dry land" (1:9). One might suppose that, knowing this, Jonah should have realized that trying to escape Yahweh's presence, whether by land or by sea, would necessarily prove futile. But Jonah is so anxious that he tries anyway. The narrator does not yet reveal why Jonah is so desperate to escape the presence of Yahweh. The pagan sailors, decent men that they are, hesitate to throw Jonah overboard; yet since this obviously is what Yahweh desires, they finally go ahead and do so. They then proceed to worship Yahweh with vows and sacrifices when the sea ceases to rage. Jonah is now swallowed by the great fish appointed by Yahweh for this purpose (1:17). Jonah at last prays to Yahweh from the belly of the fish, surely a strange place, thereby tacitly acknowledging that there is no escape from the presence of Yahweh.[243] Yahweh now speaks to the fish, which obediently deposits Jonah safely on dry land.

Again the "word of Yahweh" summons Jonah to go to Nineveh. This time he goes, though grudgingly. His message offers no hope at all, for he simply declares, "Yet forty days, and Nineveh shall be overthrown!" (3:4b). Nevertheless, in response to this terse and unpromising announcement, "the people of Nineveh believed God," one and all. Moreover, its king now decrees that not only human, but also beast, herd, and flock should fast, put on sackcloth, and pray urgently to God (cf. Ps 150:6), just in case he might be persuaded to spare them—even though Jonah has not mentioned this possibility.[244] And then God does change his mind and does not destroy them after all.

This is too much for Jonah, who now, in his angry complaint to Yahweh, clearly explains why he tried to avoid this mission to Nineveh in the first place: "For I knew that thou art a gracious God and merciful, slow to anger, and abounding in steadfast love, and repentest of evil" (4:2).[245] In short, Jonah did not want Yahweh to spare Nineveh at all and feared from the first that Yahweh would do so. Jonah is particularly outraged that he, of all people, should have been appointed the agent of that hated city's deliverance. Jonah wants Yahweh to be a tribal deity, concerned only with the well-being of Israelites, Judahites, or Jews. Rather than go on living in a world ruled by a gracious and merciful God who spares Ninevites, Jonah now prays to die. Still sulking, he clings to the hope that Yahweh may yet destroy the city, so he sets up camp overlooking it but at a safe distance, "till he should see what would become of the city" (4:5). Evidently Jonah hoped that even now Yahweh might rain down fire and brimstone, as he had long ago upon Sodom and Gomorrah.

Again Yahweh shows his rule over all creation: He appoints a plant with large leaves to give Jonah shade, a worm to attack the plant, and a hot wind and sun to make Jonah uncomfortable, all in order to try to get through to him. Jonah sorely misses the plant in his self-pity; but how much more should Jonah, like Yahweh who sent him there, care about Nineveh with its one hundred twenty thousand children "and also much cattle" (4:11)!

The story does not say whether Jonah finally gets the point or remains in the hard shell of his narrow tribal religion. But the book's author clearly wishes the reader to see that the God who made and presides over the sea and dry land is concerned for the well-being of "all creatures that on earth do dwell"—human and otherwise. This understanding is one with that of the prophet Isaiah, who looked for that time when Yahweh would bring peace among nations and within all creation (Isa 2:2–4; 11:6–9; 19:19–25). Reference to "much cattle" in 4:11 is consistent with 3:6–9, which tells that both man and beast, herd and flock, had been called on to fast, put on sackcloth, and pray to God! Yahweh's concern for "cattle," probably meaning all kinds of domestic or farm animals, and wildlife appears in numerous other biblical texts.[246]

Jonah, the parable's protagonist or antihero, is presented as a somewhat ridiculous figure if not a "schlemiehl." He knows all along that Yahweh is the God of heaven who made both sea and dry land, but he tries to escape Yahweh's jurisdiction by sea anyway. Because he also knows that Yahweh is gracious and merciful, and therefore not likely to destroy Nineveh if its citizens repent, he tries to ignore Yahweh's summons to preach there. And when Yahweh does spare the city because the Ninevites repent after hearing Jonah preach, Jonah prays that he might die rather than continue living in a world where God cares about Assyrians.[247] It is probable that the narrator drew Jonah as a caricature of xenophobic or henotheistic[248] tendencies in Judaism, represented, perhaps in milder form, in Deuteronomy 23:3, Ezra 9–10, Nehemiah 13, Esther 9:5–16, Joel 3:1–17, Obadiah, Nahum, and Additions to Esther 14:15. At any rate, on the question of Israel's relation to other nations—a major theme throughout the Bible—the *author* of the story clearly is aligned with the understanding that Israel was to be a blessing to other families of the earth (Gen 12:3), or in the words of Second Isaiah, a "light to the nations" (Isa 49:5–6).

Micah

Micah lived in the Southern Kingdom, Judah, about the same time as Isaiah (ca. 740–700 B.C.). Like other southern prophets, he took up certain Isaianic themes and may have been one of that prophet's early disciples (cf. Isa 8:16). But while Isaiah remained in Jerusalem, Micah seems to have lived in the countryside, some twenty-five miles west of the city. Little is known about Micah, but a few passages reveal his personal commitment and feelings, namely, 1:8; 3:8; 7:7. Micah's precise meaning often is obscure, a number of passages present textual problems, and several evidently are later additions, as can be seen by the number of footnotes in many English translations that indicate translators' recourse to conjecture or alternate readings, such as Greek and Syriac versions. Some verses seem to presuppose the exile, and may have been added after 586 B.C. by later hands.[249]

Despite textual uncertainties, Micah's overall message is clear. The rich and powerful have been oppressing and exploiting the poor and helpless, a point most vividly stated in 3:1–3 (cf. Isa 3:14–15). Like most prophets, Micah addresses the power structure, here the heads and rulers of Judah (3:1, 9–11).[250] Instead of giving justice and equity in the courts, they "give judgment for a bribe" (3:9–11). Some covet and seize fields and houses (2:1–2), driving women and children into the streets (2:9). Some cheat in the marketplace with false weights and measures (6:10–11; cf. Deut 25:13–16). Children treat parents with contempt (7:6a; cf. Exod 20:12 or Deut 5:16). None of the men is upright (7:2; cf. Jer 5:1–5; Ezek 22:30), all prey upon each other, and neither friends nor family can be trusted (7:26). Micah rebukes both the false prophets who prophesy for hire and tell people only what they want to hear (3:5, 11)[251] and the people who wish to hear only comforting lies (2:6). Such people would like religion to be an opiate: "If a man should go about and utter wind and lies, saying 'I will preach to you of wine and strong drink,' he would be the preacher for this people!" (2:11). In the manner of other classical prophets who stressed the central importance of the covenant's horizontal obligations, Micah resoundingly declares that Yahweh requires not sacrifice but justice, kindness, and walking humbly with God (6:6–8).[252] Like Isaiah, he proposes to walk about Jerusalem "stripped and naked" to bring home to the people of that city his message that it is doomed (1:8; cf. Isaiah 20). Because of their several offenses, Yahweh will bring catastrophe upon Samaria (the capital of Israel) and Jerusalem (the capital of Judah): "I will make Samaria a heap in the open country" (1:6); "Zion shall be plowed as a field" (3:12). (A hundred years later, Jeremiah's life will be spared when, during his trial as a traitor or security risk for so proclaiming, someone remembers that Micah preached earlier to the same effect.)[253] Micah warns his contemporaries that Yahweh will cause them to suffer hunger and privation (6:13, 15) and domination by foreign nations (1:3–16; 2:3–4).

Like most other classical prophets, Micah also promises a brighter future. In the famous "floating oracle" (4:1–3), so called because it also appears in Isaiah 2:2–4, Micah looks for an era of international peace, when many nations will come to Jerusalem to be taught the ways of God. Then "they shall beat their swords into plowshares, and their spears into pruning hooks," and every man shall sit "under his vine and under his fig tree" in peace and security (4:34; cf. Zech 3:2). Some oracles, probably added following the catastrophic events of 586 that marked the beginning of the exile,[254] emphasize further hopes. Echoing Isaiah, Micah 2:12 and 4:7 promise that Yahweh will bring back a remnant. Like Second Isaiah (Isa 35:10), Micah 4:6–7 looks for Yahweh to bring the lame and those otherwise afflicted and "cast off" back to Zion, where he will reign forevermore. The messianic oracle in 5:2–4 promises the appearance of a ruler from the tribe of Judah (cf. Gen 49:10), evidently a Davidic king—an expectation implicit also, perhaps, in 2:13 but absent from traditions more likely attributable to Micah, the eighth-century prophet. The later traditions also anticipate Israel's crushing victory over other nations, a scenario that contrasts sharply with the prospect of international peace and goodwill pictured in 4:1–4.[255] The expected expropriation of the wealth of nations for the glory of Yahweh and Jerusalem (4:13) accords with hopes expressed in various other postexilic texts, such as Isaiah 61:6; Haggai 2:6–9; Zechariah 14:14. Since other nations had plundered Judah, some Judahites or Jews understandably wished to return the favor. Such, however, was not Micah's own vision of the future.

Nahum

Here we have another of the twelve shorter prophetic writings that constitute the book of the Twelve. Nahum is concerned with a single theme: the impending defeat of Nineveh and the prospect of Judah's deliverance from Assyrian domination. Nineveh was the capital of Assyria. Since the latter third of the eighth century B.C., Judah had been under the weight of Assyrian power in the Near East. But then the neo-Babylonian empire began to emerge as a major power as Assyria weakened. Nineveh fell to Babylonian forces in 612 B.C., marking the end of Assyrian ascendency in the eastern Mediterranean world.

Nahum rejoices at the prospect of Nineveh's overthrow, which he views as Yahweh's judgment against that city for its idolatry, wickedness, and oppression. He seems to share Isaiah's understanding that Assyria has been the rod of Yahweh's anger against Judah (1:12; cf. Isa 10:5–11), but now Yahweh is about to liberate his people by breaking the Assyrian yoke "from off"[256] their necks (1:13). Not only will Yahweh punish Nineveh, he will completely destroy that hated city

(1:8–9, 14–15). The prophet confidently proclaims the imminent arrival of an era of peace and glory for Judah, and perhaps for all Israel (1:15; 2:2). Evidently he believes that Judah's troubles will be over for good: "For never again shall the wicked come against you" (1:15c). It was true that Assyria never again caused Judah grief.

But Nahum's celebration is premature. Soon the bell would toll for Judah too. Three years later, in 609, Josiah, the great reformer king of Judah, perhaps inspired by hopes like Nahum's, leads his troops against an Egyptian contingent on its way to reinforce the beleaguered Assyrians. Josiah is killed in battle, and the Egyptian pharaoh makes Judah a vassal tributary (2 Kgs 23:29–35). Soon afterward, the Babylonians come on the scene, not as Judah's liberators but as their new overlords and conquerors (2 Kings 24–25).

As with other prophetic oracles against foreign nations, Nahum testifies to the universal sovereignty of Yahweh. Yahweh rules over the affairs of all nations. Nahum's message of hatred for Nineveh, however, contrasts with the outlook of the author of the book of Jonah, who understands that Yahweh is concerned for the well-being of the people of that city, a hundred and twenty thousand young children who do not know their right hand from their left, and also much cattle (Jonah 4:11).[257] Nahum's nationalistic vision of the future also differs notably from that of Isaiah, who prophesied that in the coming age, Assyria, together with Egypt and Israel, would be Yahweh's people and enjoy his blessings (Isa 19:23–25).

Habakkuk

As at the beginning of Amos and Micah, the caption at Habakkuk 1:1 states that the words which follow are what the prophet "saw."[258] The book contains no information about the prophet or his times. The prophet Habakkuk who appears in the fictional story of Bel and the Dragon was supposedly a contemporary of Daniel's, but is not said to be the same person as the prophet whose words are preserved in this book. Reference to Yahweh's "rousing the Chaldeans" at Habakkuk 1:6 hints that this book's author lived before 586 B.C., when the Chaldeans, or Babylonians, stormed into Jerusalem and put an end to the kingdom of Judah. Nothing else in the book, however, indicates this period. References to the past or present activities of an enemy nation are vague and seem to symbolize at times an oppressive nation and at other times a wicked and oppressive individual within the community. Later writings, such as Judith and Revelation, use Babylon as a symbol for mythic or latter-day enemy nations. Habakkuk's preoccupation with the problem of theodicy seems more at home in the time of Job, Ecclesiastes, or the Wisdom of Solomon. These writings likewise address the question of why God, who is believed to be both righteous and all-powerful, permits the wicked to go unpunished while they exploit or "swallow up" the righteous (Hab 1:4, 13).

The book consists of four distinguishable sections: a dialogue with Yahweh (1:2–2:5), a list of woes in store for an unrighteous man or nation (2:6–17), a short polemic against belief in idols (2:18–20), and a psalm (chap. 3).

The first section is structured in the form of questions and answers.[259] Habakkuk complains about the violence and injustice he sees in the land (1:2–4). Yahweh replies that he is sending the Chaldeans as a judgment against the people of Judah (or the Jewish people)—although the Chaldeans do not know this (1:5–11; cf. Isa 10:5–14), supposing their own might to be their god (cf. Wis 2:11).

At the beginning of the second section, Habakkuk replies that Yahweh, who is everlasting, may well send the Chaldeans as a judgment, but he questions whether it is right for such faithless and wicked men to keep on swallowing the righteous, "mercilessly slaying nations for ever" (1:12–17). Yahweh answers by instructing the prophet to write the words set forth in a vision on a tablet for all to read (2:2; cf. Isa 8:1; Dan 12:4). It is unclear which of the following verses, if any, record the words revealed in that vision. The next verse (2:3) says that the time when the vision will be fulfilled "hastens to the end," and that though it may seem to move slowly, "it will not delay."[260] Perhaps the gist of the vision is the assurance implicit in 2:4: The righteous who remain faithful (despite oppression or persecution) shall live, or, alternately, the righteous who aspire to enjoy the time of vindication must live faithfully in the meantime.

The third section consists of a series of "woes" against a man (or men) or nations who act unjustly (2:6–19).[261] Taking and keeping pledges (2:6) is contrary to the covenant requirement that they be returned (Exod 20:26–27; Deut 24:10–13), but most of the other offenses enumerated here are more the sort that nations commit. Embedded in these warnings of "woe," is a verse drawn from or parallel to Isaiah 11:9, which looks toward the future transformation of the whole earth: "For the earth will be filled with the knowledge of the fury of Yahweh, as the waters cover the sea" (Hab 2:14).[262] This third section also briefly ridicules the futility of trusting in man-made idols (2:19). This theme, enunciated earlier by Second Isaiah (Isa 40:18–20), recurs especially in the Apocrypha (Wisdom of Solomon 13–15, Letter of Jeremiah; Bel and the Dragon).

Chapter 3 is in the form of a psalm. The term *selah* (3:3, 9, 13) commonly appears in psalms to mark a pause in the singing or recital. *Shigionoth* (3:1) means "hymns," as in the caption to Psalm 7; but the phrase "according to" usually precedes a specific hymn tune (e.g., before Pss 6 and 46) instead. Placing instructions "to the choirmaster" after Habakkuk 3:19 also is unusual. Ordinarily this sort of notation comes first (e.g., Pss 75; 76; 88). The psalm praises Yahweh, who in the past has used his terrible power to save his people. The prophet's final answer is then stated: He will quietly wait for Yahweh to bring the invaders to judgment; even though fruit and flock may fail, he will trust Yahweh and rejoice in him (3:16–19; cf. Job 1:13–21).

Zephaniah

The book begins, like Hosea, Amos, and Micah, with an editorial description of the prophet and his period (1:1). Much of the text may come from the time of Josiah (640–609 B.C.). Like that king and the Deuteronomic reformers, Zephaniah undertakes to oppose the Judahites' continuing worship of Baal and other foreign gods (1:4–6).

Zephaniah proclaims that Yahweh will punish the people of Jerusalem and Judah for their offenses, which include apostasy, adopting foreign attire, violence, fraud (1:4–9), supposing that Yahweh will not act justly (1:12), oppression, exploitation, corruption, and faithlessness, particularly on the part of the community's leaders and officials (3:1–4, 7). A number of verses seem to echo passages in Amos. Like Joel and Amos, Zephaniah refers to the "day of Yahweh": It is near or "at hand," this day of wrath, ruin, devastation, and darkness (1:7, 14–15).[263] It will not merely be punishment, nor will Judah alone bear it; Yahweh "will be terrible" against many nations, including Assyria (2:11–15; cf. Nahum). Indeed, Zephaniah looks for Yahweh's judgment against the whole earth: Humans and beasts, birds and fish, everything will be swept away, the earth and all its inhabitants (1:2–3, 18; 3:8; cf. Gen 8:8–17). The perspective here is decidedly theocentric: Yahweh can get along perfectly well without humankind or even the earth itself.

And yet the nation may still repent (2:1–3). Several passages, some containing typical Isaianic terms and tones, look for Yahweh to restore the fortunes of his people (e.g., 2:7; 3:11–20). Zephaniah's message of assurance for the future is distinctive in that it implies an intervening judgment of individuals: The "proudly exultant" will be removed and those who are "humble and lowly" will remain so that the restored Israel might constitute a righteous remnant; there will be none left who will do wrong (3:11–13). By contrast, Jeremiah expected Yahweh to transform the hearts of all his people so that they would keep the new covenant he would make with them (Jer 31:31–34).

Like Joel and several other prophetic books, Zephaniah includes oracles against certain foreign nations (2:4–15),[264] yet looks forward to the time when all nations "may call on the name of Yahweh and serve him with one accord" (3:9). The author promises that in the coming time of restoration, Judah will be "renowned and praised" by "all peoples of the earth" (3:20; cf. Gen 12:2–3).[265] Like Hosea, Zephaniah expects that Yahweh will again love his people.[266] In this new era of blessing and restoration, Yahweh himself will be Israel's king (3:2). Zephaniah does not look for the coming of a Davidic, or any other human, messiah.

Some scholars think it likely that certain of these beliefs and expectations for the future were added by a later postexilic writer or writers. On the other hand, most scholars recognize that some prophets who proclaimed Yahweh's impending judgment but did not live to see it occur also included genuine oracles of hope for the future (e.g., Hosea, Isaiah). Perhaps Zephaniah likewise looked with hope for a future beyond the time of judgment, even if he did not live to see the catastrophic events of 598–586 B.C.

Haggai

Haggai is usually dated around 520 B.C. Persia has defeated Babylon, and many Jews, liberated from exile by Cyrus's decree in 538, have returned to Judah. What once had been the independent kingdom of Judah is now a province of the Persian empire. Its governor is Zerubbabel, perhaps a grandson or great-grandson of Jehoiachin, also known as Jeconiah or Coniah, the next-to-last king of Judah, mentioned in 1 Chronicles 3:16–19 and Haggai 1:1. If so, Zerubbabel would have been a descendant of David.

Life is difficult for the returned exiles: The economy is in trouble and food is scarce, as the prophet observes in picturesque imagery (1:6, 9–11). Haggai, addressing himself particularly to Zerubbabel and Joshua, the high priest, declares that Yahweh has brought these conditions about because the temple, destroyed by the Babylonians in 586, has not yet been rebuilt: "Is it a time for you yourselves to dwell in your paneled houses, while this house lies in ruins?" (1:4–11).

Inspired by Haggai's, and also Zechariah's, preaching, Zerubbabel, Joshua, and the rest of the Jewish people get to work, and soon the temple's foundation is laid. Encouraged by subsequent agricultural and economic improvements (2:15–19), Haggai proclaims that "in a little while," Yahweh will cause the treasuries of all nations (presumably including valuables plundered from the first temple) to fill the new temple now under construction with greater splendor even than that of Solomon (2:6–9). Yahweh is about to overthrow the power of other nations (2:21–22)[267] and make Zerubbabel messiah or king over a new and once more independent nation of Judah (2:23). Since all kings of Judah have been, or were expected to be, descendants of David, Haggai's statement about Zerubbabel appears to confirm the Chronicler's genealogical data concerning his Davidic ancestry.

As a result of Haggai's preaching, as well as that of his contemporary, Zechariah, the temple was rebuilt in 515. Nevertheless, the Persians continued to rule over the Jewish people for nearly two hundred more years, and Zerubbabel vanished from the pages of history without ever becoming messiah. Although the book of Ezra (written ca. 350 B.C.) makes a point of reporting that various Persian kings furnished money and other impetus for rebuilding the temple (e.g., Ezra 1:1–4; 5:13–6:15), nothing in Haggai or Zechariah hints that the Persians provided any such assistance.

The book of Haggai presents several other important developments. Haggai is the first prophet to address his message to a provincial governor. Earlier prophets sometimes spoke Yahweh's word to kings, but now, of course, there is no king of Judah. Haggai expects Zerubbabel to become king once construction on the temple is completed and the new era begun. Haggai also addresses Joshua, "the high priest" (2:1–9). That title is first mentioned here and in Zechariah.[268] Absent kingship, the newly established high priesthood is the highest office a Jewish leader can hold, other than one to which he may be appointed by a foreign ruler. Zechariah goes so far as to proclaim Joshua, the high priest, messiah (Zech 6:9–14). The hope for a priestly messiah from the "house of Aaron" also appears in later Jewish sources.

Though earlier prophets also spoke of Yahweh's sending droughts or pestilence to warn or punish his people (e.g., Amos 4:6–10; Mic 6:14–15), they more typically proclaimed that he would bring judgment against them in the form of defeat at the hands of foreign nations. Now that the Jewish people live under foreign, Persian, domination, Haggai visualizes Yahweh's judgment only in the guise of natural disasters.[269] The preexilic prophets emphasized the horizontal dimension of the covenant, the requirements of justice, mercy, and concern for the poor and needy within the community, while often insisting that Yahweh had no interest in sacrificial offerings.[270] Haggai, however, is silent about the horizontal requirements of the covenant but preoccupied with promoting the reconstruction of the temple, which, since the Deuteronomic reform, was the only place where sacrifices might properly be offered.[271] Chapters 40–48 of Ezekiel likewise focus on a new temple in Jerusalem; there too it is associated with the coming of the messianic age. Preoccupation with the temple and the offering of sacrifices in it is even more pronounced, of course, in the Priestly Code (PC) and Chronicles-Ezra-Nehemiah, which are all dated between 450 and 350 B.C.

Zechariah

The first eight chapters of this book are generally attributed to Haggai's contemporary, the prophet Zechariah (ca. 520 B.C.). Chapters 9–14 probably are later additions, written between the fourth and second centuries B.C. These later chapters are sometimes designated "Second Zechariah."

The setting for chapters 1–8 is as follows. The Persians had defeated Babylon in 539 B.C. and become the dominant power in the Near East. Persian policy, as seen in Emperor Cyrus's decree of 538, permitted captive peoples to return to their native lands. Zechariah, speaking for Yahweh, summons Jewish exiles to return to Zion (Jerusalem), assuring them that this city and Judah, for the first time called "the holy land," will be Yahweh's future dwelling place (2:6–12). Zerubbabel, a descendant, perhaps, of one of Judah's last kings,[272] has been appointed governor of Judah, now a Persian territory.

Zechariah reports a series of symbolic visions which, in various ways, convey the message that Yahweh intends to restore Judah and Jerusalem and bring on the messianic age. In one vision, Joshua, the high priest, is told that Yahweh will bring his "servant the Branch" (messiah; cf. Isa 11:1), cleanse the land of guilt, and establish peace (3:8–10). Another vision identifies Zerubbabel as the messiah who will finish building the temple (4:6–10), a hope shared by his contemporary, the prophet Haggai. Zechariah refers in one passage to two "branches" or messiahs, one being Joshua, the high priest, and the other Zerubbabel, possibly a descendant of David, and thus a political messiah or potential king (4:1–14). Later, after Zerubbabel drops out of view, Joshua is designated the Branch who shall build the temple

(6:9–13). Unlike Haggai but like earlier prophets, Zechariah also admonishes his contemporaries to keep the horizontal requirements of the covenant (5:3; 7:8–10; 8:16–17). This first part of the book closes with more assurances of Yahweh's intent to do good to his people, especially now that the temple's foundations have been laid. Like Isaiah and Micah, Zechariah declares that the time will come when many peoples or nations will worship Yahweh in Jerusalem (2:11; 8:20–23).

Chapters 1–8 present other notable features. Satan appears here for the third and last time in the Old Testament (3:1–2).[273] Satan is not yet an evil being, much less a cosmic evil power, but only "the accuser," or attorney general, an official in the heavenly council or court of Yahweh. Here, evidently, Satan has marked Jerusalem for condemnation because of its various offenses, but Yahweh decides to spare Jerusalem, "as a brand plucked from the fire," and so overrules Satan. Like Jeremiah, Ezekiel, the writer(s) of Lamentations, and the Deuteronomic historian, Zechariah interprets the catastrophic events of the exile as Yahweh's judgment against the people of Judah and Jerusalem for breaking the covenant (7:7–14). Several of the images depicted in the visions in these chapters are particularly vivid: four horns (representing foreign nations that have defeated Judah), colored horses and chariots (which patrol the earth for Yahweh), a golden lampstand with seven lamps, and a flying scroll, thirty feet long and fifteen wide. Some of these images are later elaborated in the books of Daniel and Revelation.

Chapters 9–14 describe the final days when Yahweh is expected to intervene on behalf of Jerusalem and Judah. Mention of Greece (9:13) suggests that these chapters were composed no earlier than the latter part of the fourth century B.C. after Alexander's empire had extended into the Near East. Several neighboring peoples are condemned (9:1–7), after which the writer declares that Yahweh himself will guard Jerusalem against any further oppressors and calls the people ("daughter") of Jerusalem to rejoice because their messiah (king) comes (or will come) to establish his kingdom of peace throughout the earth (9:8–10).[274]

Chapter 14 states that Yahweh himself will fight against the nations that attack Jerusalem. Mountains will be moved, there will be continuous day, a fountain of "living" (fresh or cleansing) water will flow through Jerusalem (14:8; cf. 13:1 and Ezek 47:1–9), and Yahweh "will become king over all the earth" (14:9).[275] No Davidic king or messiah is mentioned in chapter 14, but there are allusions to such a king in chapter 9 and perhaps chapter 12. The wealth of surrounding nations will be collected (14:14),[276] and all "the families of the earth" (cf. Gen 12:3) shall worship Yahweh in Jerusalem or else be punished if they fail to do so (14:16–19; cf. 8:22).

The intervening chapters, with several cryptic passages about shepherds and the house of David, also look for the coming redemption of Judah and perhaps Ephraim or Israel (10:7). Enemy nations will be defeated (10:11), and those that make war on Jerusalem will be destroyed (12:6–9). "On that day" (in the messianic age), Jerusalem will be cleansed of sin, people will no longer worship idols, prophecy, at least the prophecies of false prophets, will cease (13:1–5),[277] and there will be no more traders in Yahweh's temple (14:21).[278]

Malachi

The book's title means "my messenger," that is, the messenger of Yahweh. The term can also be translated as "angel," meaning one who is sent by God. It probably was taken from the reference to one so designated at 3:1, though possibly the prophet himself bore this symbolic name (or, like the figures whose words are recorded in Second and Third Isaiah, this prophet remained anonymous). The setting is Jerusalem around the middle of the fifth century B.C., slightly before the time of Nehemiah. Judah still is part of the Persian empire. The temple has been rebuilt and sacrifices are being offered but living conditions still are difficult for the Jewish people. Crops are blighted or ravaged by locusts (3:10–11; cf. Joel 1–2).

Using a "diatribe" or question-and-answer format, the prophet interprets these conditions as Yahweh's judgment against the people. Why are these bad things happening? Because men have been marrying foreign women (2:11)—a serious problem also in the eyes of Malachi's near contemporaries Nehemiah and Ezra—and they have been unfaithful to their wives, even divorcing them (2:13–16). Moreover, the Jewish people have violated certain basic horizontal covenant requirements emphasized by earlier prophets[279] and have failed to fear Yahweh and keep his commandments generally (3:5, 7; 4:4). Most of all, Malachi focuses on the fact that priests and people alike have been offering blemished sacrifices: "When you offer blind animals in sacrifice, is that no evil? And when you offer those that are lame or sick, is that no evil? Present that [sort of thing] to your governor; will he be pleased with you or show you favor?" (1:6–14). The people also have been holding back their tithes (3:8–10).

To make things right, Yahweh will send his messenger to cause the sons of Levi, still equivalent to priests, once more to present proper offerings. This messenger, the prophet warns, is coming (3:1–3). The prophet urges that once right offerings are forthcoming, Yahweh will restore the fruitfulness of fields, trees, and vines (3:4, 10–12). It is unclear whether this restoration is to mark the beginning of the messianic age. The book makes no reference to a coming Davidic king or messiah. In contrast to the preexilic prophets, but like several other postexilic writings, the book of Malachi regards the offering of sacrifices as Yahweh's central requirement. Before the time of restoration, Yahweh himself will judge those Jews who have broken the covenant (3:5). At the time of judgment, the righteous and wicked will be separated: the former to rejoice but the latter to be destroyed (3:16–4:3).[280]

The book closes with what many interpreters regard as a late addition, which promises, or warns, that Yahweh will send the prophet Elijah to preach repentance "before the great and terrible day of the LORD comes" (4:5–6).[281] Since Elijah was carried to heaven, he might also someday be sent back to earth (2 Kgs 2:11–12). In Malachi, Elijah is expected to reconcile fathers and their children (4:6). In the later traditions, his task is still more inclusive.[282] As the text of Malachi stands, Elijah seems to be identified as the messenger who is to come (3:1–2).[283] Later Jewish and Christian traditions look for Elijah as the one whose appearance will herald the advent of the messianic age. Malachi is the last of the twelve shorter prophetic writings that make up the book of the Twelve, and in many Christian Bibles immediately precedes the New Testament.[284]

NOTES

Overview

1. As previously noted, little, if anything, is known about this rabbinical meeting at Jamnia. But "Jamnia" is a useful symbol for the fact that, in due course, probably in the early centuries of the Common Era, the canon of Jewish scriptures took its present form.

2. Marcion probably could be thought of within the general framework of early gnostic Christianity. See the second essay in part I.

3. For modern translation and commentary, see James H. Charlesworth, ed., *The Old Testament Pseudepigrapha*, 2 vols. (Garden City, N.Y.: Doubleday, 1983, 1985), designated hereafter in endnotes as *OTP*.

4. Many interpreters think it likely that Deuteronomic historians edited

these writings in two stages, one around 550 and the other several decades earlier. In this book, for the sake of simplicity, this editorial process is considered to have occurred around 550.

5. Interpreters sometimes suggest that the Chronicler may have been Ezra himself.

6. The term "pseudepigrapha" means, in effect, falsely or incorrectly ascribed writings.

Genesis

1. As to P, J, and other hypothetical biblical sources or traditions, see the second essay in part I.

2. These texts have been the focal point of many recent studies concerning biblical attitudes towards other creatures and the environment. For example: Bernhard W. Anderson, *From Creation to New Creation: Old Testament Perspectives* (Minneapolis: Fortress, 1994), pp. 111–31; Douglas John Hall, *Imaging God: Dominion as Stewardship* (New York: Friendship Press, 1986); Odil Hannes Steck, *World and Environment* (Nashville: Abingdon, 1980), pp. 102–8, 194–200.

3. As to the divine names in biblical texts and translations, see the second essay in part I. "Yahweh God" appears in most English translations as "the LORD God."

4. See Phyllis Trible, *God and the Rhetoric of Sexuality* (Philadelphia: Fortress, 1978), 72–105. Trible suggests that in the J narrative, *ha adam* does not become male until woman is made from its ribs.

5. Note that this is not simply "the tree of knowledge." Although its significance is much debated, it is clear that eating its fruit marks the beginning of the end of human innocence; afterward, humans know, that is, they experience, both good and evil. The fruit in question, popularly thought of as an apple, is not specified in the Genesis story.

6. Cf. Wis 2:24, where it is said that "the devil's envy" caused death to enter the world. There is no mention of "the devil" in the Old Testament.

7. Contrary to postbiblical myth and legend, there is no suggestion in the biblical garden story that the man and woman had engaged in any—let alone illicit—sexual activity or were ejected and banished from the garden for doing so. Their reported sexual interaction occurs only after their expulsion from the garden, thereby enabling the human race to continue.

8. The later and more sophisticated P writers no doubt were aware that sacrificial offerings had not been ordained until the time of Moses, and then only for Israelites to practice.

9. Holmes Rolston, *Environmental Ethics: Duties to and Values in the Natural World* (Philadelphia: Temple University Press, 1988), 94.

10. See Richard H. Hiers, "Reverence for Life and Environmental Ethics in Biblical Law and Covenant," *Journal of Law and Religion* 13 (1996–98), 127, 134–38.

11. Interpreters often suggest that Ham must have committed some kind of perverse sexual act. More likely, he simply violated an ancient tabu, namely, seeing his father drunk and naked.

12. In later times, the episode has been invoked as justification for black slavery, apartheid, and racial segregation of blacks. There is no indication that Canaan or Canaanites were black.

13. For example, see Gen 9:28–29 (Noah); 23:1 (Sarah); 25:7 (Abraham); Job 42:16 (Job); Tob 14:11 (Tobit); 14:14 (Tobias).

14 The final clause of Gen 12:3 can equally be translated "in (or through) you all the families of the earth shall be blessed," and "all the families of the earth shall seek to be as blessed as you are." Later biblical traditions reflect these contrasting understandings of Israel's relation to other nations or peoples: as a blessing to others or as uniquely privileged as others are not. See the third essay in part I.

15. In Hebrew, the two italicized words derive from the same verbal root. It is obvious that a *shophet* should do *mishpat* in the same way that a supreme court justice should do justice.

16. Here we see an early instance of the theodicy question: How or why can Yahweh, who is righteous, do something unjust?

17. This version of the story is often thought to derive from the E tradition. In this version, Sarah's true identity is revealed to Abimelech before there is any sexual impropriety.

18. Birthright referred to the status of the son who would be considered the head of the family after his father's death. It may also have included a double share of the apportioned estate (see Deut 21:15–17).

19. Note that once the blessing had been given, it could not be rescinded or transferred.

20. See also Deut 25:5–10 and the book of Ruth.

21. The story has also inspired latter-day masterpieces. See Thomas Mann's four-volume novel, *Joseph and His Brothers* (New York: Knopf, 1938); *Young Joseph* (Knopf, 1935); *Joseph in Egypt* (Knopf, 1936); and *Joseph the Provider* (Knopf, 1944).

22. The King James Version translates the special garment as "a coat of many colors." More prosaically, the RSV and NRSV read "a long robe with sleeves." In any event, it was considered elegant apparel.

Exodus

23. This is probably from the J tradition. It evidently preserves vestiges of another primitive story about a night-time attack by some sort of supernatural being (cf. Gen 32:24–32).

24. In J, Moses speaks and God sends the plagues; in E, Moses raises his hand or rod; in P, Aaron wields the rod. The P tradition views Aaron as the father of all later priests and tends to emphasize his importance.

25. The P account is concerned with how the Passover ceremony is to be

observed in later generations, Exod 12:1–20, 40–51.

26. Ancient tradition, possibly from J, explains unleavened bread—later used in commemorating Passover—on the basis of the Israelites' hasty departure: There was no time to let the dough rise before baking it (12:39).

27. In early biblical tradition, there were only two reasons why bad things happened: human perversity (as in Genesis 3–11) and God's sometimes inscrutable ways (as in the story of Job). Later other explanations are suggested. Fate or chance is first mentioned in Ecclesiastes. A demon appears in the book of Tobit. "The devil" makes his debut only in the deuterocanonical Wisdom of Solomon.

28. Scholars generally recognize that "Red Sea" is a mistranslation. As the story is told, the Sea of Reeds appears to have been close to if not still part of Egypt. Scholars suggest that the deliverance by or from the sea may have occurred in the marshy area between Baal Zaphon and Pelusium, or Lake Sirbonis.

29. For example, see Deut 5:6; Hos 11:1; Isa 43:15–17; 51:10.

30. See B. Davie Napier, *Song of the Vineyard: A Guide through the Old Testament*, rev. ed. (Philadelphia: Fortress, 1981), 11–15.

31. In recent years, some biblical scholars, finding parallels between early Israel's experience and that of recent revolutionary movements as interpreted by liberation theology, have proposed that Israel came into existence as a movement for liberation or revolution by exploited peasants. See, for instance, Norman Gottwald, et al., *The Bible and Liberation: Political and Social Hermeneutics*, rev. ed. (Maryknoll, N.Y.: Orbis, 1993). For a contrasting interpretation, see James K. Hoffmeier, *Israel in Egypt: The Evidence for the Authenticity of the Exodus Tradition* (New York: Oxford University Press, 1997).

32. See Martin Buber, *Moses* (Oxford: East and West Library, 1946), a classic study of Moses' personality and role.

33. Biblical scholars generally identify Exod 34:10–26, sometimes called "the Ritual Decalogue," as an even earlier collection of laws.

34. For example, see Exod 21:20, 26–27; 22:21–27; 23:4–5, 9–12.

35. In traditional Judaism, the total number of commandments in the several books of the law is said to be either 613 or 623.

Leviticus
36. The first codification was the Covenant Code; the second was the Deuteronomic Code, D.

37. Cf. Exod 21:22–25; Deut 19:15–21.

38. Many scholars doubt that the jubilee year laws were ever put into effect. See, e.g., Jeffrey A. Fager, *Land Tenure and the Biblical Jubilee*, Journal for the Study of the Old Testament—Supplement Series 155 (Sheffield: Sheffield Academic Press, 1993). In any event, these laws represent what were thought to be ideal social arrangements.

39. According to the P narrative in Genesis, early humans and all other creatures originally were vegetarian (Gen 1:29–30). After the flood, humans

were permitted to eat flesh, but not "with its life, that is, its blood" (9:4). According to Acts 15:20, 29, early Christians were to abstain likewise. Abstaining from eating animals' blood could be said to represent respect or reverence for the life of these, God's creatures.

Numbers

40. See, e.g., Num 1:47–53; 3:5–37; 18:2–7.

41. See chapters 27 and 36. Cf. Job 42:15, which says that Job provided for both his sons and his daughters. On biblical laws of inheritance generally, see Richard H. Hiers, "Transfer of Property by Inheritance and Bequest in Biblical Law and Tradition," *Journal of Law and Religion* 10 (1993–94), 121–55.

42. See also Num 35:9–28; Deut 4:41–43; 19:1–10; Josh 20:1–9. These cities of refuge were places where persons who had killed someone accidentally or without malice could find sanctuary from victims' families seeking vengeance, pending further investigation and trial.

Deuteronomy

43. Cf., for instance, Deut 5:6–21 with Exod 20:2–17; Deut 22:1–4 with Exod 23:4–5; Deut 23:19–20 with Exod 22:25; Deut 24:7 with Exod 32:16; and Deut 22:28–29 with Exod 23:16–17. However, most of the laws found in the Covenant Code are not repeated in D, and most of the laws found in D appear there for the first time.

44. See Deut 27; Josh 8:30–35; 24:1–28.

45. See, e.g., Judg 17:7–13; 1 Sam 2:12–17; 9:12–13; 14:33–35.

46. See 2 Kgs 22:1–23:25. Some scholars suggest that the roots of the Deuteronomic Reform go back to the time of Judah's King Hezekiah, late in the eighth century B.C. There is also some debate among scholars as to whether the Deuteronomic Reform resulted in the new legislation found in Deuteronomy 12–19 and 26, or whether this legislation, when discovered or acknowledged, resulted in the Deuteronomic Reform.

47. See, e.g., Deut 30:15–20 and 32:45–47.

48. Cf. Jacob's blessing of his sons and, implicitly, the tribes named for them (Genesis 49).

Joshua

49. Many interpreters consider it likely that the Deuteronomic editors wrote in two phases, initially some decades earlier, and then again around 550 B.C.

50. See Josh 10:40–42; 11:21–23.

51. Key theological terms here are italicized. See Josh.1:13–15; 11:23; 21:43–45; 23:1, 14.

52. See, e.g., Josh 11:22; 13:2–7, 13; 15:63; 16:10. See also Judg 1:27–36 and Num 33:55.

53. The conquest theory is advocated most notably by the late William F. Albright, John Bright, and George Ernest Wright; the gradual settlement theory

by Albrecht Alt and Martin Noth. Archeological evidence indicates the destruction of many Canaanite cities in the thirteenth century B.C. but does not show that such destruction was caused by Israelites.

54. See, e.g., Josh 17:11–18; 19:47; Judges 1.

55. See, e.g., Josh 10:28–40; 11:10–20; see also 23:11–13 (a caution against marriage with indigenous nations or peoples). To what extent the *herem* was practiced in ancient times is uncertain. Some accounts may have been exaggerated by DH in order to underscore for contemporary readers the importance of worshiping Yahweh only.

56. Cf. characteristic sermons or admonitions in Deuteronomy (e.g., Deut 6:10–15; 7:1–11; 8:11–20; 11:8–16) and the Deuteronomic formula or "theology of history" spelled out in Judg 2:11–19.

57. Cf. Num 27:1–11, which sets up an order of heirs to inherited property when a man dies without surviving sons. In Numbers, it is clear that in that circumstance, daughters, if any, inherit the estate. Neither the Joshua nor the Numbers text mentions inheritance by widows.

58. See also Josh 21:1 (an additional city); 21:21, 27, 32 and 38. Cf. Num 35:9–34; Deut 4:41–43; 19:1–13.

59. What the ark looked like, what it contained, and what later became of it are matters for speculation. See Graham Hancock, *The Sign and the Seal: A Quest for the Lost Ark of the Covenant* (London: Heinemann, 1992).

60. Archeological evidence suggests that Jericho was last destroyed ca. 3000 B.C., long before the time of Joshua, so some interpreters propose that the story originally had to do with another city conquered by Israel.

61. Glimpses of this ancient, possibly annual, ceremony may also be seen in Josh 24:1–28 and Deuteronomy 27. Ezra's reading of the law before a gathered assembly in Jerusalem many centuries later (Neh 8:1–12) may have been modeled upon this early Israelite covenant renewal observance.

62. Shiloh was an Israelite religious and political center again during the time of Eli (1 Samuel 1 and 4). Shechem's significance was underscored by the transfer and burial of Joseph's remains (Josh 24:32). It also had been the site of a vicious attack by two of Jacob's sons (Genesis 34).

63. See also Deut 6:20–23; 26:5–9.

Judges

64. The Deuteronomic historian, writing and editing during the time of the exile (ca. 550 B.C.), looked back on Israel's earlier history, trying to make sense of its meaning.

65. See also 1 Sam 8:4–18, which may reflect Israel's experience of oppression under Solomon's reign as king.

66. See Phyllis Trible, *Texts of Terror* (Philadelphia: Fortress, 1984), 93–116, which empathetically reflects on this tragedy from the daughter's perspective.

67. See also 1 Sam 13:19–22.

68. As to the initial atrocity described in Judges 19, see Trible, *Texts of Terror*, 65–91.

Ruth

69. *Levir* is a Latin term for brother-in-law.

70. But see Numbers 12 and Judg 14:1–3.

71. Some commentators suggest otherwise, proposing instead, for instance, that the underlying law concerns redemption of land as in Lev 25:25–28. See Raymond Westbrook, "Redemption of Land," *Israel Law Review* 6 (1971): 367, 373–75.

72. The family moved temporarily to Moab because of famine in the land of Judah. Today, they would be considered economic refugees. In earlier times, Jacob and his family had moved to Egypt during a period of famine (Genesis 46–47).

73. Nothing in these verses indicates that the hypothetical husband Naomi refers to would have had to be a kinsman of her deceased husband. Arguably, these verses and other texts in Ruth, such as 1:16–17 and 4:15, point to close bonding between Naomi and her daughters-in-law as basis for what follows. Thus, these texts do not necessarily implicate levirate marriage.

74. See Ruth 2:3: "She happened to come to the part of the field belonging to Boaz." But compare 2:2, where Ruth says to Naomi, "Let me go to the field, and glean among the ears of grain after him in whose sight I shall find favor." It appears that Ruth was looking for a suitable husband.

75. There is no indication otherwise that Naomi was actually selling such a parcel of land or that Boaz subsequently purchased it.

76. David Daube, a noted Jewish legal scholar, suggests that Boaz intimated that the nearer kinsman would have to marry Naomi, the senior widow. See David Daube, *Ancient Jewish Law* (Leiden: Brill, 1981), 39.

77. It is not entirely clear how marrying Ruth (or Naomi) would have "impaired" the nearer kinsman's inheritance. See Daube, *Ancient Jewish Law*, 40–41.

78. Some interpreters suggest that removing the sandal may have been simply part of standard land transaction formalities. See Ruth 4:7.

79. For example, see Ezra 9–10; Neh 13:23–31; Add Esth 14:15.

1 Samuel

80. See Judg 15:11.

81. See 1 Sam 8:1–3; 2:12.

82. See also 1 Sam 11:14–15.

83. But see 2 Sam 21:19, where a certain Elhanan is credited with having killed Goliath (cf. 1 Chr 20:5).

84. We see here an instance of what has come in more recent times to be known as "the protection racket," a source of revenue popular in Mafia circles.

2 Samuel
85. Cf. 1 Chr 21:1, which credits Satan with inspiring this census.

1 Kings
86. See, e.g., 1 Kgs 15:9–15, 33–34; 22:41–46.
87. See, e.g., Judg 8:22–23; 1 Sam 8:4–18.
88. In Canaanite religion, Baal was the god of rain, fertility, and life.
89. Evidently, when a man was charged with treason under ancient Near Eastern common law, his property would escheat to the state rather than pass to his heirs. See Raymond Westbrook, *Property and the Family in Biblical Law* (Sheffield: JSOT Press, 1991).

2 Kings
90. These are generally printed in appendices to modern study Bibles.
91. The images of entering heaven by crossing the Jordan or by means of a heavenly chariot in spirituals from the American South may derive partly from this scene and partly from Israel's crossing the Jordan on its way to the promised land (Joshua 31).
92. See Mal 4:5–6; Sir 48:1–11; Matt 17:10–12.
93. See 2 Kgs 10:32–33; 13:22.
94. See Julius Wellhausen, *Prolegomena to the History of Ancient Israel* (New York: Macmillan, 1957), 32–34. This classic study was first published in 1878.
95. See 1 and 2 Maccabees.

1 Chronicles
96. This chronological flashback or overlap may be explained as resulting from the Chronicler's concern to complete his genealogical lists, which continue into the postexilic period. His more substantial historical narrative begins in chapter 10 with a summary of Saul's final moments.
97. It is unclear whether Satan was thought of here as a member of Yahweh's heavenly council, acting only under Yahweh's authority (as in the book of Job and 1 Kgs 22:19–23), or as an independent evil being of some sort, like "the devil" in Wis 2:24.
98. Cf. 2 Sam 24:18–25 (*fifty silver* shekels).

2 Chronicles
99. See, e.g., 2 Chr 20:14–19; 23:4–7; 29:34; 34:12–13.
100. Wellhausen, *Prolegomena to the History*, 215.
101. Manasseh reigned for fifty-five years, according to 2 Chr 33:1 and 2 Kgs 21:1.
102. None of the contemporary, that is, mid to late sixth century B.C. sources report that Cyrus intended to assist in rebuilding the temple, much less rebuild it himself. See, e.g., Isaiah 40–66, Haggai, and Zechariah.

Ezra

103. See, e.g., Ezra 7:11, 12, 21; Neh 8:1–2, 4, 9. Ezra also figures prominently in 1 and 2 Esdras, in the Old Testament Apocrypha.

104. The first collection is the Tetrateuch, or first four books, edited under priestly auspices; the second is the Deuteronomic History, comprising Deuteronomy, Joshua, Judges, 1 and 2 Samuel, and 1 and 2 Kings.

105. The earliest such usage is in Jer 38:19.

Nehemiah

106. The office of royal cupbearer apparently was an important position, lest anyone attempt to poison the king. Here the cupbearer also seems to have been the king's confidant.

107. See Deuteronomy 27; Josh 8:30–35; 24:1–28.

Job

108. The book of Job, particularly its prologue and epilogue, reads like, and has been performed as, a theatrical play. The famous, modern, somewhat secular, existentialist reinterpretation of Job, of course, is Archibald MacLeish's *J. B.: A Play in Verse* (New York: S. French, 1958), for which MacLeish received a Pulitzer Prize the following year.

109. Job 1:1–5, 8, 22; 2:10; 29:11–17; 31:1–40.

110. See Job 24:18–25; 27:7–23; and perhaps 26:5–14.

111. Some annotators and commentators agree. But see Job 1:1, 8, and 2:3, where the narrator (and Yahweh) characterize Job as "blameless and upright," and Job 42:7, where, at the end, Yahweh tells Job's "friends" that, unlike them, Job has spoken rightly of Yahweh.

112. Neither Job nor the other human participants in the story know what is going on behind the scenes—namely, Yahweh's wager with Satan. The masterfully dramatic prologue reveals this background to the reader, who thereby is all the more enabled to appreciate Job's quandry and his "friends'" self-serving and fatuous responses. Surprisingly, modern commentators, like Elihu, sometimes forget or ignore the prologue and feel obliged to explain that somehow Job really did something wrong and so deserved to be treated as he was.

113. See, e.g., Job 9:14–19; 23:2–7; 31:35.

114. See, e.g., Job 5:8; 8:5–7; 11:13–20; 22:21–30.

115. See Gene M. Tucker, "Rain on a Land Where No One Lives: The Hebrew Bible on the Environment," *Journal of Biblical Literature* 116 (1997): 3–17. This theme comes to classic expression in Sir 18:13.

116. Job's righteousness is also exemplified by his providing an inheritance for his daughters as well as for his sons (42:15). Cf. Num 27:1–12, where property passes to daughters under intestate succession only if there are no sons.

117. Cf. Isa 40:2, where the prophet tells the exiles that they have already received double for their iniquities.

118. The prospect of resurrection is rarely indicated in the Old Testament: It is hinted at, perhaps, in Ezek 37:1–14 and Isa 25:8, but explicitly anticipated only in Isa 26:19 and Dan 12:2.

119. Satan is not yet a cosmic principality or even a minor evil being, but only a particularly zealous prosecuting attorney in Yahweh's court, in effect, Yahweh's attorney general. He appears only two other times in the Old Testament: 1 Chr 21:1; Zech 3:1–2. There is no mention of "the devil" in the Old Testament; cf. Wis 2:24.

Psalms

120. But see Ps 151 in the Apocrypha. The Dead Sea Scrolls and other early sources include four additional psalms, numbered 152–155. See also *OTP* 2:612–24 for additional texts, translations, and commentary.

121. The Pseudepigrapha includes an entire book captioned "The Psalms of Solomon." See *OTP* 2:639–70.

122. For these and other notations, see the RSV, NRSV, and REB; they are omitted in the NEB.

123. See also the three repeated refrains in the psalms found in the Prayer of Azariah and the Song of the Three Young Men.

124. For example, Ps 53 duplicates Ps 14, and Ps 108 evidently is based on Pss 57:7–11 and 60:5–12.

125. According to Matt 27:46 and Mark 15:34, Jesus began to pray in the words of Ps 22 as he was being crucified.

126. For instance, see Pss 13; 35; 54; 56; 71.

127. For instance, see Pss 74; 79; 137; see also the book of Lamentations.

128. For instance, see Pss 9; 18; 30; 98; 116.

129. For instance, see Pss 95; 104; 147; 148.

130. See also Ps 145:9: "Yahweh is good to all, and his compassion is over all that he has made." Cf. Sir 18:13: "The compassion of man is for his neighbor, but the compassion of the Lord is for all living things."

131. See, e.g., Pss 1; 37; 49; 112. These psalms express themes typically found (or questioned) in such biblical wisdom writings as Job, Proverbs, Ecclesiastes, and Sirach.

132. See, e.g., Pss 15; 32; 52; 62; 81; 128.

133. See, e.g., Pss 91; 100; 121; 125.

134. See, e.g., Pss 48; 84; 87; 122; 132.

135. See Deuteronomy 12 and 16.

136. See Pss 40:6; 50:9–15, 23; 51:16–17; 69:30–31; 141:2.

137. See Pss 20:3; 50:8; 51:19; 66:13–15.

138. See Pss 67; 87 (NEB); 117; 148; 150.

Proverbs

139. Other biblical wisdom writings or sayings may be found in Job, Psalms, Ecclesiastes, Tobit, the Wisdom of Solomon, and Sirach.

140. Notable examples in biblical times are found in Babylonian, Edomite, and Egyptian traditions. Jeremiah refers to "wise men," possibly functionaries or consultants in the royal court (Jer 8:8–9). The Gospel of Matthew refers to "wise men from the East" (Matt 2:1). Rabbis were sometimes known as "sages." Wisdom sayings have been collected in many other cultures: for example, Ghana, Spain, and, in early America, Benjamin Franklin's "Poor Richard's Almanac."

141. In Prov 8:22–31, *Hochmah* is represented as Yahweh's first creation, present with him "at the beginning," if not assisting in the creation and ordering of the world. Later New Testament texts sometimes ascribe a similar role to Jesus or Christ (John 1:1–3; Col 1:15–17; and Heb 1:2–3).

142. See, e.g., Prov 30:15–16, 24–28, 29–30.

143. See, e.g., Prov 25:20; 26:20–21; 30:21–23, 33.

144. See, e.g., Prov 17:28; 25:6–7; 26:17–19; 27:2.

145. See, e.g., Prov 15:22; 20:18; 29:4, 12, 14; 31:4–5.

146. See, e.g., Prov 5:1–23; 6:23–35; 7:6–27; 23:26–28.

147. See also Prov 6:6–11; 12:24; 15:19; 20:4. It is likely that the so-called Protestant work ethic derives from the biblical book of Proverbs.

148. See, e.g., Prov 14:31; 19:17; 28:27; 29:7; 31:8–9.

149. See Prov 21:9, 19; 25:24; 27:15–16.

150. See Prov 13:24; 22:15; 23:13–14; 29:15.

151. See, e.g., Prov 2:21–22; 3:9–10; 11:17–21; 12:7, 21; 15:6; 22:8–9.

152. See, e.g., Prov 10:8; 19:16; 28:7; 29:18.

153. See Prov 14:31; 22:22–23; 23:10–11.

154. See Prov 19:26; 20:20; 23:22.

Ecclesiastes

155. See also Eccl 6:8: "For what advantage has the wise man over the fool?"

156. Interpreters sometimes suggest that Qoheleth could be considered a prototypical nihilist existentialist or postmodernist deconstructionist.

157. Qoheleth's pessimism regarding human nature possibly echoes the J tradition's characterization of humankind before the flood in Gen 6:5. See also 2 Esdr 7:116–120.

158. Cf. Qoheleth's sardonic comment at 10:19: "Money answers everything."

159. See Job 42:1–6.

160. See Eccl 3:14; 5:7; 7:18; 12:13.

Song of Solomon (or Canticles)

161. Cf. Hosea 2.

162. Other wedding songs or recitations may be found in Ruth 4:11–12, Jer 33:11, and Tob 8:5–6, 15–17. See also Ps 45:10–17.

163. Song 2:7; 3:5; 8:4; cf. 5:8.

164. See, e.g., Gen 1:1–31; Pss 104; 145; 148; and Isaiah 40.

165. See, e.g., Gen 2:23–24; 29:10–11; Deut 24:5; Tob 8:4–8.

Isaiah

166. See, e.g., Isa 1; 3:11–15; 5:1–23.

167. See Isa 5:26–30; 7:10–8:8; 10:1–9.

168. See Isa 2:2; 11:10; 19:19–25.

169. This remarkable passage picks up a basic theme in Yahweh's promise to Abraham: that his descendants would "be a blessing" in whom "all the families of the earth shall be blessed" (Gen 12:1–3). Compare the perspective of the narrator in the story of Jonah.

170. See Isa 7:10, 14; 20:2–6; 37:30; 38:7–8.

171. Cf. "Immanuel" (Isa 7:14–17; 8:5–8).

172. Cf. Isa 11:6–9; Hos 2:18.

173. See Isa 48:20; 49:9; 52:11–12; 55:12.

174. See Isa 43:15–17; 44:24, 27; 51:10–11.

175. See Isa 43:4; 49:15; 54:8, 10. Cf. Deut 7:7; 10:15.

176. See, e.g., Wis 13:1–15:17; Letter of Jeremiah; Bel and the Dragon.

177. Christian interpreters often read these texts as prophetic references to Jesus' role as Messiah or Christ.

178. Cf. Hag 2:6–7; Zech 14:14.

179. See also Isa 1:3; 7:14; 9:1–7.

180. See Isa 56:3–8; 66:23; cf. 19:19–25.

181. Cf. Ps 50:9–15; see also Ps 40:6–8.

182. Cf. Jdt 16:17; Mark 9:43–49.

183. Cf. 1 Cor 15:52–54.

Jeremiah

184. See 2 Kgs 24:18–25:30.

185. This time, patriotic princes drop Jeremiah into a cistern, leaving him to sink into the mire, but he is rescued, under King Zedekiah's orders, by an Ethiopian and others. Later, Zedekiah gives Jeremiah protection and secretly seeks his advice (38:4–28).

186. See Jer 6:13–14; 8:10–11; 23:9–32.

187. See Jer 11:18–20; 18:19–23; 20:7–12.

188. See Jer 2:20–28; 17:12–13, 26; 19:4–5.

189. See Jer 6:20; 7:21–23 but also 33:18–22—possibly a later addition—which endorses sacrificial offerings by "the Levitical priests".

190. Cf. Neh 13:15–22.

191. See Isa 8:16, which orders that the prophet's testimony be preserved among his "disciples."

192. Like Isaiah of Jerusalem, Jeremiah sometimes assures his contemporaries that a new king or messiah from the house of David would again rule over Yahweh's people (see Jer 23:5–6; 30:8–9; cf. Isa 9:2–7; 11:1–10).

193. See, e.g., Jer 50:29; 51:5; cf. Isa 5:24; 10:20.

Lamentations

194. See, e.g., Lam 1:13; 2:14, 22; 3:14, 48.

195. Several psalms in the book of Psalms express similar anguish and longing for deliverance (see, e.g, Pss 44; 59; 74; 79).

196. In Lam 5:7, the writer urges that these catastrophes were to be understood as punishment for the sins of the "fathers." Cf. Jer 16:10–13, where the prophet insists that his contemporaries "have done worse than [their] fathers." See also Jer 31:29–30 and Ezek 18:1–32.

197. See, e.g., Isa 10:1–11; Jer 5:1–6:26; 9:1–11; Ezek 5:1–6:27.

198. Deut 8:11–20; 2 Kgs 24:1–4, 20.

199. See Lam 1:21–22; 5:21; cf. Pss 74; 79.

Ezekiel

200. See Ezek 2:1–3:11; cf. the calls of Isaiah (Isa 6:1–13) and Jeremiah (Jer 1:1–10) to their respective prophetic missions.

201. See Deuteronomy 12–19; 2 Kings 22–23.

202. Cf. Jer 5:1–5; Gen 18:17–33.

203. Some interpreters consider that Ezekiel may have meant here to express hope for the resurrection of the dead. Job 19:25–27 is sometimes interpreted similarly. Isaiah 26:19 and Dan 12:2 refer explicitly to the resurrection of the dead.

204. Cf. Rev 22:10, 12, 18–20.

205. Cf. Ps 137, whose author did not believe that the Jewish exiles could worship Yahweh in a foreign land, and Jonah, who tried to escape Yahweh's presence by sailing to Tarshish (Jonah 1–4).

206. Cf. Jer 31:29–31; Lam 5:7; Exod 34:6–7; Deut 24:16.

207. See, e.g., Joel 3:1–17, 19; and the books of Obadiah and Nahum.

208. See Ezek 40:46–47; 43:18–19; 44:15–16.

209. See Ezek 47:7–12; cf. the tree[s] of life in Rev 22:1–2.

210. See, e.g., Isa 25:6; Joel 3:18; Amos 9:13; *2 Apoc Bar* 29:4–5; and in the Talmud, *Shabbat* 30b.

211. See, e.g., Matt 26:29; Luke 13:29; Rev 2:7.

212. See, e.g., Isa 11:10; 19:19–25; 25:6–7; 49:6; Jer 48:47; 49:6; Mic 4:1–4; and Zech 14:16–19.

Daniel

213. See, e.g., Dan 7:19–21; 8:11–13; 12:11; cf. 1 Macc 1:20–23, 41–50, 54–64. According to 1 Maccabees, Antiochus IV attempted to induce his Jewish subjects to adopt Greek culture and worship pagan deities; moreover, he issued orders banning traditional practices including circumcision, Sabbath observance, and possession of Jewish law books, and arranged for the desecration of the Jerusalem temple.

214. Judith and Esther (in the Additions to Esther) also keep kosher, that is, refrain from eating gentile food.

215. This angel is unnamed. Two named angels, Gabriel and Michael, appear briefly in Daniel 8–10 as interpreters or agents of divine revelation and redemption.

216. See Dan 4:3, 17, 25–26; 5:18–28.

217. Dan 2:31–44; 7:14, 18–27; 8:3–25.

218. See Joel 2:30–31; Zech 14:1–5; Add Esth 11:59; Mark 13:8, 14–19.

219. See also Isa 26:19. Cf. Wis 3:1–9, assuring readers that the souls of the righteous are immortal.

Hosea

220. The notable exception is the book of Jonah, which consists largely of a story or parable about that rather peculiar prophet.

221. See Judg 8:22–23; 1 Sam 8:4–7.

222. See Hos 3:13; 4:9; 8:13b; 9:7, 9; 12:2.

223. See Hos 1:4; 9:12–16; 13:1–9, 14, 16.

224. Cf. Isa 11:6–9; 65:20–25. See also Gen 9:8–17, as to the primordial covenant with "every living creature" "for all generations."

Joel

225. See Ps 137:7; Obad 10–14.

226. Imagery referring to "a devouring enemy nation" (1:6–7; 2:4–11, 20) probably symbolizes the great plague of locusts described in 1:4.

227. Here, as in other biblical texts, both domestic animals and wildlife look to Yahweh for care and call upon him for food and other needs. See, e.g., Job 38:39–41; 39:5–8; Pss 104:10–14, 16–18, 24–30; 136:25; 145:9–16; 147:9.

228. See Joel 1:15; 2:1–2, 11; cf. Amos 5:18–20.

229. Before the exile, the prophets looked for divine judgment mainly in the form of oppression or defeat at the hands of foreign nations. After the exile, the Jewish people were already under foreign domination. Yahweh's judgment then was more often expected in the form of crop failure or other agricultural and economic disasters. See, e.g., Hag 1:10–11 and Mal 3:10–11 (if the people return to Yahweh, he will mitigate or put an end to such disasters).

230. Cf. Exod 34:6; Neh 9:17; Ps 145:8; Jonah 4:2.

231. Cf. Isa 11:10; 25:6; Ezek 47:22–23; Zech 14:16–19.

232. Cf. Matt 25:31–46, where nations will be gathered for judgment but the fate of individuals will depend on what each has done or failed to do.

Amos

233. Israel here means the Northern Kingdom, also referred to in Amos as Samaria, Joseph, Isaac, and Jacob.

234. Note the remarkable reference in 1:9 to Tyre's offense in delivering "up a whole people to Edom": They "did not remember the covenant of brotherhood."

235. Amos 5:21–24 is often cited as representing the core or essential message of the classical prophets.

236. See Amos 5:2; 8:12; 9:1–4, 8a–b.

237. See Jer 33:14–16; Ezek 37:24–25.

Obadiah

238. See, e.g., Ps 137:7; Jer 49:7–22; Lam 4:21–22; Ezek 25:12–14; Joel 3:19.

239. Cf. Amos 1:3–2:8.

240. See also Ezra 9:8; Zech 2:12; Wis 12:3; 2 Macc 1:7.

241. See also Isa 25:6–7; 49:6.

Jonah

242. In 722/21 B.C., Assyria had overrun the Northern Kingdom, Israel, and for more than a hundred years afterward generally dominated the Southern Kingdom, Judah. The story of Jonah may have been written as late as the third or second century B.C. "Assyria" may have been meant to represent other foreign nations that ruled over the Jewish people in these later times.

243. Cf. Ps 137:4: "How shall we sing the LORD's song in a foreign land?"

244. Cf. Amos 5:6: "Seek Yahweh and live, lest he break out like fire in the house of Joseph" or Jer 7:5: "For if you truly amend your ways and your doings, . . . then I will let you dwell in this place."

245. Cf. Exod 34:6; Neh 9:17; Joel 2:13. Commentators sometimes suggest that Jonah was angry because he was embarrassed since the people of Nineveh laughed at him because his prophecy of doom was not fulfilled. There is no basis whatsoever for that theory. Jonah was angry because Yahweh did not destroy Nineveh.

246. See, e.g., Gen 6:19–20; 8:1, 15–19; 9:8–17; Exod 20:10 or Deut 5:14; Exod 23:4–5; Lev 25:6–7; Deut 22:1–4; Job 39:5–6; Pss 50:9–12; 104:10–14, 16–18, 26; Isa 65:25; Hos 2:18.

247. Cf. Tob 14:4, 8, which view Jonah's prophecy as simply foretelling Nineveh's eventual destruction.

248. Jonah's attitude represents an excellent example of what H. Richard Niebuhr characterizes as henotheistic or tribal faith. See H. Richard Niebuhr, *Radical Monotheism and Western Culture* (Louisville, Ky.: Westminster John Knox, 1993).

Micah

249. See, e.g., Mic 2:12–13; 4:6–10; 5:2–4; and possibly 7:8–20.

250. Micah also condemns the Northern Kingdom for its offenses (1:1, 5–7).

251. Cf. 2 Kgs 22:6, 11–12; Jer 28:1–17.

252. Cf. Isa 1:11–17; Amos 5:21–24. Mic 6:6–8 is often considered a classic summary of the message of the classical prophets. See also Amos 5:21–24.

253. See Jeremiah 26.

254. See 2 Kings 25.

255. See Mic 4:11–13; 5:7–9; 7:8–10, 15–17.

Nahum

256. This double preposition in the RSV translation nicely renders the grammatical construction and flavor of the Hebrew text.

257. Jonah himself, as represented in the book of Jonah, would share Nahum's delight in Nineveh's destruction.

Habakkuk

258. See also Ezek 1:1 and Obad 1:1.

259. Parts of Malachi, 2 Esdras, and James have a similar structure.

260. Cf. Ezek 12:21–28; 2 Esdr 4:26–52.

261. Cf. Isa 5:8–23; Luke 6:24–26.

262. See also Hos 2:18–23; 1 Cor 13:8–12.

Zephaniah

263. Prophetic and especially apocalyptic biblical writings generally look for the fulfillment of their warnings or promises in their contemporaries' near future.

264. These include the Philistines (2:4–7), Moab and Ammon (2:8–12), Ethiopia (2:12), and Assyria—especially its capital, Nineveh (2:12–15), which will be turned into a wildlife refuge (2:14–15).

265. The Genesis verses say that Abraham's descendants "will be a blessing," but Gen 12:3b can be read to mean either that in (or through) Abraham "all the families of the earth shall be blessed" or that other nations shall "bless themselves," that is, wish that they enjoyed the same kind of status, prosperity, and other blessings as Abraham's descendants.

266. See Zeph 3:17; Hos 2:19. Cf. Hos 11:1 and Deut 10:15, referring to Yahweh's love for Israel in the past.

Haggai

267. This text appears to echo the Song of Miriam/Moses (Exod 15:1, 21).

268. The high (or chief) priest is referred to a few times in Chronicles (2 Chr 19:11; 26:20) and in the P tradition (Num 35:25, 28, 32), but these texts generally are dated after the time of Haggai.

269. The same understanding is found also in Zechariah, Malachi, and Joel.

270. See, e.g., Isa 1:10–17; Jer 7:21–23; Amos 5:21–25.

271. See Deuteronomy 12–19.

Zechariah

272. See 1 Chr 3:16–19.

273. See 1 Chr 21:1; Job 1:6–12; 2:1–7.

274. This messianic prophecy may have been enacted with Jesus' entry into Jerusalem, as noted in Mark 11:1–10 and John 12:12–15. Cf. Matt 21:5, which evidently read Zech 9:9 as visualizing the messianic king riding two animals at the same time. See also Gen 49:8–12, which evidently associated a messianic figure with an ass's colt.

275. The concept of God's kingdom, relatively rare in the Old Testament, also comes to expression in Obad 21.

276. See also Isa 60:5–7; Hag 2:6–8.

277. Cf. 1 Cor 13:8.

278. Cf. Mark 12:15–17 and parallels in the other New Testament Gospels.

Malachi

279. These include committing adultery, swearing falsely, oppressing workers, widows and orphans, and failing to do justice to sojourners.

280. Cf. Daniel 12, which also looks for the judgment of individuals.

281. Cf. similar language in Joel 2:31b.

282. Cf. Sir 48:9–10; Mark 9:11–12.

283. In Jewish Bibles, the verses found in Malachi 4 in Christian Bibles are all part of chapter 3. Thus in Jewish scriptures (the Hebrew Bible) the connection between Elijah, named at the end of chapter 3, with the messenger named at its beginning is more apparent.

284. The New Testament begins with the Gospel of Matthew. Here Elijah plays a significant role. John the Baptist sends his disciples to Jesus to ask whether he is the "one who is to come" (Matt 11:2–3). Jesus afterward explains that John himself "is Elijah who is to come" (Matt 11:14); see also Matt 17:10–13. See Alan R. Culpepper, *John, The Son of Zebedee: The Life of a Legend* (Minneapolis: Fortress, 2000); John A. T. Robinson, *Twelve New Testament Studies* (London: SCM Press, 1962); and W. Barnes Tatum, *John the Baptist and Jesus* (Sonoma, Calif.: Polebridge, 1994).

PART III
The Old Testament Apocrypha, or Deuterocanonicals

OVERVIEW

The Greek Bible commonly used by Jews from around 200 B.C. to around A.D. 100 and by Christians during the first several centuries A.D. included a number of writings that eventually were excluded from Jewish and Protestant Bibles. From these writings come all but a few of those designated in the aggregate as the Apocrypha in modern editions of the Bible. To be more precise, one should specify these writings as the "Old Testament Apocrypha," since there is also a voluminous literature known as the "New Testament Apocrypha."[1] The latter is not included in any modern version of the Bible. In Catholic Bibles, writings here designated as the Old Testament Apocrypha are known instead as "Deuterocanonical" books and considered authoritative. The Old Testament apocryphal writings that derive from the old Greek Bible (or Septuagint, as it is often called on the basis of the legend that it was translated verbatim into Greek from the Hebrew by seventy [*septuaginta*] scholars in seventy days)[2] include the following: 1 Esdras (also known as 3 Ezra), Tobit, Judith, the Additions to Esther, the Wisdom of Solomon, Ecclesiasticus (or Sirach), Baruch, the Letter of Jeremiah, the Prayer of Azariah and the Song of the Three Young Men, Susanna, Bel and the Dragon, the Prayer of Manasseh, and 1 and 2 Maccabees. Most of these constitute separate "books," but some were incorporated into other Old Testament writings, namely, Esther and Daniel.

Second Esdras (also known as 4 Ezra) was not included in the Septuagint but was found in the Old Latin translation of it (ca. A.D. 200) and was included by Jerome in his Latin edition of the Bible, the Vulgate (ca. A.D. 390). Fourth Ezra is sometimes included in scholarly editions of the Old Testament Pseudepigrapha. Jerome evidently was the first to use the term "Apocrypha" (meaning "hidden") to designate those writings that, in his time, were known in Greek or Latin but not in Hebrew texts. In prefaces before each, he suggested to readers that the apocryphal writings were not on a par as to antiquity or authority with the biblical writings known in Hebrew. Later editions of the

Vulgate—copied by hand, of course, until the age of printing—included the apocryphal writings but often omitted Jerome's qualifying prefaces. For more than a thousand years, the Vulgate was the standard Bible of Western Christianity.

Renaissance scholarship and religious concerns of the Protestant reformers occasioned further doubts about the weight to be accorded the apocryphal writings. For a variety of reasons, Martin Luther decided in 1534 that although they were "useful and good to read," the apocryphal books were not "held equal to the Scriptures." But Luther included most of the apocryphal books in his German Bible published that same year. He omitted only 3 and 4 Esdras and 3 and 4 Maccabees. Luther's Bible evidently was the first to place the apocryphal books as a group after the other Old Testament writings.[3] All later branches of Protestantism have followed Luther's more restricted canon. At the Council of Trent in 1546, however, the Roman Catholic Church reaffirmed the canonical status of the Apocrypha, except for 1 and 2 Esdras and the Prayer of Manasseh. The official versions of the Vulgate's Old Testament since Trent end with 1 and 2 Maccabees but add the Prayer of Manasseh and 1 and 2 Esdras in an appendix placed after the New Testament.

The Eastern Orthodox churches likewise maintained a more inclusive Old Testament canon, with some further additions. Thus, the Eastern churches at present include 3 Maccabees and Psalm 151 (which were in some versions of the Septuagint and other ancient texts but not in the Vulgate), as well as 1 Esdras, and some also include the Prayer of Manasseh and 2 Esdras. In Russian Orthodox Bibles, 1 and 2 Esdras are designated as 2 and 3 Esdras, respectively. Since the seventeenth century, the Apocrypha of the Eastern churches has consisted of Tobit, Judith, Wisdom of Solomon, and Sirach.

The apocryphal books do not appear at all, of course, in the old Hebrew or modern Jewish Bibles. Catholic Bibles include most of the apocryphal books. Those designated deuterocanonical are considered fully scriptural, and generally are found in the same locations or sequences as in the Greek Old Testament.[4] Those designated apocryphal—1 and 2 Esdras, and the Prayer of Manasseh—are not considered fully canonical and ordinarily appear in a separate section at the back of Catholic Bibles. Catholic Bibles do not include 3 and 4 Maccabees or Psalm 151 at all.[5]

Until 1827, editions of the King James Version (KJV) of the Bible usually included the Old Testament Apocrypha, and located it either between the Old Testament and the New Testament or following the

New Testament.[6] Uncertainty over where to place the Apocrypha is reflected in the fact that many modern Bibles omit it altogether, while some place it between the Old Testament and the New Testament, and others after the New Testament. Some editions of the RSV and NRSV include not only 3 but also 4 Maccabees, which was in some editions of the Septuagint and other ancient versions but has not been included in either the Vulgate or Eastern canons. Some also include Psalm 151. Thus it can be seen that the Apocrypha is still a somewhat open if not fluid category; this is true both in religious and scholarly circles.

1 Esdras

This writing is known in the Vulgate and Catholic Bibles generally as 3 Esdras but in Eastern Orthodox Bibles as 2 Esdras. The present nomenclature derives from the fact that in the Septuagint,[7] Ezra and Nehemiah constitute a single book (1 Esdras), whereas in the Vulgate, our present Ezra is named 1 Esdras and Nehemiah is called 2 Esdras. The Greek name Esdras was and still is generally used in the title, instead of the Hebrew name, Ezra, which, however, has always appeared in the text (chaps. 8–9). Other important Judahite and Jewish leaders are remembered in this book with considerable appreciation, especially Josiah and Zerubbabel. But Ezra "the priest and reader of the law" is the most prominent figure in the book which is, appropriately, named for him.

Most of the book parallels and apparently borrows substantially from portions of 2 Chronicles, Ezra, and Nehemiah. The main piece of new material is the story of three bodyguards and the Persian king Darius (3:1–5:3), which serves to introduce Zerubbabel, who later becomes governor over the Jewish people under Persian rule.[8]

As this story is told, the three bodyguards plan a contest in order to entertain King Darius and induce him to bestow wealth and honors upon one of their number. Each presents, for the king to judge, his written statement and oral argument about "what one thing is strongest." In turn, they argue persuasively for the relative strengths of wine, the king, women, and truth. The case for truth may have been a later addition to the story. In the present account, Zerubbabel gets two shots at the prize by arguing both for women (4:13–32) and truth (4:33–40). Here, truth—a Greek value or virtue—is linked with God, for example, in Zerubbabel's summary exclamation, "Blessed be the God of truth!" The assembled crowd shouts in reply—and in unison— the famous line, "Great is truth, and strongest of all" (4:41). Zerubbabel is then named contest winner and granted his desire, which is that he be authorized to go to Jerusalem and rebuild the city and the temple.[9] In addition, Darius issues edicts granting special privileges to all Jews who now return to Judea, expelling Idumeans (Edomites) from villages claimed by Jews, and authorizing expenditures to pay for rebuilding Jerusalem, constructing the new temple, and providing a series of burnt offerings.

The rest of 1 Esdras consists largely of material drawn from portions of 2 Chronicles, Ezra, and Nehemiah. The writer is particularly interested in traditions concerning the temple, ritual observances there, its destruction by the Babylonians, and especially its restoration under the leadership of Zerubbabel. This writer emphasizes the names of priests, Levites, and other Jewish leaders who take part in that restoration. The narrator also focuses on the support purportedly given for this project by the Persian monarchs Cyrus, Darius, and Artaxerxes, the sacrifices offered at the dedication of the new temple, and Ezra's leadership in promulgating the law and in breaking up marriages between Jewish men and foreign women.

First Esdras begins with an account of Josiah's superlative celebration of Passover and his death in battle (1:1–33), both based on 2 Chronicles 35. The last days of Judah are reviewed in 1:34–58, following 2 Chronicles 36 with slight variations and errors which are noted in most study editions of the Bible. Chapter 2 picks up, from Ezra 1, the story of Cyrus's determination to pay for rebuilding the temple and his return of the gold and silver vessels taken by the Babylonians at the beginning of the exile (2:1–15).[10] The narrative then strangely skips forward a century to the time of Artaxerxes (2:16–30). The same unfriendly neighboring officials who, according to Ezra 4:7–23, complain to Artaxerxes about Jewish efforts to rebuild the walls of Jerusalem, also object, in 1 Esdras 2:16–24, to the Jews' rebuilding of the temple. Actually, the temple already was rebuilt (in 515 B.C.). Curiously, 1 Esdras makes no mention of Nehemiah, under whose leadership the walls of Jerusalem were restored in 444 B.C., according to the book of Nehemiah.

The list of returning exiles in chapter 5 corresponds closely to lists in Ezra 2 and Nehemiah 7. All three sources distinguish several classes of temple functionaries, probably in descending order of rank: priests, Levites (including, it seems, though evidently at lower levels of status, the orders of singers and gatekeepers), temple servants, and "Solomon's servants." The report of temple building continues in 5:47–7:15, drawing from Ezra 3:1–4:5 and 4:24–6:22. Chapters 8 and 9, which concern Ezra's reading the law, leading a mass procession of exiles from Babylon, and breaking up racially (or nationally) mixed marriages, follow closely what is found in Ezra 7–10 and Nehemiah 7:73–8:12.

It may be that the author thought these earlier traditions pertinent to the situation of the Jewish people during the Maccabean period, perhaps around the time the temple was rededicated in 164 B.C., following its desecration by Antiochus IV (cf. 1 Macc 4:36–59). Copies of earlier biblical writings were always scarce and in this period might have been especially so, since many of them, including books of the law, probably had been confiscated and destroyed by Antiochus's "inspectors" (1 Macc 1:56). It would not be surprising if the author of 1 Esdras wished to assemble a compendium of these earlier traditions in order to preserve and encourage traditionalist practices. The writer emphasizes proper worship in the temple, quite possibly after its restoration under the Maccabees. The book usually is dated in the second century B.C. and, like many other books in the Apocrypha, probably was originally composed in Greek.

2 Esdras (or 4 Ezra)

Although not included in the Septuagint, 2 Esdras came into Christian Scripture through the Old Latin and Vulgate editions. Modern translations are based on Latin, Ethiopic, Syriac, Arabic, Armenian, and other early versions, which often disagree. Chapters 3–14 contain accounts of seven visions, which, according to the seventh (14:1–48), were written at Ezra's inspired dictation. These visions probably were composed in Jewish circles, possibly as late as around A.D. 100. In different ways, they affirm that God will deliver the few who are righteous, if not in this world, then in the next; condemn the many who are unrighteous; and punish the enemies of the Jewish people, particularly the Romans, who had defeated the Jews and overrun Jerusalem in A.D. 66–70.

The first three visions (3:1–9:25) are presented in the form of dialogues. Somewhat like Job and Jeremiah, Ezra (also named Salathiel; 3:1) questions God (usually referred to by a circumlocution, such as "the Most High") about why God's people suffer while unrighteous nations prosper (3:28–36), and raises concerns about the human predicament generally. The archangel Uriel answers, as God answers Job in his speeches out of the whirlwind, that there are fixed limits to human power and knowledge.[11] Not about to be put off by being told that he cannot comprehend the "things above" (4:21, NEB), Ezra insists that he wants to ask about matters of daily experience, namely, why the Gentiles lord it over "Israel," and why the meaning of life has become questionable. Uriel replies that all will soon become clear, for the present age is hastening to its end (4:26; cf. 1 Cor 13:8–12). In the new age, the righteous will have their reward. But, Ezra urges, this will do little good, for most if not all are unrighteous and so have no hope.[12] What good is paradise or the prospect of immortality if no one will qualify to receive these blessings (7:119–126)? Repeatedly, Ezra is told not to worry: God will bless the righteous, few though they be, with immortality in the world to come, which was made for the sake of the few (8:1). As for the rest, who abused their freedom by despising the Most High and forsaking his law and his ways, "So let the multitude perish" (8:55–61; 9:22).

The fourth, fifth, and sixth visions, like other apocalyptic texts, purport to be revelations to an ancient seer, here Ezra, which were written and sealed long ago for later reference. These revelations concern the subsequent course of history, most notably the "last days" of the present age and the onset of the coming age, which now, from the standpoint of those who were to read the unsealed visions, is soon to appear (see, e.g., 12:37–38; 14:8–48). The fourth vision, of a woman in mourning (9:38–10:59), refers to the plight of Zion (Jerusalem) after the temple is destroyed, probably in A.D. 70 (10:21–23). It affirms that Jerusalem will be rebuilt in splendor (10:55). The fifth vision (11:1–12:51) depicts an eagle with three heads and twelve wings that controls and oppresses the earth. This eagle evidently stands for the Roman empire. Its dominion will end (11:44–46), and the lion (i.e., the messiah) will deliver God's people (12:34). The sixth vision or dream, of a man from the sea, shows that God will defeat his enemies but protect his people (chap. 13). Here also we see an early version of the popular legend about the ten tribes of Israel dwelling in "another land" until the "last times" (13:39–50).[13]

Several other distinctive features appear in chapters 3–14. Here for the first time in biblical tradition, we find the idea that human depravity ("the evil heart") has been transmitted to Adam's descendants (3:20–27; 7:118). As in 1 Esdras, truth is an important value; here it is expected to prevail in the coming age (6:28; 7:34).[14] The two primeval sea monsters, Behemoth and Leviathan, will serve as food, evidently in the coming age, for those whom God will choose (6:49–52). Several visions refer to the coming time of judgment (e.g., 7:32–44, 61–74) and depict the fate of the spirits of those who die in the meantime. The unrighteous will dwell in seven "ways of torment" (7:79–87). The righteous, on the other hand, will dwell in seven orders of blissful habitation (7:88–99; cf. 4:35).[15] As in Ezekiel 47, the coming age is pictured as paradise, with perpetual and abundant fruit (7:123; cf. Rev 22:2). The visions tell that the world has grown old, explaining that this is why people are smaller than in earlier times (5:51–56). Nine and a half out of twelve parts of the old age have already passed, and as the world becomes weaker through old age, the evils of life in it multiply all the more (14:10–17).

Ezra himself is pictured as one of those "taken up" into heaven (8:19; 14:9; cf. 6:26), but not until, under divine inspiration, he dictates the twenty-four books of the Old Testament in order to warn those born after his ascension but before "the times are ended" (14:9), along with seventy other books reserved for the edification of the wise (14:19–48; cf. 12:37–38). It is curious that the only claim for plenary inspiration of the Old Testament, and other writings is in 2 Esdras, which itself enjoys only the most tenuous canonical status. The original book of 2 Esdras seems to have ended here, with chapter 14.

The last strata in 2 Esdras consist of Christian additions, mainly in chapters 1–2, commonly dated around A.D. 150, and chapters 15–16, which may have been written as late as A.D. 250. Both sets of additions promise their readers that the close of the age or kingdom of God will soon come (2:13, 34–35; 16:52). The time of tribulation that will herald the advent of the new age is also at hand (16:37–39, 74). The latter addition appears to reflect Christian experience of active persecution by Roman authorities, possibly in the time of the emperor Decius (see 15:52). The writer's enthusiasm for the coming destruction of the enemies of the chosen people probably reflects hatred engendered in the course of experiencing such persecution (see 15:34–45, 56–63). As in the books of Daniel and Revelation, "Babylon" is a code name for the oppressors of God's people—here, as in the book of Revelation, the Roman empire.

Chapters 1–2 reflect relatively peaceful times. Special features include the thesis that if "Judah" will not obey him, God will bestow his favor on "other nations," implicitly, gentile Christians (1:24–40).[16] The latter will enjoy the "everlasting habitations," those prepared for the former (2:11; cf. 7:88–99, and Luke 16:9), which include the tree of life and the twelve trees loaded with all kinds of fruit (2:12, 18, 38) anticipated in earlier prophetic and New Testament traditions. In the meantime, God's people are to live according to the provisions of the traditional biblical law governing love and justice in human society:

"Guard the rights of the widow, secure justice for the fatherless, give to the needy, . . . clothe the naked, care for the injured and the weak. . . ." (2:20–22).[17] Proper burial takes on new meaning, in view of the hope for the resurrection of the dead (2:23).[18]

Nothing in the visions or the later Christian additions suggests that either Jews or Christians were to concern themselves with worship at the Jerusalem temple or with offering sacrifices there, in contrast to emphasis on these activities in Ezra and 1 Esdras. The Romans destroyed the temple in A.D. 70; it was never rebuilt, and both Jews and Christians had to accommodate their traditions and practices to its absence. Instead, both the visions and the additions look for God's intervention on behalf of his people, a deliverance associated in some passages with the coming of God's Son (2:43–47; 7:28). These themes are paralleled in various New Testament writings, especially the book of Revelation (or the Apocalypse to John).

Tobit

This charming narrative provides many insights into Jewish practices and beliefs around 400–170 B.C., the period during which, at some point, it evidently was written. We see the ideal (honored, to be sure, only by Tobit) that Israelites should keep the feasts in Jerusalem (1:4–8; cf. Deut 12:1–14); the distinction between priests (sons of Aaron) and Levites (1:6–7) that emerged around 400 B.C.; the virtue of abstinence from gentile (nonkosher) food (1:10–12);[19] belief in the seven holy angels or archangels of God (12:15), guardian angels (5:21; 12:12–14), and demons, which reflects Persian (Zoroastrian) influence; the importance of a good burial (1:17; 6:14);[20] passing reference to "women's work" (2:11–12) and to "the eternal abode" (3:6); the practice of placing bread on the graves of the righteous but not on those of sinners (4:17; cf. Sir 30:18); an anxious father's advice to his only son as the latter goes forth into the world—much of it in the form of wisdom sayings (4:3–19);[21] mention of a man-eating fish (6:2); use of fish parts in demon exorcism and healing; conflicting ideas about whether angels do (6:5) or do not (12:19) eat fish;[22] an otherwise rarely reported insistence on intratribal marriage (4:12–13; 6:9–12; cf. Num 36:6–12); the idea of divinely foreordained marriage (6:17); a glimpse of the marriage service (7:11–15); the touching words of a bride's parents to the newlyweds (10:11); some fine examples of personal prayer (3:2–15; 8:5–8); a splendid psalm of praise and blessing for the marriage of two only-children (8:15–17); the entertaining quarrels of the old married couple, Tobit and Anna (2:11–14; 10:1–7); and several more wisdom sayings, this time attributed to the angel Raphael (12:6–10).

A few other features may be mentioned. "Brother" and "sister" are frequently used as terms of endearment rather than indicators of biological kinship.[23] In both Tobias's and Raguel's prayers (8:5, 15), all God's creatures are called on to bless him. The same theme appears in other prayers or psalms.[24] Tobit's last words look for the destruction of Nineveh—in accordance with Jonah's prophecy (14:4, 8). Yet at the same time, Tobit looks forward to the future when "all the Gentiles" would convert, and worship and praise God alone (14:6–7).

There are three plots: (1) the story of Tobit, a righteous Israelite now living in Nineveh, afflicted, by chance (cf. Eccl 9:11), with blindness while practicing ritual purity; (2) that of Sarah, over in Ecbatana, whose seven husbands have been killed, one after the other, by a jealous demon and who now, understandably, has little prospect of finding an eligible (and willing) spouse (3:15); and (3) the story of how Tobit recalls that he has lent a sum of money to a certain Gabael at Rages and his subsequent decision to send his son, Tobias, on a journey to collect the money.

The plots are skillfully interwoven. All on the same day, Tobit and Sarah, who, like Job, have been falsely accused by victim-blaming associates, pray that they may die and so be delivered from their troubles. The prayers of both are heard in the heavenly council,[25] and the angel Raphael is sent to cure their ills (chap. 3). Still on the same day, Tobit remembers the money (4:1). Tobias's journey, during which he is accompanied by the angel Raphael (disguised as "brother Azarias") and "the dog" (5:16; 11:4), leads to the resolution of all their problems.

Along the way, the angel instructs Tobias to catch a large fish that has tried to swallow him and set aside its inner parts for later use in smoking out the demon and healing his father's eyes. As they approach Ecbatana, Azarias advises Tobias to think about marrying his cousin Sarah, who is not only eligible and the heir to a large fortune but also beautiful and sensible (6:1–12).[26] Brother Azarias briefs Tobias about how to handle the demon—a matter about which Tobias has, quite reasonably, been concerned (6:13–17).

After they arrive, Azarias suggests the marriage to Sarah's father, Raguel, who is well disposed, and, as they sit down to dinner, tells Tobias to "eat, drink, and be merry" (7:9; cf. Eccl 2:24). He also tells him about the previous seven unfortunate husbands, but without mentioning the demon. Undaunted, Tobias insists on marriage forthwith.

The ceremony is quickly performed, Tobias and Sarah go up to bed, and Raguel, expecting the worst, goes outside to dig another grave. But the demon is overcome by the smoke from the burning fish entrails, and flees to Egypt, where the angel binds him. Now Sarah's parents put on a two-week wedding feast (chap. 8). Somewhat incidentally and anticlimactically, Brother Azarias goes to Rages and collects the money from Gabael (chap. 9).

Back in Nineveh, Tobit worries about the money, Anna about her son, and the two take the occasion to have a lively domestic argument: "Am I not distressed, my child," says Anna, "that I let you go, you who are the light of my eyes?" But Tobit tells her, "Be still and stop worrying; he is well." And she answers him, "You be still and stop deceiving me; my child has perished" (10:5–7). Then the young couple returns, along with the dog. Tobias heals his father's eyes, and all ends happily (chaps. 11–12). Before ascending back to heaven, Raphael offers Tobit and Tobias some advice, especially recommending that they praise God and give alms. He also identifies his role as observer of human conduct and mediator before God as one of the "seven holy angels who present the prayers" of the pious and enter into the holy presence (12:11–15). He then instructs Tobit to write down in a book "everything that has happened" (12:11–20), thus, implicitly, accounting for the composition of the book.

Chapters 13 and 14 may be later additions. Chapter 13 consists of a psalm. Many biblical and apocryphal books contain one or more psalms. This one praises God as Father, King of the ages, and King of heaven,[27] and looks for the messianic age when Jerusalem will become a city of gold, emeralds, and other precious stones. Chapter 14 reports Tobit's further acts of virtue (notably, giving alms) and his last words (in which he looks for the restoration of Jerusalem and the time when all the gentiles will turn to God), his death at the ripe age of 158, and his "magnificent funeral."[28] The book closes with the further information that Tobias also gives his mother-in-law and father-in-law magnificent funerals, inherits their property (as well as Tobit's), and dies at the age of 127 after hearing the good news of Nineveh's destruction at the hands of Nebuchadnezzar and Ahasuerus.[29]

Judith

This story probably was written during the first half of the second century B.C. in order to encourage the writer's fellow Jews to remain faithful to their traditions and to resist their enemies despite the seemingly overwhelming power of other peoples. Unlike the book of Daniel, which encourages its readers to expect and await supernatural deliverance, the writer of Judith implies that contemporary Jewish readers should emulate her example not only by trusting God, but also by taking up arms against their oppressors. This is what many Jews did in the time of Antiochus IV and the early Maccabean period.[30]

Bethulia, a place otherwise unknown, may stand for Jerusalem. As the story is told, it is the last bastion: If it falls, all Judah will be captured, its people enslaved, and, worst of all, the Jerusalem temple ("the sanctuary") will be captured and desecrated by the idolatrous and malicious gentiles.[31] The Syrian overlord, Antiochus IV, did, in fact, plunder and desecrate the temple in 167 B.C.[32] The historical setting described in the story is impossible: The author portrays Nebuchadnezzar as king of Assyria after the exile. This confusion may have been intended to alert readers to look for the real meaning of the book, namely, a summons to resist contemporary foes. The Syrians, of course, would have taken a dim view of any resistance literature explicitly naming them. The arrogance of "Nebuchadnezzar" and his adherents, together with the demand that conquered people give up their religion (3:8; 6:24), corresponds closely to the situation of the Jewish people at the time of Antiochus IV.

As the story goes, Holofernes, an Assyrian general, has been dispatched by Nebuchadnezzar to punish those nations, including "Israel," that had refused to help him in his earlier war against Arphaxad, the Mede. It is understood that these nations will be required to give up their religion and worship Nebuchadnezzar as god (3:8).[33] In this setting, Judith summons the elders of Bethulia to her house, speaks of God's transcendent power and purpose, exhorts them to remain true to him, and prays for his aid in carrying out her plan (chaps. 8–9). She then puts this plan into operation, thereby bringing about the deliverance so desperately needed (chaps. 10–15).

After adorning herself with elegant finery, the better "to entice the eyes of all men who might see her," Judith crosses into no-man's-land and explains to an Assyrian patrol there that she wants to tell Holofernes how he can defeat the Hebrews. All the soldiers eagerly volunteer to escort this beautiful woman to their general, but only a hundred are chosen for this pleasant duty (10:3–19). She proceeds to tell Holofernes with various ingenious double-entendres and prevarications that as soon as the people of Bethulia eat and drink the consecrated offerings, which, she says, they are on the verge of doing lest they starve, God himself will destroy them by way of punishment for so doing (11:5–19). Holofernes is impressed with Judith's wisdom but especially with her beauty. He schemes to get her alone, that he might "embrace" her (12:10–12), but when the time comes, he breaks his own previous record for wine consumption, passes out, and Judith lops off his head, a favorite scene in later Western art, placing it in her now empty kosher food bag. Back in Bethulia, she instructs her fellow Israelites what to do next (14:14). Just as she predicted, after the Israelites sally forth in the morning, the Assyrians panic on finding their general headless. The Israelites proceed to defeat them with "great slaughter" and to take possession of nearby towns and villages and a vast quantity of booty (14:11–15:7).

Led by the women of Israel, all then celebrate their deliverance with dances, branches, and songs, the women wearing olive wreaths and the men garlands (15:12–13). Judith lives out her days a widow, and dies at the age of 105 (16:21–24). The book concludes with a tribute rather like the Deuteronomic formula in praise of certain early Israelite judges: "And no one ever again spread terror among the people of Israel in the days of Judith, or for a long time after her death (16:25)."[34]

Judith's words summarize the main thrust of the book: "God, our God, is still with us, to show his power in Israel, and his strength against our enemies" (13:11; see also 16:17). Judith epitomizes the bravery of Jael against Sisera and David against Goliath, the alluring beauty of Sarah (the wife of Abraham), Esther, and Susanna, and the shrewd strategies of Tamar and Gideon. Like the book of Tobit, Judith concludes with a psalm and final biographical notes (chap. 16).

Several points of religious and cultural interest may be noted. Like Daniel and Esther (of the Additions), Judith keeps kosher (10:5). Like Tobit and Sarah in the book of Tobit, and like Esther and Mordecai in the Additions to Esther, she prays at length to God for assistance (9:2–14). Like Deborah, she rallies her contemporaries to go and fight bravely against their oppressors (8:11–27; cf. Judg 4:6–9, 15). Like Miriam and Deborah, she composes a song or psalm of victory to commemorate the events (16:2–17). The psalm looks forward to the eternal torment (by fire and worms) of all nations that oppose God's people (16:17).[35] Before she dies, she grants her maidslave freedom, an unprecedented act of liberation, and distributes her property to both her husband's and her own nearest relatives, again, an unprecedented procedure (16:23–25).[36] We also learn from the story that widows may receive substantial inheritances (or bequests) from their husbands (8:7). In general, Judith represents a model of Jewish piety, virtue, and bravery, qualities evidently not reserved to men in Judaism of the second century B.C.[37]

Additions to Esther

The Additions are those parts of the Greek version of Esther that were not known in Hebrew at the time Jewish Scripture was defined and delimited at Jamnia (ca. A.D. 90). They were probably added around the time the earlier story of Esther was translated into Greek (ca. 100 B.C.). According to 11:1, the translation, probably meaning the whole book of Esther including these additions, was the work of a certain Lysimachus of Jerusalem. Six sets of additions, not all necessarily written at the same time or by the same person, are scattered throughout the book at various points. Like the earlier writing, the Additions purport to describe events and personalities during the Persian period of Jewish history (ca. 540–330 B.C.), around the time of the emperor Artaxerxes, or Ahasuerus.[38]

The author(s) evidently wished to clarify certain matters left in doubt in the original, and, particularly, to introduce religious elements notably absent from it. For example, in the original book, God is never mentioned, and no one prays or observes any other religious practices. The Additions now explain that Mordecai (Mardochaeus, NEB) refused to bow to Haman—thereby provoking the latter's animosity against all Jews—lest he "set the glory of man above the glory of God" (13:12–14). Esther tells God that she finds her marriage to the gentile king Artaxerxes (Ahasuerus) abhorrent (14:15); moreover, lest she be thought proud of herself as queen, she explains that she wears her crown only on public occasions, not in private when she is at leisure (14:16). These explanations are set in the form of Mordecai's and Esther's prayers to God, who already knows all things (13:12; 14:15–16); thus, their actual function is to enlighten the reader.[39] Lest contemporary Jewish scruples be offended, the Additions note that Esther avoids eating gentile food; like Daniel and Judith, she keeps kosher.

The Additions try again to explain the murky connections between lots, Purim, and the story (10:10–13). Here the idea is that God has "made" one "lot" for the Jews (Israel) and another for all other nations (gentiles), some or all of whom had come to destroy Israel, and that in the course of events, God decided for and saved Israel and defeated the gentiles (10:8–12; cf. Luke 1:68, 71). Purim, implicitly, celebrates this "day of decision." The whole book of Esther, including the Additions, is now characterized as the "Letter of Purim" (11:1).

The Additions frequently refer to God, who is ultimately credited with saving his people (15:8; 10:9). Even the Persian king, Artaxerxes, testifies to God's justice, omniscience, and sovereignty (16:4, 16, 21).

The Jews' subjugation to their enemies is explained as God's punishment for their worship of other gods (14:6–7), a theory of history congruent with earlier prophetic and Deuteronomic views. Mordecai's dream (11:5–11) also is of religious interest. Earthquake, tumult on earth, the gathering of two great dragons and all the nations for battle, darkness, gloom, and the like, are standard features of Jewish and early Christian apocalyptic representations of the time of tribulation expected before the establishment of God's kingdom on earth.[40] The interpretation of some of these features in 10:5–9 may be considered a later, somewhat implausible, demythologizing attempt to explain allegorically that these apocalyptic expectations have been fulfilled in the persons of Esther, Haman, and Mordecai.[41]

The tendency of tradition to exaggerate as it grows may be seen in the characterization of Haman as an accomplice of the two conspiratorial eunuchs (12:6) and as a Macedonian plotting treason against the Persian empire (16:10–14). The Additions supply several new melodramatic touches when Esther goes before the king; for example, though "radiant with perfect beauty," her "heart was frozen" as she approaches the royal presence; the king was "most terrifying" and "glanced at her in towering anger" (NEB), with the result that she falls fainting not only once but twice (15:1–16; cf. Esth 5:1–2). Few interpreters propose that the Additions should be taken as literal history. Nevertheless, the Additions, like other writings from the same period, do provide a treasury of historical information about the beliefs, concerns, and practices of Judaism in the second and first centuries B.C.

Wisdom of Solomon (or Wisdom)

The author of Wisdom implicitly identifies himself with Solomon in chapters 7–9.[42] Unmistakably Greek terms (e.g., Hades) and ideas (e.g., 8:7, 19–20; 12:1), however, suggest that the book was not composed before the fourth century B.C., when Judaism first came into significant contact with Hellenistic culture. Usually Wisdom is dated in the first century B.C.

Like traditional biblical wisdom writings such as Proverbs, this book holds that righteous individuals are rewarded and wicked ones punished, but it differs from the orthodox wisdom theology by proposing that such rewards and punishments may be dispensed after death rather than in this life. As in Proverbs 8, wisdom itself is represented as a female being closely associated with God from the beginning of the world (9:9). Here, wisdom, which is identified with God's spirit or breath, is said to fill the whole earth, holding all things together (1:5–7; 7:22–8:1).[43]

Several other passages also evidently influenced New Testament ideas and expressions: for example, 3:7 (cf. Matt 13:43); 3:8 (cf. Rev 2:26–27; 20:4); 3:14 (cf. Matt 19:12); 5:16 (cf. Rev 2:10); 5:16–19 (cf. Eph 6:11–17); 6:3 (cf. Rom 13:1–2); 14:22–31 (cf. Rom 1:18–32). Like many New Testament writings, Wisdom looks for the time of Judgment, when the righteous will be rewarded and the unrighteous punished (chaps. 3–5). These several affinities may explain why Wisdom is listed with New Testament writings in the Muratorian fragment, an early Christian document written around A.D. 200.

The book contains several kinds of material. Like other wisdom writings, it praises wisdom, commending it particularly to the kings of the earth (1:1–15; 6:1–25). The writer reflects thematically upon the respective destinies of the wicked and the righteous (1:16–5:23), perceptively portraying the desperate and exploitive attitudes and actions of the ungodly (2:1–11). Both living and dead will come before the Lord at the time of judgment (4:16–5:14). In chapters 7–9, "Solomon" tells about himself and the wonders of wisdom and prays for its continuing gifts of knowledge, immortality, and power.

These reflections on the blessings of wisdom then lead into a review of stories about early humankind and Israel, in which wisdom is said to have delivered the ancients who heeded her (chaps. 10–11). This section blends into the concluding rumination—probably by another writer—on God's dealings with Israel and Egypt long ago (chaps. 11–19). This last also includes a brief allusion to God's attempt to bring the Canaanites to repentance, even though, in his omniscience, he knew beforehand that this "accursed race"[44] would never change (12:3–11). Then follows a longer discourse on human foolishness in making and worshiping idols and the many expressions of depravity that result from such worship (13:1–15:17). The futility of making and worshiping idols is a theme featured in other more or less contemporary writings, such as Bel and the Dragon and the Letter of Jeremiah. In this connection, the author indicates his general antipathy toward art, especially painted sculpture (15:4–6).[45]

The final chapters present a highly idealized and imaginative interpretation of Israel's early history (e.g., 16:20–21). These chapters tell that the manna given in the wilderness was made to suit the individual tastes of every Israelite.[46] An imaginary prototype of medieval and Chinese dragons appears in a list of newly created beasts that Yahweh might have sent, but mercifully did not do so, to punish the Israelites for their apostasy in the wilderness (11:18–19; cf. Job 41). These several chapters of revisionist history evidently were meant to encourage fellow Jews to believe that God would still act in history on behalf of his people when they needed his help, as he had done in the past.[47]

Like 2 Esdras, Wisdom promises immortality to the souls of the righteous (3:1–4; 5:15–16) but is more optimistic about the number that might qualify for this blessing. At times, Wisdom seems to view all Israelites as "sons" of God (12:21; 16:10) or even as "a holy people and a blameless race" (10:15; cf. Ezra 9:2). Wisdom affirms God's providence, and, like Tobit, addresses God as Father (14:3; Tob 13:4; cf. 2 Esdr 1:29). For the first time in biblical tradition, death's entry into the world is blamed upon the devil, who is mentioned here for the first and only time in the Old Testament Apocrypha.[48] Nevertheless, cosmic dualism is quite limited, for Wisdom praises God as the creator and lover of all that exists (1:14; 11:24).

Ecclesiasticus (or the Wisdom of Jesus, Son of Sirach)

Ecclesiasticus, not to be confused with Ecclesiastes, or Sirach (as it is often called), is the longest of the wisdom writings. The author reveals not only his name, Joshua (Hebrew) or Jesus (Greek), (50:27) but also various personal experiences and insights.[49] It may be inferred that he was a man with wide interests, a gentle spirit, and a firm faith. Probably a teacher and philosopher, he comments that devising proverbs "requires painful thinking" (13:26). He values priests and sacrificial offerings (7:29–31; 45:6–26) but warns against supposing that God can be bribed (7:9; 35:12) and generally urges a high standard of justice, kindness, and consideration for others. Wisdom is closely associated with the law or commandments, which are understood mainly in terms of ethics or practical reason. Sirach probably was written around 180 B.C. and translated into Greek around 130 B.C.

Few other biblical books begin with a prologue. The prologue to Sirach, written by the anonymous grandson of the Jesus who translated it from Hebrew, commends the book to those who love learning as a guide to progress in living according to the law. Chapters 1–43 consist largely of proverbs (short observations and admonitions), which often are grouped by topics. A briefer section (44:1–50:21) praises certain famous men of yore, showing how they were favored by God for their righteousness, beginning with Enoch and ending with Simon the high priest (ca. 200 B.C.). The book concludes with a psalm of thanksgiving (51:1–12) and exhortations to heed the instruction here presented.

Many traditional wisdom themes are repeated in Sirach. Wisdom is praised and said to begin with the "fear of the Lord" and to come from him (chap. 1). Those who love and heed wisdom are righteous; those who do not are foolish and wicked. The former may look for reward in the form of prosperity, long life, a famous name, and posterity, but the latter will be punished in this life. Unlike Wisdom of Solomon, Sirach offers no hope for resurrection or immortality. The reader, often addressed as "my son," is warned against the enticements of loose women and the perils of adultery (9:3–9). A bad wife is a great catastrophe; a good one, a great blessing (25:16–26:4, 13–18). Fathers are to use the rod rather than spoil their sons (30:1–13). Excessive drinking leads to trouble (31:25–31).[50] The author makes many shrewd observations and comparisons regarding the human condition.[51] Numerous sayings offer advice, particularly for those in authority and those who aspire to success in various kinds of enterprise.[52] Many also refer to matters of etiquette (e.g., 31:12–18; 32:1–13). Several are prudential in nature (e.g., 8:10–19; 13:1–13).

The author is fond of balanced statements, which often show considerable sophistication and delicate irony.[53] In a single verse, he acknowledges and articulates the ambivalent character of human nature or proclivity intimated throughout biblical traditions:

> What race is worthy of honor?
>   The human race.
> What race is worthy of honor?
>   Those who fear the Lord.
> What race is unworthy of honor?
>   The human race.
> What race is unworthy of honor?
>   Those who transgress the commandments. (Sir 10:19)

Repeatedly, the writer emphasizes the importance of giving alms and otherwise helping the poor and needy (e.g., 4:1–10; 29:9–13). Almsgiving is also commended in Tobit (Tob 4:7–11; 12:8–9) and by a later Jesus (Luke 12:33; 16:1–9). But Sirach advises against helping sinners (12:1–7). Numerous other passages are echoed later in sayings attributed to Jesus in the first three Gospels.[54] Sirach apparently opposes placing food on graves (30:18), a practice endorsed by Tobit with respect to the graves of the righteous.[55] Sirach holds a low view of women (22:3; 25:24; 42:14) but nevertheless recommends marriage (36:22–26).

Many other topics are considered: friendship (6:7–17), treating oneself well (14:3–19), freedom of the will and responsibility (15:11–20), lending and borrowing (29:1–20), matters of health and table manners relating to eating and drinking (31:12–32:13), dealing with servants (33:24–31), mourning (38:16–23), and the value of physicians, scribes, and craftsmen (38:1–25, 24–34). Throughout, God is praised as creator and sovereign of all that is, who cares for his creation and governs it well.[56]

The long section in praise of famous men highlights the great deeds of biblical heroes. Although the writer makes no mention of resurrection or immortality, he is confident that the fame and names of these men "will live for ever" (44:1–15). In several instances, the earlier tradition is expanded by legends previously unrecorded, such as the ascension of Enoch (44:16; cf. Gen 5:24), the youthful David's playing with lions and bears (47:3), and Solomon's filling the earth with parables and riddles (49:17). Most of the famous figures are somewhat idealized: Noah was perfect (44:17); Abraham was unique "in glory" (44:19), Moses, who was equal in glory to the angels (45:2), was chosen by God "out of all mankind" (45:4), Aaron was chosen "out of all the living" (45:16), and Elijah is said to have prophesied after he was dead (48:13). Elijah is remembered for his zeal and wondrous deeds and for being carried into heaven "in a chariot with horses of fire" so that he might come again "at the appointed time" to "calm the wrath of God" and proclaim repentance.[57]

Together these recitations served as reminders to Jews living early in the second century B.C. that God sustained his people in the past by raising up strong leaders and making covenants with them that would endure to all times. By implication, Sirach's contemporaries could look to God to raise up such leaders and to continue to honor his covenant promises in their time and in the future. Such hopes would have been very important in the era of Antiochus IV and in the Maccabean period.

Baruch

This book is ascribed implicitly to the Baruch who was Jeremiah's secretary (see Jeremiah 36 and 45). It is set, ostensibly, among certain Jewish exiles in Babylon around 580 B.C. Jerusalem has been burned (1:2), the temple devastated (2:26), many of the people of Jerusalem and other cities of Judah have perished miserably (2:25), and the rest are now scattered in exile (3:8). Several features point to more recent composition, however, such as references to demons (4:7) and Hades (2:17). Interpreters generally suggest that the book was written in the second or early first century B.C. during the Maccabean period. However, it is conceivable that Baruch, or at least some material in it, could have been composed earlier, possibly during the time of the exile. Unlike most other writings in the Old Testament Apocrypha, Baruch was probably first written in Hebrew.

Stylistic and substantive considerations suggest that there may have been more than one author. The book consists of four sections, each with special characteristics and concerns. The first two are in prose; the last two, which are in poetic form, seem to have been modeled on earlier psalms, proverbs, and prophetic forms and themes.

The first section (1:1–14) introduces "this book" as written by Baruch around 582 B.C. in Babylon and read to the Jewish exiles there (1:1–3), and then sent to the high priest and other priests and people in Jerusalem so that they might make their "confession" by reading it in the temple on special holy days (1:14). The first section also reports that the exiles collected money, "each giving what he could," to be sent to the priests and those with them in Jerusalem, to buy sacrificial offerings at the temple (1:5–10). Curiously, the writer seems to assume that the temple is still standing and that the customary ritual functions continue in it, despite its destruction in 586.[58] Confusion on this point would be understandable if the author was writing several generations or centuries later. He evidently meant to imply that all diaspora Jews who were unable to attend the prescribed festivals in Jerusalem themselves could, by sending money, have sacrifices and prayers offered there on their behalf (cf. Deut 14:22–26). We may see here a precedent for Paul's collecting money from the gentile churches on behalf of "the saints" in Jerusalem (e.g., 1 Cor 16:1–4), and for the later Catholic practice of making contributions for the saying of masses. In Baruch, prayers are requested not only for the contributors but for the Babylonian kings Nebuchadnezzar and Belshazzar (1:10–11).[59]

The second section (1:15–3:8) is a prayer of confession to be offered to God, along with sacrifices and other prayers, on special days (1:14). The first part, 1:15 through 2:5 (or perhaps 2:12), fits the situation of those left behind in Jerusalem after the deportations of 598 and 586.[60] The remainder of this section is written from the standpoint of the exiles (see, e.g., 2:13–14). Both sections draw on language and themes found in earlier biblical texts, especially Deuteronomy, Jeremiah, and Daniel. The confession initially acknowledges that the calamities experienced are God's punishment for the victims' sins and disobedience (1:17–21), but at the end, the confession suggests that the punishment is for the sins of the fathers after all (3:4–8; cf. Lam. 5:7). The confession concludes with a promise (attributed to Moses) that if the Israelites change their ways, God will bring them back from exile and make an everlasting covenant with them (2:28–35; cf. Jer 32:38–40), and with an extended prayer for God's mercy upon his people now still scattered in exile (3:1–8).

The third section (3:9–4:4) is addressed to "Israel" and explains that the reason its people dwell in the land of their enemies is that they have forsaken wisdom. Wisdom either has not been granted to other nations or has been foolishly ignored by them.[61] Thus, those who have lived for pleasure and glory, hunting wild animals and birds for sport or hoarding silver and gold, all have perished for lack of wisdom, along with the famous giants of old (3:16–17, 24–28, NEB). But God, who knows all things and by wisdom established the earth for all time, filling it with four-footed creatures, sending forth light, and calling to the stars, has given wisdom to Israel (3:32–36). Thus, there is hope for Israel, since through the Law, Israel knows what is pleasing to God (4:4). Wisdom here is equated with the Law or Torah (4:1).[62] This third section could be considered as another instance of biblical wisdom tradition of the sort found elsewhere in Proverbs, Wisdom of Solomon, and Sirach.

The fourth section (4:5–5:5) is likewise addressed to Israel (typically called "my children" or "my sons and daughters") and Jerusalem (in 4:30–5:5) but now develops a new and different theme. The writer summons his contemporary Israelite (or Jewish) readers to "take courage," for God will soon (4:24) bring them back to Jerusalem and act in judgment against those cities that have afflicted them (4:25, 31–35).[63] It is unclear whether the speaker in this fourth section (who addresses hearers/readers as "my people" or "my children") is meant to be Baruch (who is mentioned only in the first section), wisdom (speaking for herself as in Proverbs 8), or some prophet, pronouncing oracles on behalf of God. In this final section, the speaker frequently refers to God as "the Everlasting," which may be understood both as a circumlocution and as a way of expressing hope that God will always be with and for his people despite their present suffering. Wisdom is not mentioned in this section, but possibly the author or editor understood wisdom, which is named at the end of the third section (3:37–4:4) to be the speaker in 4:5–5:9 as well.

The message of hope in the fourth section contains numerous echoes of Second and Third Isaiah (Isaiah 40–66), from which several verses may derive. The substance of this message is that the exiles will be gathered once more to Jerusalem, "from east and west" (4:36–37; cf. Matt 8:11). In preparation for their return, "every high mountain" will be "made low" and "the valleys filled up, to make level ground," while fragrant trees will shade the exiles on their return journey (5:7–8). Certain features of prophetic and apocalyptic eschatology are notably absent, however. In Baruch, there is no expectation of the appearance of a messiah, a new covenant, the resurrection of the dead, or the judgment of the righteous and unrighteous.

Letter of Jeremiah

This writing is in the form of a letter by Jeremiah to those about to be taken into exile by the Babylonians (v. 1). A letter from Jeremiah to the Jewish exiles in Babylon is preserved in Jeremiah 29, but the letter treated here probably comes from a later author writing sometime between 331 and 100 B.C. In some ancient Bibles, the Letter is treated as a separate book and placed between Lamentations and Ezekiel; in others, it is included as part of Baruch, and so some English translations designate it as chapter 6 of that book.

"Jeremiah" wishes to warn the prospective exiles lest in Babylon they be tempted to worship images or idols as if such really were gods. Thematically, the writer asserts that idols cannot save themselves (vv. 12, 15, 49, 57) or anyone else (vv. 36–39) from the vicissitudes of life, asks rhetorically why anyone should call or consider them gods (vv. 40, 44, 52, 56), and urges readers not to fear them (vv. 16, 23, 65, 69). This is perhaps the most extensive or sustained polemic against the worship of idols in the Bible.[64] The impotence of idols is vividly and sardonically stressed: They cannot save themselves from rust and corrosion (v. 12) or from war and robbers (v. 15), their eyes are coated with dust kicked up by the feet of visitors to their shrines (v. 17), bats, birds, and cats perch ignominiously on their bodies and heads (v. 22), and they are no more than scarecrows in a cucumber patch (v. 70).

The problem of apostasy and idolatry has a long history in biblical tradition. The first two or three of the Ten Commandments were aimed at correcting the tendency of early Israelites to worship other gods, which often were represented by "graven images" or "likenesses" (Exod 20:4; Deut 5:8). The "golden calf" episode (Exodus 32) is an early and dramatic instance of that tendency. Solomon and his foreign wives (1 Kgs 11:1–8) and his descendant, King Manasseh (2 Kgs 21:1–16), were especially notorious later exemplars of this tendency. Idolatry was a special problem in the late exilic and postexilic periods, when the Jewish people were in constant close contact with people from other cultures in whose lives pagan gods or images played an important part.

Several distinctive features may be noted in this Letter. It interprets the exile as God's judgment against the exiles for their own sins (v. 2).[65] The writer warns that the exiles may remain in Babylon up to seven generations (v. 3).[66] The reference in verse 7 to God's angel watching over the exiles is reminiscent of the guardian angel Raphael in Tobit. Angels are sometimes called "watchers" in various writings in the Pseudepigrapha. The writer has no respect for priests who officiate at the idols' temples: They steal silver and gold from the idols, spend it on themselves or give it to brothel harlots (v. 10), sell the sacrifices offered to the idols and use the proceeds for their own benefit (v. 28), take the gods' clothing for their wives and children (v. 32), and in case of fire, save themselves but let the idols burn (v. 55). Like Sirach (and earlier legal and prophetic writings), the author of the Letter shows concern for the poor, the helpless, the blind, the distressed, widows, and orphans—noting that neither the idols nor their priests do anything to help them (vv. 28, 37–38).

The Prayer of Azariah and the Song of the Three Young Men
(Additions to Daniel)

Here we have the first of three sets of additions to the book of Daniel found in the Septuagint and other early versions.[67] This first set consists of three psalms or hymns joined together with a minimum of connecting narrative. Purportedly, they were recited by one or all of Daniel's three friends, Shadrach, Meshach, and Abednego, after King Nebuchadnezzar had them bound and cast into a "burning fiery furnace" because they had refused to bow down and worship the golden image erected by the king (see Dan 3:1–18). In the Additions, the friends have Hebrew names (Azariah, Hananiah, and Mishael), possibly to underscore their traditionalist character. Except for verse 66, which may have been appended to tie them into this setting, the psalms themselves do not refer to the fiery furnace. Verses 23–27 pick up the story from verse 1, presenting a vivid prose account of the events implicit in Daniel 3:19–27. Only here do we learn that the angel of the Lord "came down" and "drove the fiery flame" away. In the apocryphal or augmented versions, the Prayer and Song are inserted after Daniel 3:23. This first set of additions is dated between 170 and 150 B.C.

The Prayer of Azariah (vv. 2–22) is a psalm of communal lament (cf. Pss 83; 85). Its acceptance of national calamity as God's judgment recalls Lamentations 1. Several passages are suggestive of the era following Antiochus IV's desecration of the temple (ca. 167 B.C.): The Jewish people have been given over to lawless enemies and to an unjust king (the most wicked in the world), there is no Jewish prince, prophet, or leader, no offering of sacrifices, and no place to offer them (vv. 9–10, 15). Since sacrifices can no longer be made, God is asked to accept a contrite heart and a humble spirit instead (v. 16; cf. Ps 51:16–17). The psalmist calls on God to remember his promises to Abraham, Isaac, and Israel ("thy holy one"—a rare characterization of Jacob) and to put down those who oppress their descendants so that these oppressors will come to know that he is the only God, sovereign over all nations (vv. 11–14, 20–22). Here we see an expression of explicit monotheistic faith (cf. v. 68).

The Song of the Three Young Men comprises two psalms of thanksgiving, at verses 29–34 and 35–65, each with distinctive repeated congregational responses. Both psalms are preserved in Christian liturgy as the *Benedictus es, Domine* and *Benedicite omnia opera Domini*, respectively. In the former, God is blessed and glorified in all places: in the temple (now evidently reconsecrated), seated upon the cherubim (cf. Ezekiel 1 and 10) contemplating the seas, upon the throne of his kingdom, presumably the land, and in the firmament of heaven. In the latter psalm, celestial and atmospheric powers, along with earth and sea, mountains, springs and rivers, everything that grows, whales and all other sea creatures, all birds, all beasts, together with Israel, priests, and the souls of the righteous (including, perhaps, those who have died), are called upon to praise the Lord.[68] The celebration of creation theme appears later in such magnificent compositions as Saint Francis's "Canticle of the Sun," the hymn "Old One Hundred," Haydn's "Creation," and Beethoven's "Ode to Joy."

Verse 66 again refers to the three young men, calling on them too to "bless the Lord"—here because he has delivered them from the fiery furnace—while the last two verses, echoing earlier psalms, call on all who worship the Lord to bless and praise him. The tone of rejoicing in the Song of the Three Young Men may possibly reflect important victories by the Maccabeans in their war of liberation against the Syrians (see, e.g., 1 Macc 7:39–48).

Susanna
(Additions to Daniel)

Like several other writings from later times, Susanna is set in Babylon where a significant Jewish community flourished following the exile there (586–539 B.C.). The Greek wordplays in vv. 54–55 and 58–59 and other features, however, suggest that the story probably was written between the third and first centuries B.C. under the influence of Hellenistic culture. Its narrative qualities rank among the best of biblical writings, and it is one of the earliest known detective stories in world literature. Here, Daniel, as zealous attorney for the defense, not only saves his client but solves the case and catches the true culprits in the courtroom. In some early biblical manuscripts, the story of Susanna is placed at the beginning of the book of Daniel, thereby introducing that hero, here represented as a "young lad" (v. 45).

Its theological and moral thrust, summarized in verses 60–62, accords with the orthodox wisdom viewpoint: The righteous, also beautiful, Susanna is vindicated, and the wicked elders are punished. The book emphasizes law and, implicitly, due process. Susanna has been instructed in the law of Moses (v. 3). She is married to a certain Joakim, who figures only slightly in the narrative.

The story begins with mention of Joakim's wealth, spacious garden, and high status in the Jewish community. Two unnamed elders have recently been appointed judges and often hold court in Joakim's house. Susanna naturally strolls about the garden from time to time, including during lunch hour. At such times, these two elders, the original "dirty old men," ogle her, thinking lustful thoughts. One day they conspire to put their wicked desires into effect as Susanna is alone in the garden and about to bathe in the privacy of her courtyard. They threaten to accuse her of adultery if she refuses to lie with them. Adultery was a capital offense. But Susanna refuses to violate the Seventh Commandment even to save her own life (vv. 22–23; cf. Deut 22:22). The two elders not only covet their neighbor's wife but maliciously bear false witness against her and want her killed to cover up their own wicked scheme (see Exod 20:13–14, 16–17). So in retaliation, they tell their tale (v. 27), and the matter proceeds to trial at Joakim's house. These shameless elders even order Susanna unveiled during trial so "that they might feast upon her beauty" (v. 32). Believing the false charges, for the accusers are elders and judges, the assembled people, acting as jury, condemn Susanna to death (v. 41).

Susanna's piety is shown in her refusal to sin, her trust in God, and her prayer for his help. The Lord hears her prayer (cf. Tob 3:16–17) and arouses Daniel to rescue her. This inspired youth declares her innocent and proceeds to so prove at trial, urging attention to "the facts," ordering witnesses sequestered, and cross-examining them separately. They offer conflicting testimony, thereby revealing that Susanna is innocent and that they have lied. In accordance with the law about false witnesses (Deut 19:16–21), the perjuring elders suffer the punishment that would have been inflicted upon the falsely accused (vv. 61–62).

A few incidental points of interest may be noted. The story illustrates the Old Testament law requiring at least two witnesses to sustain a criminal allegation (Num 35:30; Deut 19:15). Daniel is the only biblical figure who appears as an attorney, that is, an advocate for someone else at trial (but see Gen 18:22–33). Among other elements of what might be considered judicial due process, Daniel calls for sequestration of the witnesses and then interrogates them separately. In conducting his interrogation, he badgers the witnesses, accusing the first of making unjust judgments and the second of having Canaanite (rather than Judahite) ancestors. The writer also has Daniel aim an ethnic slur at Israel: The wicked judges might be able to intimidate *Israelite* women into compliance with their lustful schemes, but not a daughter of *Judah* (vv. 52–57)![69]

The central point of the story is underscored in verse 60: God "saves those who hope in him." The writer evidently intended the story to encourage Jews to remain faithful to their law and moral tradition despite temptations and pressures toward acculturation to the ways of their gentile neighbors. Similar concern appears in the book of Daniel and its other additions, and in such stories as Tobit and Esther and in the many other relatively late writings, such as the Wisdom of Solomon, the Letter of Jeremiah, and the books of the Maccabees.

Bel and the Dragon
(Additions to Daniel)

These two stories of rather uneven literary quality present Daniel as an exemplary disbeliever in all gods except God and an iconoclast who literally smashes or destroys false gods.[70] As in Daniel and the other Additions, the setting is Babylon, but now, supposedly, in the days of Cyrus, the sixth century B.C. Persian emperor hailed by Second Isaiah as God's messiah (Isa 45:1). Here, as elsewhere in Daniel and in some other relatively late Old Testament and apocryphal writings such as Esther, Baruch, and the Letter of Jeremiah (as well as Revelation in the New Testament), "Babylon" probably is to be understood as a code term for latter-day enemies or oppressors of the Jewish people. These

Additions, like the others, probably were written in the third, second, or first century B.C. In the Greek versions of Daniel, these two stories are added at the end, either before or after Susanna.

According to the first story, Bel is a Babylonian god represented by a large statue (cf. Isaiah 46) that regularly has been served huge quantities of food and drink by seventy priests. Because these offerings are consumed each day, it seems that the image really is a living god (v. 6). But Daniel knows that there is only one living God, the creator and sovereign of all that is (v. 5). Consequently, he knows that Bel must be bogus. To show that Bel really has been eating all these offerings, however, the priests instruct the king to place food and wine once more in its temple. But this time, in the king's presence, Daniel secretly sprinkles a layer of ashes on the floor of Bel's temple, a stratagem worthy of heroes in modern detective novels. In the night, the priests and their families, as usual, enter the temple by a hidden tunnel and eat and drink up all the offerings. The next morning, in a moment of high melodrama,[71] Daniel draws the king's attention to fresh footprints: "Look at the floor and notice whose footsteps these are." The king now realizes what has been happening and orders the priests and their families who have been perpetrating this fraud put to death. Here, as in Letter of Jeremiah 6:28, priests who worship idols are seen not only as idolaters but as self-serving swindlers preying upon the piety of a gullible pagan populace. The story of Bel stands with Susanna among the world's earliest detective stories. It might also be regarded as a precursor to the famous scene in *The Wizard of Oz* in which Dorothy unmasks the man behind the machine.

The story of the Dragon, or Snake, follows. "You cannot deny that this is a living god," the king tells Daniel (v. 24), pointing to some kind of large reptile, evidently moving about its cage at another shrine. This obviously is alive. But since the Lord is the only living God (v. 25), Daniel knows that this can be no god either. He feeds the poor creature poisonous pancakes and it promptly dies, to the great consternation of its worshipers, who force the king to hand Daniel over to them for retribution. They throw Daniel into the lions' den—his second time there, it seems (cf. Dan 6:16–24). The lions' rations (two human bodies and two sheep a day) are suspended in order to encourage them to eat Daniel. At this point, the plot becomes badly muddled.

The prophet Habakkuk has been innocently carrying dinner to some local farmworkers in Judea (v. 33; cf. 1 Sam 17:17–18). Suddenly "the angel of the Lord" orders him to take the dinner to Daniel in the lions' den in Babylon. When Habakkuk protests (understandably) that he has never been in Babylon and knows nothing about the den, the angel abruptly seizes him by the hair and carries him—while he carefully balances the dinner bowl—to within a few feet above the den, apparently just beyond the zone of danger. Daniel gets the dinner, and the angel returns the prophet safely home. Why the lions refrain from eating Daniel is never explained. Possibly the story mixes the lions' den plot with another version in which Daniel faces starvation. At any event, when the king discovers Daniel alive and well six days later, he declares that Daniel's God is great, releases Daniel from the den, and throws Daniel's enemies to the lions, who devour them on the spot. Again we see an instance, albeit fictive, of "death to the idolaters."[72]

As in canonical Daniel, the Letter of Jeremiah, Wisdom of Solomon 13–15, and Isaiah 40:18–28, 44:6–20, and 46:1–9, the basic theme in these Additions is that God alone is to be worshiped, never idols and false gods, however plausible they may appear. The latter may have posed a serious temptation to Jews living in the midst of pagan neighbors and under domination of foreigners who were devoted to their gods. From the standpoint of biblical faith, religion is not necessarily a "good thing." Daniel, like all righteous Israelites and Jews, is portrayed as a disbeliever or atheist regarding the existence of other gods.[73] In positive terms, the two stories illustrate obedience to the first two commandments (see Exod 20:3–5) and persistent faith in God, despite social or political pressures.

The Prayer of Manasseh

This shortest book in the Apocrypha, indeed, in the Old Testament, is also distinguished by its quality of personal piety. It resembles certain psalms of individual lament (e.g., Pss 69–71) but makes no mention of enemies or desire for vengeance. Instead, the writer consistently acknowledges his own sin (cf. 2 Esdr 7:116–126). Unlike the writer of 2 Esdras, "Manasseh" looks with hope to God for the gift of repentance and forgiveness for all who have sinned. Unlike Jonah, he knows himself as a sinner and therefore rejoices that God is "of great compassion, long-suffering, and very merciful, and repentest over the evils of men" (v. 7a; cf. Jonah 4:1–3). While the prophets called for repentance by the whole people of Israel or Judah, this writer assures readers that God has appointed repentance for individual sinners, and he identifies himself as one of these (vv. 7c–8). He uses a striking metaphor for repentance: "Now I bend the knee of my heart" (v. 11). Several apparent parallels are found to New Testament passages: verse

6 and Romans 11:33; verse 8 and Luke 5:32; verse 9 and Luke 18:13; and verse 15c and Matthew 6:13 (added ending to the Lord's Prayer). The Prayer may well have been familiar at least to Greek-speaking Jews and Christians in the first century A.D.

According to the Deuteronomic editor of 2 Kings 21, Manasseh was the worst of Judah's kings: In particular, he worshiped the gods or "abominations" of other nations and peoples, and, like earlier and later moguls and dictators, "shed very much innocent blood" (cf. 1 Macc 1:37). Later, the Chronicler undertook to rehabilitate Manasseh, probably in order to understand and explain why so wicked a king could have reigned fifty-five years, longer than any other king of either Judah or Israel. According to the Chronicler, after Manasseh prayed to God, who received his entreaty, he changed his ways for the better (2 Chr 33:12–19). The present book purports to tell what Manasseh said in that prayer. Only verses 9–10 correspond with what is known of Manasseh, however: that he had practiced apostasy and idolatry on a grand scale. Like many other texts, this Prayer acclaims God as maker of heaven and earth.[74] In accord with the first creation story (Gen 1:2, 9–10) and Job 38:8–11, the writer does not say that God created the sea; rather he "shackled" or confined it (v. 3).[75]

Later biblical tradition often sanctifies earlier figures whose character, as originally described, was less than impeccable, such as David (2 Kgs 22:2) and Jacob (Prayer of Azariah 12). Here the writer states that neither Abraham, Isaac, nor Jacob sinned against God (v. 8). The present writer implicitly views Manasseh quite favorably, as a model repentant and rehabilitated sinner.

This outstanding example of Jewish devotional writing is commonly dated in the second to first century B.C. Notwithstanding its religious quality, which he highly valued, Luther, followed by all other Protestants, concluded that the Prayer belonged in the Apocrypha. Later in the sixteenth century, the Council of Trent decided to exclude the Prayer of Manasseh, together with 1 and 2 Esdras, from the Catholic Bible. Some Eastern Orthodox Churches, however, still include the Prayer, with most of the rest of what Jews and Protestants call the Apocrypha, in their Bibles. Charlesworth includes the Prayer of Manasseh, along with full commentary, in his edition of the Pseudepigrapha.[76]

1 Maccabees

Here we have a detailed history of the Jewish people during the brief but tumultuous period of 175–135 B.C. Most of the book probably was written within a few decades of the events described in it. Generally it is considered an accurate account, though obviously told from a partisan Jewish standpoint. The writer emphasizes the heroic and splendid accomplishments of "the family": Mattathias, his three sons (Judas, Jonathan, and Simon), and Simon's son John Hyrcanus. Judas was nicknamed the Maccabee or Maccabeus, probably meaning "the hammer," in recognition of his military prowess. The members of Mattathias's family are known both as Hasmoneans and Maccabeans or Maccabees. The era in Jewish history from 167–63 B.C. is commonly designated the Hasmonean or Maccabean period because of the leadership roles played by various family members during these years.

A cursory introduction reports the triumphs of the Greek conqueror, Alexander the Great, his death (ca. 323 B.C.), his generals' succession to power, and the appearance of Antiochus IV ("Epiphanes"), who gained control over the Syrian portion of Alexander's former empire in 175 B.C. Even before Antiochus's time, certain renegade Jews began to follow gentile, that is, non-Jewish practices (1:11–15). For reasons that are not entirely certain, Antiochus determines to put an end to Jewish religion, condemns to death any Jews who persist in their religious practices, desecrates the temple, and orders Jews to sacrifice to pagan gods (1:20–2:18). Mattathias, a traditionalist Jew of priestly lineage, refuses to offer such sacrifice, kills a Jew who has done so, along with the Syrian officer who has been enforcing the order, and thereby initiates a movement for religious freedom that soon has major military and political consequences.

Emphasis on Sabbath observance apparently increased during the course of the four centuries since Jews last had occasion to fight for their nation. Consequently, when attacked on the Sabbath, the first group of Jewish traditionalists chooses to die rather than break the law by "working," that is, fighting back on that day. Jewish leaders quickly recognize that such a policy can only lead to further disaster and so determine that in the future, Jews will fight if attacked on the Sabbath (2:29–41). Mattathias and the Hasideans, ardent traditionalists, enforce orthodoxy upon those less zealous for the law, massacring backsliding "sinners," and forcibly circumcising Jewish youths whose parents have neglected to attend to that requirement (2:42–48; cf. 3 Macc 7:10–15).

Subsequently, under Judas's direction and invoking the help of Heaven, a circumlocution for the name of God, Jewish forces begin to win a series of battles, usually against much larger armies. By 164 B.C., Jerusalem is regained, the temple restored, a new altar built, and sacrificial worship resumed (4:36–59). This restoration is commemorated in the later Jewish festival of Hanukkah. Chapter 5 reports numerous additional victories by the Jews, sometimes called Israelites, over their gentile enemies, under Judas's formidable leadership.

In the following years, the Jews find themselves now on one side, now another, of the numerous contenders for control of the Syrian or Seleucid kingdom. As he lies dying, Antiochus names his friend Philip as regent (6:14–15). Lysias, who has been Antiochus's chief of staff, now puts forward the latter's son, also named Eupator, as King Antiochus V. Lysias leads a great army (including thirty-two elephants, each with its Indian driver) against Judas, but upon hearing that Philip is trying to seize the throne, Lysias comes to terms with the Jews and hastens back home to fight Philip. Soon (chap. 7), Antiochus IV's nephew, Demetrius (or Demetrius I), makes himself king and has both Antiochus V and Lysias put to death. Alcimus, "an ungodly Jew" who aspires to be high priest, ingratiates himself with King Demetrius and accuses Judas of sedition. Demetrius sends an army under General Nicanor against Judas. Nicanor's army is defeated, and his head is cut off and displayed in Jerusalem (cf. Judith 13–14). This event was to be memorialized by celebration of "Nicanor's Day" (7:49; 2 Macc 15:36).[77]

Hoping to gain support against Demetrius, Judas makes alliance with the Romans (chap. 8) but then dies fighting a huge Syrian army under Bacchides, another of Demetrius's generals. Judas's brother Jonathan becomes leader of the traditionalist Jewish forces, which succeed in compelling Bacchides to withdraw (chap. 9). Alexander Epiphanes (or Balas) now comes forward as king. Both he and Demetrius bid for the Jews' support (chap. 10). The latter side with Alexander, who offers Jonathan the high priesthood. After Demetrius dies in battle, Alexander honors Jonathan, making him provincial governor under the Syrians (10:59–66). Demetrius's son Demetrius II then arrives with an army commanded by Appolonius, which Jonathan's men put to rout, much to the delight of King Alexander.

Next, Ptolemy, king of Egypt, invades the land. In the course of further intrigue, battle, and insurrection, Alexander is killed and Ptolemy dies. Demetrius II becomes king of Syria, and Jonathan pledges allegiance to him; in return, Demetrius awards Jonathan the office of high priest and releases the Jews from the requirement of paying taxes. At this point, Trypho, an adherent of the late Alexander, pushes Alexander's son forward as King Antiochus VI, and Jonathan eventually agrees to accept the latter's sovereignty. Miraculously,

Jonathan defeats a large army sent by Demetrius II (11:63–74) and attempts to renew relations with Rome and Sparta. But then, through a devious stratagem, Jonathan is captured and later killed by Trypho, who now wants to be king himself (chap. 12).

The third Maccabean brother, Simon, is chosen leader of the Jews and negotiates a treaty with Demetrius II. The treaty results in virtual Jewish independence (ca. 142 B.C.) and the beginning of an ideal, if brief, era under Simon's leadership as high priest and ethnarch (chaps. 13–14). Next, Antiochus VII (son of Demetrius I) bids for the Seleucid throne, but when his initially promising relations with the Jews break down, he sends his commander Cendebeus (Kendebaeus, NEB) to attack them. Simon, now old, appoints his sons Judas and John (or John Hyrcanus) to lead the nation, and they rout the forces of Cendebeus (16:1–10). A certain Ptolemy, evidently hoping to gain control of the country, treacherously, assassinates Simon and two of his sons, but John Hyrcanus survives the plot, kills the assassins, and becomes high priest (ca. 134 B.C.).

The first Hasmonean to claim the title of king of the Jews probably was John's successor and son, Aristobulus I (ca. 104–103 B.C.). Thereafter, a quasi-independent Jewish kingdom under Hasmonean rule survived until 63 B.C., when the Romans annexed what they were to call Palestine and made it a province of their own mighty empire.

The period described in 1 Maccabees may well have been the context for other writings, such as Esther, Daniel, and Judith, that also report persecution of the Jews, their brave resistance, and hopes for the future. Other traditions and lore purporting to describe events in the early Maccabean period are to be found in 2 and 4 Maccabees. Third Maccabees appears to have an entirely different setting.

2 Maccabees

This writer's main purpose is to encourage his readers (or hearers; 15:39) scrupulously to maintain their Jewish traditions and practices despite both constant temptations to assimilate to the ways of gentile, particularly Greek, culture and the danger of religious persecution. In a somewhat self-conscious preface (cf. prologue to Sirach), he states that he is summarizing a detailed five-volume history by an earlier writer, Jason of Cyrene (2:19–32). Jason may have written in the last quarter of the second century B.C., while the anonymous final author of 2 Maccabees possibly composed his summary fifty to seventy-five years later. We may assume that Jason was primarily responsible for the stories and most of the details, while the present author provided most of the commentary and interpretation.

The book begins with what purport to be two letters intended to encourage Jews living in Egypt to observe the festival of Hanukkah, which celebrates the rededication of the temple by Judas Maccabeus in 164 B.C. (1:1–2:18; cf. 1 Macc 4:36–61). The writer later returns to the temple purification scene, noting that Judas and his followers voted that all Jews should observe this festival each year (10:1–8). Subsequently, they also vote to require celebration of Nicanor's Day, commemorating the defeat of that hated enemy (15:36). (Neither observance, of course, was contained or authorized in the Torah) Pious legends about Nehemiah and Jeremiah stress continuity with ancient rituals and artifacts (1:30–2:8), and the writer claims to possess all the old books and records, in order to authenticate his ties to earlier tradition (2:13–15).

The main narrative (3:1–15:37) covers the relatively brief period from the time of the high priest Onias III to Judas's defeat of Nicanor (ca. 180–160 B.C.) and tells the story of traditionalist Judaism's struggle for survival and religious freedom against Syrian oppression. Judas is still alive and is the main leader of the Jews ("Israel") at the close of the book (cf. 1 Macc 9:14–22).

Some information adds to that given in 1 Maccabees, such as descriptions of the corruption of the high priests Jason and Menelaus and the apostate zeal of these and other priests for Hellenistic (Greek) culture. Examples of the latter include the priests' enthusiasm for the gymnasium, the Greek hat, the wrestling arena, and the discus—to the neglect of their proper priestly duties (4:7–34). However, historians generally do not consider 2 Maccabees a source of reliable information. The author passes along several legendary stories illustrative of the importance of fidelity to Jewish religion and of God's power to deliver his people, such as the stories of Heliodorus's attempt to plunder the temple bank (chap. 3), the martyrdom of Eleazar (6:18–31) and of the seven brothers and their mother (chap. 7) for refusing to eat pork, and Razis's death at his own hand for the sake of Judaism (14:37–46). Apparitions—typically featuring goldclad horsemen and golden weapons—regularly inspire faithful Jews and terrify their enemies.[78] The author's perspective is suggested at 11:13: "The Hebrews were invincible because the mighty God fought on their side."

As in Judith, the focal interest is preservation of the "holy place," the temple (15:17–18). Throughout, the author presents incidents demonstrating that God punishes oppressors of the Jews but defends the latter—at least those who remain true to the law (e.g., 8:38; 10:38). Several episodes concern the Jews' slaughtering gentile enemies pursuant to the will of God (e.g., 12:1–28). The writer interjects numerous interpretive comments, somewhat along the lines of the Deuteronomic and orthodox wisdom theologies, to the effect that God brings disaster on Jews who commit idolatry and that individuals suffer because they have sinned.[79]

The book contains a number of other points of religious interest. Here we see several instances of belief in the future resurrection of martyrs and, perhaps, of other righteous Jews.[80] Those who are among the living may make atonement for the dead by prayer and offerings, looking to their resurrection (12:43–45), and certain righteous dead are visualized as praying for the benefit of Jews who are alive (15:12–14). Throughout most of the period described here, Jews refrain from fighting on the Sabbath, sometimes to their detriment,[81] but eventually Judas is granted the vision of a golden sword, apparently understood as authorization for doing battle on Sabbath days (chap. 15). As in Tobit, burial, including a magnificent funeral, is a matter of great importance (4:49; cf. 5:10; 13:7). The temple's function as a bank of deposit is noted (3:10–21; cf. 4 Macc 4:3–10). Second Maccabees contains the first references to "Judaism" (2:21; 14:38)—which accords with the book's emphasis on keeping Jewish tradition—and refers in passing to belief in God's creation of the world out of nothing (7:28; cf. Gen 1:1–2).

Two distinctive religious developments appear frequently. One is the common use of the term "holy" for entities other than God: the holy city (3:1), the holy place or temple (e.g., 5:15, 17), holy vessels (5:16), the holy Sabbath day (5:25; 6:11), the holy book (8:23), and the holy people (15:24). The other is the use of new and special titles or circumlocutions for the name of God. He is not only the Most High (3:31), but also the Sovereign of spirits (3:24), the Savior of one's life (3:35), Creator of all things or of the world (7:23; 13:14), the Defender of the Jews or their nation (8:36; 14:34), the Great Sovereign of the world (12:15), the King of kings (13:4), and the Sovereign in heaven (15:4). The most frequently used title is simply the Almighty.

3 Maccabees

Unlike the other books of the Maccabees, this writing contains no references to the Maccabean period. Instead, it purports to tell about the harrowing experiences of traditionalist Jews in Egypt during the reign of that nation's "audacious" (and intermittently befuddled) ruler, Ptolemy Philopator. Though a king by that name did rule Egypt (ca. 220–203 B.C.), it is more likely that 3 Maccabees reflects the experience of Jews, possibly in Egypt, during the course of the next two or three centuries.

The precipitating incident in the plot is Ptolemy's thwarted attempt to enter the "holy of holies," that is, the inner temple at Jerusalem. According to 2 Maccabees, one Heliodorus entered the temple to plunder bank deposits around 175 B.C., a story similar in several respects to that in 3 Maccabees about Ptolemy.[82] Antiochus IV entered the holy of holies around 170 B.C. in order to take its treasures, the Roman general Pompey entered it in 63 B.C., and the mad Roman emperor Caligula proposed to erect a statue of himself there around A.D. 40. Which of these episodes, if any, may be reflected here is uncertain. Several interpreters think that 3 Maccabees was written in the first century A.D. Though present in some important ancient biblical manuscripts, 3 Maccabees was omitted in Jerome's Vulgate and generally does not appear in Western Christian Bibles. It is included with the scriptures of the Eastern Orthodox Churches.[83]

The story line is relatively simple, in contrast to the complexities of 1 or 2 Maccabees. Ptolemy, while touring shrines around his realm, develops a compulsion to enter the holy of holies, which was supposedly barred not only to gentiles but to everyone other than the high priest (1:11–15). In response to the anguished cries of the faithful and the prayer of Simon the high priest, God intervenes, shaking and temporarily paralyzing the audacious and profane Ptolemy (1:16–2:24). Later, back in Egypt, and egged on by his drinking companions, this impious king resolves to take revenge by harassing Jews both in Alexandria and in the countryside.

Still smarting because he has been prevented from entering the inner temple, and further enraged at what he perceives as the Jews' subsequent ingratitude (i.e., their refusal to renounce Judaism in exchange for initiation into the mystery cults), Ptolemy orders his soldiers to arrest all the Jews in Egypt so that he may inflict "sure and shameful death" upon them (chap. 3). Amid the joyous shouts of bloodthirsty gentiles, the Jews are rounded up and herded into a large racetrack or amphitheater, known as the hippodrome, to be tortured and destroyed (chap. 4). "Filled with overpowering anger and wrath," King Ptolemy orders his elephant keeper, a certain Hermon, to drug five hundred elephants so that they will be all the more ferocious when they are made to charge the bound and hapless Jews the next day. The Jews cry to their God and Father in heaven, who then sends the king into such a deep sleep that the hour appointed for their destruction passes and they are spared for the time being. The eager crowd of would-be spectators eventually arouses the king, but instead of getting on with the bloodshed, he resumes drinking and calls on all his guests to join in partying with him. The Jews' execution is then rescheduled for the next day.

Next morning, however, again answering the Jews' entreaties, God confuses Ptolemy's mind so that he forgets his evil design and instead threatens Hermon and his other officials for plotting against the Jews, whom he praises for their "full and firm loyalty." Later, however, Ptolemy reconvenes the drinking party and demands to know why Hermon has not yet sent the elephants to trample the Jews. He then reschedules their destruction for the following day. But when his officers complain that he is treating them like idiots by his frequent changes of orders, Ptolemy swears that he will get on with the massacre immediately. The thundering herd of elephants, again maddened by substance ingestion (5:45–48),[84] now charges toward the hippodrome, while "countless masses" of depraved gentiles surge in, eager to witness the impending gory spectacle (chap. 5).

An old priest named Eleazer (cf. 2 Macc 6:18–31) now calls at length (6:2–15) on God to remember the descendants of Abraham and "the sainted Jacob" (6:3; cf. Prayer of Azariah 12), as he had done in the days of Pharaoh, Sennacherib, Daniel and his three friends, and Jonah.[85] When all the Jews raise a great cry to heaven, the sound terrifies the Egyptian army, which has been following the elephants into the hippodrome, and when two fearful angels suddenly appear, the great beasts turn round, trampling many of the Egyptian troops to death. The king now repents of his wicked scheme, blames it all on his officials, orders the Jews released from their bonds, and gives provisions for a seven-day festival so that the Jews might celebrate their deliverance. The king also holds a great banquet in celebration of the occasion and grants the Jews' petition that they be allowed to return to their homes (chap. 6).

Chapter 7 reports the king's letter to all his officials, in which he professes his faith in God and blames the plot against the Jews on certain malicious "friends" or officials in his court (7:1–9; cf. Add to Esth 16:1–14). Before departing, the Jews request and receive permission to massacre fellow Jews who have transgressed the law, which they proceed to do joyfully, praising God. Finally, the good traditionalist

Jews return home safely, there to enjoy great prestige and to recover all their property.

Like the writer of 2 Maccabees, the present author characterizes the temple as the holy place (1:23; 2:14) and faithful Jews or Israel as holy people (2:6; cf. Ezra 9:2, 8). He introduces even more new or uncommon titles for God than are found in 2 Maccabees. Some of the more unusual are as follows: Ruler over the whole Creation (2:7), the First Father of all (2:21), Ruler of all Power (5:7; 7:9), Almighty God Most High and King of Great Power (6:2), Eternal One (6:12), Honored One (6:13), the Eternal Savior of Israel (7:18), and the Deliverer of Israel through all times (7:23). God's providence is implicit in several such titles, in certain explicit expressions (e.g., at 4:19–21; 5:30), and in the story as a whole. The book's theme is that God will deliver faithful Jews who call on him, even when there is no hope in sight. Deliverance is conceived as providential rescue of the living from torment and death rather than as the resurrection of the righteous (cf. 2 Maccabees) or the reward of eternal life (cf. 4 Maccabees).

4 Maccabees

Fourth Maccabees has not been accorded full canonical status in any known Jewish or Christian Bibles, but it is found in the appendix section of Greek Orthodox Bibles. Many early Christian bishops and theologians found the book inspiring, if not authoritative, and frequently cited it with approval. It consists largely of an elaboration upon the stories of the martyrdom of Eleazer and of the anonymous seven brothers and their anonymous mother that appeared earlier in 2 Maccabees 6:18–7:42. Here these stories are retold and embellished in order to illustrate the present author's concern, which is to present Judaism as a reputable philosophy and to demonstrate that Jews, who through reason control their emotions and thereby remain faithful to the law, will be rewarded with immortality or eternal life, at least if they die as martyrs. Like 3 Maccabees, 4 Maccabees is included in standard editions of the Pseudepigrapha.[86]

The author's characterization of Judaism as a philosophy recalls Philo's and Josephus's attempts to so represent Judaism in order to find an acceptable place for it in the world of Greek culture. The present author reflects acquaintance with Platonic and Stoic concepts but is concerned to stress the necessity of keeping strict Jewish tradition at all cost by refusing to eat pork or food previously sacrificed to idols.[87] Repeatedly, he relates reason to Jewish law, at times equating the two.

Both reason and law function to control or restrain the emotions, which include, particularly, pleasure and pain, which affect both body and soul (1:20). Other important emotions that are of special concern in the book are brotherly and maternal love (14:1, 20; 15:20). Virtue, self-control, and knowledge also figure frequently in the writer's argument.

The central theme is that Jews, who know that eternal life awaits those who keep the law zealously, act with reason when they preserve their virtue by fidelity to the law, notwithstanding the prospect of torture and death for so doing.[88] Clearly, the writer's intention is to summon fellow Jews to keep the law and tradition despite persecution (see, e.g., 17:8–10; 18:1–2). The emphasis on persecution suggests that the writer lived at a time when Jews were seriously threatened for practicing their religion. The rather persuasive arguments advanced by "the tyrant Antiochus" (5:5–13; 8:5–14) may contain echoes of real controversies in the author's time. The book, probably written in Greek, seems dependent on 2 Maccabees, and dates from sometime between the late second century B.C. and A.D. 120. Jews were subjected to persecution or other forms of hostility several times during those years under Seleucid and Roman authorities.

The embellished accounts of the martyrs purportedly illustrate the supremacy of reason over the emotions. Reason, however, is understood broadly as "devout reason" (16:1, 4). Thus, the martyrs undergo torture and death not so much for the sake of reason as such as for their religion or that of their fathers (6:22; 9:7, 29; cf. 11:21) or just plain "religion" (9:24; 13:27; 16:13), the law, or their ancestral law (6:27, 30; 16:16), virtue (11:2; cf. 9:18), or God (16:19). They thereby serve and vindicate "the way of the Hebrew people" and their nation (17:9–10).

Unlike 2 Maccabees, which looks for the *resurrection* of the martyrs (if not of all the righteous who have died), 4 Maccabees gives assurances that those martyred for keeping the law will enjoy *immortality* or *everlasting life*, with God in the presence of Abraham, Isaac, Jacob, and other patriarchs who, though they have died, "live in God."[89] The martyrs, the author tells us, now stand before the divine throne (17:18; cf. Rev 20:4–6). Fourth Maccabees 10:15 suggests that all pious Jews will experience everlasting life when they die. Jews who transgress the commandments of God, however, face the prospect of eternal torment by fire (13:15).[90] The wicked oppressors of the Jews also will suffer eternal torment by fire and otherwise (9:9; 12:12).[91] Some other possible echoes of 2 and 4 Maccabees appear in the book of Revelation.

Several passages suggest that God might accept the martyrs' deaths in exchange for those of the rest of the Jewish people.[92] The underlying rationale is similar to that of the Deuteronomic theology of history: When God's people break the commandments, he will punish them for doing so. Here the idea seems to be that God might accept the deaths of some, rather than punish all. The writer explains that God ("the Divine Justice") moved Antiochus to oppress the Jews because under the influence of the wicked high priest Jason, they had changed their ways in favor of Hellenism, even to the extent of abandoning the temple service (4:17–21).[93] Prior to that time, they enjoyed peace and prosperity because they observed the law (3:20). Thus, unlike the author of Revelation, the writer does not invoke cosmic dualism in order to explain the disasters that befall the martyrs and other righteous persons. There is no mention of Satan in this connection. Instead, the writer understands that Antiochus has received his kingdom from God (12:11). Consistent with this affirmation of God's universal sovereignty, the author refers to him three times as Providence.[94] This God is not only Creator of all things (11:5) but also Ruler over all history. One passage probably does refer to a demonic figure, "the destroyer, the deceitful serpent" (18:8). That being, however, functions only in the limited role of one who goes about defiling the virginity of young women.[95]

The mother of the seven brothers receives special attention in 4 Maccabees. The writer mentions, in passing, that "mothers are the weaker sex" (15:5), but then goes on to praise this mother in striking terms. She is "mother of the nation, vindicator of the law and champion of religion" (15:29). Moreover, she is "more noble than males in steadfastness, and more manly than men in endurance" (15:30), a "soldier of God in the cause of religion" and an "elder" (16:14). Clearly she is an exemplar par excellence of the kind of "reason" the author commends to all his Jewish readers.

Psalm 151

Both the RSV and the NRSV include two versions of Psalm 151. The longer is translated from the Hebrew version in the Dead Sea Scrolls (DSS), the shorter is from the Septuagint (LXX). No other modern Western Bible contains this psalm (or 3 and 4 Maccabees), but it was present in several important LXX manuscripts, and the LXX version of Psalm 151 (along with 3 Maccabees) is recognized as fully canonical in

Bibles of the Eastern Orthodox Churches, where it appears at the end of the book of Psalms. The DSS version, which is in Hebrew, seems to have been part of the scriptures of the Qumran sect. A Syriac version of Psalm 151 was also found among the DSS. The psalm probably was first composed sometime between 200 B.C. and A.D. 70.

Both the DSS and LXX versions of this short psalm take the form of an autobiographical statement by David, which might be paraphrased as follows: I was smaller and younger than my brothers; I tended my father's flock; my hands and fingers fashioned a lyre to play for the glory of God, who sent his messenger or prophet to take me from following the flock and anoint me; even though my brothers were tall and handsome, the Lord did not choose them.

Verses 3, 4, and 7b of the DSS psalm are without parallels in the LXX version. The last two verses of the LXX version, which refer to David's encounter with "the Philistine" (presumably Goliath), may have paralleled a description of the encounter found at the beginning of another psalm that follows immediately afterward in the DSS, identified in *OTP* as Psalm 151B. Psalm 151 contains several echoes of passages and events in 1 Samuel 16 and 17. Some of the psalms ascribed to David in the book of Psalms are set in particular situations in the course of his career, but these are in the form of prayers to God for deliverance from personal or national enemies generally rather than autobiographical reminiscences.[96] Four additional psalms found among the DSS in Syriac and Hebrew versions are included in the *OTP* as Psalms 152, 153, 154, and 155.

NOTES

Overview

1. The two main collections of the New Testament Apocrypha are J. K. Elliott, ed., *The Apocryphal New Testament* (New York: Oxford University Press, 1994), a new revised edition that updates the earlier classic volume by M. R. James; and Edgar Hennecke, ed., *New Testament Apocrypha*, 2 vols. (Philadelphia: Westminster, 1963, 1965).

2. The Septuagint is often referred to as the LXX, the Roman numeral for seventy.

3. On this matter, see Luther's "Prefaces to the Apocrypha" in *Luther's Works* 35:337 n. 1 (Philadelphia: Fortress, 1960).

4. In recognition of this practice, the *New Oxford Annotated Bible with the Apocrypha* (New York: Oxford University Press, 1991) includes on its title

page the enlarged caption, "The New Oxford Annotated Bible with the Apocryphal/Deuterocanonical Books."

5. In deference to these traditional practices, the *New Oxford Annotated Bible with the Apocrpypha* includes 1 Esdras, the Prayer of Manasseh, Psalm 151, 3 Maccabees, 2 Esdras, and 4 Maccabees, in that order, at the end of the Deuterocanonical books, just before its New Testament section.

6. In subsequent years, many publishers found that they could economize by omitting the Old Testament Apocrypha from the Bibles they produced.

1 Esdras

7. The Septuagint is the name given commonly for the Greek Bible of Judaism in the last two centuries B.C. and the first century A.D. At that time, Greek was the common language of many people in the Mediterranean world, and possibly more Jews spoke and read Greek than Hebrew.

8. See Ezra 3–5, Zechariah 4, and Haggai.

9. Cf. Neh 2:1–8, where another Persian king authorizes Nehemiah to rebuild Jerusalem.

10. Cf. 1 Esdr 4:57, where Darius orders these same vessels returned.

2 Esdras (or 4 Ezra)

11. Uriel is one of seven biblical and intertestamental archangels, each of whose name ends in "el." Another is Jeremiel, who appears in 2 Esdr 4:36. Gabriel and Michael are mentioned in the Book of Daniel, and Raphael in the Book of Tobit. See Tob 12:15 and 1 Enoch 20:1–8.

12. See 2 Esdr 4:38; 7:46–48, 68; 8:35.

13. In popular imagination and lore, these are known as "the lost ten tribes of Israel."

14. Cf. 1 Esdr 4:33–41.

15. As to the "habitations" of the righteous, cf. Tob 3:6 and Luke 16:9, 23.

16. Cf. Paul's reflections on related matters in Romans 9–11.

17. Cf. Matt 25:31–46; Luke 10:29–37.

18. Cf. the book of Tobit, where proper burial is a recurrent concern.

Tobit

19. Cf. Dan 1:8, Jdt 12:2; Add to Esth 14:17.

20. See also Tob 14:11, 13; cf. 2 Esdr 2:23; Mark 15:43–46.

21. As in Proverbs and especially Sirach, these sayings commend consideration for others, including charitable giving. See also the angel's wisdom admonition in Tob 12:8–9.

22. The issue here is whether angels do or do not have physical (corporeal) bodies. These texts may have given rise to the purported medieval theological preoccupation with the question of how many angels can dance on the head of a pin. The answer to that one is fairly simple: If corporeal, at most one; if incorporeal, any number up to and including infinity. There is no evidence

that medieval theology was seriously concerned about this question, however popular this notion may have been with later detractors of religion.

23. See, e.g., Tob 5:20; 7:4, 16; 8:4, 7.

24. See, e.g., Pss 148:7, 10; 150:6; Song of the Three Young Men 57–59. See also the traditional Christian doxology: "Praise God from whom all blessings flow, Praise him all creatures here below . . ."

25. The most notable biblical scenes set in the heavenly council are Job 1:6–12 and 2:1–6. See also Tob 12:15.

26. The latter verse includes the angel's remarkable statement: "I know that Raguel, according to the law of Moses, cannot give her to another man without incurring the penalty of death, because you rather than any other man are entitled to the inheritance." There is no such biblical law.

27. Here as in other later biblical writings, the divine names "God" (Elohim) and "the LORD" (Yahweh) are often replaced with circumlocutions such as these. See also Tob 4:11, "the Most High."

28. Cf. Gen 6:3; Job 42:16.

29. Cf. the books of Jonah and Nahum, which offer contrasting views of Nineveh's destruction.

Judith

30. See 1 and 2 Maccabees.

31. Jdt 4:2, 12–13; 8:21–24; 9:8.

32. See 1 Macc 1:21–24, 54; cf. Dan 8:9–13.

33. Cf. 1 Macc 1:14–50; Dan 3:3–15.

34. Cf. Judg 3:30; 8:25.

35. See also Isa 66:24; Sir 7:17; Mark 9:43–48.

36. Cf. Num 27:8–11; Job 42:15.

37. See also 4 Macc 15.

Additions to Esther

38. Artaxerxes I ruled approximately from 464 to 425, Artaxerxes II from about 404 to 358.

39. Cf. John 11:41–42, where Jesus prays in order to be heard by the people standing around him.

40. See, e.g., Isa 27:1; Ezekiel 38–39; Dan 12:1; Zechariah 14; Mark 13; Revelation 12; 13; 20.

41. Many other biblical writings attempt, in one way or another, to account for the nonfulfillment of earlier apocalyptic hopes and expectations. See, e.g., Dan 12:9–13 (extending the expected time from 1290 to 3335 days), John 21:20–23 (explaining that the expectation of Jesus' early return was based on a misunderstanding of Jesus' saying about Peter), and 2 Peter 3:1–10 (explaining, among other things, that the Lord reckons time differently than humans do and that, anyway, the delay shows his forebearance, so "that all should reach repentance").

Wisdom of Solomon (or Wisdom)
42. Cf. Eccl 1:12–2:12.
43. Cf. John 1:1–5; Col 1:15–17.
44. Cf. Gen 9:24–26.
45. Cf. Exod 20:4 and Deut 5:8, which can be read to prohibit not only worshiping but even making artistic representations of anything.
46. Cf. Num 11:4–6, where, as elsewhere in earlier biblical tradition, Israelites repeatedly complain that manna was scarcely fit to eat.
47. See esp. Wis 16:7–8; 19:22.
48. See Wis 2:24. Cf. Genesis 3, which refers only to the serpent, one of the creatures God had made, and understands human mortality as part of God's punishment for the first couple's disobedience.

Ecclesiasticus (or the Wisdom of Jesus, Son of Sirach)
49. See, e.g., Sir 34:11–12; 39:32–34; 51:13–22.
50. Cf. Prov 23:29–35.
51. See, e.g., Sir 20:18, 29; 21:2, 14; 40:17–27.
52. See, e.g., Sir 10:1–3; 11:7–9; 20:27–28; 37:7–35.
53. See, e.g., 5:1 (on financial transactions); 5:13 (on speaking); 6:13 (on enemies and friends); 10:23, 31 (on neither honoring nor despising); 11:2 (on praising and loathing); 33:14–15 (on good and evil); 41:1–2 (on death).
54. See, e.g., Sir 7:14b, 35; 9:5a; 11:19; 19:17; 27:6; 28:3–4.
55. See Tob 4:17; cf. Let Jer 27.
56. See Sir 10:4; 39:16–35; 42:15–43:33.
57. Cf. Mal 4:5–6; Mark 9:11–13; Luke 1:17.

Baruch
58. See 2 Kgs 25:9. Sacrifices were again being offered at the temple site in Jerusalem following its purification and rededication early in the Maccabean period (see 1 Macc 4:36–59).
59. Cf. Jer 29:7, where the prophet instructs the exiles in Babylon to seek the welfare of that city and pray to Yahweh on its behalf, and Matt 5:44 = Luke 6:28, where Jesus tells his hearers to love and pray for their enemies.
60. See the book of Lamentations.
61. Cf. Rom 1:18–2:16.
62. Cf. the equation of reason and law in 4 Maccabees.
63. The writer's description of the unnamed shameless foreign nation (4:15, 25) contrasts with the first section's positive attitude toward the Babylonian kings (1:11–12).

Letter of Jeremiah
64. See also Ps 115:4–8; Isa 40:18–20; 41:7; 44:9–20; 46:1–2, 5–7; Jer 10:2–16; Wisdom of Solomon 13–15; and Bel and the Dragon.
65. Cf. Lam 5:7 and Bar 3:5, 8, which blame the exiles' "fathers."

66. Cf. Jer 29:10, which anticipated that the exile would last for seventy years. In fact, a significant Jewish community remained in Babylon for several centuries. It was in Babylon that the Babylonian Talmud was later set down.

The Prayer of Azariah and the Song of the Three Young Men

67. The other "additions" are the stories of Susanna and Bel and the Dragon.

68. Cf. Pss 148; 150:6; also Job 38–40, which likewise affirms Yahweh's creation of, compassion for, and dominion over all creation and all living beings.

Susanna

69. Cf. Sus 48, where Daniel refers to Susanna as "a daughter of Israel."

Bel and the Dragon

70. Bel and the Dragon is the title as rendered in the RSV and NRSV. The NEB and REB translate the title as Bel and the Snake.

71. Cf. Esther 7; Additions to Esther 15.

72. Cf. Exod 32:21–29; Deuteronomy 13; and 1 Kgs 18:40.

73. Cf. Revelation 13–14 and 20, where Christians face persecution for refusing to acknowledge the deity of the Roman gods or emperor.

The Prayer of Manasseh

74. See, e.g., Psalm 148; Isaiah 45; Song of the Three Young Men; and the Apostles' Creed.

75. Cf. Jonah 1:9, where that prophet acknowledges—unhappily, it seems—that Yahweh "made the sea and the dry land."

76. See the suggested reading list at the end of this book.

1 Maccabees

77. Second Maccabees presents a detailed if possibly less historically reliable account of events in the Maccabean era that ends with the defeat and death of Nicanor.

2 Maccabees

78. See, e.g., 2 Macc 3:24–30; 5:1–4; 11:18.

79. See, e.g., 2 Macc 6:12–16; 7:18, 32; 8:36; 12:40–42.

80. See, e.g., 2 Macc 7:9, 14; 14:46; cf. Dan 12:2–3.

81. See, e.g., 2 Macc 5:25–26; 6:11; 8:26.

3 Maccabees

82. See 2 Macc 3:8–40; cf. 3 Macc 1:8–2:23.

83. For an alternate translation and additional commentary, see *OTP* 2:509–29.

84. Cf. 3 Macc 5:1–3 and 1 Macc 6:34.

85. Jonah here is regarded as a model of piety; cf. his characterization in the book of Jonah.

4 Maccabees

86. See *OTP* 2:531–64 for another modern translation and detailed commentary and notes.

87. Cf. 1 Cor 8:1–13; 10:14–11:1.

88. See especially the homilies in chaps. 1–2; 13; 16; and 18.

89. See, e.g., 4 Macc 5:37; 7:19; 13:17; 16:25; cf. Mark 12:26–27. Cf. Dan 12:1–3, which looks for the resurrection of the dead, with Wis 3:1–9; 5:1, 15–16, affirming the immortality of the righteous or of their souls.

90. Cf. Isa 66:24; Rev 14:9–11.

91. Cf. Jdt16:17; Rev 20:10.

92. See 4 Macc 6:28–29; 17:21–22; 18:4.

93. Cf. 2 Macc 4:7–20.

94. See 4 Macc 9:24; 13:19; 17:22.

95. Cf. the role of the demon Asmodeus in Tob 3:7–8.

Psalm 151

96. See, e.g., Pss 56; 59; 60; 63 (captions included in RSV, NRSV, and REB but omitted in NEB).

PART IV
The New Testament, or Canonical Early Christian Writings

OVERVIEW

The Bible of the early Christian churches was the same as that of their Jewish contemporaries, namely, the collection of writings known among later Christians as the Old Testament. Both Jews and Christians during the first century A.D. mainly used the Greek translation of the Old Testament, the Septuagint, and other Greek versions, which included most of the writings contained in what later was called the Old Testament Apocrypha. There was as yet no New Testament, and no one yet referred to the Old Testament. The earliest references to an Old and a New Testament appeared around A.D. 200, but it was not until near the end of the fourth century that Christians generally agreed on which writings were to be included in this supplement to their earlier scriptures.

"New Testament" is a misleading translation of Hebrew and Greek expressions meaning a "new covenant." Jeremiah had looked for the time when God would make a new covenant with Israel and Judah, one written on people's hearts.[1] The book of Hebrews draws directly on the Jeremiah passage in characterizing the new covenant Christians have with God,[2] arguing that Christ mediates better promises and a better covenant.[3] In the course of time, the term was extended to refer to Christian writings that, in general terms, described this new covenant, and in time came to be regarded as Scripture.

By A.D. 140, if not earlier, many Christians came to regard Paul's letters as authoritative writings and as a supplement to the Old Testament.[4] Marcion was the first Christian known to have proposed the creation of an entire new set of scriptures for Christianity (ca. A.D. 140). He observed that the God described in Jewish scriptures delighted in bloody sacrifices and revenge, and concluded that this God must be evil by nature, since he had created such an evil world as the one in which humans were condemned to live. He rejected both the God of Judaism and its Bible. Instead, he urged Christians to worship Jesus, a previously unknown God, and to use as Scripture his own edited version of Luke's Gospel and some of Paul's letters. Marcion's radical proposal (which in time other Christians rejected as heretical), along with other deviant, and generally gnostic, teachings and writings,[5] prompted Christian leaders to begin to try to identify precisely the writings that were to be considered authoritative or canonical for the faith and life of their growing communities.

Bishops and other church fathers, such as Irenaeus, Tertullian, Origen, and Eusebius, tried to distinguish canonical from noncanonical writings, beginning in the late second century and into the first part of the fourth. Some authorities included writings that eventually were excluded from the canon, such as the *Gospel of Peter* and the *Revelation of Peter*, *1–2 Clement*, the *Shepherd of Hermas*, and the *Epistle of Barnabas*,[6] while omitting several writings that ultimately were included, such as the Gospel of John, Colossians, Hebrews, James, 1–2 Peter, 2–3 John, Jude, and Revelation. By the end of the fourth century, Christians had all but reached universal agreement that the New Testament canon would consist of its present twenty-seven books. At least officially, then and ever since, Christians have also agreed, against Marcion, that the Old Testament would remain part of their Bible as well.

Paul's letters, probably the earliest New Testament writings, were composed between A.D. 50 and 60. If a written source Q existed (see below), it may have been set down as early as A.D. 40, but no such document is extant. The Gospel of Mark could have been written as early as A.D. 60. The latest New Testament writings probably are 1–2 Timothy and Titus (the Pastoral Letters; ca. A.D. 110–20), Jude (ca. A.D. 120–140), and 2 Peter (ca. A.D. 120–140). The other canonical Gospels are generally dated between A.D. 70 and 100, and the other New Testament writings between about 90 and 110.

The New Testament writings eventually were arranged according to the following scheme. First, the Gospels, taken together, report on Jesus' birth, his public ministry or activity and teaching, and his trial, death, and early resurrection appearances. Next comes Acts, which describes Christianity's growth from Jerusalem and its environs into a universal religion, open to gentiles (non-Jews) as well as Jews. Then follow Paul's letters—or those believed to have been written by Paul—arranged in approximate order of length: the longest (Romans) first, then the next longest (1 Corinthians), on down to the shortest (Philemon).[7] Next come letters attributed to other writers, again beginning with the longest (Hebrews), followed by the next longest (James), and ending with Jude, the shortest of the non-Pauline letters apart from 2 and 3 John, which are grouped with 1 John. These non-Pauline letters generally deal with problems arising in the churches a decade or more after Paul's time. Finally, the New Testament closes with the book of Revelation, which probably was written in response to the persecution of Christians in the Roman province of Asia around A.D. 96. This writing looks for the return of Jesus and the beginning of the new age of salvation in what was then the near future.

The first three Gospels are called the Synoptic Gospels because when read or "seen together," they present similar accounts of Jesus' message and activity. Some interpreters urge that Matthew was the earliest Gospel, and that Mark and Luke based their versions on it. Most interpreters, however, view Mark as the earliest Gospel, and suggest that Matthew and Luke both used its narrative framework and many of its sayings when writing their own Gospels.

Approximately two hundred verses consisting mainly of Jesus' sayings that do not appear in Mark are found in both Matthew and Luke. Most interpreters agree that these verses derived from an earlier written or oral source commonly called Q.[8] The exact extent of the Q material is unknown, however, since, if there was such a source, we can only identify its contents from those texts both Matthew and Luke drew from it. Neither Matthew nor Luke necessarily used all of it, and either may have drawn on it at times when the other did not. Thus, some sayings found only in Matthew or only in Luke may also have come from Q. Many, but not all, interpreters believe that Matthew had an additional special source (M) and that Luke had his special source (L). Interpreters also generally credit the evangelists with the composition of some verses and the editorial revision or modification of others. The Synoptic evangelists, then, may be seen not only as collectors and editors or redactors, but also as authors of some of the traditions we find in their Gospels.

The first three, or Synoptic Gospels, are generally regarded as the main sources of information about Jesus' own activities and words. Since the latter part of the eighteenth century, a great deal of attention has been focused on "the historical Jesus," that is, on the effort to determine what can be said with some degree of probability about him. The classic scholarly account of such efforts, originally published in 1906, is Albert Schweitzer's *The Quest of the Historical Jesus*.[9] Schweitzer regarded Reimarus as the first serious writer to pursue this quest.[10] Among many issues Schweitzer identified, two remain central in current scholarship. First, how much really can be known about the historical Jesus? Both the nineteenth and twentieth centuries have seen publication of highly skeptical conclusions.[11] Several members of the Jesus Seminar express their doubts that more than a few of Jesus' sayings in the Gospels are accurately attributed to him.[12] The Jesus Seminar has not been without its critics.[13] It is safe to say that contemporary scholarly opinion remains divided on this issue.

The other significant issue Schweitzer identified was the problem of eschatology. Did Jesus, as the Synoptic Gospels clearly indicate, expect the coming of the kingdom of God or the parousia of the Son of man to take place in the very near future, perhaps during his own lifetime but at least during the lifetime of some of his own contemporaries? Schweitzer credited Johannes Weiss with having first clearly and boldly so concluded.[14] But that conclusion posed serious problems for both traditional and liberal Christian faith. For the former, the question was: How could Jesus, the Son of God incarnate, have been in error? For liberal Christianity, Jesus was the great teacher of the moral life. What meaning or relevance could his words have for later times if he really intended his teaching only for people in his own time? Schweitzer noted the beginning of what he called "the struggle against eschatology" in the aftermath of Weiss's work.[15] This struggle has been a central feature of historical Jesus studies in the twentieth century. Both traditionalist and liberal interpreters have undertaken to preserve their respective images of a Jesus without eschatology.[16] Schweitzer observed that writings about Jesus that failed to take account of his eschatological orientation tended to fill that vacuum with all sorts of imaginative, but historically unfounded, representations of his mission and message, and that these representations typically depicted Jesus as a founder of the writer's own particular religious or ideological schools. That observation still seems an apt characterization of many recent books, and dramatic or media productions about Jesus.

Readers of the Gospels, at any rate, may wish to consider to what extent these accounts report with some accuracy what Jesus may have said and done, and to what extent they represent the interests or concerns of the Gospel writers or the communities in and for which they wrote. Like most other New Testament authors, the Synoptic evangelists themselves evidently believed that the end of the present age was near, and they cautioned their readers to be ready for the coming of the kingdom of God and the parousia of the Son of man. So, they wrote, Jesus himself had advised and proclaimed.

Luke is generally regarded as the author/editor of the book of Acts. Evidently when the Gospel of John was included, it was placed after the Synoptic Gospels and between the two volumes of Luke-Acts. John's Gospel has a few features in common with the Synoptics, but for the most part it gives a rather different account of the course of events in Jesus' ministry and a very different account of his sayings and his self-understanding.

Most of Paul's letters, or "epistles," were written to churches he himself had founded, and deal with problems there about which he had learned. The exceptions are Romans, his own theological letter of introduction to this significant church that he had neither founded nor, as yet, visited, and his letter to Philemon, a person who, under his influence, had converted to Christianity. Interpreters use the term "Deutero-Pauline" to refer to Ephesians, Colossians, and sometimes 2 Thessalonians. These letters purport to have been written by Paul but may well have been composed by associates or followers of Paul who used his name. We learn from 2 Thessalonians 2:1–2 that people other than Paul had already been writing letters in Paul's name. Many interpreters think that Paul did write one or more of these letters. Few, however, believe that Paul wrote 1 and 2 Timothy and Titus, which, together, are commonly designated the Pastoral Letters. These letters (or tracts) may have been composed by someone who wished to invoke Paul's authority in dealing with problems of the early second century, notably those presented by deviant doctrines and questionable moral standards among the churches and their leadership.

Most of the non-Pauline letters were written as treatises or tracts for the guidance and instruction of Christians during the late first and early second centuries A.D. They are commonly called "catholic" or general epistles, since they were addressed, in effect, to all Christians everywhere.[17] Possible exceptions are 1 Peter, which was addressed to churches in certain provinces of Asia Minor, 2 John, which may have been written to a particular church, and 3 John, which is in the form of a letter to a single person named Gaius. Revelation might be considered in this connection also, since it was addressed to seven churches in the Roman province of Asia and may not have been intended for Christians elsewhere. Other than Hebrews, whose writer remains anonymous, the other non-Pauline letters purport to have been authored by (or were later attributed to) persons who had been apostles of Jesus (Peter and John) or else his brothers (James and Jude).

The term "Christian" is rarely used in the New Testament,[18] and "Christianity" does not appear at all. The New Testament writers used a wide variety of terms to name the adherents of the new religion and the religion itself. Acts frequently refers to followers of "the Way."[19]

Other common terms for Christians are "(the) brethren"[20] and "the saints."[21] Somewhat less common terms for Christians are "believers,"[22] "the elect,"[23] those "of the truth,"[24] "beloved,"[25] "children" or "little children,"[26] and "children of God."[27] Christians are also referred to as those "called to belong to Jesus Christ" (Rom 1:6) and "friends" (3 John 15). Christianity is known variously as "the faith,"[28] or "our faith" (1 John 5:4), "the truth,"[29] "the mystery" (Eph 3:3–4, 9; 6:19), "(our) religion" (1 Tim 3:16; 2 Tim 3:5), "the doctrine" (2 John 9), "the brotherhood" (1 Pet 3:17), and "the way of truth" or of "righteousness" (2 Pet 2:2, 21). As a convenience, we shall use "Christian" and "Christianity" in the following chapters as if these terms had already been current during the New Testament period.

Matthew

Early Christian tradition attributes this writing to Matthew, presumably the apostle named at 9:9 and 10:3. That some time has passed between the events and the writing of the Gospel is suggested by the phrase "to this day" at 27:8 and 28:15. The author's apparent use of Mark (written ca. A.D. 60–70) and his probable reference to the destruction of Jerusalem (22:7) suggest a date after A.D. 70, perhaps as late as 90. Some modern scholars nevertheless urge that Matthew's was the earliest Gospel. Its use by Ignatius of Antioch (ca. 110) and the prominence assigned to Peter (16:18–19) indicate that it may have been written in Antioch, Syria, where Peter seems to have been a leading figure.

Matthew evidently reproduces Mark's basic narrative framework, adding, at the beginning, Jesus' genealogy and stories about his birth, the wise men, and Herod (chaps. 1–2), and at the end, stories about the appearance of the risen Jesus to the Marys and to the eleven (28:9–20). Within Mark's narrative structure, Matthew presents five collections of Jesus' sayings, each concluding with an editorial statement marking the end of the sayings and the resumption of narrative.[1] The first collection is the famous Sermon on the Mount.[2] Matthew also has collected and arranged several subgroups of sayings, for example, the "antitheses" or sayings about the law ("You have heard that it was said . . . But I say to you. . ."; 5:21–48), and sayings about practicing piety (6:1–18), John the Baptist and himself (11:2–19), the kingdom of God (13:18–50), and the coming judgment (24:36–25:46).

Many of the sayings parallel Mark, and probably were drawn from sayings found in Mark. Some two hundred verses, consisting largely of sayings, are similar to sayings found in Luke's Gospel but not in

Mark's. These verses are commonly designated as "Q" sayings.[3] Several hundred additional sayings are found only in Matthew's Gospel. These may have been drawn from sources known only to Matthew, or may represent Q sayings omitted by Luke. Numerous sayings are given twice, usually with slight variations, such as sayings on the excision of bodily members that cause sin,[4] divorce and remarriage (5:31–32; 19:3–9), good and bad trees and their respective fruit (7:16–20; 12:33), God's desire for mercy rather than sacrifice (9:13; 12:7), the sign of Jonah (12:39–41; 16:4), and the disciples' authority to bind and loose (16:19; 18:18). These considerations indicate that Matthew meant his writing (later called a Gospel) as a complete account of Jesus' ministry and message that could guide and instruct the Christian community for which he prepared it on matters of belief and conduct.[5] Interpreters generally agree that this was a Jewish Christian community, that is, a community of Christians who had been, and in some ways still were, Jews.

All the earliest Christians had been Jews. Matthew's Gospel shows that questions about the place of Jewish law in the Christian life of that early era had not yet been resolved (cf. Galatians). Here, Jesus not only commands observance of the written law (5:17–19) but also requires obedience to the oral law (tradition) of the Pharisees (23:2–3, 23). At the outset (1:1), Matthew states that Jesus is descended from Abraham, thus a Jew, and from David, thus qualified to be the Messiah (Christ), a term that had meaning only in Jewish circles. Throughout the Gospel, Matthew interprets events associated with Jesus as fulfilled messianic prophecies.[6] Yet clearly Matthew's Jesus rejects the leadership of the scribes and Pharisees (23:2–33). Instead, the church is to be guided by the will of God as set forth in the words of Jesus (7:21–29), which require a standard of righteousness beyond that determined by the scribes and Pharisees (5:20–28). Interpreters suggest that Matthew organized Jesus' sayings into the five collections following the model of Moses' five books of the Law. Thus, Matthew's Jesus is presented as a new or second Moses; he is the authoritative teacher of what God requires of those who would enter his kingdom.

As in Mark, Jesus proclaims that the kingdom of God is near and calls his hearers to repent before the Son of man comes to judge the world (4:17; 24:29–44); he casts out demons, heals the sick (8:1–6), and sends his twelve disciples to extend this mission of preaching, exorcism, and healing to all Jews or "Israel" (10:1–15). Matthew 10:23 even suggests that Jesus expects the parousia (the coming of the Son of man and the beginning of the kingdom of God or messianic age) to occur before the Twelve return. Later, after their return, Jesus "feeds" his followers the meal of bread and fish in the wilderness (chaps. 14–15), perhaps to consecrate them for the joys of life together in the coming kingdom.[7] As in Mark, Jesus then turns to Jerusalem to purify the temple, preach, eat the Last Supper with the Twelve, suffer, die, and be raised from the dead (chaps. 16–28).

Matthew emphasizes Jesus' miraculous or supernatural power. For instance, Matthew says that Jesus did not do many mighty works in his own country, rather than that he could not do so (13:59; cf. Mark 6:5). In Matthew's version, when Jesus "cursed" the fig tree, it withered at once (21:19; cf. Mark 11:20), and he fed not only five and four thousand men but also unnumbered women and children (14:21; 15:38; cf. Mark 6:44; 8:9).

Matthew also stresses the coming judgment and the fate of the unrighteous. He alone depicts the great judgment scene with its separation of the sheep from the goats, based on people's response to those in need—or lack of same (25:31–46). More than any other Gospel writer, he underscores the punishment awaiting the condemned in eternal fire or "outer darkness," where there will be "weeping and gnashing of teeth."[8]

A further characteristic is Matthew's concern to reinterpret certain problematic sayings found in Mark. Thus, Matthew's Jesus does not deny that he is good (19:16–17; cf. Mark 10:17–18), it is the mother of James and John who asks that they be given special status in the coming kingdom (20:20–21; cf. Mark 10:35–37), and divorce is allowed in cases of unchastity (5:32; 19:9; cf. Mark 10:11–12).[9] In these and other ways, Matthew gave his community a record of Jesus' words and deeds that could guide their faith and life at that time and, as it turned out, in the following centuries. During the course of these centuries, Christians placed it first not only among the Gospels but among all the writings they came to call the New Testament.

Mark

This Gospel, probably written around A.D. 60–70, perhaps in Rome, was intended for gentile (non-Jewish) Christians, as is evidenced by the author's numerous explanations of Jesus' Aramaic expressions and of Jewish practices.[10] The term "gospel," meaning "good news," represents a later addition to the title. None of Jesus' twelve disciples was named Mark.[11] Interpreters sometimes suggest that the author may have been the young man mentioned at 14:51–52. In any case, the author is traditionally called Mark; as early as the second century, the Gospel came to be captioned "according to Mark."

Mark describes Jesus' adult activity or career, beginning with his baptism by John and ending with the empty tomb (16:8). This Gospel is characterized by a sense of urgency and mystery. Terms such as "immediately" and "and" continuously drive the narration forward. Mystery and wonder are expressed not only in the Gospel's abrupt conclusion but in the "messianic secret," the recurrent amazement of the crowds,[12] the disciples' chronic lack of comprehension,[13] and Jesus' announcements of the impending suffering ("passion"), death, and resurrection of "the Son of man"—with whom he only indirectly identifies himself.[14]

Mark describes two periods in Jesus' career. In the first, Jesus summons his hearers to repent, for the kingdom of God has come near (1:15). He teaches, casts out demons, and heals the afflicted; he sends his disciples to preach, exorcise, and heal; he feeds multitudes with bread and fish; and he argues with the Pharisees. Near Caesarea Philippi, he asks his disciples who they think he is, and Peter answers, "the Messiah," whereupon Jesus tells them "to tell no one about him" (8:27–30). He then begins teaching his followers that the Son of man—and perhaps many of them as well—must suffer and die before the kingdom of God and the Son of man will be revealed, but that the parousia will occur while at least some of them are still alive.[15]

In the second phase, Jesus moves with his disciples toward Jerusalem, exorcising demons and teaching the Twelve and others as he goes (chaps. 9–10). He enters Jerusalem on a colt amid his followers' enthusiastic shouts,[16] and the next day "curses" a fig tree,[17] takes charge of the temple area,[18] and teaches there for several days, arguing with the religious authorities.[19] A woman anoints him with ointment, and Judas leaves in order to betray him (14:1–11). Jesus eats the Passover with the twelve, looking forward to the time when he will drink wine in the kingdom of God (14:12–25). Then he goes to Gethsemane with the Twelve and prays, and there he is betrayed by Judas, arrested, tried before a night session of the Sanhedrin, or Council, and handed over to the Romans, who execute him in the morning as "King of the Jews" (14:43–15:30). On the cross, he begins to repeat the Twenty-second Psalm in Aramaic, and soon afterward dies (15:33–39). He is buried, but on the third day, the women find his tomb empty and flee in astonishment, saying nothing to anyone about it—"for they were afraid" (16:8).

The question of Mark's historical value has often been debated since it has come to be widely regarded as the earliest Gospel. Many scholars consider it a generally reliable account of Jesus' message and the pattern (if not precise sequence) of events during his public activity; others view it primarily as an expression of Mark's theological interests. Controversy has centered especially on the "messianic secret,"[20] the passion pronouncements, and the Marcan "apocalypse" (chap. 13). Several sayings in chapter 13 indicate that although some time would lapse before the parousia (appearance or arrival) of the Son of man, he would indeed come before the complete passing of the generation of Jesus' followers (13:30; cf. 8:38–9:1). Mark evidently wanted his contemporaries (ca. A.D. 60–70) to understand that the Son of man could come at any time, so they must "watch" in constant readiness for that event (13:32–37).

Among Mark's concerns, two are particularly prominent: to encourage Christians to believe in Jesus' (or God's) power to deliver the faithful from danger, demons, or illness,[21] and to urge them to hope and prepare for the coming of the Son of man, the time of judgment, and eternal life in the coming kingdom of God.[22]

Two sets of additions to chapter 16 are often printed in modern editions of the text. The longer of these includes verses 9–20. According to these added verses, the risen Jesus appears to Mary Magdalene, then to two of the disciples, and afterward to the remaining eleven disciples, commanding them to preach the gospel to "the whole creation" (cf. Matt 28:16–20). He commends belief and baptism as the way to salvation (cf. John 3:5), and promises that his adherents will handle serpents (cf. Isa 11:8–9) and drink poison without being harmed. Finally, he ascends to heaven.[23] Some interpreters, perhaps a majority, believe that Mark originally ended with 16:8; others think that more followed, but has been lost. The most reliable early manuscripts end here, and nearly all modern scholars agree that verses 9–20 and the alternative or additional two verses contained in various other versions are secondary. The abrupt ending at verse 8 accords with the terse narrative style and the element of mystery seen throughout Mark's Gospel.

Luke

This is the first of a two-volume history of Jesus and the early church, sometimes referred to as Luke-Acts. The author may have been the physician named in Colossians 4:14, but this is not certain.[24] A person named Luke is mentioned as one of Paul's "fellow workers" in Philemon 24. Luke probably was a gentile, writing in Greek for gentile Christians and also, perhaps, for the edification of non-Christian gentile readers, symbolized by the name Theophilus (1:3; Acts 1:1). Luke evidently wrote after the destruction of Jerusalem in A.D. 70, perhaps as late as 90.[25]

Luke, a second-generation Christian (1:1–2), sets out to write an "orderly account" (1:3) and gives many dates and other pieces of information, some of which may be accurate.[26] Like Matthew, he follows Mark's narrative, though omitting more of it than Matthew does.[27] He adds both a preface, which consists largely of traditions not found in the other Gospels (chaps. 1–3),[28] and a conclusion, which describes appearances by the risen Jesus near Jerusalem.[29] Luke inserts two collections of material, mainly sayings (6:20–8:3; 9:51–18:14), within Mark's narrative framework. Some of the sayings in Luke evidently derive from Mark. Those found only in Luke are commonly identified by the symbol "L." Other sayings that appear also in Matthew (but not Mark) may derive from a sayings source (Q) used by both of these later evangelists.

Like the Jesus depicted in Mark and Matthew, Luke's Jesus proclaims the kingdom of God and the need for repentance (4:43; 13:1–9), eats and otherwise associates with "sinners,"[30] exorcises demons and heals the sick, sends the Twelve (and also seventy others) to extend this activity more widely (chaps. 9–10), and feeds the five thousand. He then turns to go to Jerusalem, enters it to the acclaim of his disciples, and teaches in the temple precincts. He eats the Passover with the Twelve, looking for its fulfillment in the coming kingdom of God (22:14–18). Afterward, he is arrested by Jewish authorities, tried and executed by the Romans as a revolutionary (23:38), and then is raised from the dead.

In various ways, Luke suggests that Christianity was meant for gentiles (non-Jews) from the very beginning. Simeon quotes the "light to the Gentiles" passage from Isaiah 49:6 in his psalm of blessing (2:32), Jesus' ancestry is traced back to Adam—the father of all humankind (3:23–38; cf. Matt. 1:1–2), Jesus points to God's care for gentiles in ancient times (4:25–27), and two Samaritans exemplify neighbor-love and faith (10:29–37; 17:11–19). Luke also sets out to show that Christianity is no threat to Roman order by reporting that the several Roman officials in charge of Jesus' execution found him innocent.[31]

Frequently, Luke omits traditions that might be difficult to understand: the derogatory comment of Jesus' friends about his mental health (Mark 3:21), the request of James and John (or their mother) for special honors (Mark 10:35–40), the seemingly unintelligible fig tree incident (Mark 11:12–14), and Jesus' cry of dereliction on the cross, which gentiles might not recognize as the first words of Psalm 22 (Mark 15:34). Instead of the latter, Luke's Jesus prays for God to forgive those who are crucifying him, assures one of the criminals crucified with him that "today" they will both be in Paradise, and commits his spirit to God.[32] Perhaps to demonstrate Jesus' physical (as opposed to merely spiritual) resurrection, Luke reports that the risen Jesus takes and eats a piece of broiled fish (24:36–43),[33] and interprets the Old Testament law, prophets, and psalms as prophecies now fulfilled (24:41–47). The risen Jesus is then carried up into heaven. The community of his followers return to Jerusalem, where the story of the church continues in the early chapters of the book of Acts.

Luke's Jesus particularly insists that those who have wealth should use it to aid the poor, who are heirs to the promised kingdom.[34] Those who respond to people in need may themselves hope for life in the kingdom of God, but those who keep their possessions to themselves have nothing more to hope for.[35] As in Matthew and Mark, Luke's Jesus eats and otherwise associates with "sinners" (5:29–32; 15:1–2), and he gives assurances that God will forgive those who repent.[36]

The promised kingdom had not yet come when Luke wrote his Gospel. Consequently, he omits Jesus' announcement at the beginning of his ministry that it was near (Mark 1:15), adds that Jesus' disciples incorrectly supposed it near as they approached Jerusalem (19:11), and changes Jesus' words to the high priest accordingly (22:69; cf. Mark 14:62). Nevertheless, Luke preserves and adds sayings that urge his own contemporaries to continue to hope and prepare for the coming of the kingdom of God and the Son of man, for these parousia events could now occur at any time.[37] Other New Testament authors who wrote toward the end of the first century A.D. likewise indicated their belief and expectation that the parousia was near.[38]

John

The author of this Gospel is commonly identified as John, though no disciple by this name is mentioned in the text.[39] The only John mentioned in the Gospel is John the Baptist, the first person named therein who "came for testimony."[40] The anonymous writer's implicit source was "the Counselor" or Holy Spirit (14:25–26; 16:12–13). This account of Jesus' ministry and message differs considerably from that of the first three, or Synoptic, Gospels. To what extent John gives reliable historical information is still debated.

John's Jesus does not proclaim the kingdom of God or repentance, and he exorcises no demons but does heal some who were sick. He typically speaks in long, complicated, and somewhat repetitious discourses about himself and his relationship to God. In particular, Jesus calls people to believe that he himself is the way to eternal life (3:36; 6:40). He performs "signs" or "works" in order to manifest his glory so that people may believe (2:11; 5:36; 14:11). In what often is considered the original conclusion, the writer states that his purpose is to report the signs provided by Jesus in order to promote the reader's belief "that Jesus is the Christ, the Son of God," thereby enabling the reader to "have life in his name" (20:30–31).

These emphases contrast with the Synoptic Gospels, where Jesus never calls on people to believe in himself and never performs miracles, signs, or works in order to prompt belief. Instead of proclaiming the coming of the kingdom of God (as in the Synoptics), John's Jesus assures the faithful that he will come again and bring them to the place he will prepare for them in his "father's house," presumably in heaven (14:13).[41] In the meantime, they will be guided by the Spirit or Counselor, who can come only after he, Jesus, goes (16:7–11); and they are to live in obedience to the "new" commandment, to love one another.[42]

Jesus is portrayed in terms of a high Christology: He is identified in the prologue (1:1–18) as the Word that was with God and was God from the beginning (cf. Prov 8:22–31), and elsewhere he is represented as identical or one with God.[43] John's Jesus is omniscient (4:17–18; 18:4) and omnipotent: He voluntarily lays down his life and can regain it when he wishes (10:17–18), he himself assigns Judas the task of betraying him (13:21–26), and he says "I thirst" on the cross only to fulfill Scripture (19:28). He has no need of others' advice, though sometimes he later does as they suggest.[44] He prays aloud, not to be heard by God, who always hears him, but for the edification of those standing by (11:41–42). When he learns that his friend Lazarus is sick, he purposely delays coming until Lazarus has definitely died so that he can raise him from the dead, and so be glorified that others may believe in him (11:1–44).

Interpreters generally regard the Fourth Gospel as a theological treatise in which the faith-understanding or theology of a particular Christian writer or church is attributed to Jesus himself. Most of the New Testament treatises are in the form of letters, such as Hebrews and James. Certain sayings clearly represent the perspectives of later

Christianity.[45] There is no messianic secret in John's Gospel. Instead, Jesus is identified publicly and repeatedly as the Son, Son of God, Son of man, and Messiah (Christ) all through the Gospel.[46] Jesus' contemporaries are labeled indiscriminately "the Jews," and from early in his career, they seek to kill him (5:16–18; 7:1). John even implies that "the Jews" did execute Jesus (19:12–16), though the Roman official Pilate's sentence actually was carried out by Roman soldiers (19:23). Interpreters also find traces of antignostic or antidocetic interests in the Gospel: Jesus was the "true light" (1:9; 8:12), the word become flesh (1:14; cf. 1 John 4:2; 2 John 7), and "the truth"; and he experienced bodily resurrection (20:27). These polemical interests indicate that the Gospel was written toward the end of the first century, probably in a Hellenistic, gentile Christian setting. Gnostics generally held that salvation came through secret knowledge (*gnosis*), and they viewed the material world as inferior or evil. Docetists urged that Jesus had only *appeared* to have a physical body but was actually spiritual and immaterial. Gnostic and docetic motifs were emerging within Christianity (as is evidenced in the Nag Hammadi writings) by the end of the first century.

Certain discrepancies also puzzle interpreters: Jesus baptizes (3:22) but does not baptize (4:2); he will not bear witness to himself (5:31), but he bears witness to himself (8:14, 18); disciples ask where he is going (13:36; 14:5), but he complains that they do not ask where he is going (16:5). These and other considerations have prompted various theories about possible editorial rearrangements and revisions of the text. Chapter 21 is commonly viewed as a later supplement, concerned, among other matters, with rehabilitating Peter by reporting his threefold pledge of devotion to Jesus (21:15–17; cf. 18:17, 25–27), and with the problem presented by the unexpected death of the beloved disciple prior to Jesus' return (21:20–23). Several other New Testament writings likewise attempt to account for the unexpected delay of Jesus' coming as Christ or Lord.[47]

Acts

Here Luke continues the narrative begun in his Gospel (see Acts 1:1–2). The sections written in the first person plural imply that the author was, at times, a companion of Paul's (chaps. 16; 20–21; 27–28). Acts concludes with Paul reportedly still alive in Rome, which could mean that it was written before A.D. 64, when, according to early extrabiblical tradition, Paul and Peter were executed there. Another possibility is that Luke may have wished to end his account on a more positive note and so brought this volume to its close where he did, even though he was writing after Paul's death. Luke-Acts is usually dated around A.D. 70–90.

The structure of Acts is straightforward: It describes the expansion of "the Way" (Christianity, first designated as such at 11:26) from its beginnings in Jerusalem and Judea into Samaria and to the end (or political center) of the earth (1:8), represented by Rome. The narrative begins with a report of the risen Jesus' several encounters with his followers in Jerusalem for forty days and then his ascension on a cloud into heaven (1:3–10). Luke thematically reports increasing numbers of believers in Jerusalem;[48] the persecution of the church there, causing its members to scatter throughout Judea and Samaria (8:1); Philip's preaching in Samaria and elsewhere (8:4–40); and, in particular, the mission of Paul (and others) to the gentile (non-Jewish) world, while converts continue to increase in number.[49] Luke frequently reports that various women—including several of "high standing"—are among this growing numbers of believers.[50]

Acts supplies many details not recorded elsewhere, concerning such matters as developments and practices within the communal life of the Jerusalem church (2:42–47; 4:32–37) and biographical information about Paul: that he had studied with Rabbi Gamaliel (22:3), was a tentmaker by trade (18:3), and a Roman citizen (22:25). Some features, however, seem legendary: Angels appear frequently, apostles are miraculously rescued from prison on three different occasions[51] and often experience visions and perform signs and wonders, some approximating magic.[52] Acts' account of the death of Judas Iscariot (1:15–19) differs significantly from the account found in Matthew 27:3–10.

In Acts, Luke especially wished to show that the eventual mission to the gentiles was divinely inspired as well as officially approved by the leaders of the church. The initial proclamation to gentiles is endorsed by the apostles at Jerusalem, who send Peter and John to baptize Philip's Samaritan converts (8:5–17). An "angel of the Lord" sends Philip to instruct the Ethiopian treasurer, whom he then baptizes (8:26–38). An angel directs the Roman Cornelius to Peter, and in a vision, and by order of "the Spirit," Peter is made to understand that not only Jews but also gentiles may become Christians, for "God shows no partiality" (10:34–35). Since the Holy Spirit sanctions the conversion of these uncircumcised persons, Peter sees no reason not to baptize them (10:44–48), and soon even the circumcisionist faction in Jerusalem is persuaded that gentiles too may be received into the church (11:1–18). Acts states explicitly that God (or the Spirit) has initiated the gentile mission, in particular, Paul's activity among them (e.g., 13:2–4; 14:27). Paul's final statement epitomizes the point: "This salvation of God has been sent to the Gentiles; they will listen" (28:28).

The Jewish Christian faction in Jerusalem, however, is not initially convinced that Paul's gentile converts can be "saved" unless they are circumcised. Luke reports in Acts 15 that James (probably Jesus' brother referred to in Gal 1:18–19) and other apostles and elders there agree that circumcision will not be required of such converts. Instead, gentile Christians need only abstain from food that has been sacrificed to idols,[53] blood, animals that have been killed by strangling,[54] and refrain from unchastity.[55] Luke's threefold repetition of these terms indicates that he considers them important. Paul's own recollection of the agreement, however, is substantially different (see Gal 2:1–10).

Paul is the main figure in Acts 13–28. Though formerly a zealous persecutor of "the Way," his experience on the road to Damascus turns him into the leading proponent of the gentile mission.[56] In Acts, Paul typically begins by preaching (and arguing) in the local synagogue, persuading many Jews and God-fearers (gentile converts to Judaism) to become Christians, but then "the Jews," prompted by jealousy, reject Paul and his message. After that, Paul condemns them, declaring that now salvation will be for the gentiles (e.g., 13:42–47; 18:4–6).[57] As in the Fourth Gospel, "the Jews" generally appear as a hostile aggregation, here plotting against Paul, when not actually attacking him.[58]

Luke evidently is also concerned with showing that Rome has no reason to view Christianity as a threat to its sovereignty. Paul is a Roman citizen and had subjected himself to Roman law.[59] Jesus was innocent in the eyes of Roman officials (Luke 23:14–15, 47); in Acts, Luke says repeatedly that Jesus really was killed by "the Jews."[60] Roman officials likewise pronounce Paul innocent of any crime (23:29; 26:31).

As in the Gospel, so in Acts, Jesus' disciples heal the sick, cast out demons, and proclaim the kingdom of God and repentance; here they add as a central article of faith that Jesus·is the Christ (5:42; 18:28). Those who believe in Jesus will have their sins forgiven (10:43; 13:38–39), receive eternal life (13:48),[61] or be saved (16:31).

Several times Luke reports that many were baptized, suggesting the increasing importance of baptism in his time.[62] Though the kingdom of God was still an important topic in Christian preaching, it is unclear in Acts what the reported speakers meant to say about it.[63] Passages quoted frequently by Christians in later times include 5:29

("We must obey God rather than men"), 17:28 ("In him we live and move and have our being"), and 20:35 ("It is more blessed to give than to receive").

Romans

Paul, "an apostle to the Gentiles," as he calls himself here and elsewhere (e.g., 11:13; Gal 2:2, 8), has already traveled and preached widely in the gentile (non-Jewish) world. Belief that the time of salvation would not come until the gentile mission was completed may have given impetus to Paul's and other early Christians' missionary zeal.[64] Now Paul plans to visit the Christian church in Rome on his way to Spain (15:18–29). In the meantime, he intends to deliver the contributions he has been soliciting from various gentile congregations to the Jerusalem church, in order to assist "the poor among the saints" there (cf. Gal 2:10; 1 Cor 16:1–4).

Since he has not previously visited the church at Rome (1:10; 15:22), he writes here at some length, describing his gospel, or his understanding of the substance of Christian faith and life (2:16; 16:25). Thus Romans is the fullest statement we have of Paul's beliefs or "systematic theology." Frequently, he echoes or anticipates thoughts and concerns developed in his other letters, especially 1 Corinthians, Galatians, and Philippians. He did not found the church in Rome, but does not hesitate to mention, though somewhat delicately, his apostolic authority over it, while remarking graciously upon the faith and knowledge these Roman Christians already enjoy.[65]

Romans is a real letter, written to an actual congregation in the course of Paul's busy life (see Acts 18–21), perhaps around A.D. 58. He begins, as he usually does in his other letters, by identifying himself and stating his authority and role as apostle (1:1–16), naming the community addressed, saluting the intended recipients in distinctive theological terms (1:7), and mentioning his thanks, constant prayers, and concerns for them (1:8–15). He concludes the letter with various personal comments, including a benediction (15:13), reference to his travel plans (15:14–32), another benediction (15:33), greetings and words of commendation for a number of acquaintances in (or bound for) Rome (16:1–15), further exhortations, still another benediction (16:17–20), greetings from various companions, including his secretary (16:21–23), and the final benediction (16:25–27).

In between, the letter includes the following: his thematic statement that righteousness by faith is for both Jews and gentiles (1:16–17), his reflections on the moral responsibility and destiny of gentiles (1:18–2:16), his description of the situation of Jews in relation to the law and justification (2:27–4:25), his definition of the character of Christian existence under grace and faith (5:1–8:39), his assurance that salvation is for gentiles as well as for "Israel" (9:1–11:36), various admonitions to right living (12:1–15:6), and a concluding affirmation that gentiles as well as Jews are heirs to the promise of hope (15:7–12).

Several basic Pauline terms recur throughout the first eleven chapters: faith, grace, works, sin, death, wrath, justification, righteousness, and the law. In brief, Paul's argument is as follows. Those gentiles who do "by nature" what the law demands "show that what the law requires is written on their hearts" (2:14–15). But Jews do not keep the law of Moses (2:17–24); indeed, all people, "both Jews and Greeks," are under the power of sin (3:9–18). The law brings "knowledge of sin," prompts disobedience, causes sin to be "counted," and so results in death.[66] Therefore, no one can hope to be justified (that is, considered or accounted as righteous or acceptable) before God by doing the "works" of Jewish law (3:20). Yet without justification, there can be no deliverance from death. The good news is that God has manifested his righteousness apart from the law, as the gift of redemption in Jesus Christ, a gift that is to be received by faith (3:21–28; 10:1–13). Paul sometimes refers to this gift as the grace of God (e.g., 5:2, 20). The various elements of Paul's understanding are not always clearly integrated, and at times he seems to say that God justifies people because of their faith (e.g., 3:26; 10:9–10). Generally, however, Paul seems to mean that Jesus' death and resurrection overcome the power of sin for those who believe, by reconciling them to God, thus sparing them the wrath of God they otherwise deserve (4:23–5:11), and giving them assurance of eternal life (5:18–21; 6:22–23). Therefore, they can be confident of God's continuing care for them during the interim before the parousia, despite all tribulation and persecution (8:18–39).

As to the moral life, Paul insists that those "in Christ" are no longer "under law" but are "under grace" (6:15). This does not mean, however, that people are free to do as they please. Liberated from the power of sin, they should be obedient to the teachings they have received, becoming servants or slaves to righteousness and God (6:1–23).[67] Paul urges his readers to live according to the guidance of God's indwelling Spirit (8:2–14), in obedience to the Roman authorities, who are God's ministers (13:1–7),[68] and with love or concern for the good of their neighbors and fellow believers (13:8–10; 14:1–15:6),[69] conducting themselves as persons who know that the day of salvation is near (13:11–14).

1 Corinthians

Like most of Paul's letters, 1 Corinthians was written to a gentile (non-Jewish) Christian church that he himself had founded (4:15), and addresses problems he was concerned about there. Paul had established the church at Corinth around A.D. 40 and was now writing to them twelve or thirteen years later. Corinth was a sea port city located in the Roman province of Achaia, not far from Delphi, Athens, and Sparta.

In 1 Corinthians, Paul treats matters he has learned about both from members of Chloe's household (1:11) and from a letter the church has sent asking his advice (7:1) but possibly also from other sources.[70] As usual, he begins by stating his name (also that of his associate, here "brother Sosthenes") and identifying the addressees; he adds a characteristic theological salutation and mentions his constant thanks and concern for them (1:1–9). The conclusion (chap. 16) refers to the collection he is raising for the church in Jerusalem (cf. Gal 2:10) and to his travel plans, then includes a summary exhortation peculiarly appropriate to this letter (16:13–14). Paul finally ends the letter with various personal commendations and greetings, a final warning, or execration, (16:22a), an Aramaic prayer for the Lord's coming (v. 22b), a benediction, and one last affirmation about love— this time, his for them.

Paul's main concern is that some of these Corinthian Christians consider themselves better than others and are behaving in ways that are harmful to the church and to other members. In particular, they are "puffed up" with pride about their spiritual gifts, especially "knowledge," "wisdom," and "speaking in tongues." They like to boast about and show off what they consider their religious superiority.

All through the letter Paul reminds these self-styled spiritualists that their wisdom and knowledge are still imperfect,[71] that what matters is the power of God, not the wisdom of humans, which at best, by contrast, is foolishness.[72] Their knowledge should not be used to dazzle and confuse new converts, who may not know, for instance, that idols have no real existence. Instead, it should be tested and improved by love: "'Knowledge' puffs up, but love builds up" (8:1–13; 10:23–33). In their zeal to claim superior status, the spiritualists have divided the church into factions that are "puffed up in favor of one against the other" (4:6), each pretending to be the only true Christians

(1:10–15). Moreover, their sense of freedom from "the law" has led some of these proud spiritualists to follow an anything goes morality with respect to their bodily life (5:1–2). "All things are lawful," they claim, but, Paul counters, "not all things are helpful," either to themselves or to others (6:12–20).

These factional spiritualists should recognize that there is one and the same Spirit, Lord, and God, who inspires all spiritual gifts alike (chap. 12). Those who have received such gifts—whether the ability to speak in tongues, prophetic powers, knowledge, and even faith and the ability to practice self-sacrifice—gain and give nothing if they do not also have and act from love (13:1–3). Present knowledge is incomplete or imperfect, as is prophecy, for both will "pass away" when the "perfect" (parousia or kingdom of God) comes, but love never ends. In the coming age, love, the greatest of the spiritual gifts, will abide, along with faith and hope (13:8–13).

Paul is particularly concerned about the spiritualists' practice of speaking in tongues (presumably inspired, but incoherent utterance). He insists that this practice be restricted for the sake of "building up the church" (14:6–12). In their worship services, Paul urges, "let all things be done for edification" (14:26). Paul therefore especially commends the gift of prophecy (intelligible and inspirational discourse; 14:1–5); urges that those who speak in tongues also pray for power to interpret so that others may be edified (14:13–20); recommends that not more than three persons speak in tongues during the course of a worship service, and then each in turn, but not at all, unless someone is present to interpret; and rules that those who prophesy do so only one at a time (14:26–33). He adds—without further explanation or rationale—that women should keep silent in church (14:33b–35).

Paul reviews several other questions as well. "The saints" (Christians) are "to judge the world" in the last days (cf. Matt 19:28); therefore, in the meantime, they should settle matters among themselves rather than go before pagan law courts (6:1–8; cf. Matt 18:15–17). Sexual and marital guidelines are given, along with advice to the circumcised and the uncircumcised and to slave and free. All should remain in whatever state they are, if possible, for the present age is soon to pass away (chap. 7). Women are to have their heads (especially their hair) covered when they pray or prophesy (11:2–16).[73] The Lord's Supper is to be observed with due regard for the feelings of others (11:17–22, 33–34). Paul recites the tradition he "received from the Lord" as to the Last Supper, which, unlike the Gospels' accounts, includes the so-called words of institution: "Do this in remembrance of me" (11:24–25). Thereby, Paul says, they will "proclaim the Lord's death until he comes" (v. 26).

Chapter 15 is devoted to concerns about Jesus' resurrection and the future resurrection of Christians whose deaths will have occurred before his coming. (Paul never refers to Jesus' "second coming" but only to his "coming.") Paul recalls the tradition he has received concerning Jesus' resurrection appearances, including an otherwise unrecorded report of the risen Jesus' appearance to some five hundred people, most of them still alive in the author's day (cf. Matt 16:28; 24:34), an appearance to James (presumably the brother of Jesus; cf. Gal 1:19), and finally, "as to one untimely born," an appearance to himself (15:1–8).

Some, perhaps many, Christians in Corinth had died, but Christ had not yet returned, and these dead had not been raised. Some were saying there would be no resurrection (15:12–51). Others were asking what kind of body those raised from the dead would have. Responding to their concerns, Paul declares that Christians who have died ("fallen asleep") will indeed be raised, with a "spiritual body," and that those who are still alive when "the man of heaven" comes likewise will be transformed ("changed") and will thus put on immortality. Paul's writings reflect his expectation that Jesus would come and that the related parousia events would occur within his own lifetime and that of his contemporaries (15:51–52; cf. 1 Thess 4:15–17). Appropriately, as he concludes the letter, he repeats the primitive Aramaic prayer, "Our Lord, come!" (16:22).[74]

The congregation at Corinth evidently continued to experience serious problems. Second Corinthians incorporates correspondence of Paul's in which he attempts to set them straight on a number of issues.

2 Corinthians

Several common themes appear throughout 2 Corinthians, but it is not clear whether we have here the letter as Paul wrote it, or whether the present writing is a composite of parts of two or perhaps three originally separate letters. Paul evidently visited and wrote to this fractious congregation at Corinth on several occasions. Interpreters sometimes suggest that 2 Corinthians 6:14–7:1 is a fragment of an earlier letter, perhaps the one alluded to in 1 Corinthians 5:9–11. The rest of 2 Corinthians may include all or parts of two other letters: a "hot" or agitated one (chaps. 10–13) and a calmer one, possibly written somewhat later, after the passing of the crisis in Paul's relation with this troubled and troublesome church (chaps. 1–9). When Paul's letters were collected, possibly several decades after he wrote them, these separate units might then have been put together to form the present writing. Or it may be that chapters 1–13 originally constituted a single letter, in which, as happened elsewhere, Paul's mood shifted somewhat abruptly. This theory could be supported by the fact that the two main sections share some similarities: Chapters 1–9 do reflect some strain between Paul and the Corinthians, and in chapters 10–13 he does mention his love and concern for them; in both sections, Paul refers to a previous visit (2:1–5; 13:2) and is sensitive to the charge of self-commendation or boasting. Thus, a good case can be made for both the composite and the original integrity theories. Commentators agree that Paul authored all the contents of the letter.

Chapter 1 begins typically: Paul names himself, also Timothy, "our brother," notes his own apostolic status, designates the addressees, and greets them with the double salutation, "grace and peace." There follows, atypically, a lengthy review of his relationship with the church, in which he reminds them of his own career, his apostolic role, and his hopes for the future, intermittently and uneasily justifying and commending himself.[75] His tone, generally, is conciliatory, especially in chapter 7, where he affirms his "great confidence" in them. His central concern is to declare that in Christ, God was reconciling the world to himself and that, therefore, those "in Christ" can and must now be reconciled to God (5:16–20). Chapters 8–9 conclude this unit, which may have been a separate, perhaps later, conciliatory letter urging the Corinthian Christians to contribute generously to the collection he is raising for the church in Jerusalem, a concern that appears elsewhere toward the end of Paul's letters.[76]

Paul's warning against association with unbelievers (6:14–7:1) interrupts his calling on the Corinthians to widen or open their hearts to him (6:11; 7:2). Conceivably, this warning section may be a fragment from a letter of the sort Paul refers to in 1 Corinthians 5:9–11 that had been preserved and was added to the present writing when Paul's letters were collected in later years. On the other hand, Paul sometimes does interrupt himself (see, e.g., 1 Corinthians 8–10), and may have done so here as well. It is not clear whether 2 Corinthians 6:14–7:1 refers to marriage with non-Christians (cf. 1 Cor 7:12–16) or, more generally, to associating with those who worship other gods and practice what from a Christian standpoint would be considered "iniquity" and "defilement."

In the unit that begins in chapter 10—possibly part, if not the beginning, of an earlier, agitated letter—Paul starts by identifying himself, but without adding any further preliminaries, and then angrily asserts his authority against those in the Corinthian church who would belittle him. He notes that it was he who first brought the gospel to them, then indulges in some "foolish" boasting over his Jewish credentials, his hardships, and his religious experience in order to refute the "superlative" or false apostles who have tried to undermine his authority (10:7–12:13). That these false apostles claim Jewish descent (11:22) suggests that they may be Jewish Christians like the "circumcisionists" who troubled Paul's churches in Galatia and Philippi. Paul warns that he plans to come, hinting that he may have to use his authority severely (12:14–13:10). In a somewhat abrupt conclusion to this unit (if not to the original letter in its entirety), he tells the Corinthians that if they mend their ways, heed his admonitions, agree with one another, and live in peace, the God of love and peace will be with them (13:11). Such advice seems appropriate, given the factional character of this church as we know it also from 1 Corinthians. Paul then ends the letter with an unusual Trinitarian benediction (13:11–14; cf. Matt 28:19).

In the course of this letter, Paul expresses several of his basic ideas, in particular, that believers are in Christ or Christ is in them, that they are being transformed into his likeness and are thus already "new creatures,"[77] that they may look for an eternal dwelling in the heavens (4:17–5:5),[78] but that they will be judged according to their deeds done "in the body" (5:10; cf. Gal 6:7–9). Paul does not say when the parousia will take place, but as in 1 Corinthians 15, he evidently expects it in the near future, probably in the lifetime of some of those to whom he is writing (1:13–14).[79] Two of Paul's often quoted affirmations are found in 2 Corinthians: "We have this treasure in earthen vessels" (3:7); and "We can do nothing against the truth, but only for the truth" (13:8).

Galatians

Paul wrote this letter around ca. A.D. 55 to some churches in Galatia that he himself apparently founded several years earlier (4:13). Galatia was the Roman province situated diagonally across central Asia Minor, now modern Turkey. The Christians addressed, as in all of Paul's letters, are gentiles (i.e., former pagans rather than former Jews). Here, as elsewhere, he describes himself as an apostle to the gentiles (1:16; 2:2, 8).

We learn from Acts and from some of Paul's letters that he was one of the first and principal Christian missionaries to the gentile world.

Paul confronts a major problem, for Christianity began entirely within the context of Judaism. That Jesus was the Messiah or the Christ would have made sense only in the thought world of Judaism. All the first Christians had been Jews. According to Matthew, Jesus had told his followers that they must observe all of Jewish law, both written and oral (Matt 5:17–19; 23:2–3, 23); according to Luke, Christians in Jerusalem had continued to worship in the temple there (Acts 2:46; 3:1). Whether gentiles might also become Christians was an open question at first (see Acts 10:1–11:18).

Paul has been telling his gentile converts that their standing before God, or "justification," is by the grace of God, received by faith, and grounded in Christ's death and resurrection. Paul's main concern as he writes this letter is that some people have been telling these gentile converts that in order to be real Christians, they must first become Jews by being circumcised and observing Jewish holidays (4:10; 5:2–6). The circumcisionists, sometimes called "Judaizers," seem to have been associated with, if not officially sent by, the "pillars" (leaders) of the Jewish Christian church in Jerusalem.

Arguing against the position of the circumcisionists, Paul contends for the independence and authenticity of his understanding of the gospel: He had received it directly by divine revelation, not from others (1:11–17); only much later did he consult with Cephas (Peter), James (the brother of Jesus and leader of the Jerusalem congregation) and John; then, Paul insists, they made no stipulations about circumcision (1:18–2:10). Paul's point is that requiring circumcision now is contrary to the understanding he and the "pillars" agreed to years ago in Jerusalem. The only condition then, Paul says, was that gentile Christians were to "remember the poor"—that is, contribute to the well-being of the "poor among the saints" in the Jerusalem church, a condition to which Paul gladly agreed (Gal 2:6–10; cf. Rom 15:25–27; Acts 15:1–29).

In this context, Paul goes on to charge that Peter was unduly responsive to the wishes of the circumcisionists who came to Antioch "from James," insisting that Jewish Christians must not eat with gentile Christians (2:11–12). Paul accuses Peter of backing away from his earlier ecumenicity. It is not certain exactly where Paul's summary of his confrontation with Peter ends and the statement of his present faith-understanding to the Galatians begins, but his argument is clear. Justification or righteousness before God is never attained by keeping Jewish law but only through faith in Jesus Christ (2:15–16). If one tries to keep part of the law, that person must keep all of it (3:10; 5:3).

But no one is able to keep the whole law (3:21–22).[80] Moreover, and more to the point, to try to keep even part of the law is to ignore the grace of God, who gives righteousness through faith (2:18–21; 5:4–5). These themes are developed more fully in Paul's letter to the Romans, probably written near the same time as this letter to Galatian Christians.

Paul insists that neither being circumcised nor being uncircumcised is important. What matter are faith and love. Through faith, all are children of God and one in Christ; externals such as being Jew or Greek, slave or free, male or female, no longer mean anything (3:26–28; 6:15). The only thing that counts is "faith working through love" (5:6; cf. 1 Corinthians 13).

But now another question arises. If gentile Christians are not obliged to follow Jewish law, what should be the basis for their moral life? Obviously reverting to their prior pagan standards will not do. Paul now argues that freedom from Jewish law does not mean license to do what one pleases. Life is to be lived under the law of neighbor-love (5:13–14) and in accordance with the Spirit, not according to the lower nature or "flesh" (5:16–26). By "flesh," Paul means not only sensuality but also, and more centrally, self-centeredness, that is, envy and selfish ambition. The "fruits of the Spirit" include love, joy, peace, patience, kindness, gentleness, and self-control. The standard by which people live, then, is crucially important. Those who live according to the flesh will not inherit the kingdom of God (5:19–21),[81] but those who live by love and the Spirit, Paul assures the Galatians, will receive the harvest of eternal life (6:7–10).

Ephesians

It is not certain whether Ephesians was written by Paul or by a later Christian who was familiar with Paul's thought. Some stylistic and conceptual features suggest authorship by someone other than Paul himself, for instance, such atypical expressions as "the heavenly places" and "forgiveness" (1:3, 7, 20), and the idea of Christ's uniting or filling "all things" (1:10; 4:10), or his self-giving love for the church (5:25–27). Secondary authorship is also suggested by the fact that many passages parallel and possibly were taken from Colossians, authorship of which likewise is in doubt. Paul does not elsewhere say that Christians have been "sealed with the Holy Spirit" (1:13; 4:30) or refer to the gospel he preaches as a "mystery" (3:3–4; 6:19).[82] The idea that Christians were predestined "before the foundation of the world"

(1:4–5) goes beyond Paul's claim to have been "set apart" before his birth to be an apostle (Gal 1:15; cf. Jer 1:5). The author's prayer that "Christ may dwell in [the] hearts" of his readers and that they might "be filled with all the fulness of God" is unparalleled in Pauline writings and may contain gnostic overtones. The letter makes no mention of the collection Paul was raising for the poor among "the saints" in Jerusalem or of his travel plans—standard features of some of his genuine letters. According to Acts chap.19, Paul spent considerable time in Ephesus, but the author of Ephesians writes as if he has never been there before (1:15; 3:1–3). Early versions of the letter do not mention Ephesus, and it may be that it was written, like the catholic or general letters (e.g., Hebrews and Jude), to all Christians everywhere.[83] If written by Paul, it would be the only such letter of his that we have.

On the other hand, a strong case can be made for Paul's authorship. Ephesians begins and ends in Paul's usual fashion (1:1–2; 6:21–24). Much of its substance resembles that of unquestionably authentic letters, especially Galatians and 1 Corinthians. The letter states, even more clearly than in Paul's usual fashion, that salvation is by the grace of God through, but not because of, faith (2:4–9).[84] Emphasis is placed upon the unity of the church (4:3–6), as in 1 Corinthians 12–14, though in Ephesians, the principle of unity applies to the church universal rather than the local congregation. The author implies that he is in prison (3:1; 4:1; 6:20), which was Paul's lot several times. Here, as in unquestionably Pauline letters, the author presents himself as a missionary to the gentiles (3:2, 8; cf. Gal 2:8–9) and as only "least" of all the saints or apostles (3:8; cf. 1 Cor 15:9).

The letter's main concern is to emphasize that gentiles are no longer separated from Jews as they were before Christ but are now fellow heirs to the promise and members of the same body—the universal church—through the grace of God (2:1–22). This is the great "mystery" now revealed to the apostles so that they might preach it to all, even to the "principalities and powers" (3:1–10). Paul elsewhere urged that Christianity was not only for Jews but also for gentiles (see especially Romans and Galatians). Not only the church but all creation is now under the lordship of Christ (1:20–23; cf. Phil 2:1–1).

The writer is also concerned with encouraging his late first-century readers to live worthily of their "calling" (4:1), recognizing their common unity in the church: There is one body, one Spirit, one hope, one Lord, one faith, one baptism, "one God and Father of us all" (4:3–6). In this connection, the writer summons readers to live in accordance with their new "nature," in patience, peace, and love, "building up" the church (4:1–5:20; cf. 1 Corinthians 12–14). Such moral instruction was particularly important for gentile Christians who previously had known only paganism and its low moral standards.

The admonitions to wives and husbands, children and fathers, and slaves and masters also are in the context of concern for the unity of the church, love and respect for one another, and the lordship of Christ over all (5:21–6:9). Relations here commended are hierarchical rather than equally mutual or reciprocal. Wives are to respect and be subject to their husbands, but husbands are to love their wives (5:21–32). Children are to obey their parents, but fathers must not provoke their children to anger (6:14). And slaves are to be obedient to their masters "doing the will of God from the heart," but masters are "to do the same" and "forbear threatening," knowing who is master of both and that "there is no partiality" with the Master in heaven (6:5–9).[85]

Finally, the writer urges Christians to "put on the whole armor of God"[86] in order to withstand the devil in "the evil day" and to pray "at all times in the Spirit" for all of God's people, including himself (6:10–20). Because they are sealed by the Holy Spirit, these readers may be confident that they will acquire possession of their "inheritance" on the day of redemption (1:13–14; 4:30).[87]

Philippians

Paul is writing from prison, perhaps in Rome (1:13–14; 4:22), in which case this may be the last letter of his that we have. He looks back fondly on his long and special association with these good Macedonian Christians. The church at Philippi was the first he established in Europe, and since early times they have supported his work (1:5; 4:15–16). This church has had time to develop a leadership structure that includes bishops (or supervisors) and deacons. This is the first and only mention of such church officers in Paul's unquestionably genuine letters.[88]

Paul wants his friends in Philippi to know that his imprisonment should not cause them concern (1:12–26); even if he is put to death, they should rejoice (2:17–18). He wishes to reassure them about their mutual friend Epaphroditus's health and so sends him back to them, perhaps carrying this letter (2:25–30). He urges two women there, his "fellow workers," to be reconciled (4:2–3). Paul goes on to thank the Philippian Christians for the gifts they have sent him by

Epaphroditus (4:10–18). Twice he seems about to conclude the letter (3:1; 4:8), but each time he goes on, unwilling, it seems, to bid farewell to these people of whom he is so fond (1:8).

The most striking feature here is Paul's completely peaceful frame of mind. The verb "rejoice" is woven through the letter like a scarlet thread: He rejoices, and he calls on the Philippians to do so as well. He is in prison awaiting trial, but his imprisonment has served to "advance the gospel" (1:12–14). Some preach Christ for wrong reasons, yet he rejoices because Christ nevertheless is proclaimed (1:15–18). Whether he lives or dies, he looks forward to the outcome (1:19–26). Not even the circumcisionists upset him now (3:1–3; cf. Gal 5:12). He reviews his Hebrew credentials but refuses to claim merit or perfection (3:3–14; cf. 2 Corinthians 10–12). Some may disagree with him, but he only urges that they all hold true to the understandings they have attained.[89] Lyrically, he urges his readers to rejoice always and have no anxieties (4:4–6; cf. Matt 6:25–34).

As in most of his letters, Paul exhorts its recipients to live worthily of the gospel or the new life that has been given them, and so to be concerned not only for themselves but also for others (1:27–2:4). In this connection, perhaps quoting from an early Christian hymn or creed, he refers them to the example of Jesus' own self-giving love (2:5–11). "Work out your own salvation," he urges them, being confident that "God is at work in you" (2:12–13). Moreover, they are to live blameless lives, so that "in the day of Christ," he may be proud of them (2:14–16; see also 1:6, 9–11). He tells them to imitate him in striving for the goal of the "upward call" of God, sure of their "prize" or "end"—the transformed existence of life in the heavenly commonwealth, which will be theirs when Christ comes (3:12–21). As in 1 Cor 15:50–53 and 1 Thess 4:15–17, where Paul expresses similar hopes and assurances, he expects that both he and those to whom his letter is addressed will experience this great transformation soon, surely in their own lifetime, for "the Lord is at hand" (4:5).

Colossians

This letter may have been written either by Paul or in Paul's name, perhaps after his death, by someone interested in advising Colossian (and Laodicean) Christians in the spirit of Paul (see 2:1, 5; 4:16). Since the author says he is Paul (1:1, 23; 4:18), we so name him here, leaving open the question of his actual identity.

Much of the letter is typically Pauline. The writer begins by identifying himself as "Paul, an apostle of Christ Jesus" and mentioning Timothy, his coworker. He refers to his continual thanks and prayers for the church (1:3, 9), and calls on his readers to live according to the new life (or nature) that is theirs (3:1–17). As in many of Paul's authentic letters, the concluding verses mention certain persons (4:7–17). Among these are Onesimus and several others named in Paul's letter to Philemon.[90] Only in Colossians is it said that Luke, who may or may not have been the author of Luke-Acts, is a physician (4:14). As in Ephesians, Philippians, and Philemon, Paul is in, and writing from, prison (4:3, 10). He did not found the church at Colossae but has heard of the faith and love of Christians there (1:4), and writes to give them guidance and directions on various related matters. All of these considerations could argue for Paul's authorship.

Nevertheless, several features suggest that the author may have been someone other than Paul. The writer says nothing about hoping to visit the church (cf. Phil 1:27; Phlm 22) and hints that Paul will be seen no more (2:1, 5). Certain basic terms here are not used in Paul's normal sense: "The grace of God" is something to be heard and understood (1:6), "the faith" means the substance of Christian teaching (1:23; 2:7), and, as in Ephesians, "forgiveness" replaces justification (1:14; 2:13; 3:13).[91]

Some passages in Colossians closely parallel parts of Ephesians, for instance, 3:9–10 (cf. Eph 4:22–24, on the "old nature" and Christians' "new nature"), 3:16–17 (cf. Eph 5:19–20, on Christian worship and conduct), 3:18–4:1 (cf. Eph 5:21–6:9, on relations between husbands and wives, fathers and children, and masters and slaves). As in Ephesians, Paul refers to the substance of the gospel as a "mystery" (1:26–27; 2:2; 4:3). From these similarities, it might be concluded either that Paul, or someone else, wrote both, perhaps near the same time, when these concerns were on his mind, or that someone else copied from the earlier letter while writing the other.

But Colossians and Ephesians also differ on significant points. In Ephesians, the author says that Christ has begun to unite and fill all things and that this mission either was or will be accomplished in the "fulness of time" (Eph 1:9–10, 16–23; 4:10). In Colossians, however, the author affirms that Christ ("the Son") "is before all things," the "first-born of all creation," "the beginning," in whom all things were created (1:16–18),[92] in whom "all things hold together" (1:17),[93] and in whom "the fulness of deity dwells bodily" (2:9).

Other unusual ideas and expressions include "making peace by the blood of [the] cross" (1:20), the completion of the preaching of the gospel to "every creature under heaven" (1:23),[94] and God's canceling the bond (of the law) by "nailing it to the cross" and disarming "the principalities and powers" (2:14–15). The idea that Christians' baptism represents their being buried with Christ (2:12) is not found in Paul's other letters (cf. 1 Cor 1:13–17). Another unique idea is that the Son (Christ) is the image of the invisible God (1:15).[95]

The writer's main concerns are to warn against various heresies and to urge readers to live up to the standard of their new Christian morality, putting aside old, pagan ways. The heresies include: philosophy based on mere human tradition or belief in the *stoicheia* ("elemental spirits"), which, in Greek thought, gave structure to the universe (2:8, 20);[96] some sort of legalism, possibly of the sort Paul undertook to refute in Galatians;[97] ascetic self-denial (2:18, 23);[98] angel worship; and possibly a docetic belief that Jesus did not have bodily existence (1:22; 2:9, 18).[99]

Several moral admonitions characterize the way of the old or earthly nature that Christians are to "put to death" or "put off" (3:5–10), and the way of the new nature, which they are to "put on" (3:12–4:6). Those who conduct themselves properly, "making the most of the time" (4:5), will receive "the inheritance" as their reward at the parousia, when Christ appears (3:4, 6, 24).[100]

1 Thessalonians

The congregations in Philippi and Thessalonica probably were the first Christian churches established in Europe, at least the first established there by Paul. First Thessalonians is commonly regarded as the earliest of Paul's letters, datable perhaps as early as A.D. 50 or 51, though no evidence particularly compels this conclusion. The authors of the letter identify themselves as "Paul, Silvanus, and Timothy" (1:1) and generally write in the first person plural, though Paul seems to be the principal spokesman (2:17–18). The authors recall their earlier work with the Thessalonian Christians, noting that they had supported themselves so as not to be a burden to the church there (2:1–9). The letter begins and ends in Paul's characteristic fashion (1:1–2; 5:23–28), and critics generally agree that this is one of his authentic letters.

Paul has several concerns here. He wants to strengthen the Thessalonian "believers" in the face of persecution from their fellow countrymen (2:14). The afflictions they suffer, he says, are part of the tempter's (Satan's) efforts to undermine faith (3:3–5; cf. Matt 6:13). Paul is encouraged now that Timothy has brought back good news about their steadfast faith (3:6–10). He urges them to live according to the moral standards he has taught them (4:1–12). Men are to marry and hold their wives in holiness and honor; all "brethren" are to love one another, live quietly, mind their own affairs, work with their hands, and be dependent on no one. Especially, Paul wishes to reassure them that fellow believers who have "fallen asleep" (died) have not perished forever but will return with Christ when he comes (4:13–18; cf. 3:13).[101] Paul expects this to happen while many, including himself, are still alive; at that time, those who are still alive, "who are left until the coming of the Lord," will be "caught up together with them in the clouds" (4:14–17). Paul does not say here that those still alive would first be "changed" or transformed so as to have "spiritual bodies" like the resurrected dead; but that understanding may be implicit (see 1 Cor 15:35–52; Phil 3:20–21).

When exactly the parousia will be is not known, but it will come "like a thief in the night" (5:1–4), that is, unexpectedly, at any time.[102] In the meantime, Christians are to live a life of faith, hope, and love (5:5–8; cf. Eph 6:10–17), building one another up (5:11; cf. 1 Corinthians 12–14). Various other passages underscore the expectation of Christ's coming and likewise urge readers to live in the interim with faith, love, and hope.[103] These Christians are to love one another (4:9–10; cf. John 13:34–35), but love is not limited to "the brethren" or fellow believers; instead, it is to be all-inclusive (3:12; cf. Matt 5:43–48).

One peculiarity of the letter is the animus Paul expresses toward "the Jews." Here he says that they killed "the Lord Jesus" (2:15; cf. John 19:14–18), in contrast to Matthew 27:27–36 or Mark 15:16–25, according to which Jesus was crucified by Roman soldiers. Moreover, Paul reports that "the Jews" have interfered with his work among gentiles (2:15–16; cf. Acts 14:1–2). (Evidently he is not referring here to Jewish Christians or "circumcisionists" of the sort that troubled the Galatian churches.)

Another special feature of the letter is Paul's affectionate attitude toward these Christians,[104] equaled only, perhaps, in his letter to the Philippians. Here, as there, he calls on the readers to "rejoice always" (5:16). Although Paul may not have known that he was composing Scripture for all later Christianity, he did intend the letter as authoritative instruction for the whole church at Thessalonica (5:27; cf. Col 4:16).

2 Thessalonians

Some interpreters consider this a genuine letter of Paul's. Most others, perhaps, regard it as deutero-Pauline, that is, actually written by someone else, possibly as late as the A.D. 90s. At points, it is quite similar to 1 Thessalonians; for example, the opening (1:1–2a) duplicates 1 Thessalonians 1:1, and the concluding benedictions are nearly identical. Both purport to be from "Paul, Silvanus, and Timothy" and are written largely in the first person plural. Both refer to afflictions experienced by members of the church at Thessalonica.

But there are significant differences. In 1 Thessalonians, the parousia is characterized as a time of salvation for both the living and "those who have fallen asleep."[105] Here, on the other hand, it is represented as a time of vengeance, when Jesus and his "mighty angels in flaming fire" will inflict eternal punishment upon unbelievers and the disobedient (1:7–9) and Jesus will slay "the lawless one," a minion of Satan, "with the breath of his mouth" (2:8–9). The whole scene more nearly resembles what is anticipated in Revelation than anything found elsewhere in Paul's writings.

In 1 Thessalonians, Paul urges, and warns, that the parousia will occur without any prior signs or notice (5:1–3), but here the author clearly and forcibly insists that there will be prior indications, namely, the appearance of "the man of lawlessness" or "the son of perdition" (associated with Satan), whose coming will be marked by false "signs and wonders" (2:1–3, 8–9). A similar expectation is found in 1 John 2:18, but not in the letters of Paul that are generally recognized as authentic. In the meantime, the "lawless one" is being restrained but will be revealed "in his time," when he will try to deceive unbelievers (2:6–7; cf. Rev 20:1–3, 7–8). The specific meaning is uncertain; however, the writer's apparent point is that believers should not be among those deceived into believing that the Lord has already come (2:2–3) but should hold fast to truth and righteousness in preparation for his doing so (2:9–12). The parousia has been delayed, but clearly it is expected in the near future. We hear for the first (and only) time in the New Testament of Christians assembling to meet Jesus when he comes at the parousia (2:1). Perhaps the reason some have stopped work and are living in idleness (3:6, 11–12) is that they suppose that the kingdom of God either has come or is on the verge of doing so.[106] Alternatively, these idlers may have been prompted by ordinary laziness. In any event, the writer admonishes them to earn their own way in the interim: "If anyone will not work, let him not eat" (3:6–12).

There are additional hints that someone other than Paul wrote the letter. The "reminder" of what Paul said while still with them (2:5) and the admonitions to keep "the tradition" he taught (2:1; 3:6) suggest that the letter was written after Paul's time. References to Paul's giving commands (3:6, 10, 12) also suggest secondary authorship, since Paul only once so characterized his instruction in the authentic letters.[107] The writer's unparalleled insistence on Paul's "mark" (3:17) as proof of his authorship may protest too much.[108]

Whoever the writer may have been, his intent, certainly, was to encourage Christians at Thessalonica to endure their present sufferings (cf. 1 Peter and Revelation), to look for vindication at the parousia, which was still to come, and would not come until after the appearance of "the man of lawlessness," and to urge them to remain steadfast in the meantime, each one earning his own living rather than depending on the others.[109] Unlike Paul's (other) letters, 2 Thessalonians contains virtually nothing else in the way of moral instruction or guidance. There is no indication whether the suffering or affliction the Thessalonians were experiencing was at the hands of their pagan neighbors, hostile Jews (cf. 1 Thess 2:14), or, perhaps, Roman authorities, as in the case of those addressed by the authors of 1 Peter and Revelation.

1 Timothy

Most modern interpreters regard 1 and 2 Timothy and Titus as treatises by an anonymous Christian pastor concerning problems common among the churches in the first quarter of the second century. These Pastoral Letters, as they are usually called, are written in the form of instructions by Paul to his associates Timothy and Titus. The writer sets out, in Paul's name, to advise the rising generation of church leaders, symbolized by these two former companions of Paul's, how they should conduct their ministries and deal with problems arising in their own time. Above all, they are to train themselves in "godliness" (4:7–8). The letters offer guidance on such issues as the importance of "guarding" or preserving "sound doctrine" and of avoiding theological disputes and speculations, the duties and qualifications of bishops and deacons, and the care of widows. In the ancient world, writers frequently attributed their own compositions to honored predecessors. It is understandable that someone concerned about these matters would have written in Paul's name, since Paul was the most important authority figure in first-century gentile Christianity.

All the Pastoral Letters reflect Christianity's emergence as a gentile religion. No longer do we find references to Judaizers or Christian circumcisionists. "The law" is now viewed favorably as a restraint upon "the lawless" and "the ungodly," and as the moral dimension of "sound doctrine" or "the glorious gospel," which the writer espouses (1 Tim 1:7–11). The first and perhaps second generation of apostles and other early church leaders have all died. Now there arises the problem of maintaining not only correct doctrine but also proper moral standards within the churches. As yet there is no "canon," or authoritative collection of Christian writings; there are no creeds, and there is no recognized structure of church governance other than bishops or supervisors and other local leaders such as elders and deacons.

Several passages in 1 Timothy have to do with preserving orthodoxy ("right teaching") and right conduct, as over against different doctrines and practices.[110] References to "endless genealogies" and "silly myths" (1:4; 4:7) may indicate that early gnostic versions of Christianity were current in the author's time.[111] The writer urges that prayers be offered "for all men," because "God our Savior . . . desires all men to be saved" (2:1–4).[112] Women are to dress modestly, adorning themselves with good deeds, not with braided hair or costly attire. They are to be silent and submissive to men (cf. 1 Cor 14:34–35; Eph 5:22–24), since woman, not man, was deceived by the serpent (2:9–14).[113] Notwithstanding this great error, a woman may be saved if she bears children, provided she also maintains the virtues of faith, love, holiness, and modesty (2:15). Bishops and deacons should be good husbands and fathers and men of reputable character, and neither drunkards nor lovers of money (3:1–13). Women also have some place as church leaders, possibly as deacons (3:11). Ministers are advised how to handle their responsibilities and various delicate situations that arise from time to time in their congregations (4:11–5:22).

Ruling "elders" may possibly represent still another new category of leadership, but see Titus 1:5–9, in which the terms "bishop" and "elder" appear to be used synonymously. Those elders who preach and teach (cf. 1 Cor 12:28), are worthy of special honor (and due remuneration) and may not be charged with offenses unless at least two witnesses testify against them (5:17–19).[114] Evidently such elders were understood to have authority to ordain ministers by the laying on of hands (4:14; cf. 5:22).

In keeping with the writer's affirmation that "everything created by God is good" (4:4; cf. Gen 1:31), he commends use of "a little wine" for the sake of one's health (5:23). Christian slaves should not be disrespectful toward their Christian masters just because now "they are brethren," but they "must serve all the better" (6:1–2; cf. Phlm 15–17). Christians should be content if they have food and clothing, and not desire wealth, for such desires "plunge men into ruin" (6:6–10). In this connection, the writer sets forth what becomes an often misquoted warning: "The love of money is the root of all evils" (6:10). Ministers should "fight the good fight," holding on to the eternal life that is already theirs, looking for the coming of Christ "at the proper time," and should charge wealthy members of their congregations "to be rich in good deeds" and generosity, setting their hopes on God, not on "uncertain riches," and thereby "laying up for themselves a good foundation for the future" (6:11–19).[115]

Like the author(s) of Ephesians and Colossians, the present writer refers to the substance of the Christian faith as "the mystery" (3:8, 16). Like the author of the Gospel of John, he declares that those who believe in Jesus already have eternal life (1:16; cf. John 6:40). Like the author of Hebrews, he represents Jesus as "mediator" between God and humanity (2:5). There is no mention of the coming of, or of entry into, the kingdom of God.

A number of passages and expressions have been absorbed into later Christian liturgy and hymns, such as "The saying is sure and worthy of full acceptance, that Christ Jesus came into the world to save sinners" (1:15), the characterization of God as "immortal, invisible, the only God" (1:17), and the admonitions to "fight the good fight," "take hold of [the] eternal life," and "be rich in good deeds, liberal and generous" (6:12, 18).

2 Timothy

This letter, or treatise, like 1 Timothy and Titus, probably was written well after Paul's lifetime by a church leader who wished to encourage Christian pastors to practice their ministries bravely and effectively, upholding "the truth" against false teaching and myths (1:6–8; 4:1–5). "Timothy" is a third-generation Christian (1:5) who represents such pastors. "Paul" mentions his own appointment as preacher and teacher and his consequent suffering as an example and encouragement to later preachers and teachers who—in the writer's time— might expect to "share in suffering for the gospel" (1:8–12; 3:10–12; 4:5). The letter is written as if from Rome, where Paul is a prisoner

(1:8; 2:9), expecting soon to die, having fought the good fight (cf. 1 Tim 6:12) and kept the faith (4:6–8).

As in 1 Timothy, the writer offers advice for pastors in coping with their tasks and responsibilities. He is particularly concerned that ministers should "guard" the teaching received from earlier times and avoid being confused by other teachings.[116] They should pursue their aims single-mindedly and conscientiously, like good soldiers, athletes, farmers, and workers (2:3–6, 15). The "man of God" (Christian minister; 3:17) is to use Scripture in his work. This, being inspired by God, is a sure guide to faith and righteousness (3:16). "Scripture" here probably refers to the Greek Old Testament (Septuagint or other versions), which would have included most of the Old Testament Apocrypha. There was, as yet, no New Testament.

The author warns that in "the last days" people will be lovers of self, money, and pleasure (3:1–9). Such people, he writes, are to be avoided (cf. 1 John 2:15–17). Implicitly, he believes that he and his readers are living in the "last days" (cf. 2 Pet 3:3; 1 John 2:18). He opposes the "realized eschatology" of those proponents of the idea that the resurrection has already occurred (2:18).[117] The writer also looks in hope for "that Day" when Christ Jesus will appear "to judge the living and the dead" (4:1, 8), language later reflected in the Apostles' and Nicene Creeds. He is also confident of the salvation already manifested in the One who "brought life and immortality to light" (1:9–10). Like Paul and the author of the Fourth Gospel, the present writer evidently expected that salvation would be experienced in heaven—the apparent meaning of the new expression "heavenly kingdom" at 4:18.[118]

Titus

Here we find many of the same themes and expressions as in 1 and 2 Timothy. Interpreters generally agree that all three of these Pastoral Letters probably were written by the same person. The author probably understood that he was stating what Paul would have said about problems confronting the churches' ministers a generation or two later. Timothy and Titus stand for or symbolize such ministers. The three Pastoral Letters or treatises are usually dated around A.D. 110–120.

Again the writer urges that Christian leaders maintain sound doctrine and refute contrary teachings (1:9–2:1). At the same time, they are to avoid "stupid controversies, genealogies, dissension," and the like (3:9). Genealogies may refer to gnostic myths about divine emanations (cf. 1:14).[119] References to circumcisionists (1:10) and arguments about "the law" (3:9) suggest the existence of a problem with Jewish Christian legalism, though this is not indicated in the other Pastoral Letters (cf. Galatians). In any event, Christians are to adhere to "the faith," meaning, evidently, Christian doctrine or tradition, also referred to as "the truth" (1:13–14).[120] Christian doctrine was just beginning to take shape early in the second century.

Several basic ethical concerns are addressed here. Pastors and all Christians are to be "zealous for good deeds" (2:7, 14; cf. Jas 2:14–22), helping those in urgent need (3:14).[121] Bishops or elders—here evidently two names for the same leadership office—must be able to manage their own households and otherwise be qualified as worthy leaders (1:5–9; cf. 1 Tim 3:1–7). "Paul" advises ministers how they should instruct different kinds of people in the congregations: older men and women, younger women and men, and slaves (2:2–10). As in 1 Timothy 6:1–2, the writer says nothing here about masters' obligations to slaves (cf. Eph 6:9; Col 4:1). He declares God's intent to save all humankind (2:11; cf. 1 Tim 2:3–4), but also refers to "the elect" (1:1; cf. 2 Tim 2:10), an expression which implies belief that God has decided to save only some.

As in most New Testament writings, hope for the future is associated with the parousia, or appearing of Christ, which the writer and his readers still await (2:13). Christians have already been saved or justified by God's mercy or grace and are therefore "heirs in hope of eternal life" (3:5–7; cf. 1:2). In the meantime, pastors should use their authority to insist that all live "sober, upright, and godly lives in this world" based on the mercy and grace of God (2:11–3:8). Also, during this interim, Christians are to be submissive to "rulers and authorities," meaning, probably, Roman rulers of the time (3:1).[122]

Philemon

When the New Testament writings were collected, beginning sometime during the second century, the letters then ascribed to Paul were arranged by order of length, with Romans first and Philemon last. Philemon may also have been the last letter Paul wrote. As in Philippians, Paul is a "prisoner" (vv. 1, 9), perhaps in Rome, around A.D. 62. Paul's other letters are to churches; this one is to a single individual, Philemon, though indirectly also to others, including those who constituted the church that met in Philemon's house (vv. 1–2).

Paul begins much the same way he does in his letters to churches: He names himself and his "brother" Timothy as writers, names individual recipients of the letter (vv. 1–2), sets down his customary salutation (v. 3), and states that he thanks God always in his prayers for Philemon because of his love and faith. He closes the letter with greetings from a "fellow" prisoner and four fellow workers[123] and a characteristic Pauline benediction (v. 25).[124]

Paul's apparent purpose in writing is that he wants Philemon to free his slave Onesimus. He puts the matter graciously but firmly. He begins by saying that although he might command, "for love's sake" he prefers to appeal to Philemon's free will, so that his "goodness might not be by compulsion" (vv. 8–14). Though he would be glad to have Onesimus continue to serve him, Paul sends him back to Philemon—not, it seems, so that Philemon might once again send him to serve Paul in prison but in order that Philemon might receive him "no longer as a slave" but "as a beloved brother" (v. 16). Paul here makes operative his understanding that in Christ "there is neither slave nor free" (Gal 3:28). He offers to pay anything that Onesimus may owe Philemon, but reminds Philemon that such payment would hardly be fitting since Philemon owes his "own self" to Paul (vv. 18–19). Apparently both Philemon and Onesimus have been converted to Christianity through Paul's efforts. Paul states that he is confident of Philemon's obedience and that Philemon will do even more than Paul expressly asks, namely, give Onesimus his freedom. At the same time, he adds, not too subtly, that Philemon should prepare a guest room for him, hinting that he plans to come for a visit to see whether Onesimus has in fact been freed (vv. 21–22).

Interpreters sometimes state as an established fact that Onesimus was a runaway slave[125] who had stolen money or property from Philemon. The text of this letter, our only source of information on these matters, does not necessarily support such conclusions. It seems as likely that Philemon had sent Onesimus to wait upon Paul during his imprisonment, which is just what Onesimus was doing, but that after Onesimus's conversion, Paul determined that he should become a free man and so wrote Philemon to this effect. That Onesimus might have done Philemon any wrong or owed him anything could be interpreted in terms of damages to Philemon's property or debts incurred in the course of Onesimus's servitude, matters that would need to be settled in connection with his manumission.

Paul did not categorically call for the abolition of slavery, nor did anyone else in the ancient world. Paul did believe that the present age would soon pass away, and with it such institutions as slavery and even marriage (1 Cor 7:17–31; cf. Matt 22:30). In the meantime, Paul urged people in all his churches, including slaves, to remain in whatever estate or condition God had called them (1 Cor 7:17–24). Either Paul or, more likely, one or two later Christian writers who still looked for the parousia in the near future subsequently added that in the interim, Christian slaves should be obedient and serve their masters with goodwill, while Christian masters should be considerate of their slaves, "knowing that he who is [the Master of both] is in heaven, and that there is no partiality with him" (Eph 6:5–9; Col 3:22–4:1). A still later author, who likewise apparently expected the parousia in his and his readers' lifetime, rather more harshly insisted that slaves be required to be submissive, "give satisfaction in every respect," not be "refractory" or pilferers, and that they "show entire and true fidelity" to their masters, not presuming upon the fact that masters and slaves were now "brethren" (Titus 2:9–10, 13; 1 Tim 6:1–2). The author of these Pastoral Letters did not include anything about the equality of masters and slaves in Christ or any advice or admonitions to masters about how they should treat their slaves. By contrast, in Philemon, Paul says nothing about Onesimus's owing obedience as a slave; instead, it is Philemon who is to be obedient to Paul, by giving Onesimus his freedom (v. 21).

Hebrews

Although a few verses (13:18–19, 22–25) parallel the substance and format of typical Pauline letters, Hebrews is widely regarded as a treatise by someone other than Paul; indeed, it constitutes a distinctive interpretation of the essence of Christianity. Early Christian authorities who eventually arranged the New Testament writings in their present sequence placed Hebrews as the first (since it was the longest) of the non-Pauline letters, or "catholic epistles." Shorter non-Pauline letters follow in order of approximately diminishing length, concluding with Jude. Like the other catholic epistles, Hebrews was written for the author's contemporary Christians generally and so is not addressed to any particular congregations or individuals. Its emphasis on holding fast "the confession" (2:1–3; 4:14) and eschewing "strange teaching" (13:9) suggests that it was composed during a period when the defense of orthodoxy against variant doctrines was a serious problem, perhaps as early as A.D.100–120.[126] Although the author writes as if Jewish priests were still offering sacrifices in the temple (which the Romans destroyed in A.D. 70), his knowledge of Judaism seems to have been based on Old Testament scriptures or on "testimonies" rather than on firsthand acquaintance with ongoing Jewish or Jewish Christian practices and concerns.[127] There is no mention of circumcision or keeping Sabbaths or other holy days. His references to the Old Testament are sometimes vague (2:6; 4:4) and fanciful (10:28; 11:26; 12:16–17). Notwithstanding the traditional title, there is no indication that the treatise was written to or for Jews or Jewish Christians.

The author's main concern is to set out an understanding of the meaning of Christianity for gentile Christians of his time. These Christians had inherited as their Scripture the Greek Old Testament. There was as yet no New Testament. Core beliefs and institutions in the Old Testament, however, meant little to gentile Christians, who were largely unfamiliar with Jewish traditions. Hebrews renders Old Testament traditions relevant to the author's era by showing how Christianity was grounded in the Old Testament, and, at the same time, how it was something new, indeed, the fulfillment of the hopes and promises set down in the Old Testament. The author uses several strategies in this connection, for instance, by invoking the Platonic distinction between shadow and reality (10:3). More frequently, he contrasts earlier Israelite/Jewish persons and institutions with Christ, who is presented as superior to, or the fulfillment and perfection of, all earlier persons, practices, and promises. Thus, the Son is superior to biblical angels (1:4–2:8), Christ to Moses (3:3–6), Jesus, as "high priest," to the whole Levitical priesthood (5:1–7:19), and the heavenly sanctuary to the earthly one (8:5; 9:1). Christians enjoy a better covenant (7:22), better promises (8:6), better sacrifices (9:23), and, ultimately, a better country (11:16) than those afforded or offered their precursors in the Old Testament.

The Christology (understanding of Christ) set out in Hebrews differs in significant respects from the understandings found elsewhere in the New Testament. Not only were all things created through Christ (1:2; cf. John 1:1–3)—though God was "the builder" (3:4)—and the universe upheld by Christ's word (1:3; 2:10; cf. Col 1:15–17), but all things were created *for* him (2:10), and he is the appointed "heir of all things" (1:2; cf. 1 Cor 15:28). By suffering death, he tasted death "for every one" (2:9), and through his death, he destroyed the devil, thereby delivering all who were in bondage through fear of death (2:14–15).[128]

Most characteristically and distinctively, Hebrews' Christology focuses on Christ's role as the new and ultimate high priest. Various Old Testament passages, especially in Psalms, are read as testimony by the Holy Spirit (3:7; 9:8; 10:15) to Jesus' priestly mission in the role of "high priest for ever after the order of Melchizedek" (6:20).[129] The author explains that Melchizedek's name means "righteous king" and "king of peace" and that Melchizedek, unlike later Levitical priests, was a priest forever. In these respects, he says, Jesus is like Melchizedek (chap. 7). Perhaps the author also means to relate Jesus to Melchizedek because, like that ancient figure, Jesus did not have any Aaronic or Levitical ancestors (7:14).[130] His main point is that whereas the Levitical priests had to offer sacrifices daily, Jesus "did this once for all when he offered up himself" (7:27; 10:10–14). Jesus is now enthroned as high priest in the heavenly sanctuary (8:12); there he mediates a new covenant, the one promised by Jeremiah.[131] In this connection, he also makes intercession for those who "draw near to God," thereby saving them "for all time" (7:25).

Several passages indicate the writer's belief that the "present age" was about to end and that Christ soon would come again. The writer refers to his own time as "these last days" (1:2) and urges his readers to live rightly as they "see the Day drawing near" (10:25). He quotes from Habakkuk to the effect that in "yet a little while . . . the coming one shall come and shall not tarry" (10:37),[132] and promises that Christ will appear a *second* time "to save those who are eagerly awaiting him" (9:28). This is the only text in the Bible to speak of Christ's second coming. Christian hopes for the future are also described in terms of the true "rest" promised the fathers of old (3:7–4:11) and as the "heavenly city" which is to come (11:16; 13:14).[133] Christians should "strive to enter" or "seek" (4:11; 13:14)[134] this "rest" or "city" by faith and righteous living.

Hebrews also contains several other distinctive ideas and texts. Here we find the famous definition of faith as "the assurance of things hoped for, the conviction of things not seen" (11:1). Yet in Hebrews, "faith" also seems to mean doing or acting rightly in accordance with the divine intent (cf. Gal 5:6; Jas 2:18–26), as is illustrated by a series of Old Testament personalities and scenes (11:4–38). The need for authoritative leadership is indicated in the admonition, "Obey your leaders and submit to them" (13:17; cf. Titus 2:15). There was, as yet, no overall church hierarchy. The book cautions against some Christians' habit of neglecting to attend common meetings for worship and mutual encouragement (10:25). The writer addresses the problem whether Christians who lapse into apostasy or sin may be restored to the community and have any hope of salvation. The answer given here is no (6:4–8; 10:26–31).[135] In Hebrews, God's promise is characterized in striking language, as "a sure and steadfast anchor of the soul" (6:19)—an image that may have been important to later Christian catacomb artists, who adopted the anchor as one of the earliest Christian symbols. Passages from Hebrews, more than from most other New Testament writings, are commonly repeated in later Christian preaching, liturgy, and aphorism.[136]

Several concluding exhortations set forth the kind of life befitting those who aspire to enter the heavenly city or promised rest. They are to accept the Lord's discipline, strive for peace with all people, let brotherly love continue, show hospitality to strangers (cf. 3 John 5–8), remember those in prison and the ill-treated (cf. Matt 25:31–46), honor marriage, renounce love of money (cf. 1 Tim 6:10), share possessions (cf. Acts 2:44–45), and obey their leaders (12:1–13:17).

James

Like Ephesians and Hebrews, James is a tract or treatise, written for Christians everywhere ("the twelve tribes in the Dispersion"; 1:1). Though not claiming to be an apostle, the writer gives authoritative advice and instruction on several subjects. Some interpreters see traces of Jewish Christianity here and suggest that the author was James, the brother of Jesus.[137] But typical Jewish Christian interests, such as circumcision and Sabbath observance, are not mentioned. The writer does not commend works of the *Jewish* law, but instead urges fidelity to the laws of liberty and love (2:8, 12) and performance of "works" that complete faith and give expression to love (2:14–26; cf. 1:27). James may have been composed by a gentile Christian pastor around A.D. 90–100.

The author particularly wishes to correct the notion that faith or belief is all that matters. Interpreters sometimes call this mistaken notion "fideism." Such a misunderstanding could have been prompted by Paul's emphasis on faith. Like Paul, however, James insists that what matters is faith working through love (2:14–26).[138] In addition, James is concerned to encourage Christians to be humble, peaceable, and gentle, rather than proud, jealous, ambitious, and judgmental.[139] He warns against misusing the tongue, that "little member" which is "a fire" and a "restless evil, full of deadly poison," urging that it be controlled and directed toward right speaking (1:26; 3:2–12).[140]

Similarly, he warns that passions or desires, if not restrained, lead to sin, strife, and death (1:14–15; 4:1–3). Christians must keep themselves from "friendship with the world" (4:4; cf. 1 John 2:15–17), but this does not mean indifference to those in need. On the contrary, "religion that is pure and undefiled" includes visiting "widows and orphans in their affliction" (1:27). Such, indeed, is the test of faith: Whether it is helpful to those in need (2:14–17; cf. Luke 10:25–37). It is a question of doing, not simply hearing, the word (1:22–26; cf. Luke 6:46–49). The author's attitude toward the rich is related to this: They busy themselves with the pursuit of gain and luxury, not only ignoring, but even exploiting laborers and killing the righteous (5:1–6; cf. Wisd 1:16–2:20). Therefore, Christians should be careful not to defer to the rich or humiliate the poor. Indeed, the poor are heirs to the kingdom of God (2:1–5).[141]

Like most New Testament authors, James understands that the "coming of the Lord is at hand," indeed, "the Judge is standing at the doors" (5:8–9). But James admonishes his readers to be patient and steadfast in the meantime (5:7, 10–11). Those who suffer should pray, and those who are cheerful should sing praise (5:13). If one is sick, he should summon the church elders, who are then to pray over him and anoint him with oil (5:14).[142] This text may have given rise to the later Christian rite or sacrament of anointing the sick and dying, known popularly as "last rites." Christians, according to James, are to confess their sins to one another and pray for one another (5:16), a text that later may have led to the Christian rite or sacrament of confession, though here there is no suggestion of offering one's confession to a priest. Elijah is then presented as an example of the efficacy of prayer (5:17–18).

In contrast to Hebrews, James holds that sinners and those who wander from the truth can indeed be brought back. Moreover, whoever helps bring a sinner back from his way of error "will save his soul from death" and "cover a multitude of sins" (5:19–20). Several passages in James echo sayings of Jesus found in Matthew's Gospel.[143] The author evidently was familiar with that Gospel.

1 Peter

The writer identifies himself as Peter, an apostle (1:1), and sends greetings from the church at "Babylon" (probably Rome, 5:13; cf. Rev 17:1–18:24). The letter might have been written by the apostle Peter, who, with Paul, was executed in Rome in A.D. 64, according to extrabiblical tradition. Many interpreters, however, think it more likely the composition of a later Christian, and that its references to sufferings and trials should be understood in connection either with the experienced persecution of Christians in Asia Minor around A.D. 96 (see Revelation 1–3) or possibly with the common apocalyptic expectation that the messianic age would be preceded by a time of severe suffering or tribulation (see, e.g., Dan 12:1; Mark 13:7–23). The author also identifies himself as an elder (5:1), a category of Christain leadership otherwise mentioned only in relatively late New Testament writings. First Peter's several affinities to Ephesians, the Pastorals, Hebrews, and James also point toward probable post-Petrine authorship.

The author begins in the fashion of Paul's letters, addressing certain persons or communities, here "the exiles of the Dispersion" (cf. Jas 1:1), specifically, Christians located in several of the Roman provinces of Asia Minor (1:1). These probably were first- or second-generation converts from paganism to Christianity (1:14, 18). Christians in two of these provinces, Galatia and Asia, are also addressed, respectively, in Paul's letter to the Galatians, and in the book of Revelation. First Peter likewise concludes in terms reminiscent of Paul's letters (5:12–14). According to Paul (Galatians 1–2), Peter (or Cephas) was a missionary to Jews and was associated with Jewish Christian concerns in Jerusalem and Antioch. The present letter gives no indication of these connections or concerns. To this writer, Christians are "a chosen race" and "holy nation" (2:9). When he mentions gentiles, he seems to mean non-Christian gentiles (2:12; 4:3). Jews are not mentioned at all.

The writer is particularly concerned with encouraging Christians in Asia Minor to remain steadfast despite the trials they are suffering or may have to undergo.[144] Suffering is associated with the evil designs of the devil (5:8–9; cf. Matt 6:13) but not with Roman persecution, in contrast to Revelation, where both Satan and Rome are implicated in the tribulation experienced by Christians. Here readers are instructed to be subject to and to honor the emperor (2:13–17).[145]

Like most other New Testament writings, 1 Peter warns then-contemporary readers that the present age will soon end. Christ's previous coming marked the beginning of the end of the old era (1:20); now "the end of all things is at hand" (4:7), and "the time has come for judgment" (4:17).[146] Evidently the writer expects God to be the judge (1:17; 4:5). Afterward, those whose previous conduct has been found sufficiently righteous will receive the imperishable "inheritance . . . kept in heaven" for them (1:4). Whether that inheritance will be experienced in heaven[147] or on earth[148] is not indicated. In the meantime, "for a little while," Christians may have to suffer various trials (1:6; 5:10).

During the interim, Christians should live soberly and righteously, above all, with love for one another (1:22; 2:16; 3:8; 4:8).[149] Love, the writer urges, "covers a multitude of sins" (4:8; cf. Jas 5:20). In this connection, Christians should "practice hospitality ungrudgingly to one another" (4:9).[150] Like Paul, the present writer understands that this new life of love has been made possible by the death and resurrection of Christ, in whom Christians are now "born anew" (1:3, 22–23; cf. John 3:3). Righteous living is essential, for at the judgment, God will judge each person "impartially according to his deeds" (1:17; 2:12).[151]

So important is the matter of right living that the author devotes most of chapters 2–5 to moral advice and instruction. Such advice was particularly important since the gentile Christians to whom he was writing had grown up in the midst of degraded pagan culture without the benefit of guidance from biblical law. Particularly, the writer is concerned that Christians should control the "passions of the flesh" (2:11; 4:2).[152] Though formerly not God's people, now through God's grace, gentiles have become his people (2:9–10; cf. Hos 1:6–2:23). But they must live up to the standard of their new being. Therefore, they should "put away" malice and envy, and use their gifts for one another's good (2:1; 4:10–11.)[153] Many other specific precepts and guidelines are enumerated (e.g., in 2:11–3:17; 4:15; 5:1–6).

First Peter has a number of unique or unusual features. The idea that the Spirit of Christ inspired Old Testament prophetic utterances (1:10–11) is not found elsewhere.[154] Only in 1 Peter do we find the idea that when Christ died he was "put to death in the flesh" but remained or became "alive in the spirit" (3:18). This spiritual Christ then "preached to the spirits in prison," namely, the dead in Hades (3:19–20; 4:6; cf. Eph 4:8–10). These texts probably were the basis for the later creedal affirmation that after he was buried, Christ "descended into Hell." Here the idea is that he preached to those in Hades in order to make salvation possible for the dead of earlier generations. Like some other post-Pauline writings, 1 Peter calls on servants (here "house servants") to be submissive to their masters, showing "all respect," "even to the overbearing," thereby "following" in Christ's "steps." The author says nothing about how masters should treat their servants.[155] Likewise, the author calls on wives to be submissive to their husbands, evidently so as to "win" (convert) those who are pagans (3:1–6), a rather extraordinary missions strategy (cf. 1 Cor 7:12–17). However, he calls on husbands to be considerate of their wives (3:7),[156] honoring them "as the weaker sex" (an expression found earlier in 4 Macc 15:5), since they are "joint heirs of the grace of life."

Some form critics suggest that 1 Peter was originally a baptismal sermon.[157] Baptism is mentioned, somewhat indirectly, at 3:21, where the deliverance of Noah (and others on the ark) "by water" is compared with baptism, which saves "as an appeal to God for a clear conscience through the resurrection of Jesus Christ" (cf. John 3:5). Most New Testament writings do not refer to baptism; it is not clear to what extent this rite was considered important within the New Testament period.[158] At all events, baptism does not seem to be one of the central interests indicated in 1 Peter.

Implicitly, elders are seen as "shepherds," charged to care for their flocks (5:1–3; cf. Ezekiel 34). Elders are also referred to as church leaders in Acts and the Pastoral Letters. Perhaps the principal leaders in each congregation, or possibly each town, were known as elders or bishops (see Titus 1:5–9). In 1 Peter, Christ is twice designated the chief Shepherd (2:25; 5:4),[159] an unusual christological title in the New Testament.[160]

Finally, "the devil" plays a special role in 1 Peter. He "prowls around like a roaring lion, seeking those he can devour" (5:8). The devil, Satan, or "the Evil One" is associated with tribulation or the suffering of the faithful, and is regarded as a danger to be reckoned with in several other New Testament writings.[161] This understanding contrasts with that in Hebrews 2:14–15, which seems to say that Jesus has already destroyed the devil (cf. Mark 3:23–27).

2 Peter

Although the writer presents himself as Peter the apostle (1:1, 16–18), New Testament scholars generally agree that this letter was written well after Peter's time, possibly as late as A.D. 120–140. The generation of the "fathers" (or apostles) has passed away (3:4; cf. John 21:20–23). Paul's letters have been collected and are considered authoritative if not yet scriptural (3:15–16). The writer notes that some things in Paul's letters are hard to understand (a word of consolation to later interpreters of Paul, no doubt). Since Paul's letters are well known, the present author does not write in his name, as some earlier New Testament writers apparently did.[162] Instead, so that his advice would carry weight, this author writes to "remind" Christians what "Peter" had said they should remember or recall in years to come (1:12–15; 3:1). Attribution to Peter indicates Peter's importance in early second-century church circles. Another (or possibly the same) author undertook to offer fellow Christians much of the same advice, writing under the name of Jude. Like other "catholic epistles," such as Hebrews, James, and 1 John, 2 Peter is a general letter or tract that was written for all Christians of the time, not for a particular congregation.

Second Peter emphasizes three related concerns. First, Christians should live godly lives, supplementing their faith with virtue, so that at the time of judgment they might be found fit to enter into the kingdom of Christ (1:3–11; 3:11, 14). The author does not use the terms "Christian" or "Christianity," but refers to the latter as "the way of truth" (2:2) and "the way of righteousness" (2:21). "Knowledge" and "godliness" are recurrent expressions characterizing the Christian life (e.g., 1:3–8). Self-control, steadfastness, and brotherly affection (*philadelphia*) are also commended (1:6–7). Second Peter has a distinctive theory of salvation: Christians are to "become partakers of the divine nature" (1:4; cf. 1 Cor 15:35–54). Implicitly, they will do so when they enter "the eternal kingdom" of their "Lord and Savior Jesus Christ" (1:11).[163] The writer suggests that by their holiness and godliness, Christians can hasten the coming of the parousia (3:11–12; cf. Acts 3:19–21).

Second, the writer urges his readers to beware of false prophets and teachers who promote heresies and entice or exploit gullible persons with their licentiousness and greed (2:1–3). These deviants have been promoting "cleverly devised myths" and other heresies (1:16; 2:1).[164] Christians should recognize that the interpretation of Scripture is not a matter for each individual's opinion (i.e., heresy, 1:20–21). False teachers and prophets also promote ungodly wickedness (2:2–22). The writer refers frequently to the "destruction" that awaits such persons (2:3, 12; 3:7). Unlike other New Testament writers, 2 Peter looks for their punishment not only on the day of judgment but in the meantime as well (2:9–10).

Finally, the writer attempts to explain why the promised parousia or coming of Christ has not yet occurred. He anticipates that in the last days, "scoffers" will raise this question (3:3–4). Evidently the writer believed that his readers were then living in these "last days," for such scoffers have evidently appeared. He suggests several explanations for the delay of the parousia.

For one thing, God has created and destroyed the earth before by his word (3:5–6); he will "by the same word" destroy the heavens and earth that now exist (3:7) and make new heavens and a new earth (3:11–13). In other words, God did it before, and he will surely do it again, as the scoffers and the ungodly will discover to their sorrow on the day of judgment when it eventually dawns.

Next, the writer suggests that God reckons time differently than humans do: "With the Lord, one day is as a thousand years" (3:8; cf. Ps. 90:4). Therefore, the passing of two or more generations since the parousia was expected to have occurred need not be a matter of concern, despite earlier promises and hopes.[165]

Another explanation is that this delay is to be understood as God's forbearance; by postponing the day of judgment, God desires that none should perish and that all might reach repentance (3:9, 15). Nevertheless, "the day of the Lord" may come at any time, "like a thief" (3:10);[166] therefore, Christians must be ready, awaiting it in "lives of holiness and godliness" (3:10–14).

The idea that the old heavens and earth would be completely destroyed at the time of the parousia (3:10–12) is unusual. The Old Testament prophets typically looked for the transformation or restoration of the earth, when humans and other creatures would live together on earth in peace under the sovereignty of God.[167] In Revelation (21:1–22:5), which shares the expectation that the present world is to "pass away," as here (3:13), the redeemed are expected to inhabit a new earth.

1 John

Here again, we have a treatise written to or for all Christians of the author's time, rather than a letter to a particular congregation. It is, the writer says, "the message" he proclaims (1:3, 5). Both in style and substance, 1 John resembles the Gospel of John so closely as to suggest to many scholars that the same author might have written both. There are, however, important differences, and the question of authorship remains open. Both the letter and the Gospel probably were written around A.D. 100. Some interpreters think that the same person who wrote 1 John also wrote 2 and 3 John, but this theory is less well founded.

Both 1 John and the Gospel use the term "abiding" prominently,[168] and both make much of the contrast between light and darkness and of the ambiguous character of the world. Both refer frequently to "the truth" as the essence of Christianity (1 John 3:19; John 18:37) and to "eternal life" (rather than the kingdom of God) as the ultimate blessing for those who believe in Jesus (1 John 5:13; John 20:30–31). Both stress the commandment to love one another or "the brethren" (1 John 2:7–10; 3:23; John 15:12–17). Both refer to believers as "children of God" (1 John 3:1; John 1:12). Unlike most New Testament writings, each mentions the forgiveness of sins (1 John 2:12; John 20:23). Each twice records the unusual promise that God will grant those who pray whatever they wish.[169] Both insist that Jesus was "in the flesh," evidently in order to counter some incipient docetic, possibly gnostic, heresy that regarded him only as a spirit or spiritual being (1 John 4:2; John 1:14; 20:27).[170]

Many features in 1 John, however, contrast with those of the Gospel. The author of 1 John consistently addresses his readers rather condescendingly as "little children" or "children" (e.g., 2:1, 18, 28), a characterization found elsewhere only in the appendix to the Fourth Gospel (John 21:5). First John is the only New Testament writing to say that those who commit sins are "of the devil" (cf. Wis 2:24) or that Jesus "appeared to destroy the works of the devil" (3:8, 10).[171] Only in 1 John do we find a distinction between "mortal" and "nonmortal" sins (5:16–17). Somewhat in passing, the author of the letter cautions against believing "false prophets" (4:1) and worshiping idols (5:21)—concerns not present in the Gospel. First John also diverges from the Fourth Gospel in its understandings that the world is dominated by "the evil one" (5:19) and that the parousia is imminent (2:18).

The basic purpose of the letter (or treatise) is to urge Christians both to hold fast to the Christian message (1:5), particularly that Jesus is the Christ or Son of God (5:1, 5), and to live in accordance with the love commandment; in short, to believe and love (3:23). Various "antichrists" (heretics) have split off from the church, denying that Jesus is the Christ (2:18–23). Anyone who denies this belief or doctrine is a "liar" (2:22). So is anyone who claims to "know" Christ but disobeys his commandments (2:4); thus, "if any one says 'I love God,' and hates his brother, he is a liar" (4:20). The test of love is whether it prompts one to help his brother who is in need (3:17–18).[172] Love is "of God"; indeed, "God is love" (4:7–8, 16)—the only biblical passages to say this in so many words. Those who abide in love "may have confidence for the day of judgment" (4:17).

The writer is mainly concerned with the moral life of his Christian contemporaries. Repeatedly, he urges them to live according to Christ's commandment to love one another. Those who do so may thereby know and show that they are "children of God" (3:10). First John holds that Christians (those "born of God") do not sin (3:4–9; 5:18). Yet he insists that those who say they have no sin deceive themselves, and he urges Christians to confess their sins so that God may forgive them (1:8–10). Indeed, he says that his reason for writing this letter or tract is so that his intended readers may not sin (2:1).

Like most New Testament writers, the author of 1 John expected the coming of Christ in the near future. According to apocalyptic doctrine, "antichrist" was to come first—that is, before the parousia, or the coming of Jesus as Christ.[173] Since *many* antichrists have now come, the author logically concludes, it must be "the last hour" (2:18; cf. 4:3). Like Paul, 1 John anticipates that when Christ comes, believers will be transformed, becoming like him (3:2).[174] In the meantime, those who so aspire should live in purity of life, in love, and in righteousness, renouncing sin (3:3–10) and "the world," which "passes away" (2:15–17)[175] but in the meantime continues to be "in the power of the evil one" (5:19; cf. 1 Pet 5:8–9). Implicitly, perhaps, as in John 14:1–3 and some of Paul's letters,[176] the future realm of salvation was thought to be in heaven, not on earth.[177]

2 John

Second John is written in the form of a letter from "the elder" (or "old man" or "presbyter") to "the elect lady and her children." The Greek term for church (*ekklesia*) is feminine; the "elect lady" evidently stood either for some particular church and its members or for the whole church. If the latter, it would be in effect a catholic, or general, letter, like 1 Peter, James, and 1 John. The writer could have been the same person who wrote 1 John (ca. A.D. 100) or may have been a church leader writing, perhaps, near the time the Pastoral Letters were composed (ca. A.D. 110–120). "Elders" are mentioned as church leaders in the latter chapters of Acts, in Titus, and in James 5:14, and seem to have been local leaders or bishops. The author or authors of the Gospel of John and of 1, 2, and 3 John are all anonymous: None of these writings itself states that it was written by a person named John. Third John likewise purports to have been written by "the elder." No single person is so named or identified in the other Johannine writings or elsewhere in the New Testament.

Like 1 John, 2 John addresses those who already know "the truth," meaning, in effect, sound doctrine (vv. 1, 4). Second John also uses the term "abiding," but does so with reference to maintaining true doctrine (v. 9), in contrast to what we find in 1 John 4:13–16, where it is a question of abiding in love and in God and of God's abiding in believers (cf. John 15:4–7). Nothing is said in 2 John about "light" and "darkness" or "the world"—central themes in 1 John. Concern with maintaining sound doctrine is characteristic of New Testament writings composed after A.D. 100, notably the Pastoral Letters, Jude, and 2 Peter. Language used in urging adherence to the love commandment here (vv. 5–6) suggests some literary relationship to 1 John,[178] though the instruction to "follow love" (v. 6) is unparalleled. The salutation (v. 3) may have been borrowed from one of Paul's letters, several of which were familiar to Christians by the time of 2 Peter (2 Pet 3:15–16), if not in earlier years.[179]

The main concern in 2 John is to warn Christians against heretical teachers or "deceivers," who deny that Jesus came in the flesh (v. 7; cf. 1 John 4:2). These docetists presumably held that Jesus only seemed (*dokein*) to have been in human form. Like the author of 1 and 2 Timothy and Titus, this writer exhorts his readers to hold to "the truth" or traditional "doctrine." He warns especially against receiving such heretics "into the house," and thereby contributing to their "wicked work" (vv. 10–11). Receiving "into the house" probably means welcoming into the local church.[180] Interpreters generally read this warning as referring to offering hospitality. Both receiving strangers into church and offering such persons hospitality were difficult or delicate questions. Given the absence of a central structure of church government that could issue credentials and the lack of any common creedal standards, it might well have been unclear at first encounter whether a newly arrived visitor or traveling missionary was heretical or not. Heretics, that is, persons with different religious opinions or beliefs, could unsettle early Christian communities. Nevertheless, Hebrew 13:2 and 3 John 5–8 advocate offering hospitality to strangers. Unlike the author of 1 John, the writer of 2 John does not construe the appearance of many deceivers or "antichrists" as a sign that the parousia is near (v. 7; cf. 1 John 2:18). The letter ends with greetings from the children of "your elect sister," presumably another early Christian congregation. The terms "elect lady" and "elect sister" are not used in other New Testament writings; if they refer to particular churches or congregations, we have no way to identify the ones for which these greetings may have been intended.

3 John

As in 2 John, the writer identifies himself as "the elder" or "presbyter." The "beloved disciple" to whom the Gospel of John is attributed, implicitly, presumably lived to a considerable age (John 21:20–24). The assertion in 3 John 12 that its writer's "testimony is true" seems intended to associate him with this elderly disciple, of whom the same is said in John 21:24. That disciple might have been known as "the elder" in view of his age, and no doubt would have been acknowledged as a person of some authority.[181] So it is possible that the author of the Fourth Gospel also wrote 3 John, but it is by no means certain. No disciple or writer named John is mentioned in either the Gospel or any of the letters of John, but ascriptions to John appear in the earliest New Testament manuscripts. Like 2 John, 3 John mentions "truth" several times; the expression "follow the truth" appears in both (v. 4; 2 John 4), and some concluding remarks are nearly identical (2 John 12; 3 John 13–14). Third John contains a striking summary of the Christian life: "He who does good is of God; he who does evil has not seen God" (v. 11).[182] Unlike 1 and 2 John, 3 John mentions neither heretics nor the love commandment; likewise, it does not mention "antichrist" or "the evil one." Like 2 John, 3 John does not explicitly refer to the coming parousia or to moral readiness or preparation for that critical future event. Interpreters generally think it likely that the same person wrote 2 and 3 John, but are less certain about whether this person was the author of 1 John.

The writer's main concern is to encourage a person named Gaius (and perhaps others in his church; v. 9) to show hospitality to traveling Christian missionaries, to support their future travels, and to resist efforts by a certain misguided Diotrephes to the contrary. Interpreters suggest that 3 John was meant to correct a misreading of the warning in 2 John against welcoming heretics (2 John 10–11). Other New Testament writings also encourage hospitality (Heb 13:2; 1 Pet 4:9). Whether strangers or traveling missionaries were heretical or orthodox might not have been immediately apparent to early Christian communities where doctrinal lines were just beginning to be established. This writer wishes to vouch for the credentials of Demetrius, as a well-attested Christian, perhaps a missionary, and possibly the bearer of this letter, and evidently asks Gaius to welcome him into the church (v. 12).

Gaius was a common Roman name. We know nothing more about him from other sources. Like Philemon, in Paul's letter by that name, he may have been an actual person. Or, perhaps like Theophilus in Luke 1:3 and Acts 1:1, he may have been a hypothetical person, representing or standing for early Christian readers generally. References to Diotrephes and Demetrius suggest that this letter may have been a genuine one, that is, to and about real persons in real circumstances. The concluding greeting to and from "the friends" (v. 15) is distinctive, and may have been the basis for the Quakers' later self-designation as the Society of Friends.

Jude

The author describes himself as the brother of James (v. 1). Jesus had brothers named James and Judas, or Jude.[183] Nevertheless, the letter's concern about ungodly heretics (vv. 4, 8–9) suggests a setting somewhat after the time of the generation of Jesus' contemporaries, perhaps during the period when 1 and 2 Timothy and Titus were composed, ca. A.D. 110–120. Similar concerns are prominent in these Pastoral Letters. The present writing probably was ascribed to Jude in accordance with the later Christian practice of attributing authoritative writings to major figures of the apostolic age, namely, to Paul, the twelve apostles, or Jesus' brothers. If Jesus' brother James was thought to have written a letter for the guidance of all Christians, why should his brother Jude not have done so as well? But the writer reveals that the age of the apostles was already over by calling on readers to remember their predictions (v. 17). Jude and 2 Peter are so similar that one must have drawn from the other: Compare Jude 3–8, 10–13, and 17–18 with 2 Pet 2:1–17 and 3:1–3. If used by 2 Peter, Jude would have been written by A.D. 120–140 at the latest.

This general letter or tract for all Christians urges "those who are called" to defend "the faith" given to their holy predecessors from certain heretics who have infiltrated the churches (vv. 3–4). As in Colossians 1:23 and 2:6, and Titus 1:13, "faith" here refers to the body of authoritative doctrine that the present generation of Christians received from those before them. Here is the only place in the New Testament where we find the expression "holy faith" (v. 20). Like the wicked men and angels of old, the worldly and licentious people of the writer's time are being or surely will be punished severely (vv. 10–13). Among other offenses, these people have been carousing during church love feasts; v. 12).[184] On the other hand, those who are "beloved in God the Father and kept for Jesus Christ" (v. 1) should confirm their "most holy faith," remaining in the love of God, awaiting Christ's mercy "until eternal life" (vv. 20–21). The fact that "scoffers following their own ungodly passions," a phenomenon of "the last times," have now already appeared (vv. 17–19),[185] can be construed as evidence of the writer's belief in the imminence of this mercy.

The author shows a tendency to incorporate and expand upon earlier legends and lore. He seems to have drawn upon Wisdom of Solomon 10:6 regarding the destruction not only of Sodom and Gomorrah but also of neighboring towns, adding that they were all punished by eternal fire (v. 7).[186] His use of the book of *Enoch* suggests that he considered it authoritative as Scripture (vv. 6, 13–15).[187] His reference to the archangel Michael's debate with the devil over possession of Moses' body comes from some other extrabiblical tradition, possibly a lost fragment of the pseudepigraphic *Assumption of Moses*.

The unusually elaborate benediction or doxology at the end of the letter (vv. 24–25) may derive from earlier Christian liturgy or may have been composed by the author of the letter. Its reference to God's being "before all time" is unparalleled in biblical tradition, though belief in God's pre-existence is certainly implicit in the Genesis creation stories and various psalms.[188]

Revelation

The writer of this extraordinary composition identifies himself several times as John, but does not claim to be one of the apostles. Reference to his bearing witness and testimony (1:2) might suggest a connection with the "beloved disciple" mentioned in John 21:24, whose witness and testimony are there noted. At any rate, these terms probably were intended to authenticate the "words of prophecy" set forth in the rest of the book of Revelation. The "revelation" (i.e., apocalypse) is in two parts: first, a group of letters by John to seven churches in the Roman province of Asia in western Asia Minor (1:4–3:22), and then a series of apocalyptic visions and auditions experienced by the author while "in the spirit" (4:1–22:5). A concluding section affirms the validity and importance of "these words." For the most part, the words of the "prophecy" or "revelation" are attributed to Jesus himself, either directly (1:10–19) or through his "angel" (1:1; 22:16). Revelation is the only New Testament work apart from the Gospels and Acts 1:7–8 to attribute verbatim statements to Jesus.

In 1:4–20, John writes a "cover letter" introducing the separate letters that follow, which are addressed to the "angels" of each of the seven churches. Intertestamental tradition (influenced by Persian religion) visualized seven angels as intermediaries between "the saints" and God (e.g., Tob 12:15; cf. Rev 1:4). The fact that seven churches, each with a separate angel, are named here is suggestive of that tradition. On the other hand, Jewish thought of the time also understood that God had appointed a patron angel (or "prince") to have charge over the affairs of each nation (e.g., Dan 10:13; 12:1). Revelation seems to extend the idea of patron angels to local cities. In the context of Revelation 2–3, however, the angels appear in the role of corresponding secretaries, receiving the message of revelation that God had given to Jesus, who then gave it to John (1:1), who then writes to the angels of each of the churches. These seven "letters," along with the apocalyptic visions and prophecies that come later in the apocalypse, have one common theme. They all call on their intended first-century

Christian readers to endure the many trials and tribulations they must suffer, remaining faithful despite persecution, for Jesus is coming soon. When he comes, he will deliver them and punish both their persecutors and any Christians who have succumbed to pressure and worshiped the image of the emperor. The visions and prophecies go on to promise that all forces of evil will be overcome and that the heavenly city, the New Jerusalem, will come down and be established on a new or completely transformed earth.[189]

The writer concisely sums up the purpose of this book: "Here is a call for the endurance and faith of the saints" (13:10; 14:12).[190] John knows that his readers are suffering persecution and tribulation, or expects that they are about to do so (2:10; 3:10). They are urged to "hold fast" to what they have (2:25; 3:11), meaning both the traditions they previously received (3:3),[191] and the words of the present book (1:3; 22:7). They can do so with hope for the future because—John declares repeatedly—Jesus is coming soon (3:11; 22:7, 12, 20), "like a thief" in the night (3:3; 16:15).[192] The book is written to show Christians "what must soon take place" (1:1; 22:6). "The time is near" (1:3; 22:10);[193] there will be "no more delay" (10:6).[194] And the book ends, appropriately, with the eager prayer: "Come, Lord Jesus!" (22:20).[195]

Satan either already has been or soon will be defeated in heaven (12:7–11), but for a short time he will cause much grief among the faithful on earth (12:12–17). Satan (sometimes identified here as "the devil" and "the dragon") is associated with various beasts that evidently represent the Roman empire and certain of its emperors (chaps. 13; 16). Rome is also pictured (chap. 17) as "Babylon" and "the great harlot," who is seated on seven mountains (i.e., the seven hills of Rome), which persecutes "the saints" (i.e., faithful Christians). But "Babylon" is soon to fall (chap. 18) and Satan will be bound, while those martyred for their faith will come to life and reign with Christ a thousand years (20:1–6).[196] After that, Satan will be loosed for a while but then be destroyed forever, along with Death, Hades, and all unrighteous persons (20:7–15; cf. 1 Cor 15:23–26). Here Satan is conceived more as an independent supernatural evil being than a mere symbol for the Roman empire.

The old heaven and earth will pass away, and new ones will come in their place. The glorious New Jerusalem will come down from heaven to earth (cf. Matt 6:10). Here the faithful and righteous shall dwell forever in the presence of God and the Lamb (Christ), by the river of life with trees of life on either side (21:1–22:5).[197] There will be no temple in this new era (21:22).[198] By the time Revelation was written, the Jerusalem temple had been destroyed, and both Jews and Christians were adjusting their beliefs and practices to its absence. Here the writer says that all Christians (who remain faithful) are "priests" (1:6; 5:10), an understanding that anticipates the Protestant idea of the "priesthood of all believers." Necessarily, these priests would not be involved in offering animals or any other kinds of sacrifices at the temple.

Many interpreters think that Revelation was written to strengthen the faith of Christians in the Roman province of Asia during a persecution by Roman authorities there (ca. A.D. 96). Several passages suggest that Christians had been required to worship the emperor's image on pain of economic sanctions or death, and that many already had been persecuted and some executed for failing to do so.[199] Little is known about this persecution, which may also have been the historical setting for 1 Peter, which likewise was addressed to Christians in Asia (and other Roman provinces in Asia Minor).

In the second and third centuries, Romans persecuted Christians after plagues broke out or barbarians (Western Europeans) defeated the legions, apparently on the theory that the Roman gods were displeased at not receiving the homage due them from their Christian subjects, who were therefore responsible for such disasters. In order to appease these deities, Christians should be compelled to make some show of worshiping them or their images. Something of the sort seems to have been going on in the background for the book of Revelation. The "image of the beast" probably was a statue or portrait of the current Roman emperor Domitian. A hundred years earlier, the emperor Augustus had introduced the cult of the deity of the emperor and revived the worship of the old Roman gods in order to cement the loyalty of Roman citizens and subjects from many ethnic backgrounds to the empire and its emperor, or Caesar.[200] The number 666 (13:18) probably stands for Nero Caesar, the first and most flamboyant persecutor of Christians. His name, like that of Haman in the book of Esther, might then apply to latter-day persecutors, in the same way that Zimri's name was applied to a latter-day traitor in 2 Kings 9:31. The author of Revelation actually uses Jezebel's name in this way, referring to a contemporary idolatress (2:20). It is likely that "Nero" was meant to symbolize the emperor who was persecuting the Christians to and for whom the book of Revelation was written. In the Roman province of Asia[201] in the 90s, Christians apparently were required to offer a pinch of incense or a libation of some sort to the emperor's image. Those who did so would receive a "mark," perhaps a tattoo, to show they had met this requirement; in this way, they would be spared persecution.[202] Christians confronting this requirement faced a terrible choice: Either they would be persecuted by the Romans or else they would suffer eternal torment in fire and sulfur (14:9–11). Fear and hatred generated by the experience of such persecution may partly account for the writer's lurid depiction of the torment in store for both the unrighteous and the apostate.[203]

Use of the number seven is typical of the writer's interest in mysterious and symbolic meanings.[204] Another special characteristic is the composition or incorporation of numerous early Christian hymns or psalms of praise.[205] George Frideric Handel later drew on some of these as texts for his famous composition, *The Messiah*, as did later Christian hymn writers. Chapter 18, a psalm of rejoicing over the prospective fall of Rome, echoes similar Old Testament texts, such as Ezekiel 26:17–28:23 and the book of Nahum.

Modern readers sometimes view the book of Revelation as a series of "Bible prophecies" meant for "us" and unfolding in our time "before our very eyes." It is clear, however, that Revelation was written to give hope and encouragement to readers in its author's time: The faithful could withstand Roman persecution, for Jesus was coming soon, and both Satan and Rome would soon be overthrown. But Jesus did not come, martyred Christians did not rise from the dead and there was no thousand-year reign of Christ. If Satan was bound, tragedy and evil were not noticeably diminished in subsequent times: It was more than three hundred years before the Roman empire in the West began to collapse, and its doing so marked the beginning of the "Dark Ages" in Europe. The fact that the anticipated course of events did not materialize does not, of course, justify the invention of some modern, imaginative substitute scenario in their place. Yet the underlying hopes and assurances expressed in Revelation need not be taken as inextricably tied to the specific circumstances and expectations of that time. Revelation 21–22 in particular look for the reconstitution of the conditions of life: a transformed existence much like that which, according to Genesis 1–2, God had intended humankind to enjoy forever. Once more God would dwell on earth with people, death would be no more, and a river and the tree(s) of life would again be there to bless the human race, which would embrace the full range of descendants of the first human couple—the nations (21:24–26; 22:1–2). Such hopes accord with much else that is central in the biblical tradition. Moreover, like Daniel in the Old Testament and many other biblical writings, the book of Revelation expresses supreme confidence in

God's almighty power to deliver his people from seemingly hopeless circumstances. Understandably, religious people have found its message relevant in other times of crisis during the past two thousand years.

NOTES

Overview
1. See Jer 31:31–34; cf. 32:38–40; Hos 2:18–20; Ezek 11:19–20.
2. See Heb 8:8–12; 10:16–17; cf. 1 Cor 11:25.
3. See Heb 8:7, 13; 9:15; 12:24.
4. See 2 Pet 3:15–16.
5. Several such writings turned up in Egypt in the late 1940s. See the second essay in part I. Extracanonical "gospels" have also been collected in modern editions of the New Testament Apocrypha. See above, p. 185, note 1.
6. Among the excluded writings were several "gospels."
7. First and Second Timothy, however, are longer than some of the letters that precede them.
8. See literature on Q in Suggested Reading, pp. 271–72. Cf. Mark Goodacre, *The Case Against Q: Studies in Markan Priority and the Synoptic Problem* (Harrisburg, Pa.: Trinity Press International, 2001).
9. Schweitzer published a much expanded revision of this book in 1913, with a series of new prefaces, the latest in 1951. This expanded revision, edited by John Bowden, appeared for the first time in English in 2001: *The Quest of the Historical Jesus: The First Complete Edition* (Minneapolis: Fortress, 2001). Its publication marked the hundredth anniversary of Schweitzer's first groundbreaking study, which has since appeared in English under the title, *The Mystery of the Kingdom of God.* See also a somewhat parallel study: Vincent A. McCarthy, *Quest for a Philosophical Jesus: Christianity and Philosophy in Rousseau, Kant, Hegel, and Schelling* (Macon, Ga.: Mercer University Press, 1986).
10. See Charles H. Talbert, *Reimarus, Fragments* (Philadelphia: Fortress, 1970).
11. See, e.g., David F. Strauss, *The Life of Jesus Critically Examined* (Mifflintown, Pa.: Sigler Press, 1994), originally published in 1835. See also, Schweitzer, *Quest of the Historical Jesus*, chaps. 7–11. In the early and mid-twentieth century, Rudolf Bultmann proposed in various writings that most of the Synoptic Gospels derived from the early church.
12. See Robert W. Funk, Roy W. Hoover, and the Jesus Seminar, *The Five Gospels: The Search for the Authentic Words of Jesus* (San Francisco: HarperSanFrancisco: 1993). The fifth Gospel is the *Gospel of Thomas*, discovered among other Coptic writings at Nag Hammadi in 1954. (See the second essay in part I.) However, the Jesus Seminar members find few possibly authentic sayings of Jesus here either.

13. For a detailed, though rather unsympathetic critique of the Jesus Seminar, see Luke Timothy Johnson, *The Real Jesus: The Misguided Quest of the Historical Jesus and the Truth of the Traditional Gospels* (San Francisco: HarperSanFrancisco, 1996). See also John Dominic Crossan, Luke Timothy Johnson, and Werner H. Kelber, *The Jesus Controversy: Perspectives in Conflict* (Harrisburg, Pa.: Trinity Press International, 1999).

14. Johannes Weiss, *Jesus' Proclamation of the Kingdom of God* (Philadelphia: Fortress, 1971; Chico, Calif.: Scholars Press, 1985), first published in 1892. See Schweitzer, *Quest of the Historical Jesus*, chap. 15.

15. See Schweitzer, *Quest of the Historical Jesus*, chap. 16.

16. As to the former, see, e.g., Martin Kahler, *The So-Called Historical Jesus and the Historic Biblical Christ* (Philadelphia: Fortress, 1964), first published in 1892; and Johnson, *Real Jesus* (cited above). Modern liberal interpreters, in one way or another, endeavored to interpret away (or ignore) the Synoptic evidence for Jesus' eschatological expectations. See, e.g., Adolf von Harnack, *What Is Christianity?* (New York: Harper & Brothers, 1957), first published in 1901; Rudolf Bultmann, *Jesus and the Word* (New York: Scribner's, 1934, 1958), first published in 1926; C. H. Dodd, *The Parables of the Kingdom*, rev. ed. (New York: Scribner's, 1961), first published in 1938; and most of the Jesus Seminar members' publications. Modern efforts to discover a non-eschatological historical Jesus have been questioned by Richard Hiers, *Jesus and the Future: Unsolved Questions for Understanding and Faith* (Atlanta: John Knox, 1981); Clayton Sullivan, *Rethinking Realized Eschatology* (Macon, Ga.: Mercer University Press, 1988); and Wendell Willis, ed., *The Kingdom of God in Twentieth Century Interpretation* (Peabody, Mass.: Hendrickson, 1987).

17. See Lewis R. Donelson, *From Hebrews to Revelation: A Theological Introduction* (Louisville, Ky.: Westminster John Knox, 2000).

18. "Christian" is found only in Acts 11:26; 26:28; and 1 Pet 4:16.

19. See Acts 9:2; 18:26; 24:14; cf. John 14:6; Heb 10:20.

20. See Acts. 15:1, 23; 28:14; 1 Cor 7:29; 10:1; Phil 3:1; 1 Thess 5:25–27; Heb 3:1; Jas 2:1, 14; 3:1; cf. Phlm 2 ("our sister").

21. See Acts 26:10; Rom 1:7; 2 Cor 1:1, 8; Eph 3:18; Jude 3.

22. See Acts 16:1; 1 Tim 6:2; Heb 4:3.

23. See 2 Tim 2:8; 2 John 1, 13.

24. See John 18:37; 1 John 3:19.

25. See 1 Pet 4:12; 1 John 3:2; 4:1; Jude 3, 20.

26. See 1 John 2:1, 12, 28; 3:7.

27. See 1 John 3:1–2, 10; 5:1.

28. See Col 1:23; 2:6; 1 Tim 3:9; Titus 1:13; Jude 3.

29. See John 8:31–32; 2 Tim 3:8; 2 John 4; 3 John 3–4, 8; Jude 3.

Gospel According to Matthew

1. See Matt 5:1–7:29; 9:35–11:1; 13:1–53; 18:1–19:1; 23:1–26:1.

2. Cf. the "sermon on the plain" in Luke 6:17–7:1.

3. The letter "Q" stands for the German word *Quelle*, meaning "source." The Q source remains hypothetical, since it has not been found independently; however, several studies have undertaken to reconstruct and analyze it. See the overview to part IV.

4. See Matt 5:29–30; 18:8–9; cf. 19:12.

5. These several duplicate passages also could mean that Matthew was drawing from at least two different sources, both of which included these texts.

6. See, e.g., Matt.1:22–23; 2:5–6, 17–18; 3:3.

7. Cf. Matt 6:11; 8:11; 26:29, which refer to the prospect of eating and drinking together there.

8. See Matt 8:12; 13:42, 50; 22:13; 24:51; 25:30, 41, 46.

9. These changes indicate religious and ethical concerns in the developing early church.

Gospel According to Mark

10. See, e.g., Mark 5:41; 7:3–4, 34; 15:34. Scholars generally agree that Jesus spoke mainly in Aramaic, and some scholars suggest that at least Matthew's Gospel was written originally in Aramaic. See Matthew Black, *An Aramaic Approach to the Gospels and Acts* (Peabody, Mass.: Hendrickson, 1999).

11. See Acts 12:12 and Philemon 23, which mention a person named Mark as one of Paul's companions or coworkers. Some interpreters suggest that this Mark was the author of the Gospel that bears that name.

12. See Mark 1:27; 2:12; 7:37; 11:18.

13. See Mark 4:10–13, 38–41; 8:16–21; 9:6, 32.

14. See Mark 8:31; 9:31; 10:32–34. Biblical scholars have written at length on the problematic meaning of the expression "son of man," especially as used in Mark's Gospel. In some sayings, Jesus seems to be referring simply to himself, but more often to his present or prospective suffering and his death. The term also refers often to the supernatural figure who would appear in the future (or at the parousia) as messiah or judge.

15. See Mark 8:31–9:1; cf. 13:9–32.

16. See Mark 11:7–10; cf. Zech 9:9.

17. It may be that when Jesus went looking for figs—even though it was not the season for figs—as he entered Jerusalem, he did so because he shared the expectation that fruit would always be in season in the messianic age, as in Exekiel 47. See Richard Hiers, "Not the Season for Figs," *Journal of Biblical Literature* 87 (1968): 394–400.

18. See Mark 11:15–17; cf. Mal 3:1–3; Zech 14:21b. See Richard Hiers, "Purification of the Temple: Preparation for the Kingdom of God," *Journal of Biblical Literature* 90 (1971): 82–90.

19. See Mark 11:27–13:1; cf. 14:49.

20. That is, Jesus' reported warnings to tell no one about him (e.g., at 1:44; 3:12; 8:30). See Christopher Tuckett, *The Messianic Secret* (Philadelphia:

Fortress, 1983); and the earlier classic study, Albert Schweitzer, *The Mystery of the Kingdom of God* (New York: Macmillan, 1950), originally published in 1901.

21. See, e.g., Mark 1:32–34, 40; 4:37–41; 5:34, 36; 13:9–27.

22. See Mark 8:34–9:1; 10:17–31; 13:9–37.

23. Cf. Tob 12:20; Luke 24:51; Acts 1:9–11, which also report ascension traditions.

Gospel According to Luke

24. The author of the Gospel of Luke does not clearly show more interest in Jesus' healing procedures than the other evangelists do.

25. See Luke 19:41–44; 21:20, 24.

26. See, e.g., Luke 2:1–2; 3:1–2, 23.

27. Most notably, he omits all of Mark 6:45–8:10, sometimes designated "Luke's great omission."

28. In his preface, Luke reports the angel Gabriel's annunciation to Zechariah that his wife, Elizabeth, would bear a son whom they would name John, and then the angel's annunciation to Mary that she would bear a son whom she would name Jesus. The story of Jesus' birth in a manger (or barn) and the shepherds' visit are also found only in Luke's preface.

29. See Luke 24:13–53; cf. Matthew 28, where Jesus' main appearance is in Galilee.

30. "Sinners" often may refer to persons who failed to live according to the Pharisees' interpretations of biblical law and so, from the standpoint of the Pharisees, were sinners.

31. See Luke 23:4, 14–15, 22, 47; cf. Mark 15:5, 39.

32. See Luke 23:34, 43, 46.

33. Cf. Tob 6:5; John 21:9–14.

34. See Richard Hiers, "Friends by Unrighteous Mammon: The Eschatological Proletariat, *Journal of the American Academy of Religion* 38 (1970): 30–36.

35. See Luke 6:20, 24; 12:15–21, 33; 14:12–14; 16:1–9, 19–31; cf. 19:1–8.

36. See, e.g., the parables of the Prodigal Son (15:11–32) and the Pharisee and the tax collector in the temple (18:9–14).

37. See Luke 9:27; 11:2; 12:32; 18:1–8; 21:29–36.

38. See, e.g., Jas 5:7–9; 1 Pet 4:7; Rev 1:1–3; 22:7, 10, 12, 20.

Gospel According to John

39. See John 21:2, which refers to two unnamed disciples, one of whom might have been John.

40. See John 1:7, 19–23; cf. 21:24.

41. The prospect of salvation in heaven is reflected also in Phil 3:20 and 1 Thess 4:15–17. Other New Testament writings generally look for salvation on earth or a transformed or new earth.

42. See John 13:34–35; 15:12–17; cf. Matt 5:43–46, where Jesus commands his hearers to love their enemies as well as their neighbors.

43. John 8:58; 10:30; 14:7–11; 20:28; cf. Mark 10:18, where Jesus distinguishes himself from God, who alone is good.

44. See John 2:3–10; 4:31–32; 7:3–10.

45. See, e.g., John 3:11, 13; 4:22; 17:3.

46. See, e.g., John 1:41; 4:25–26; 9:35–37.

47. See, e.g., Acts 1:6–7; 1 Cor 15:12–58; and 2 Pet 3:3–13.

Acts

48. See Acts 1:15; 2:41; 4:4; 5:14; 6:7.

49. See Acts 9:31; 11:24; 16:5; 18:8; 19:20.

50. See Acts 5:14; 9:36; 16:14–15; 17:4, 12, 33.

51. See Acts 5:17–24; 12:6–17; 16:25–34.

52. See Acts 5:12–15; 13:9–12; 19:11–12.

53. Cf. 1 Corinthians 8 and 10.

54. Cf. Gen 9:4; Deut 12:16.

55. See Acts 15:19–28, 28–29; cf. 21:25.

56. The "Damascus road" experience is described three times in Acts (9:1–22; 22:6–16; 26:12–18), but is not clearly mentioned in Paul's own writings. Cf. 2 Cor 12:1–4.

57. Cf. Matt 10:5–6, where Jesus tells the Twelve to go only to Jews, but after his resurrection instructs them to make disciples of all nations (28:19).

58. See Acts 9:23; 14:19; 17:5; 18:12; 20:3; 23:12; 24:9.

59. Cf. Rom 13:1–7.

60. See, e.g., Acts 2:36; 3:14–15; 4:10; 10:39; cf. 13:28.

61. Cf., e.g., John 3:36; 6:40.

62. See, e.g., Acts 8:36; 9:18; 10:47–48; cf. John 3:5; 1 Cor 1:13–17; Eph 5:25–27; Mark 16:16.

63. See, e.g., Acts 8:12; 14:22; 28:23, 31.

Romans

64. See, e.g., Matt 28:18–20; Acts 1:8; Rom 11:25; 15:8–24.

65. See Rom 1:5–6, 11–12; 15:14–16.

66. See Rom 3:20; 4:15; 5:12–14; 7:7–11.

67. See also 1 Cor 6:9–20; Gal 5:1–26.

68. See also 1 Pet 2:13–17.

69. Cf. 1 Corinthians 12–14; Phil 2:1–4.

1 Corinthians

70. See 1 Cor 5:1; 11:18; 16:15–18.

71. See 1 Cor 3:1–3; 8:2; 13:8–12.

72. See 1 Cor 1:17–2:13; 3:18–21.

73. It is unclear how Paul relates this requirement to his insistence that women keep silent in church (14:33b–35); perhaps he means that women

might pray and prophesy (provided they cover their hair) so long as they do not do so in church. Or, his thinking about the matter may have been inconsistent.

74. Cf. Rev 22:20, "Come, Lord Jesus!"; and Matt 6:10 or Luke 11:2, "Thy kingdom come!"

2 Corinthians

75. See 2 Cor 3:1; 4:2; 5:12; 6:3–10.

76. See Rom 15:25–28; 1 Cor 16:1–4; cf. Gal 2:6–10.

77. See 2 Cor 3:18; 4:16; 5:17; 13:5; cf. Gal 6:15.

78. Cf. Phil 3:20–21; 1 Thess 4:13–17; John 14:2–3.

79. Cf. 1 Cor 13:12; 15:51–52; 1 Thess 5:1–23.

Galatians

80. Cf. Rom 7:4–25; 2 Esdras 7.

81. Cf. 1 Cor 6:9–10. Paul, like Jesus in the Synoptic Gospels, often refers to the coming of, entering into, or inheriting the kingdom of God. Most other New Testament writings mention the kingdom of God only rarely if at all.

Ephesians

82. See also in Colossians; cf. 1 Cor 13:2; 15:51.

83. See Eph 1:1: "To the saints who are also faithful in Christ Jesus."

84. Cf. Rom 3:21–26; Gal 2:15–16.

85. Cf. Philemon, where Paul urges the master to free his slave Onesimus.

86. Cf. Wisd 5:17–20.

87. Cf. Col 3:24.

Philippians

88. Cf. 1 Cor 12:27–31, where Paul's list of church leaders makes no mention of bishops or deacons, and 1 Tim 3:1–12, where the writer lays out guidelines for bishops and deacons.

89. See Phil 3:15–16; cf. 1 Cor 11:16; 14:36, where Paul disallows dissent.

Colossians

90. See Phlm 1, 10, 23–24.

91. Cf. Rom 4:25; Gal 2:16.

92. Cf. Prov 8:22–31; John 1:1–3.

93. Cf. Wisd 1:7.

94. Cf. Mark 16:15 (calling on Jesus' followers to "preach the gospel to the whole creation") and Pss 148:7–10; 150:6; Jonah 3:6–8 (where all kinds of creatures praise or pray to God). Such texts may have inspired Saint Francis of Assisi to preach to birds or other creatures, or at least the legends about his doing so.

95. Cf. 2 Cor 4:4; Gen 1:26–27.

96. Cf. Col 1:15–19, where Paul says that Christ has this function.

97. See Col 2:13, 16, 20–21; 4:11.

98. Cf. Paul's rejection of asceticism and martyrdom in 1 Cor 13:3.

99. Cf. 1 John 4:2 (insisting that Jesus had "come in the flesh").

100. Cf. Matt 25:31–34; Gal 5:21; and Eph 1:13–14; 4:30.

1 Thessalonians

101. Cf. Paul's reassurances to Corinthian Christians who were concerned because the resurrection of the dead had not yet taken place (1 Cor 15:12–32).

102. Cf. Matt 24:34–44; Acts 1:7; Rev 3:3.

103. See 1 Thess 1:3; 2:19; 3:11–13; 5:12–23.

104. See, e.g., 1 Thess 2:8, 17–20; 3:9–10.

2 Thessalonians

105. See 1 Thess 4:13–17; cf. 1 Cor 15:51–57.

106. Numerous Old Testament and intertestamental texts suggest that in the coming age, food and drink would abound; from these, it could have been inferred that working would no longer be necessary in that age.

107. See 1 Cor 11:17; commands are also referred to in the Pastoral Letters.

108. Cf. 1 Cor 16:21, where Paul notes that the final greeting is in his "own hand."

109. Cf. 1 Thess 4:10–12.

1 Timothy

110. See 1 Tim 1:3–11; 4:1–5, 7; 6:1–2.

111. The concluding verses, 1 Tim 6:20–21, also may address gnostic claims: "Avoid the godless chatter and contradictions of what is falsely called knowledge, for by professing it some have missed the mark as regards the faith."

112. See likewise 1 Tim 4:10; Rom 5:18; 1 Cor 15:22; but see 2 Thess 2:9–12.

113. Cf. 2 Esdr 7:7, 118, which give the man, Adam, full credit for this primordial transgression. Milton's *Paradise Lost* reflects the account found in 1 Timothy.

114. Cf. Num 35:30; Deut 19:15; and Susanna.

115. Cf. Matt 6:19–20 and parallels, and Luke 16.

2 Timothy

116. See 2 Tim 1:13–14; 2:2, 14–18, 23.

117. Cf. 2 Thess 2:1–5, where "Paul" cautions against the notion "that the day of the Lord has come."

118. Cf. Phil 3:20; John 14:1–3.

Titus

119. See also 1 Tim 1:4; 4:7.

120. Cf. Col 1:23; 2:6.

121. Cf. Matt 25:31–46; Luke 10:30–37.

122. Cf. 1 Tim 2:1–2; Rom 13:1; 1 Pet 2:13–17.

Philemon

123. Two of these are named, Mark and Luke.

124. Cf. Phil 4:23; 1 Thess 5:28.

125. In that case, had Paul been guided by Deut 23:15–16, he should not have returned Onesimus to his former master.

Hebrews

126. Cf. 1 Tim 1:3–6; 2 Pet 2:1–3; and the gnostic Christian writings of the early second century found at Nag Hammadi in the 1940s.

127. See, e.g., Heb 9:1–10.

128. Cf. Rom 6:23; 1 Cor 15:24–26, 54–57; Rev 20:14.

129. Cf. Gen 14:18–20; Ps 110:4.

130. Cf. Matthew 1 and Luke 3. Relatively late Old Testament writings, such as the P tradition, the Priestly Code, 1 and 2 Chronicles, Ezra, and Nehemiah, insist that only descendants of Aaron could be legitimate priests.

131. See Heb 8:6–12; 9:15; 12:24.

132. Cf. Hab 2:3; Mal 3:1; Luke 18:8.

133. Cf. Rev 21:2–27.

134. Cf. Matt 6:33; Luke 13:24.

135. Cf. Jas 5:19–20. This issue also reverberated in Christian controversies for several centuries following the New Testament period.

136. See, e.g., Heb 4:12, 14–16; 10:31; 11:1; 12:1–2; 13:8, 20–21.

James

137. See Matt 13:55; Mark 3:31–32; Galatians 1–2.

138. Cf. Gal 5:6; 1 Cor 13:2.

139. See Jas 3:13–18; 4:2, 6, 10–12.

140. Cf. Mark 7:14–23.

141. Cf. Luke 6:20, 24; 16:19–31.

142. Cf. 1 Tim 4:14; Titus 1:5.

1 Peter

143. Examples include Jas 1:22 (cf. Matt 7:24, 26); 2:13 (cf. Matt 6:14–15; 18:23–35); 3:11–12 (cf. Matt 3:17–18); 4:10 (cf. Matt 23:12); 4:11–12 (cf. Matt 7:7); and 5:12 (cf. Matt 5:34–37).

144. See 1 Pet 1:6–7; 3:14; 4:12–19.

145. Cf. Rom 13:1–7.

146. See also 1 Pet 1:5; 2:12; 4:5.

147. Cf. John 14:2–3; Phil 3:20–21.

148. Cf. Matt 6:10; Heb 12:22; 13:14; Rev 21:2.

149. Cf. John 13:34–35; Heb 13:1.

150. Cf. Heb 13:12; 2 John 10–11; 3 John 5–8.

151. Cf. 1 Cor 6:9–10; Gal 6:7–9; Matt 25:31–46.

152. Cf. 1 Cor 6:9–20, where Paul confronted the same kind of problem.

153. Cf. 1 Corinthians 12–14.

154. Cf. Heb 3:7; 9:8; 10:15, where the Holy Spirit is said to have done so.

155. Cf. Eph 6:5–9, which speaks to this matter, and Titus 2:9–10, which does not do so..

156. Cf. Eph 5:22–30, which also gives such advice, and Titus 2:4–5, which does not.

157. Form critics are interpreters who tend to place biblical traditions in possible cultic settings within the early Christian communities. See Rudolf Bultmann and Karl Kundsin, *Form Criticism: Two Essays on New Testament Research* (New York: Harper & Brothers, 1962).

158. Cf. John 4:2; Acts 8:36; 1 Cor 1:13–17.

159. Cf. Ezek 34:11–15, where God is said to be his people's shepherd.

160. See also John 10:1–4 and Heb 13:20.

161. See, e.g., Matt 6:13; Eph 6:11; 1 John 5:19; Rev 12:7–12.

2 Peter

162. Nearly all modern scholars conclude that the Pastoral Letters, 1 and 2 Timothy and Titus, were written by someone other than Paul. Scholars are divided as to Paul's authorship of Ephesians, Colossians, and 2 Thessalonians.

163. Cf. "kingdom of God," the usual term in earlier New Testament writings (e.g., at Mark 1:15; 1 Cor 6:9–10; and Gal 5:19–20).

164. As in the Pastoral Letters, such terms may refer to early Christian gnostic beliefs.

165. See, e.g., Matt 24:33–34 = Mark 13:29–30 = Luke 21:31–32; 1 Thess 4:13–17; Rev 1:1–3; 22:10, 12, 20.

166. See also Matt 24:43–44; 1 Thess 5:2–3; Rev 3:3; 16:15.

167. See, e.g., Isa 11:69; 19:19–25; 25:6–9; Hos 2:18–23; Mic 4:1–4.

1 John

168. See, e.g., 1 John 3:23–24; John 15:4–10.

169. See 1 John 3:22; 5:14–15; John 14:13–14; 16:23–24; cf. Matt 7:7–11; Mark 11:23–24.

170. Cf. Luke 24:39–43; Phil 2:5–8.

171. Cf. 1 John 3:5, which says that he appeared "to take away sins"; and Heb 2: 14.

172. Cf. Jas 1:27; 2:14–17; Matt 25:31–46.

173. See, e.g., Mark 13:21–23; 2 Thess 2:3–4.

174. Cf. 1 Cor 15:49; Phil 3:21.

175. Cf. 1 Cor 7:29–31; 13:8–10.

176. See, e.g., Phil 3:20 and 1 Thess 4:15–17.

177. Cf. Matt 6:10; Rev 21:2–22:5.

2 John

178. Cf. 1 John 2:7; 3:11; 5:3.

179. For instance, compare 2 John 3 with Rom 1:7 and 1 Cor 1:3.

180. In the New Testament period, many churches met in peoples' houses. See, e.g., 1 Cor 16:19; Phlm 2.

3 John
181. See 3 John 9; cf. Matt 18:18 (Peter's authority).
182. Cf. 1 John 3:11–18.

Jude
183. See Matt 13:55 = Mark 6:3; cf. Luke 8:20.
184. Cf. 1 Cor 11:20–22.
185. See also 2 Pet 3:3–6; 2 Tim 3:1–9; 1 John 2:18.
186. Cf. Genesis 19; Deut 29:23.
187. See *1 Enoch* 1:9; also *1 Enoch* 6–10 and 86–88.
188. See, e.g., Pss 104 and 148.

Revelation
189. See Revelation 21–22. Cf. earlier biblical visions of a new or restored future Jerusalem: Isa 54:11–14; Ezek 40–48; Tobit 13; cf. Ezek 28:13–14, referring to ancient Tyre.
190. See also Rev 1:9; 3:10.
191. Cf. 2 Tim 1:13–14; Jude 3.
192. Cf. Matt 24:42–44 = Luke 12:39–40; 1 Thess 5:2; 2 Pet. 3:10.
193. Cf. Matt 4:17 = Mark 1:15.
194. Cf. 2 Pet 3:3–10; 2 Esdr 16:37–39, 74.
195. Cf. Matt 6:10 = Luke 11:2; 1 Cor 16:22. It appears that the earlier prayer, "Thy kingdom come," which Jesus taught his disciples, was transformed into a prayer by the church for Jesus' coming at the parousia.
196. Cf. 2 Esdr 7:28, which looks for a four-hundred-year interregnum during which the Messiah will be manifested.
197. Cf. Ezek 47:12.
198. Cf. Ezekiel 40–48, Haggai, and Zechariah, which looked for a new temple as the central feature of the coming or messianic age.
199. See Rev 6:9–11; 13:13–17; 17:6; 20:4.
200. This policy evidently was grounded on the theory that those who pray together were more likely to stay together.
201. This was the western end of what was called Asia Minor (present-day Turkey). The seven churches addressed early in the book of Revelation are all located in this province.
202. See Rev 13:16–17; 14:9–11; 19:20; 20:4.
203. See Rev 9:1–21; 14:9–11, 14–20; 19:17–21.
204. Cf. the seven visions set out in 2 Esdras.
205. See Rev 4:8, 11; 11:15; 14:13; 15:3–4; 19:6–8.

SUGGESTED READING

Introduction

Bible Dictionaries

The Anchor Bible Dictionary. 6 vols. New York: Doubleday, 1992.

Eerdmans Dictionary of the Bible. Grand Rapids: Eerdmans, 2000.

HarperCollins Bible Dictionary. San Francisco: HarperSanFrancisco, 1996.

Harper's Bible Dictionary. New York: Harper & Row, 1985.

The Interpreter's Dictionary of the Bible. 5 vols. Nashville: Abingdon, 1976.

Single-volume Bible introductions and commentaries

Adam, A. K. M. *Postmodern Interpretations of the Bible: A Reader.* St. Louis: Chalice Press, 2000.

Bird, Phyllis A., ed. *Reading the Bible as Women: Perspectives from Africa, Asia, and Latin America.* Atlanta: Society of Biblical Literature, 1998.

Brown, Raymond E., Joseph A. Fitzmyer, and Roland E. Murphy. *The New Jerome Bible Commentary.* Englewood Cliffs, N.J.: Prentice-Hall, 1990.

Buber, Martin. *On the Bible: Eighteen Studies.* Edited by Nahum H. Glatzer. Syracuse: Syracuse University Press, 2000.

Chance, J. Bradley, and Milton P. Horne. *Rereading the Bible: An Introduction to the Biblical Story.* Upper Saddle River, N.J.: Prentice-Hall, 2000.

Collins, Adela Yarbro. *Feminist Perspectives on Biblical Scholarship.* Atlanta: Society of Biblical Literature, 1985.

Dube, Musa W. *Postcolonial Feminist Interpretation of the Bible.* St. Louis: Chalice Press, 2000.

Ewert, David. *How to Understand the Bible.* Scottsdale, Pa.: Herald Press, 2000.

Flanders, Henry Jackson, Jr., et al. *People of the Covenant: An Introduction to the Bible.* New York: Oxford University Press, 1996.

Guthrie, Donald, and J. A. Motyer. *The Eerdmans Bible Commentary.* 3rd ed. Grand Rapids: Eerdmans, 1987.

Harris, Stephen L. *Understanding the Bible.* 4th ed. Mountain View, Calif.: Mayfield Press, 1997.

Hauer, Christian E., and William A. Young. *An Introduction to the Bible: A Journey into Three Worlds.* 3rd ed. Englewood Cliffs, N.J.: Prentice-Hall, 1993.

Mays, James L., ed. *HarperCollins Bible Commentary.* Rev. ed. San Francisco: HarperSanFrancisco, 2000.

Martens, Elmer A., and Willard M. Swartley. *Believers Church Bible Commentary.* Scottdale, Pa.: Herald Press, 1987.

Riches, John. *The Bible: A Very Short Introduction.* New York: Oxford University Press, 2000.

Rogerson, J. W. *An Introduction to the Bible.* New York: Penguin, 2000.

Tate, W. Randolph. *Biblical Interpretation: An Integrated Approach.* Rev. ed. Peabody, Mass.: Hendrickson, 1997.

Multivolume Bible commentaries

The Anchor Bible. New York: Doubleday, 1964–2000.

Concordia Commentary Series. St. Louis: Concordia, 1968–1970.

The Interpreter's Bible. Nashville: Abingdon, 1951–1957.

The Jewish Publication Society Commentary Series. Philadelphia: Jewish Publication Society, 1937–1965.

New International Biblical Commentary. Peabody, Mass.: Hendrickson, 1988–1999.

The New Interpreter's Bible. Nashville: Abingdon, 1994–present.

The Westminster Bible Companion. Louisville, Ky.: Westminster John Knox, 1995–present.

Part I: Background Essays

A. The Historical Context

Binder, Donald D. *Into the Temple Courts: The Place of the Synagogue in the Second Temple Period.* Atlanta: Society of Biblical Literature, 1999.

Coogan, Michael D., ed. *The Oxford History of the Biblical World.* Oxford: Oxford University Press, 2001.

Jagersma, Henk. *The History of Israel from Alexander to Bar Kochba.* Philadelphia: Fortress, 1986.

Jatte, Martin S. *Torch in the Mouth: Writing and Oral Tradition in Palestinian Judaism 200 B.C.E–400 C.E.* Oxford: Oxford University Press, 2000.

Richardson, Peter. *Herod: King of the Jews and Friend of the Romans.* Minneapolis: Fortress, 1999.

Sasson, Jack, ed. *Civilizations of the Ancient Near East.* 2 vols. Peabody, Mass.: Hendrickson, 2000.

B. The Biblical Literature

Major Categories or Literary Genres

Blenkinsopp, Joseph. *A History of Prophecy in Israel: From the Settlement in the Land to the Hellenistic Period.* Louisville, Ky.: Westminster, 1983.

Hanson, Paul D. *The Dawn of Apocalyptic: The Historical and Sociological Roots of Jewish Apocalyptic Eschatology.* Philadelphia: Fortress, 1975.

Heschel, Abraham Joshua. *The Prophets.* 2 vols. New York: Harper & Row, 1962.

Koch, Klaus. *The Prophets,* vol. 1: *The Assyrian Period* (1982); vol. 2: *The Babylonian and Persian Periods* (1984). Philadelphia: Fortress.

——. *The Rediscovery of Apocalyptic.* London: SCM Press, 1972.

Lindblom, J. *Prophecy in Ancient Israel.* Philadelphia: Fortress, 1973.

Rankin, O. S. *Israel's Wisdom Literature.* Edinburgh: T. & T. Clark, 1954.

von Rad, Gerhard. *The Message of the Prophets.* New York: Harper & Row, 1962.

——. *Wisdom in Israel.* London: SCM Press, 1972.

Narratives, Gospels, Parables, and Letters

Damrusch, David. *The Narrative Covenant: Transformation of Genre in the Growth of Biblical Literature.* Ithaca, N.Y.: Cornell University Press, 1991.

Gunn, David M., and Danna Nolan Fewell. *Narrative in the Hebrew Bible.* New York: Oxford University Press, 1993.

Sources and Editorial Units

Ackroyd, Peter R. *First and Second Chronicles, Ezra, Nehemiah.* London: SCM Press, 1973.

Bloom, Harold, and David Rosenberg (translator). *The Book of J.* New York: Vintage, 1991.

Campbell, Antony F., and Mark A. O'Brien. *Unfolding the Deuteronomistic History: Origins, Upgrades, Present Text.* Minneapolis: Fortress, 2000.

Nicholson, Ernest. *The Pentateuch in the Twentieth Century: The Legacy of Julius Wellhausen*. New York: Oxford University Press, 1998.

Canon, Manuscripts, and Translations
Burrows, Millar. *The Dead Sea Scrolls*. New York: Viking, 1955.
———. *More Light on the Dead Sea Scrolls*. New York: Viking, 1958.
Childs, Brevard S. *The New Testament as Canon: An Introduction*. London: SCM Press, 1992.
———. *Old Testament Theology in a Canonical Context*. Philadelphia: Fortress, 1986.
Ehrman, Bart D., ed. *After the New Testament: A Reader in Early Christianity*. New York: Oxford University Press, 1998.
Gamble, Harry Y. *The New Testament Canon: Its Making and Meaning*. Philadelphia: Fortress, 1985.
Gaster, Theodor H. *The Dead Sea Scriptures*. Garden City, N.Y.: Anchor, 1956; 3d ed., 1976.
Halbental, Moshe. *People of the Book: Canon, Meaning, and Authority*. Cambridge: Harvard, 1997.
Kugler Robert A., and Eileen M. Schuller. *The Dead Sea Scrolls at Fifty: Proceedings of the 1997 Society of Biblical Literature Qumran Section Meetings*. Atlanta: Society of Biblical Literature, 1999.
McDonald, Lee Martin. *The Formation of the Christian Biblical Canon*, rev. ed. Peabody, Mass.: Hendrickson, 1995.
Pagels, Elaine H. *The Gnostic Gospels*. New York: Random House, 1979.
Perkins, Pheme. *Gnosticism and the New Testament*. Minneapolis: Fortress, 1993.
Robinson, James M. *The Nag Hammadi Library: The Definitive New Translation of the Gnostic Scriptures, Complete in One Volume*, rev. ed. San Francisco: Harper & Row, 1988.
Sanders, James. *Torah and Canon*. Philadelphia: Fortress, 1978.
Trobisch, David. *Paul's Letter Collection: Tracing the Origins*. Minneapolis: Fortress, 1994.
Vermes, Geza. *The Complete Dead Sea Scrolls in English*. New York: Penguin, 1998.
von Campenhausen, Hans. *The Formation of the Christian Bible*. Philadelphia: Fortress, 1972.

C. Basic Themes and Issues in Biblical Faith and Understanding
Good and Evil
Crenshaw, James L., ed. *Theodicy in the Old Testament*. Philadelphia: Fortress, 1983.

Israel and the Other Nations
Kaiser, Walter C., Jr. *Mission in the Old Testament: Israel as a Light to the Nations*. Grand Rapids, Mich.: Baker Academic, 2000.

Part II: The Old Testament, or Hebrew Scriptures

Overview

Albright, William F. *From the Stone Age to Christianity: Monotheism and the Historical Process*. 2d ed. New York: Doubleday-Anchor, 1957.

Anderson, Bernhard W. *Understanding the Old Testament*. 4th ed. Upper Saddle River, N.J.: Prentice-Hall, 1998.

Barr, James. *History and Ideology in the Old Testament: Biblical Studies at the End of a Millennium*. New York: Oxford University Press, 2000.

Bright, John. *A History of Israel*. 4th ed. Louisville, Ky.: Westminster John Knox, 1999.

Buber, Martin. *The Prophetic Faith*. New York: Macmillan, 1949.

Burrows, Millar. *An Outline of Biblical Theology*. Philadelphia: Westminster, 1946.

Coggins, R. J. *Introducing the Old Testament*. New York: Oxford University Press, 1990.

Dempsey, Carol J. *The Prophets: A Liberation-Critical Reading*. Minneapolis: Fortress, 2000.

Driver, S. R. *An Introduction to the Literature of the Old Testament*. New York: Meridian, 1956.

Gaster, Theodor H. *Myth, Legend, and History in the Old Testament*. 2 vols. Gloucester, Mass.: Peter Smith, 1981.

Gordon, Dane R. *The Old Testament: A Beginning Survey*. Englewood Cliffs, N.J.: Prentice-Hall, 1985.

Gunkel, Hermann. *The Legends of Genesis: The Biblical Saga and History*. New York: Schocken, 1964.

Harrelson, Walter. *Introduction to the Old Testament*. New York: Holt, Rinehart & Winston, 1964.

Heschel, Abraham J. *The Prophets: An Introduction*. New York: Harper & Row, 1969.

Isserlin, B. S. J. *The Israelites: Introducing Israel's Social, Historical, Geographical, and Archeological Contexts*. Minneapolis: Fortress, 2001.

Koch, Klaus. *The Growth of the Biblical Tradition: The Form-Critical Method*. New York: Scribner's, 1968.

Mann, Thomas W. *The Book of the Torah: The Narrative Integrity of the*

Pentateuch. Louisville, Ky.: Westminster John Knox, 1988.

Matthews, Victor H. *Old Testament Themes*. St. Louis: Chalice Press, 2000.

Meek, Theophile James. *Hebrew Origins*. New York: Harper Torch, 1960.

Miller, Patrick D. *The Religion of Ancient Israel*. Louisville, Ky.: Westminster John Knox, 1999.

Muilenberg, James. *The Way of Israel: Biblical Faith and Ethics*. New York: Harper & Row, 1961.

Napier, B. Davie. *Song of the Vineyard: A Guide through the Old Testament*. Rev. ed. Philadelphia: Fortress, 1981.

Nogalski, James D., and Marvin A. Sweeney, eds. *Reading and Hearing the Book of the Twelve*. Atlanta: Society of Biblical Literature, 2000.

Noth, Martin. *The History of Israel*. New York: Harper & Brothers, 1958.

Rendtorff, Rolf. *Introduction to the Old Testament*. Philadelphia: Fortress, 1986.

Robinson, Theodore H. *Prophecy and the Prophets in Ancient Israel*. London: Duckworth, 1953.

Schmidt, Werner H. *Old Testament Introduction*. 2d ed. Louisville, Ky.: Westminster John Knox, 1999.

Scott, R. B. Y. *The Relevance of the Prophets*. Rev. ed. New York: Macmillan, 1968.

Steck, Odil Hannes. *The Prophetic Books and their Theological Witness*. St. Louis: Chalice Press, 2000.

Trible, Phyllis. *Texts of Terror: Literary-Feminist Readings of Biblical Narratives*. Philadelphia: Fortress, 1984.

de Vaux, Roland. *Ancient Israel*. New York: McGraw Hill, 1961.

Walton, John, et al. *The IVP Bible, Background Commentary: Old Testament*. Downers Grove, Ill.: InterVarsity Press, 2000.

Wright, George Ernest. *Biblical Archeology*. Abridged ed. Philadelphia: Westminster, 1960.

Genesis

Armstrong, Karen. *In the Beginning: A New Interpretation of Genesis*. New York: Ballantine, 1997.

Kierkegaard, Søren. *Fear and Trembling*. Princeton: Princeton University Press, 1954. (On Abraham's near-sacrifice of Isaac)

Moyers, Bill. *Genesis: A Living Conversation*. New York: Doubleday, 1997.

Rosenblatt, Naomi. *Wrestling with Angels: What Genesis Teaches Us about Our Spiritual Identity, Sexuality, and Personal Relationships.* New York: Delta, 1996.

Westerman, Claus. *The Genesis Accounts of Creation.* Philadelphia: Fortress, 1964.

———. *The Promises of the Fathers.* Philadelphia: Fortress, 1980.

Exodus

Harrelson, Walter. *The Ten Commandments and Human Rights.* Philadelphia: Fortress, 1980.

Leviticus

Noth, Martin. *The Laws of the Pentateuch.* London: SCM Press, 1966.

Joshua

Gottwald, Norman. *The Tribes of Yahweh: A Sociology of the Religion of Liberated Israel, 1250–1050 B.C.E.* Maryknoll, N.Y.: Orbis, 1979.

Judges

Ackerman, Susan. *Warrior, Dancer, Seductress: Women in Judges and Biblical Israel.* New York: Doubleday, 1999.

Bal, Mieke. *Death and Dissymetry: The Politics of Coherence in the Book of Judges.* Chicago: University of Chicago Press, 1988.

Schneider, Tammi J. *Judges: Studies in Hebrew Narrative and Poetry.* Collegeville, Minn.: Liturgical Press, 2000.

Yee, Gale A., ed. *Judges and Method: New Approaches in Biblical Studies* Minneapolis: Fortress, 1995.

Ruth

Fewell, Danna Nolan, and David Miller Gunn. *Compromising Redemption: Relating Characters in the Book of Ruth.* Louisville, Ky.: Westminster John Knox, 1990.

Kates, Judith A., and Gail Twersky, ed. *Reading Ruth: Contemporary Women Reclaim a Sacred Story.* New York: Ballantine, 1996.

Leggett, Donald A. *The Levirate and Goel Institutions in the Old Testament, with Special Attention to the Book of Ruth.* Cherry Hill, N.J.: Mack Publishing, 1974.

Linafelt, Tod. *Ruth and Esther: Studies in Hebrew Narrative and Poetry.* Collegeville, Minn.: Liturgical Press, 1999.

Ostriker, Alicia Suskin. *The Five Scrolls: The Song of Songs, the Book of Ruth, Lamentations, Ecclesiastes, the Book of Esther.* New York: Vintage, 2000.

1 Kings

Knoppers, Gary N., and J. Gordon McConville, eds. *Reconsidering Israel and Judah: Recent Studies on the Deuteronomistic History.* Winona Lake, Ind.: Eisenbrauns, 2000.

Mowinckel, Sigmund. *He that Cometh.* Nashville: Abingdon, 1954.

2 Kings

Klein, Ralph. *Israel in Exile: A Theological Interpretation.* Philadelphia: Fortress, 1980.

Sweeney, Marvin A. *King Josiah of Judah: The Lost Messiah of Israel.* New York: Oxford University Press, 2000.

Esther

Linafelt, Tod. *Ruth and Esther: Studies in Hebrew Narrative and Poetry.* Collegeville, Minn.: Liturgical Press, 1999.

Ostriker, Alicia Suskin. *The Five Scrolls: The Song of Songs, the Book of Ruth, Lamentations, Ecclesiastes, the Book of Esther.* New York: Vintage, 2000.

Job

Pope, Marvin H. *Job: A New Translation with Introduction and Commentary*, Anchor Bible. Garden City, N.Y.: Doubleday, 1973.

Terrien, Samuel. "The Book of Job: Introduction and Exegesis," in *The Interpreter's Bible*, vol. 3. Nashville: Abingdon, 1954, 877–1198.

Psalms

Bellinger, W. H., Jr. *Psalms: Reading and Studying the Book of Psalms.* Peabody, Mass.: Hendrickson, 1990.

Crenshaw, James L. *The Psalms: An Introduction.* Grand Rapids, Mich.: Eerdmans, 2001.

Gillingham, S. E. *The Poems and Psalms of the Holy Bible.* New York: Oxford University Press, 1994.

Murphy, Roland E. *The Gift of the Psalms.* Peabody, Mass.: Hendrickson, 2000.

Proverbs

Crenshaw, James. *Education in Ancient Israel.* New York: Doubleday, 1998.

Weeks, Stuart. *Early Israelite Wisdom.* New York: Oxford University Press, 1994.

Song of Solomon (or Canticles)

Neusner, Jacob. *Israel's Love Affair with God: The Song of Songs*. Harrisburg, Pa.: Trinity Press International, 1993.

Walsh, Carey Ellen. *Exquisite Desire: Religion, the Erotic, and the Song of Songs*. Minneapolis: Fortress, 2000.

Isaiah

Childs, Brevard S. *Isaiah*. Louisville: Westminster John Knox, 2001.

North, C. R. *Isaiah 40–55*. London: SCM Press, 1964.

Ezekiel

Odell, Margaret S., and John T. Strong, eds. *The Book of Ezekiel: Theological and Anthropological Perspectives*. Atlanta: Society of Biblical Literature, 2000.

Daniel

Gowan, Donald. *Eschatology in the Old Testament*. Edinburgh: T. & T. Clark, 2000.

Hanson, Paul D. *Old Testament Apocalyptic*. Nashville: Abingdon Press, 1987.

———. *The Dawn of Apocalyptic*. Philadelphia: Fortress, 1975.

Koch, Klaus. *The Rediscovery of Apocalyptic*. London: SCM Press, 1972.

Reddish, Mitchell, ed. *Apocalyptic Literature: A Reader*. Boston: Hendrickson, 1986.

Part III: The Old Testament Apocrypha, or Deuterocanonicals

Overview

Charles, R. H. *Apocrypha and Pseudepigrapha of the Old Testament*, 2 vols. Oxford: Clarendon, 1913.

Charlesworth, James H. *The Old Testament Pseudepigrapha*, 2 vols. Garden City, N.Y.: Doubleday, 1983–1985.

Harrington, Daniel J., S.J. *Invitation to the Apocrypha*. Grand Rapids, Mich.: Eerdmans, 1999.

Jobes, Karen H., and Moises Silva. *Invitation to the Septuagint*. Grand Rapids, Mich.: Baker Academic, 2000.

Marcos, Natalio Fernandez. *The Septuagint in Context: Introduction to the Greek Version of the Bible*. Boston: Brill, 2000.

Nickelsburg, George W. E. *Jewish Literature between the Bible and the Mishnah.* Philadelphia: Fortress, 1987.

Russell, D. S. *The Old Testament Pseudepigrapha: Patriarchs and Prophets in Early Judaism.* Philadelphia: Fortress, 1987.

Sparks, H. F. D., ed. *The Apocryphal Old Testament.* New York: Oxford University Press, 1985.

1 Esdras

Talshir, Zipora. *I Esdras: From Origin to Translation.* Atlanta: Society of Biblical Literature, 1999.

2 Esdras

Koch, Klaus. *The Rediscovery of Apocalyptic.* London: SCM Press, 1972.

Judith

Vanderkam, James C., ed. *"No One Spoke Ill of Her": Essays on Judith.* Atlanta: Society of Biblical Literature, 1992.

Wisdom of Solomon (or Wisdom)

Hahneman, Geoffrey Mark. *The Muratorian Fragment and the Development of the Canon.* New York: Oxford University Press, 1992.

Baruch

Burke, David G. *The Poetry of Baruch: A Reconstruction and Analysis of the Original Hebrew Text of Baruch 3:9–5:9.* Atlanta: Society of Biblical Literature, 1982.

Susanna

Spolsky, Ellen, ed. *The Judgment of Susanna: Authority and Witness.* Atlanta: Society of Biblical Literature, 1996.

I and II Maccabees

Kampen, John. *The Hasideans and the Origins of Pharisaism: A Study of 1 and 2 Maccabees.* Atlanta: Society of Biblical Literature, 1989.

Part IV: The New Testament, or Canonical Early Christian Writings

Overview

Achtemeier, Paul J., Joel B. Green, and Marianne Meye Thompson. *Introducing the New Testament: Its Literature and Theology.* Grand Rapids, Mich.: Eerdmans, 2001.

Cameron, Ron, ed. *The Other Gospels: Non-Canonical Gospel Texts.* Philadelphia: Westminster, 1982.

Gamble, Harry Y. *Books and Readers in the Early Church: A History of Early Christian Texts.* New Haven, Conn.: Yale University Press, 1997.

——. *The New Testament Canon: Its Making and Meaning.* Philadelphia: Fortress, 1985.

Synoptic Gospels and the Historical Jesus Question

Allen, O. Wesley, Jr. *Reading the Synoptic Gospels: Basic Methods for Interpreting Matthew, Mark, and Luke.* St. Louis: Chalice Press, 2000.

Allison, Dale C., Jr. *The Jesus Tradition in Q.* Harrisburg, Pa.: Trinity Press International, 1997.

Cadbury, Henry J. *The Making of Luke-Acts.* Peabody, Mass.: Hendrickson, 1999.

Crossan, John Dominic, Luke Timothy Johnson, and Werner H. Kelber. *The Jesus Controversy: Perspectives in Conflict.* Harrisburg, Pa.: Trinity Press International, 1998.

Dungan, David L. *A History of the Synoptic Problem: The Canon, the Text, the Composition, and the Interpretation of the Gospels.* New York: Doubleday, 1999.

Farmer, William R. *Jesus and the Gospel: Tradition, Scripture, and Canon.* Philadelphia: Fortress, 1982.

——. *New Synoptic Studies.* Macon, Ga.: Mercer University Press, 1983.

——. *The Synoptic Problem: A Critical Review of the Problem of the Literary Relationships between Matthew, Mark and Luke.* New York: Macmillan, 1964.

Hayes, John H. *Son of God to Superstar: Twentieth Century Interpretations of Jesus.* Nashville: Abingdon, 1976.

Jacobson, Arland. *The First Gospel: An Introduction to Q.* Sonoma, Calif.: Polebridge, 1992.

Kloppenborg, John S. *Excavating Q: The History and Setting of the Sayings Gospel.* Minneapolis: Fortress, 2000.

——. *The Formation of Q: Trajectories in Ancient Wisdom Collections.* Harrisburg, Pa.: Trinity Press International, 1999.

——., ed. *The Shape of Q: Signal Essays on the Sayings Gospel.* Minneapolis: Fortress, 1994.

Koester, Helmut. *Ancient Christian Gospels: Their History and Development.* Philadelphia: Trinity Press International, 1990.

Robinson, J. M., et al. *The Critical Edition of Q.* Minneapolis: Fortress, 2000.

Tyson, Joseph B. *Luke, Judaism and the Scholars: Critical Approaches to Luke-Acts.* Columbia, S.C.: University of South Carolina Press, 1999.

Weaver, Walter P. *The Historical Jesus in the Twentieth Century, 1900–1950.* Harrisburg, Pa.: Trinity Press International, 1999.

Studies on Paul
Ashton, John. *The Religion of Paul the Apostle.* New Haven, Conn.: Yale University Press, 2000.
Das, A. Andrew. *Paul, the Law, and the Covenant.* Peabody, Mass.: Hendrickson, 2000.
den Heyer, C. J. *Paul: A Man of Two Worlds.* Harrisburg, Pa.: Trinity Press International, 2000.
Dibelius, Martin, and Werner Georg Kümmel. *Paul.* Philadelphia: Westminster, 1953.
Eugberg-Pedersen, Troels. *Paul and the Stoics.* Louisville, Ky.: Westminster John Knox, 2000.
Horsley, Richard, ed. *Paul and Politics: Ekklesia, Israel, Imperium, Interpretation.* Harrisburg, Pa.: Trinity Press International, 2000.
Neumann, Ken. *The Authenticity of the Pauline Epistles in the Light of Stylo-statistical Analysis.* Atlanta: Society of Biblical Literature, 1990.
Nock, Arthur Darby. *St. Paul.* New York: Harper & Row, 1964.
Reicke, Bo. *Re-examining Paul's Letters: A History of the Pauline Correspondence.* Harrisburg, Pa.: Trinity Press International, 2001.
Roetzel, Calvin J. *Paul: The Man and the Myth.* Minneapolis: Fortress, 1999.
Sampley, J. Paul. *Paul in the Greco-Roman World.* Harrisburg, Pa.: Trinity Press International, forthcoming.
Schweitzer, Albert. *The Mysticism of Paul the Apostle.* New York: Macmillan, 1960.
Wiles, Virginia. *Making Sense of Paul: A Basic Introduction to Pauline Theology.* Peabody, Mass.: Hendrickson, 2000.
Ziesler, J. A. *Pauline Christianity,* rev. ed. New York: Oxford University Press, 1991.

Multivolume commentaries
Abingdon New Testament Commentaries. Nashville: Abingdon Press, 1996–1998.
The New International Commentary on the New Testament. Grand Rapids, Mich.: Eerdmans, 1955–1997.

Single-volume introductions or commentaries
Brown, Raymond E. *Introduction to the New Testament.* New York: Doubleday, 1997.

Drane, John. *Introducing the New Testament.* Rev. ed. Minneapolis: Fortress, 2001.

Ehrman, Bart D. *The New Testament: A Historical Introduction to the Early Christian Writings.* New York: Oxford University Press, 2000.

Eisen, Ute E. *Women Officeholders in Early Christianity: Epigraphical and Literary Studies.* Collegeville, Minn.: Liturgical Press, 2000.

Epp, Eldon Jay, and George W. MacRae. *The New Testament and Its Modern Interpreters.* Atlanta: Scholars Press, 1989.

Evans, Craig A., and Stanley E. Porter, eds. *Dictionary of New Testament Background.* Downers Grove, Ill.: InterVarsity Press, 2000.

Feine, Paul, et al. *Introduction to the New Testament.* 14th ed. Nashville: Abingdon, 1966.

Fredriksen, Paula. *From Jesus to Christ: the Origins of the New Testament Images of Jesus.* New Haven, Conn.: Yale University Press, 1988.

Hays, Richard B. *The Moral Vision of the New Testament.* San Francisco: HarperSanFrancisco, 1996.

Johnson, Luke Timothy. *The Writings of the New Testament: An Interpretation.* Philadelphia: Fortress, 1986.

Koester, Helmut. *Introduction to the New Testament.* 2 vols. Berlin and New York: Walter de Gruyter, 1995, 2000.

Ladd, George Eldon. *A Theology of the New Testament.* Rev. ed. Cambridge: Lutterworth Press, 1994.

Metzger, Bruce M. *The New Testament: Its Background, Growth, and Content.* Nashville: Abingdon, 1965.

Perrin, Norman. *The New Testament: An Introduction.* New York: Harcourt Brace Jovanovich, 1974.

Puskas, Charles B. *An Introduction to the New Testament.* Peabody, Mass.: Hendrickson, 1989.

Smith, D. Moody, and Robert A. Spivey. *Anatomy of the New Testament: A Guide to its Structure and Meaning.* 5th ed. Englewood Cliffs, N.J.: Prentice-Hall, 1995.

Stambaugh, John E., and David L. Balch, *The New Testament in its Social Environment.* Philadelphia: Westminster, 1986.

Strecker, Georg. *Theology of the New Testament.* Berlin and New York: Walter de Gruyter, 2000.

Matthew

Charlesworth, James H. *Jesus' Jewishness: Exploring the Place of Jesus in Early Judaism.* New York: Crossroad, 1991.

Jeremias, Joachim. *The Sermon on the Mount.* Philadelphia: Fortress, 1963.

Sanders, E. P. *Jesus and Judaism.* Philadelphia: Fortress, 1985.

Stendahl, Krister. *The School of St. Matthew, and Its Use of the Old Testament.* Mifflintown, Pa.: Sigler Press, 1991.

Zeitlin, Irving M. *Jesus and the Judaism of His Time.* Oxford: Polity Press, 1988.

Mark

Hare, Douglas R. A. *The Son of Man Tradition.* Philadelphia: Fortress, 1990.

Malbon, Elizabeth Struthers. *In the Company of Jesus: Characters in Mark's Gospel.* Louisville, Ky.: Westminster John Knox, 1999.

Luke

Conzelmann, Hans. *The Theology of St. Luke.* Philadelphia: Fortress, 1982.

Fuller, Reginald H. *The Formation of the Resurrection Narratives.* Philadelphia: Fortress, 1980.

Hiers, Richard. "The Problem of the Delay of the Parousia in Luke-Acts," *New Testament Studies* 20 (1974): 145–55.

Keck, Leander E., and Louis J. Martyn, eds. *Studies in Luke-Acts.* Nashville: Abingdon, 1966.

Marxsen, Willi. *Jesus and Easter: Did God Raise the Historical Jesus from the Dead?* Nashville: Abingdon, 1990.

John

Ashton, John. *Understanding the Fourth Gospel.* New York: Oxford University Press, 1991.

Carroll, John, et al. *The Return of Jesus in Early Christianity.* Peabody, Mass.: Hendrickson, 2000.

Smith, D. Moody. *The Gospel of John.* Nashville: Abingdon, 2000.

Acts

Keck, Leander E., and J. Louis Martyn, eds. *Studies in Luke-Acts.* Nashville: Abingdon, 1966.

Romans

Meeks, Wayne A. *The First Urban Christians: The Social World of the Apostle Paul.* New Haven, Conn.: Yale University Press, 1983.

2 Corinthians

Georgi, Dieter. *The Opponents of Paul in Second Corinthians.* Philadelphia: Fortress, 1986.

Galatians
Perkins, Pheme. *Abraham's Divided Children*. Harrisburg, Pa.: Trinity Press International, 2001.

1 Thessalonians
Jewett, Robert. *The Thessalonian Correspondence: Pauline Rhetoric and Millenarian Piety*. Philadelphia: Fortress, 1986.

1 Timothy
Bauer, Walter. *Orthodoxy and Heresy in Earliest Christianity*. Mifflintown, Pa.: Sigler Press, 1996.
Grant, Robert M. *Heresy and Criticism: The Search for Authenticity in Early Christian Literature*. Louisville, Ky.: Westminster John Knox, 1993.
Houlden, J. L. *The Pastoral Epistles: 1 & 2 Timothy, and Titus*. Philadelphia: Trinity Press International, 1989.
Kidd, Reggie M. *Wealth and Beneficence in the Pastoral Epistles: A Bourgeois Form of Early Christianity?* Atlanta: Society of Biblical Literature, 1990.

Titus
Logan, Alistair H. B. *Gnostic Truth and Christian Heresy: A Study in the History of Gnosticism*. Peabody, Mass.: Hendrickson, 1996.

Hebrews
Eisenbaum, Pamela Michelle. *The Jewish Heroes of Christian History: Hebrews 11 in Literary Context*. Atlanta: Society of Biblical Literature, 1997.

James
Cargal, Timothy Boyd. *Restoring the Diaspora: Discursive Structure and Purpose in the Epistle of James*. Atlanta: Society of Biblical Literature, 1993.

1 Peter
Balch, David. *Let Wives Be Submissive: The Domestic Code in 1 Peter*. Atlanta: Society of Biblical Literature, 1981.

Revelation
Friesen, Steven J. *Imperial Cults and the Apocalypse of John: Reading Revelation in the Ruins*. New York: Oxford University Press, 2001.
Grant, Robert M. *The Sword and the Cross*. New York: Macmillan, 1955.

Malina, Bruce J., and John J. Pilch. *Social Science Commentary on the Book of Revelation*. Minneapolis: Fortress, 2000.

Metzger, Bruce M. *Breaking the Code: Understanding the Book of Revelation*. Nashville: Abingdon, 1993.

Schüssler Fiorenza, Elisabeth. *The Book of Revelation: Justice and Thought*. Minneapolis: Fortress, 1999.

Smith, Robert H. *Apocalypse: A Commentary on Revelation in Words and Images*. Collegeville, Minn.: Liturgical Press, 2000.

Thompson, Leonard J. *The Book of Revelation: Apocalypse and Empire*. New York: Oxford University Press, 1990.

INDEX

Definitions or discussions of terms or names are indicated by page citations in boldface type.

About the Cover Art

The early Christian catacomb painting reproduced on the cover depicts a particularly dramatic moment in the Balaam-Balak story (Numbers 22–24). This story is set in the context of a major turning point in Israel's early history. Following their escape from Egypt, the Israelites have wandered about in the Sinai wilderness for many—traditionally forty—years. Now, at last, moving on the way to Canaan, "the promised land," they cut across a corner of Moab.

Their presence alarms Moab's king, Balak. Therefore Balak sends for Balaam, a professional (non-Israelite) execrator, to come and put a curse on this horde of advancing Israelites. Two versions of the story evidently have been blended in the present account. In one, the LORD tells Balaam not to go; in the other, Balaam may go but must speak only as the LORD instructs him. Balaam then proceeds toward Balak's headquarters, mounted on his faithful she-ass; but on the way, they are confronted by an angel brandishing a drawn sword, as shown in this fresco. At first Balaam does not see the angel, but the she-ass does, balking and eventually lying down under him. Exasperated, Balaam strikes the ass, who promptly asks him why he has done so, and for a while Balaam and the ass discuss the matter. Finally, Balaam sees the angel, who likewise reproaches him and tells him to go on to Balak, but to speak only what the angel tells him.

Balaam arrives at Balak's camp. Balak offers sacrifice and calls on Balaam to curse Israel. Instead of cursing, however, Balaam blesses Israel, much to Balak's chagrin. Balaam's classic response ("Must I not take heed to speak what the LORD puts in my mouth?") anticipates later Israelite prophets' understanding of their task. Again Balak offers sacrifice, but again Balaam blesses Israel. If that's all you can do, "neither curse them at all, nor bless them at all," just shut up, exclaims Balak. Nevertheless, still hopeful, he offers sacrifice yet a third time, but once more Balaam blesses Israel. Enough already—get out of here, an angry Balak shouts, and don't expect me to pay ("honor") you for this performance. The story concludes with Balaam volunteering a fourth oracle of blessing, for no extra charge, after which Balaam and Balak go their respective ways, while the Israelites continue on toward the land of Canaan.